Harm and Offence in Media Content

A Review of the Evidence

Revised and updated second edition

Acknowledgements

The authors gratefully acknowledge funding from Ofcom and the BBFC for the second edition of this volume. The first edition was funded by AOL, BBC, BBFC, BT, ICSTIS, Ofcom and Vodafone Group Marketing.

Thanks also to Vanessa Cragoe, Ellen Helsper, Shenja Vandergraaf and Yinhan Wang for their work on the production of this review.

Biographies

Andrea Millwood Hargrave provides independent advice on media regulatory policy and research issues. Formerly Research Director of the United Kingdom's Broadcasting Standards Commission and the Independent Television Commission, she is author of many publications on media content issues. She has an active working interest in emerging communications technologies and developments in Europe and globally.

Sonia Livingstone is a Professor of Social Psychology in the Department of Media and Communications at the London School of Economics. She is author of many books and articles on the television audience, children's relation to media, and domestic uses of the Internet. Recent books include *Young People and New Media, The Handbook of New Media, Audiences and Publics*, and *The International Handbook of Children, Media and Culture*.

Harm and Offence in Media Content

A review of the evidence

Revised and updated second edition

By Andrea Millwood Hargrave and Sonia Livingstone

With contributions from David Brake, Jesse Elvin,
Rebecca Gooch, Judith Livingstone and Russell Luyt

intellect Bristol, UK / Chicago, USA

First published in the UK in 2009 by
Intellect Books, The Mill, Parnall Road, Fishponds, Bristol, BS16 3JG, UK

First published in the USA in 2009 by
Intellect Books, The University of Chicago Press, 1427 E. 60th Street, Chicago,
IL 60637, USA

A catalogue record for this book is available from the British Library.

Cover designer: Holly Rose
Copy-editor: Rhys Williams
Typesetting: Mac Style, Beverley, E. Yorkshire

ISBN 978-1-84150-238-0

Printed and bound by Gutenberg Press, Malta.

CONTENTS

PREFACE

This volume offers a critical review of the evidence for harm and offence from media content on different platforms. The first edition, published in 2006, included research undertaken and published up to 2005. Since then, the Audio Visual Media Services Directive has been adopted in Europe (2007), replacing the earlier Television Without Frontiers Directive. This has had repercussions throughout Europe as plans are implemented to reflect the extended scope of the new Directive in a complex and converging media and communications environment. In the United Kingdom, the Culture, Media and Sport Select Committee heard evidence for harm caused by the Internet and video-games while Dr Byron has undertaken a review of the potential for harmful effects on children of the Internet and video-games. In the United States, concerns about the way in which young people, in particular, are using new technologies has given rise to partnerships between the legislature in some states and commercial Internet protocol based companies.

Indeed, regulators throughout the world are discussing how to approach the regulation of content delivered via newer delivery mechanisms. It is against this background that the UK regulator, Ofcom, approached the authors to update the 2006 literature review. This second edition examines the published evidence regarding the potential for harm from television, the Internet, video-games and filmic content (this last commissioned by the BBFC, the UK classification body for film), as well as for radio, print, advertising and mobile telephony. Since the literature is expanding more in some areas than others, with most focus on audio-visual and online media, some parts of this volume have been updated and rewritten more than others.

To produce effective, evidence-based policy, an assessment of the evidence for content-related harm and offence is required. Research on the question of harm is often scattered across different academic disciplines and different industry and regulatory sectors. Much of this research has been framed in terms of 'media effects', occasioning considerable contestation over research methods. Research on offence is more often conducted by regulators and the industry than by academics, being seen by some academics as either unmeasurable in a reliable fashion or as a policy tool for undermining civil liberties. This review seeks to identify and integrate different sources of knowledge, recognizing the strengths and weaknesses of the main research traditions, in order to offer a critical evaluation of key findings and arguments relevant to policy-formation.

The comparative scope of such a review is needed because, typically, literature reviews focus on a single medium, prefer one or another methodology, examine just one type of potential harm and/or position the analysis within one disciplinary specialism. Although there are many reviews of psychological experiments on the effects of exposure to television violence, most notably, what is lacking is a review that is as 'convergent' as the communications environment itself. Yet in developing regulatory policy, considerations of harm and offence must increasingly be evaluated in the context of a converging media environment. The present review integrates published research conducted on diverse media and using diverse methodologies – including epidemiological studies, tracking surveys and in-depth qualitative analyses. It also encompasses diverse theoretical approaches, given the various conceptions of harm and offence employed in different disciplines.

This volume offers:

- An analysis of the definition(s) of harm as distinguished from offence, so as to inquire into the basis for distinguishing harmful from offensive and other kinds of media contents.

- An up to date review of the empirical evidence regarding media harm and offence, recognizing the strengths and limitations of the methods used and identifying where findings apply to particular media or particular audience/user groups.

- A critical inquiry into the attempt to generalize from research on older, mass media to the challenges posed by the newer, converging and online media forms, noting emerging issues and research gaps.

The body of empirical published research reviewed here is expanding fast, especially in relation to the Internet. In undertaking this review, albeit within the limits of practical constraints on time and resources, a sustained search was conducted of extensive electronic and library sources across a range of academic disciplines including media and communication studies, education, psychology, psychiatry, paediatrics, gender studies, social/family studies, sociology, information and library science, criminology, law, cultural studies and public policy.[1] We draw upon relevant policy and industry-sponsored research where publicly available, and on information obtained from key researchers in the field.[2]

Given the vast amount of reading that this generated, several strategic decisions were necessary to prioritize those most relevant to current debates regarding content regulation. Specifically, we focus on empirical evidence for harm and offence, rather than on descriptive data about media markets and use.[3] We concentrate mainly, though not exclusively, on recent material (post-2000). Emphasis is given to UK-based material where this exists, though a considerable body of material from elsewhere is included as appropriate, much of it conducted in America. We also prioritize high quality (i.e. academic peer-reviewed) original publications that report empirical research evidence rather than discussions of theory or method. As a result of our search strategy and the selections noted above, this review is based on an electronic database containing some 1,000 items.

This review does not examine evidence for positive or pro-social benefits of the media[4] and so does not aim to offer an overall judgement on the relative benefits versus harms of the media. It is also beyond the scope of this review to consider the moral or legal arguments for or against content regulation, though these are many and complex. There is a substantial literature on the history of regulation in the United Kingdom and elsewhere, detailing how policies have been formulated and implemented, cases contested, complex judgements made, and precedents established and overturned.[5] Note further that some interpretation is required in matching the regulatory framework of 'harm' and 'offence' to academic publications, given that neither term is widely used other than in the psychological or legal fields.

Given the complexity of this field of research, and the persistent gaps in the evidence base, we would urge our readers to retain a sceptical lens in assessing the evidence. Questions such as the following should be asked over and again. What specific social, cultural or psychological problem is at issue? Which media contents are hypothesized to play a role? Which segments of the public are particularly vulnerable or give rise to concern? What are the strengths and weaknesses of the research methods used to generate the relevant evidence? Under what conditions are these media contents being accessed in everyday life? What kind of risk, and what scale of risk, does the evidence point to, if at all, and for whom?

Our review finds that the evidence for harm and offence is significant but constantly qualified, resulting in contingent answers that do not make life easy for regulators, policy-makers or the industry. When dealing with complex social phenomena (violence, aggression, sexuality, prejudice, etc.), many factors – including but not solely the media – must be expected to play a role. Hence we argue for a risk-based approach to media-related harm and offence that enables decisions based on proportionality.

Although there is less evidence regarding the effectiveness of possible interventions, there is considerable evidence that regulatory interventions on a proportionate basis are welcomed and expected by the public. In looking to the future, paramount consideration must be given to the dynamic nature of the technological change that is driving these questions anew, with evolving uses and developing forms of practice, especially among the young.

As homes become more complex multi-media environments, and as media technologies converge, it must be a priority to develop and extend the available evidence base, so that we sustain our understanding of the differences across, and relations among, the changing array of media and communication technologies. The challenge is to seek ways of minimizing risks, while also enabling the many benefits afforded by these technologies for our society and for the socialization of our children. Nonetheless, while new research will always be needed, this volume seeks to understand how best to formulate continuing and new regulation on the basis of present evidence.

NOTES

1. Efforts were made to contact known researchers in the field so as to identify and include the latest research. We thank Martin Barker (University of Aberystwyth), Arianna Bassoli (LSE), Kevin Browne (University of Birmingham), Karen Diamond (Purdue University), Jeffrey G Johnson (Columbia University), Keith Negus (Goldsmiths College, University of London), Kia Ng (University of Leeds) and Don Roberts (Stanford University).

2. We requested information/empirical research reports from a range of organizations. We thank those who provided or directed us towards materials for the review. These include Camille de Stempel at AOL, Claire Forbes at the Advertising Standards Authority, Claire Powell, Chris Mundy and Caroline Vogt at the BBC, Sue Clark at the BBFC, Emma Pike at British Music Rights, Nick Truman at BT, Tom Atkinson, Paul Whiteing at ICSTIS, John Carr at NCH (CHIS), Julia Fraser, Jan Kacperek, Helen Normoyle, Fran O'Brien, Ian Blair and Alison Preston from Ofcom, Annie Mullins and Rob Borthwick from Vodafone Group Marketing.

3. Since our focus is specifically on content-related harm and offence, we include issues of violence, sexual portrayal, pornography, racism, stereotyping, and so forth but exclude consideration of financial harms (online scams, fraud, etc.), physical harms (eye strain, sedentary lifestyle, 'phone masts etc.) and illegal content (child abuse images, etc.). Nor do we examine the effect of media use on children's scholastic performance (Anderson and Pempek, 2005; Heim, J., et al., 2007; Zimmerman and Christakis, 2005).

4. Though a substantial literature exists, including that concerned with the educational benefits for children, the media's contribution to civic or public society and its positive entertainment and cultural role (Davies, 1997; Fisch and Truglio, 2001; Gunter and McAleer, 1997; D.G. Singer and Singer, 2001).

5. For discussions see Akdeniz (2001), Ballard (2004), Machill, Hart, and Kaltenhauser (2002), Oswell (1998), Penfold (2004), Verhulst (2002) and Wheeler (2004).

EXECUTIVE SUMMARY

AIMS AND SCOPE OF THE REVIEW

The concepts of 'harm' and 'offence' are gaining ground, especially as policy-makers and regulators debate the possible effects of the contents and uses of the new media technologies. The debate mainly concerns the exposure of minors to potentially harmful or offensive material, although there are other sensibilities such as offence or harm caused to those from minority groups.

This research review is designed to examine the risk of harm and offence in relation to the usage of media content. Uniquely, it asks what evidence is available regarding content-related harm and offence, looking across the range of media from television to electronic games, from print to the Internet. It focuses on recent research, mainly published between 2000 and 2007, and has been thoroughly updated in this second edition of the review.

This review has the following aims:

- To offer a comprehensive and up to date review of an important, policy-relevant body of research literature, combining empirical research from diverse disciplines across the academy, together with research conducted by industry and regulatory bodies.

- To distinguish and to seek to understand the relation between harm and offence, identifying such evidence as exists for each as it relates both to the general population and to specific 'vulnerable' subgroups, notably children and young people.

- To compare findings obtained across the major forms of media (both established and new), evaluating these in the context of critical debates regarding theory, methodology and the politics of research in order to contextualize and qualify as appropriate the empirical claims in the published literature on media harm and offence.

- To draw on the latest research conducted in the United Kingdom and internationally, while recognizing that, in different regulatory contexts cross-nationally, different findings may be obtained and, therefore, culturally-specific conclusions may be required.

WHAT THIS REVIEW DOES NOT COVER

The field of research examining claims regarding media harm and offence is vast, and so the parameters of the present review must be made clear at the outset.

■ The review does not cover research evidence for the positive or pro-social benefits of the media, though these have been extensively researched elsewhere, except where they are discussed in relation to harm and offence. The review should not be read, therefore, as offering an overall judgement on the benefits and harms, taken together, of the various media.

■ It also does not consider other issues of public health being debated, such as the potential for physical harm caused by media content triggering epilepsy for example, or the possible effects of using mobile telephone handsets. Nor does the review consider areas of consumer detriment such as financial risk.

■ It is important also to note that the review only reflects the changing nature of media consumption insofar as it has been the subject of research which refers to harm and offence. Since there are many gaps in the empirical research base, a number of questions must remain unanswered. Further it is clear that the changing patterns of media use continue to be significant in framing the ways in which people relate to different media (in terms of access, expectations, media literacy, etc). Such changes should remain a priority for the future research agenda.

THE ORGANIZATION OF THIS REVIEW

The review of the literature is organized according to the following rationale:

■ We begin with the policy-context within which the debate about the potential for harm and offence is framed. In Europe the Audio Visual Media Services Directive (adopted in 2007) is to be implemented. In the United Kingdom the Byron Review (2008) has undertaken a critical and comprehensive analysis of the evidence for the potential for harm to children from the Internet and video-games. A parliamentary Select Committee is, at the time of writing, undertaking a similar review, and several other initiatives are underway to 'protect' young people from the risk of harm. In America, the regulator (FCC, 2007) has called for a review of the way in which violent content is made available to the public, using not only technical access management systems and scheduling conventions but also financial incentives for viewers. In other countries too, the policy-debate spills over into a debate about the possibility, and feasibility, of regulating content in an almost-infinite space.

■ We then move on to an account of the research in this field, arguing that it is important to distinguish theories of short-term and long-term effects, direct and indirect effects. We review the advantages and disadvantages of the main research methods in use (experiments, surveys, qualitative social research), noting the ethical and political issues that structure the field of research. We stress the value of integrating qualitative and quantitative research findings, discussing each in the light of the other, where available.

■ The review presents recent research conducted for each medium in turn, examining evidence for different types of potential harm and offence and according to categories of audiences or users (i.e. types of vulnerability). Research methods and findings are critically evaluated to identify the strengths and weaknesses of the empirical research base. They are also contextualized so as to identify factors that may mediate any media effects (e.g. conditions of access to media, the cultural/regulatory context in which the research was conducted, and the media literacy of parents or carers in managing their children's media access).

This review identified empirical studies primarily by searching a range of extensive electronic and library resources, these being largely but not exclusively academic, though it also draws on information obtained from key researchers in the field. The body of empirical published research is expanding fast in some areas – especially in relation to the Internet, though as in the earlier review, that published in the English language remains largely American.

It is worth noting that, although in policy-discussions 'harm and offence' is often used as a single phrase, it is not always clear just what the difference between them is taken to be, nor how they differently relate to legal or regulatory frameworks. Similarly, harm and offence are often not clearly distinguished in terms of academic research evidence, though, in the main, academic research is concerned with harm rather than with offence.

FINDINGS BY MEDIUM

TELEVISION

■ Television is still an important medium, especially for young children. The research included here primarily concerns violence, sexualization and stereotypes, as these have attracted the most research attention. Other effects research is noted (though not discussed here), such as effects on scholastic performance and the effect of commercial activity.

■ Over the decades, significant research effort has been expended on this ubiquitous and accessible medium, and many studies of other media are based on those from television. There is also a body of research that examines the benefits of exposure to television content but this is not considered here unless it also refers to a consideration of harm and offence.

■ The evidence suggests that, under certain circumstances, television can negatively influence attitudes in some areas, including those which may affect society (through the creation of prejudice) and those which may affect the individual (by making them unduly fearful, for example). Thus, it seems that television plays a part in contributing to stereotypes, fear of crime and other reality-defining effects, although it remains unclear what other social influences also play a role, or how important television is by comparison with these other factors.

■ The primary subjects of research have been children and young people,[1] as they are thought to be most vulnerable to negative influences which may, in turn, affect long-term attitudes or behaviour. However, there is a growing body of evidence which suggests that there are also vulnerable groups of adults who may be negatively affected by certain types of media content; for example, people with particular personality disorders.

■ The lack of longitudinal tracking data makes it difficult to determine whether there are longer-term changes to attitudes or behaviour that result from watching violent content.

■ Methodologically, one must accept the research evidence is flawed, partly because much of it derives from a different cultural and regulatory environment from that of the United Kingdom (most of the research was conducted in the United States). However, it is important to evaluate what the findings are, focusing on those studies that have minimized the methodological and cultural difficulties so as to understand the indications of influence and effect that they provide.

■ Many of the studies use experimental methods, and are subject to considerable criticism. They demonstrate short-term effects on attitudes and behaviours, among a particular research sample (e.g. college students) and under particular conditions. It is also the case that too little of the research evidence examines the viewing of age-appropriate material, although a number of studies use content popular among the target group being examined.

■ Other studies use content analysis techniques to examine the nature of content, making assumptions about the way in which the images might be received. However, in the United Kingdom and elsewhere, qualitative and social research techniques show it is valuable to talk to audience groups to understand their reasoning and reactions to content they view.

■ The review of research showed the importance to the audience of certain variables in making sense of or justifying a portrayed act. These include the context within which the act is set and the importance of identification and empathy with the protagonists.

■ Transmission time remains an important variable within audience attitudes towards broadcast television content, with established conventions designed to reduce the potential for offence.

■ Much of the research evidence shows that most audiences are generally able to distinguish fact from fiction. The evidence also suggests that the viewing of fictional content does not diminish the distress that may be caused by violence in real-life.

■ There are clear audience differences based on gender (in particular, boys seem to be more influenced by violent content) and age; but also family settings, a predisposition for a particular programme genre, the way in which the content is used and other such variables all appear to play a part in the way content is viewed and assimilated.

■ Much of the research has been less equivocal in demonstrating evidence for areas of offence caused (such as with regard to offensive language, violence or the depiction of sexual activity) in comparison with harm. Contextual and demographic variables are seen particularly to affect the levels of offence felt.

■ Importantly, some of the research literature argues that the influences or effects of television need to be understood and recognized not only by researchers and policy-makers but also by those in the industry.

FILM, VIDEO AND DVD

■ The empirical research evidence for harm and offence in relation to film has been concerned primarily with 'adult' or relatively extreme sexual and violent content, such material being more available, though restricted by age, on film and video than – at present – on television.

■ Although concerns are consistently raised regarding the reality-defining or stereotyping effects of film, we found little recent research on this. Evidence for emotional responses to film, particularly fear, exists and is relatively uncontentious, though whether this constitutes longer-term harm is more difficult to determine given the absence of longitudinal research studies.

■ Considerable attention has been paid to pornography, focusing variously on harm to those involved in production, to male consumers, to children, and to society (especially, attitudes towards women) more generally. The evidence for harm to men viewing non-violent (or consensual) pornography remains inconclusive or absent. However, the evidence for harm from viewing violent (non-consensual) pornography is rather stronger, resulting in more negative or aggressive attitudes and behaviours towards women as well as supporting the desire to watch more extreme content.

■ The evidence that viewing pornography harms children remains scarce, given ethical restrictions on the research, though many experts believe it to be harmful. Other vulnerable groups have been researched, however, with some evidence that the harmful effects of violent content especially are greater for those who are already aggressive, for children with behaviour disorders, for young offenders with a history of domestic violence and – for pornographic content – among sexual offenders.

■ Public attitudes to film content are, generally, more tolerant than for television. This is partly because the public is aware, and supportive of, current levels of regulation in film, and partly because people understand the decision process behind choosing to watch violent or sexual content. Tolerance is lowest (or offence is greatest) for the portrayal of sexual violence. Studies of audience interpretation of potentially harmful or offensive content in film throw some light on the complex judgements made by the public in this area.

■ As the conditions for viewing film – both at home and in the cinema – are changing, too little is known regarding the conditions under which people, especially children, may gain access to different kinds of potentially harmful content.

ELECTRONIC GAMES

■ Although research on electronic games is relatively new, it is strongly polarized between the psychological/experimental approach that argues that electronic games have harmful effects, and the cultural/qualitative approach that defends games as merely entertaining, even beneficial on occasion.

■ Possible outcomes of game-playing, including harmful ones, depend on the type of game and the context in which it is played.

■ In the psychological/effects approach, a growing body of research is accumulating which suggests harmful short-term effects, especially for games with violent content, and especially on boys or men who play them. There is some evidence to suggest the effects may be as much associated with games containing unrealistic or cartoon violence as they are with those employing realistic and sophisticated computer graphics.

■ However, this research remains contested in terms of how far it can be applied to aggressive situations in everyday life. It also remains unclear how much this evidence concerns media violence in general and how much it is video-game specific. One empirical comparison across research studies found that the effect of violent video-games on aggression is smaller than that found for television violence. However, more research is required to compare the effects of, for example, violent television and video-games. On the one hand, it has been argued that television imagery has hitherto been more graphic/realistic and hence more influential (although technical advances in video-game technology are allowing them to 'catch up'). On the other hand, it has been argued that video-games require a more involved and attentive style of engagement – a 'first person' rather than a 'third person' experience – which may make games more harmful.

■ There is also growing evidence about excessive game playing, which some researchers suggest shows addictive behaviour among a minority of players.

INTERNET

■ The authors found a fast-growing body of research in this area, particularly for research examining the ways in which social networking sites and services are being used.

■ While the positive social benefits of these sites are noted, these were not the subject of this review. The present focus was instead on the evidence for the potential for harm that these sites create – primarily by facilitating the easy uploading and accessing of inappropriate content, sharing and disseminating personal information, and extending the possibilities for inappropriate contacts.

■ While some argue that there is little new about online content, familiar contents merely having moved online, most disagree, expressing concern about the accessibility of more extreme forms of content that are, potentially, harmful and offensive.

■ Much of the research shows that young people using these sites are aware of the risk of harm, and are generally aware of both the technical measures and codes of behaviour that they should adopt. It also suggests that they often ignore these or, for various reasons, open themselves up to inappropriate or risky experiences.

■ For children, there is a growing body of national and international research on children's distress when they accidentally come across online pornography and other unwelcome content.

■ There is a limited, but growing, literature on the potentially harmful consequences of user-generated contact, this including everything from the school or workplace bully to the grooming of children by paedophiles. It has become evident that many children and adults experience minor versions of such contact, with some evidence also of criminal (paedophile) activity.

■ Further, research shows that when people – adults and children – receive hostile, bullying or hateful messages, they are generally ill-equipped to respond appropriately or to cope with the emotional upset this causes. Similarly, parents are unclear how they can know about, or intervene in, risky behaviours undertaken – deliberately or inadvertently – by their children. As for pornographic content, the consequences of exposure seem to be more harmful for those who are already vulnerable.

■ People's responses to 'hateful' content tend to be more tolerant, on the grounds of freedom of expression, though they find it offensive. Little as yet is known of how the targeted groups (mainly, ethnic minorities) respond.

■ The lack of clear definitions of levels or types of pornography, violence, etc on the Internet, where the range is considerable, impedes research, as do (necessarily) the ethical restrictions on researching the potentially harmful effects of online content, especially but not only on children.

■ As many defend online pornography as suggest it to be harmful, though there is a growing body of research – though still small – suggesting such content to be particularly harmful for vulnerable groups – specifically, people who are sexually compulsive and/or sexual abusers.

■ In general, the case for further research seems clear, firstly in relation to the characteristics of vulnerable groups (including strategies for intervention) and secondly in relation to the ways in which the Internet seems to support or facilitate certain kinds of harmful peer-to-peer activity.

TELEPHONY

■ There is growing evidence that mobile telephony may cause harm through the creation of fear and humiliation by bullying, for example. Although it is evident that new communication technologies are being incorporated into practices of bullying, harassment and other forms of malicious peer-to-peer communication, it is not yet clear that these technologies are responsible for an increase in the incidence of such practices.

■ There is little substantive academic evidence for the potential risk of harm or offence caused through access to the professionally-produced content market for mobiles, although inferences are being made about such possible effects from other media.

■ It is questionable whether mobile technologies are used in the same way as other fixed media, particularly because they have rapidly become personal and private forms of communication. This is an area where the lack of research evidence is especially felt.

RADIO

■ Despite being the background to so many people's lives, little recent research of radio was found in relation to questions of harm. Such concern as does arise is concentrated particularly on talk shows and similar programmes based on call-ins or user-generated content, and in relation to the lyrics of popular music.

■ Research shows that radio is found to be offensive on occasion by a substantial minority of the audience – particularly in relation to the treatment of callers by presenters, offensive language and racism.

MUSIC

■ There is little research which examines harm and offence in relation to music. The research that exists is mainly content analytic rather than based on audience reactions, except for occasional opinion surveys, and is mainly focused on popular music lyrics.

■ These studies reveal consistent messages in music lyrics that may be considered harmful and are considered offensive by some – including messages promoting violence among boys/men, homophobic messages, or those encouraging early sexuality among young girls/women. Some argue that these are particularly damaging for ethnic minority audiences.

■ There is a small body of experimental evidence suggesting that, as for other media, these messages can negatively influence the attitudes or emotions of their audience.

PRINT

■ The history of the print media and the precedents set in terms of policy- making have helped frame debates about other media and have also provided a framework for the way in which much media content is regulated.

■ Research suggests the print media, especially the press, can frame public discourse, providing important civil information. The potential complicity of the media in misinformation is questioned in many studies reviewed here. It is argued that the potential of harm that may occur not only affects the individual but also has broader consequences for society.

■ The importance of the public or private nature of different types of print media has not been widely researched but the evidence suggests that how strongly one is affected by print content is closely linked with this distinction.

ADVERTISING

■ There is a moderate body of evidence pointing to modest effects of both intentional (i.e. product-promoting) and incidental (i.e. product context) advertising messages. This suggests that advertising has some influence on product choice, and that the nature of its portrayals has some influence on the attitudes and beliefs of its audience.

■ Specifically, a range of reality-defining effects[2] have been examined – in relation to the stereotyping of population segments and, most recently, in relation to obesity and products with other health consequences. This tends to show modest evidence for harmful effects of advertising, particularly on children, although it remains contested. Since the influence of advertising is not large, according to the evidence, research is needed to determine what other factors also influence these harmful outcomes (stereotyping, obesity, smoking, etc).

■ This question of intent has implications for media literacy. In relation to advertising, the intent to persuade is generally considered acceptable provided the public recognizes this intent. In relation to children, considerable research exists on the development of 'advertising literacy' with age, though it has not been clearly shown that more media literate, or advertising literate, consumers are less affected by advertising (or other media), nor that interventions designed to increase literacy have the effect of reducing media harm.

■ Little is yet known of how all audiences – adults as well as children – recognise advertising, sponsorship, product placement etc in relation to the new media environment.

■ There is also a body of research linking advertising to offence. This research reveals the considerable cultural variation, both within and across cultures, in what content is found offensive and by whom.

REGULATION IN THE HOME

■ Research shows that users are generally accepting of regulation of content and have particular areas of concern such as violence in the media. Evidence also suggests that both parents and children are increasingly aware of the risks associated with media use.

■ There is a move away from content regulation towards the provision of more information and more access prevention tools for users. Many respondents in research say they welcome this. It is clear however, that they accept this greater 'empowerment' only within a (currently) regulated framework. Thus there is growing support for the importance of media literacy and for systems of content labelling and information, together with an increasing awareness of the difficulties in ensuring that such knowledge is fairly distributed across the population.

■ Many parents have long employed various strategies for mediating their children's television use, notably those that restrict the child's viewing (by restricting time spent or content viewed), that promote parental values and media literacy by discussing viewing with the child, and by simply sharing the viewing experience with the child. These and other strategies have been extended to electronic games and, more recently, to children's use of the Internet.

■ However, research points to a range of difficulties parents encounter, especially in managing their children's Internet use and, in consequence, some may do little to intervene in their child's online activities. Particularly, parents underestimate risks compared with those reported by the child; further, children report receiving lower levels of parental mediation than are claimed by their parents.

■ Notably, there is not yet much evidence that parental regulation effectively reduces the extent or nature of media-related risks, unless parents take a generally restrictive approach to their child's access to the medium altogether.

■ Similarly, although research is growing on children's media literacy, as are the number of initiatives designed to increase this literacy, it is not yet established that increased media literacy either reduces children's exposure to risk or increases their ability to cope with risk. Hence more research is needed.

CONCLUSIONS

■ *The meaning of harm and offence.* As noted at the outset, 'harm and offence' is often used as a single phrase, with little clarity regarding the difference between them or how they may each relate to legal and regulatory frameworks. It is suggested that harm is widely (though not necessarily) conceived in objective terms; harm, it seems, is taken to be observable by others (irrespective of whether harm is acknowledged by the individual concerned), and hence as measurable in a reliable fashion. By contrast, offence is widely (though not necessarily) conceived in subjective terms; offence, it seems, is taken to be that experienced by and reported on by the individual.

■ *Conclusions regarding offence.* Looking across all media, the research evidence shows a sizeable minority of the population find certain content offensive. This is especially the case for women and older people, though most are nonetheless tolerant of the rights of others to engage with the media of their choice. In particular, new forms of media occasion greater public concern and anxiety than do more familiar media. For these latter, the public is, in the main, supportive of the current regulatory framework. However, findings are mixed on whether people are satisfied with (or even aware of) the available processes for making a complaint about media content.

■ *Conclusions regarding harm*. Drawing conclusions about harm is more difficult, for the evidence base is more strongly contested. This review notes a range of theoretical, methodological and political difficulties, resulting in a patchy and somewhat inconsistent evidence base, while questions remain difficult to research for ethical, theoretical and practical reasons. Thus, research can only inform judgements based on the balance of probabilities rather than on irrefutable proof.

■ *Key gaps in the evidence base*. Priorities for future research include:

☐ research on the range of marginalized and/or vulnerable groups (including the elderly, gay, ethnic minorities, and those with psychological difficulties);

☐ research on new media technologies (especially Internet, mobile, other new and interactive devices) and new contents (interactive content, new forms of advertising and promotion, niche/extreme content);

☐ longitudinal or long-term panel studies, to follow up the effects of short-term harm, to track changes in levels and kinds of offence, and to identify changing expectations and understandings of media (including the access conditions) among the public;

☐ research on reality-defining/stereotyping effects that relates to recent changes especially in UK-originated media content, as well as imported content; research on the new issues arising from new media, particularly in relation to user-generated and malicious peer-to-peer content and contact;

☐ research that puts media effects in context, seeking to understand how the media play a role in a multi-factor explanation for particular social phenomena (e.g. violence, gender stereotyping, etc), this to include a comparative account of the relative size of effect for each factor (including the media) in order to enable regulatory decisions based on proportionality;

☐ research that directly compares the public's responses to the 'same' content when accessed on different media (e.g. violence on television, in film, in computer games, online) so as to understand whether and how the medium or the conditions of access to a medium, make a difference;

☐ research on the range of factors that potentially mediate (buffer, or exacerbate) any effects of media exposure (e.g. level of media literacy, role of parental mediation, difference between accidental and deliberate exposure).

■ *A risk-based approach*. This review argues that the search for simple and direct causal effects of the media is, for the most part, no longer appropriate. Rather, this should be replaced by an approach that seeks to identify the range of factors that directly, and indirectly through interactions with each other, combine to explain particular social phenomena. As research shows, each social problem of concern (e.g. aggression, prejudice, obesity, bullying, etc) is associated with a distinct and complex array of putative causes. The task for those concerned with media harm and offence is to identify and contextualize the role of the media within that array. In some cases, this may reduce the focus on the media – for example, by bringing into view the many factors that account for present levels of aggression in society. In other cases, it may increase the focus on the media – for example, in understanding the role played by the Internet in facilitating paedophiles' access to children. Further, the risks of media harm may be greater for those who are already 'vulnerable'. The conclusions to this review consider a range of key claims for media harm, on a case by case basis.

■ *The importance of a balanced approach*. To those who fear that the media are responsible for a growing range of social problems, we would urge that the evidence base is carefully and critically scrutinized, for such findings as exist generally point to more modest, qualified and context-dependent conclusions. But to those who hold that the media play little or no role in today's social problems, we would point to the complex and diverse ways in which different media are variably but crucially embedded in most or all aspects of our everyday lives, and that it seems implausible to suggest that they have no influence, whether positive or negative.

■ *Convergence*. In a context of converging technologies and media content, we are particularly concerned at the lack of evidence providing a secure basis for making comparisons across media platforms. Audits of the media used by different segments of the population provide cross-media information regarding both use and skills for a range of platforms but there is not sufficient research about attitudes to, or the influences of, cross-media content. We note that comparisons across different media regarding the nature or size of effects are difficult in methodological terms; however, such research could and should be attempted.

■ Research on the conditions under which people access and use media in their daily lives makes it clear that many contextual variables are important in framing the ways in which people approach the media, this in turn impacting on the kinds of effects these media may have. This points to difficulties with the premise of regulation that is technology-neutral, since research shows that the public does not treat technology as equivalent and that the domestic and technological conditions of access vary; these and other factors differentially affect, at least at present, how people approach and respond to different media.

■ Regulation, as currently implemented, draws on and is in many ways justified by reference to a complex base of media- and audience-specific research evidence. The balance to be struck between individuals (often parents) and institutions (industry, regulators) in managing conditions of access should, we have suggested, vary for more established and newer media. As homes become more complex, multi-media environments, and as media technologies converge, it must be a priority to develop and extend the available evidence base, so that we sustain our understanding of the differences across, and relations among, the changing array of media and communication technologies. The challenge is to seek ways of minimizing risks, while also enabling the many benefits afforded by these technologies for our society and for the socialization of our children.

NOTES

1. Where appropriate, ages of research subjects have been given. However, it should be assumed that the term 'children' generally refers to primary school-age children and 'young people' to secondary school-age children, though the latter sometimes includes young adults (i.e. students).

2. McQuail (1987) defines these as the systematic tendencies of the media, through the repetition of many similar messages, to affirm and reinforce the particular cognitions that fit one version of social reality (e.g. stereotyping or exclusion of certain groups or experiences).

1

THE POLICY CONTEXT

INTRODUCTION

Harm: material damage, actual or potential ill effect. (Soanes and Stevenson, 2004)

Offence: an act or instance of offending; resentment or hurt (ibid.), something that outrages the moral or physical senses. (Merriam-Webster, n.d.)

Recent and ongoing policy initiatives in Europe and elsewhere are typically set against a background of concern regarding the potential for harm from exposure to media content. These concerns arise especially for children and especially for content delivered in easily accessible ways through platforms such as the Internet or in ways less easily regulated than content delivered through a scarce and limited spectrum (as in traditional analogue broadcasting). One of the key changes has been the acceptance of the concepts of 'harm' and 'offence' as a legitimate reason to legislate or regulate, replacing notions of 'taste' and 'decency' that had predominated previously in broadcasting regulation in the United Kingdom and Europe. Although the debate, and the evidence base, is largely focused on the exposure of minors to potentially harmful or offensive material, there are other sensibilities such as offence or harm caused to those from minority groups.

Although harmful and offensive material is, in principle, distinguished from that which is illegal (obscenity, child abuse images, incitement to racial hatred, etc), it remains difficult to define the boundaries in a robust and consensual fashion. What contents are considered acceptable by today's standards, norms and values, and by whom? Borderline and unacceptable material may include a range of contents, most prominently though not exclusively 'adult content' of various kinds, and these may occasion considerable concern on the part of the public or subsections thereof. While norms of taste and decency can be tracked, with some reliability, through standard opinion measurement techniques, methods for assessing harm especially are much more contested and difficult. Arguably too, the research evidence – of which there is a huge amount – remains concentrated on a media environment and a regulatory regime that is still in a period of rapid change, rendering the evidence potentially out of date.

With the arrival of newer media content, particularly through the Internet (though also digital television, mobile phones, etc), it is not clear how far the public recognizes or feels empowered to respond to the expanding array of content on offer. It is likely that these newer, more interactive media pose a challenge particularly to ordinary families as well as to regulators. Can they apply familiar domestic practices of regulation and restriction to newer media? What range of concerns do people have regarding new media forms and contents? What do they need to know about whether the greatly-expanded range of contents now available to children have been shown to cause harm or not?

Policy debates attempt to balance the often-conflicting concerns over possible harms against other concerns (most notably, civil liberties and freedom of speech, children's rights to exploration and privacy, and parents' capacities or otherwise to regulate their children's media use). Difficult issues arise. How do we draw the line between the offensive and the harmful? Is it a matter of particular kinds of contents, particular forms of media or particular groups of children? What kinds of harms, if any, have received robust empirical support? What is the evidence for offence across diverse sectors of the population? How far should the regulator and policy-maker concern themselves with audiences other than children?

To produce effective, evidence-based policy looking towards the media environment of the future, an assessment of the evidence for content-related harm and offence is clearly required across as many of the current forms of evolving media as possible. That is the purpose of this updated review.

REGULATING AGAINST RISK OF HARM – THE UK PERSPECTIVE

In the United Kingdom, the Communications Act 2003 requires that the regulator (Ofcom) draws up a code for television and radio, setting standards for programmes, on matters such as protecting the under-eighteens, harm and offence, sponsorship, fairness and privacy. The Act outlines that in carrying out its functions, Ofcom is required to secure:

> Section 3 General duties of OFCOM (Office of Public Sector Information [OPSI], 2003) 2(e) The application, in the case of all television and radio services, of standards that provide adequate protection to members of the public from the inclusion of offensive and harmful material in such services;

This was a change from previous content regulatory regimes which had talked of regulating for 'taste and decency'. Issues of taste and decency are fluid and arguably subjective, especially taste. The Broadcasting Standards Commission (set up by the Broadcasting Act, 1990) recognized this and made a distinction between issues of taste and those of decency:

> A distinction has to be made between attitudes which are subject to rapid changes of fashion, such as style of dress or modes of address, and those which reflect more enduring views of right and wrong. Matters of taste are ephemeral, while matters of decency, such as the dignity to be accorded to the dead and bereaved, reflect ideals that acknowledge our shared values. (Broadcasting Standards Commission, 1998)

Ofcom has welcomed this change to a notion of 'harm and offence', codified in the Communications Act. The former Chairman of the Content Board, Richard Hooper, said in Ofcom's 'Annual Report' (2005a:15):

> In content regulation, the Act also supports a move away from the more subjective approach of the past, based on an assessment of taste and decency in television and radio programmes, to a more objective analysis of the extent of harm and offence to audiences. The result is a Code that is much shorter and is, more importantly, focused on providing protection to those who need it most, particularly children and young people.

In performing its duties, Ofcom (if it appears relevant to Ofcom in the circumstances) must have regard to:

> 3 (4)(h) The vulnerability of children and of others whose circumstances appear to OFCOM to put them in need of special protection.

In addition, the Communications Act 2003 (Section 127) states:

> 127 (1) A person is guilty of an offence if he:
>
> (a) Sends by means of a public electronic communications network a message or other matter that is grossly offensive or of an indecent, obscene or menacing character; or
>
> (b) Causes any such message or matter to be so sent.

In terms of broadcasting standards regulation a key change in the Act is the standards objective which requires:

> 319 (2)(f): That generally accepted standards are applied to the contents of television and radio services so as to provide adequate protection for members of the public from the inclusion in such services of offensive and harmful material.

There is also a specific requirement within the Act (319 (2)(a)) which sets as a standards objective that people under eighteen are protected.

Within the United Kingdom, a diverse range of laws set the legal framework for considerations of harm and offence, in addition to the Communications Act 2003. These include laws regarding public decency, electronic commerce, indecent display, obscene publications, protection of children, public order, video recordings and so forth; brief accounts of these, as they relate to media content and harm/offence are outlined in Annex II.

Additionally to the legal and statutory framework considering the risk of harm, there have been two recent inquiries considering the potential for harm of the Internet and video-games. The Byron Review (2008) was an independent review, tasked with considering the risks to children in particular and much of the updated material presented here was used by Ofcom in its submission to the Review.[1] Byron's report suggested a simplification and clarification of the classification system. Regarding the Internet, recommendations include the establishment of a UK Council for Child Internet Safety, reporting to the Prime Minister. The task of this Council should be:

> to lead the development of a strategy with two core elements: better regulation – in the form, wherever possible, of voluntary codes of practice that industry can sign up to – and better information and education, where the role of government, law enforcement, schools and children's services will be key.

Byron suggests that the Council should also have an ongoing research role and that it should re-examine the legislation surrounding sites that may contain harmful and inappropriate material. Further, she makes specific requests of the industry, including a recommendation that computers sold for use in the home should have kitemarked parental control software which is easy to install and use. Across both sectors Byron calls for raising awareness of the issues, especially for parents and carers, and for clear information. She also calls for 'whole-school' policies regarding e-safety and improving awareness.

In addition to the Byron Review, there has been a Culture, Media and Sport committee inquiry into harmful content on the Internet and in video-games, which looked at all consumers, not just children. Other initiatives have also taken place – the Department for Children, Schools and Families produced an action plan which includes an anti-cyber-bullying pack and a Virtual Cyber-bullying Taskforce.[2] In its 'Action Plan' on tackling violence, the Home Office commits to 'working with the technology and communications industries to tackle violence and offensive content on the internet, and in video games, films and other media'.[3]

Similarly, the Home Office Taskforce on Child Protection on the Internet has published guidance for social networking, aimed at parents and children, and the providers of social networking sites.[4] It makes several recommendations including those relating to safety information, editorial responsibility (including appropriate advertising), registration, user profile and associated controls, identity authentication and age verification. The 'Kitemark for Child Safety Online' has been launched (2008) – a collaboration between the British Standards Institute, the Home Office, Ofcom and representatives from ISPs and application developers.[5] This allows manufacturers to get their products certified, increasing control over the standard of filtering, monitoring and blocking applications.

REGULATING AGAINST RISK OF HARM – THE EUROPEAN PERSPECTIVE

The change in content regulation from 'good taste and decency' was driven in part by the European Union's formulation of 'harm and offence' (see also Shaw, 1999). Article 22 (1) of the Television Without Frontiers (TVWF) Directive (2003) required Member States to take appropriate measures to ensure that television broadcasts 'do not include programmes which might seriously impair the physical, mental or moral development of minors, in particular those that involve pornography or gratuitous violence.' The same Directive said that 'programmes which are likely to impair the physical, mental or moral development of minors' may be broadcast as long as scheduling or other access control systems are put in place.

In 2007 the Audio Visual Media Services (AVMS) Directive was adopted by the Member States of the European Union.[6] It replaces the TVWF Directive and is a response to what the Commission saw as the increasing convergence of technologies and markets and the way in which content could be accessed. The AVMS Directive extends regulation to all audio-visual media services, regardless of how they are transmitted, that offer the same or similar 'television-like' services. So content such as online games and user-generated videos, as well as electronic versions of newspapers and magazines, fall outside the scope of the AVMS Directive. The Directive refers to the need to protect minors:

> (44) The availability of harmful content in audiovisual media services continues to be a concern for legislators, the media industry and parents. There will also be new challenges, especially in connection with new platforms and new products. It is therefore necessary to introduce rules to protect the physical, mental and moral development of minors as well as human dignity in all audiovisual media services, including audiovisual commercial communications.

The Directive mentions the importance of media literacy to create a knowledgeable user base. The Directive is expected to be implemented in the United Kingdom in 2009.

The relevance of media literacy was amplified by the Commission's 'Communication on Media Literacy' (2007) which focuses on three areas:[7]

■ media literacy for commercial communication, covering issues related to advertising;

■ media literacy for audio-visual works, which is in part about raising awareness of European film and enhancing creativity skills;

■ media literacy for online which, for example, will give citizens a better knowledge of how Google and other Internet search engines work.

A separate recommendation on the protection of minors and human dignity and the right of reply in relation to the competitiveness of the European audio-visual and information services industry was adopted in 2006.[8] This recommendation focuses on the content of audio-visual and information services covering *all* forms of delivery, from broadcasting to the Internet. It encourages cooperation and the sharing of experience and good practices between self- and co-regulatory bodies that deal with the rating or classification of audio-visual content. Thus, it is hoped, viewers can assess the content and suitability of programmes, in particular parents and teachers. The recommendation particularly mentions the importance of media literacy.

Alongside these European initiatives, the European Union has continued with its Safer Internet plus Programme, with a budget of 55 million Euros.[9] It will:

- Reduce illegal content and tackle harmful conduct online: providing the public with national contact points for reporting illegal content online and harmful conduct, focusing in particular on child sexual abuse material and grooming.

- Promote a safer online environment: especially through self-regulatory initiatives.

- Ensure public awareness: targeting children, their parents and teachers. Exchange best practices within the network of national awareness centres.

- Establish a knowledge base: bringing together researchers engaged in child safety online at a European level.

While it is clear that content which may not conform to generally accepted standards or which may offend can be identified through opinion research, complaints and other tests of public tolerance, it is unclear how harm is to be objectively measured. The key objective of this review therefore, is to examine notions of harm and offence across key media, identifying the evidence that exists, while recognizing that regulatory practice and policy may not necessarily be based on direct evidence. It will be important for the industry (from broadcaster to content provider), the regulator and other policy-makers to be able to identify what may cause harm especially, as this is a more profound concept in its implications than offence. It is also important to identify whether and when offence may become harmful, again in relation to the available evidence.

MODES OF ACCESS

The distinction between types of content services, long established within UK legislation and regulatory practice, has been superseded – or updated – by the adoption of the AVMS Directive. Broadcasting, 'linear' programming or a 'push' technology, means that content is pushed at the viewer according to a schedule or transmission timetable set by the content provider (or broadcaster). Content that is 'pulled down' (i.e. provided as a result of selection by the viewer), such as video-on-demand or Internet-based services, is non-linear and has not been regulated thus far. It does not fall outside the legal framework, however, for it is subject to the criminal law.

With the convergence of broadcasting and Internet protocol-based technologies, the Commission argued that certain regulatory practices should apply to all audio-visual content regardless of its mode of delivery (Eurobarometer, 2004; European Commission, 1997). The AVMS Directive continues to distinguish between linear and non-linear services, but allows for some regulation of 'television-like' services based on judgements about audience expectations and editorial responsibility, regardless of delivery platform. Thus, regulation will continue for linear services such as traditional broadcasting, but will also be extended to include television schedules delivered over the Internet (IPTV), streamed content and near video-on-demand. Non-linear services (including video-on-demand) will, for the first time, be regulated, although less prescriptively than linear services. While the Directive argues that transfrontier communications should remain unrestricted, it recognizes that nation states will have to interpret the Directive's principles according to their own systems. Importantly, the newer technologies such as IPTV remove geographical obstacles. Thus, the ability of Member States to regulate for national cultural sensitivities is uncertain when material crosses geographical boundaries. It is not clear that the new Directive, yet to be implemented, has taken sufficient account of this when seeking to create a European content regulatory system (see Wheeler, 2004).

In the United Kingdom, Ofcom regulates the BBC's broadcasting output through the Ofcom Broadcasting Code on fairness and privacy and on programme standards (excluding impartiality and accuracy). Television production quotas and certain programme genre quotas set by the BBC must also be consulted on or agreed with Ofcom. However, like all broadcasters, the BBC assumes responsibility for its own output. To this end the BBC produces editorial guidelines that set out its 'values and standards' (2005). Key to these is the determination 'to balance our rights to freedom of expression and information with our responsibilities, for example, to respect privacy and protect children'. Further, the guidelines cover all the BBC's output, including its websites (while Ofcom has no control over the Internet). The BBC's Director General says that this creates guidelines 'designed for a multi-media world: the guidelines apply across all BBC content on radio, television, new media and magazines' (2005).

This literature review will examine the challenges posed by the new technologies as regards regulating for the individual, or regulating the individual, in comparison with regulating the industry that offers content to individuals. The growing focus on modes of access recognizes both that individuals have responsibilities in making content decisions but also that they make choices within constraints set by others and that they may need support in framing appropriate decisions. Oswell (1998) draws together the three groups involved in child protection on the Internet – government, industry and those who have guardianship of children – when arguing that it is important to think carefully about the levels of parental accountability being assumed and the 'consistency' of responsibility and regulation being expected of parents. This offers a sceptical framing of the increasingly popular solution, namely to seek to increase media literacy among audiences and users. For media literacy is widely seen as reducing the need both for regulation of firms and for restrictions on freedom of speech. Coming from an anti-censorship lobby in the United States, Heins (2001) argues:

> There is urgent need for coherent, objective, and clear-sighted exploration of the best 'tools and strategies' for addressing concerns about minors' access to pornography and 'other inappropriate internet content'. In the final analysis, affirmative educational approaches are more likely to be effective than technological 'fixes'.

Others call for better regulation of media content. For example, Webb, Jenkins, Browne, Afifi and Kraus (2007: e1227) call for improved film classification, noting from their content analysis of the violence portrayed in films rated PG-13 in the United States 'the use of violence as a common means by which conflicts are resolved and stated goals are obtained'. Since, they judge, these films are viewed by teenagers, many of whom are 'already embroiled in social violence', responsibility for what is viewed cannot be left solely to the individual viewer. This challenge has been taken up by the Federal Communication Commission regarding violent content on television, with an information guidance system in place which uses a technical solution, the V Chip, embedded in television sets, to restrict viewing when activated (FCC, 2007). The FCC has suggested a scheduling-based convention for television as well as asking cable operators to consider how they structure their programme packages.

In sum, there is increasing evidence that policy-makers and industry are seeking to work together to obviate an unnecessary regulatory burden while also protecting users of the media. For example, in the United States, the New York Attorney General has announced models of behaviour and good practice in association with a social networking site (Facebook) to ensure improved complaints procedures which allow, among other things, for children to report harassment (2007). Similarly, the new kitemarking scheme launched in the United Kingdom in 2008 to promote Internet safety, resulted from collaboration between government departments, the regulator and the industry. Indeed, in calling for enhanced multi-stakeholder cooperation regarding children's online safety in the United Kingdom, the Byron Review (2008) asserts three linked strategic objectives – reducing availability of harmful content, restricting access by children, and increasing children's resilience to harmful material if and when accessed.

MEDIA CONTENT REGULATION

Within this wider framework that recognizes the importance of regulating both modes of access and the promotion of media literacy, media content regulation is based on a number of key considerations. These include:

- The concept of detriment (or risk of harm).

- Proportionality (what weight is to be attached to the detriment).

- Disadvantaged or vulnerable groups (who suffers?).

The notion of preventing harm has guided many of the concerns about media content and subsequent regulation. In the United States, the Parents Television Council, a lobby group, have argued that the FCC (the converged regulator in the United States) should 'make a priority of reducing TV violence and expand the definition of broadcast indecency to include violence' (Parents Television Council, n.d.).

In the United Kingdom, the *criminal* offence in the area of harm is that governed by the 1959 Obscene Publications Act (OPA) and it involves an explicit effects-based test. Section 1 of the Act defines a publication to be obscene 'if its effect…is, if taken as a whole, such as to tend to deprave and corrupt persons who are likely, in all the circumstances, to read, see, or hear the matter contained or embodied in it'. For a description of legal processes in place in the United Kingdom, and legislation being discussed, see Annex II.

Barnett and Thomson (1996) point out the definition of depravity and corruption has been left to jurors in individual cases, but it is clear that some kind of change in mental or behavioural orientation is implied. It is not enough merely to have offended people, even in large numbers. In describing the OPA, and pointing to cases where it has been called upon, Murphy (2003) observes:

It is the tendency to deprave and corrupt which is important. This can refer merely to the effect on the mind in terms of stimulating fantasies and it is not necessary that physical or overt sexual activity should result…obscenity is not necessarily concerned with sexual depravity but also includes material advocating drug taking or violence…The persons likely to be depraved or corrupted need not be wholly innocent to begin with: the further corruption of the less innocent is also included. Nor is it necessary that all those who are likely to read, see or hear the article should be corrupted. It is sufficient that the article should tend to deprave or corrupt a significant proportion of them.

Due to a perception of the limitations of the OPA to deal with certain significant issues raised by the advent of the Internet (in particular), there is current debate in the United Kingdom about whether or not the Act should be strengthened (United Kingdom Parliament, 2004). Other legal mechanisms for the prevention of harm exist such as those that restrict the dissemination of child pornography, for example, covered by the Protection of Children Act 1978 or the Suicide Act 1961. However, these are also being challenged by new technologies that make access to certain information both easer and quicker. Hendrick, in a debate in Parliament about websites that promote suicide, said:[10]

I have researched the matter and it is abundantly clear that the Suicide Act 1961 is woefully inadequate to deal with the use of the Internet for the promotion of suicide. I say that for the reasons that I have outlined: cyberspace does not respect national boundaries or legislation, and both the physical location and author of a source of information can be concealed.

The OPA is used more sparingly now, though cases continue to be brought in relation to OPA offences. What has been created in the area of content regulation is a series of organizations designed to regulate what Barnett calls an 'affective' notion of harm, that is, 'offence' caused by content. In the United Kingdom, as in many other countries, various regulatory bodies oversee different media. (For a comprehensive review of the practices of many regulators in the field of negative audio-visual content regulation, see Millwood Hargrave, 2007).

Within the United Kingdom, several organizations are involved in content regulation, as shown in Table 1.1.

REGULATION OF HARMFUL AND OFFENSIVE MEDIA CONTENT

Media content regulation is not limited to minors, and may include a number of issues as outlined in Ofcom's Broadcasting Code (2005b):

2.3 In applying generally accepted standards broadcasters must ensure that material which may cause offence is justified by the context. Such material may include, but is not limited to, offensive language, violence, sex, sexual violence, humiliation, distress, violation of human dignity, discriminatory treatment or language (for example on the grounds of age, disability, gender, race, religion, beliefs and sexual orientation). Appropriate information should also be broadcast where it would assist in avoiding or minimising offence.

Table 1.1 The regulation of media content in the United Kingdom.

Organization	Industry	Role	Code	What it does
ASA	Advertising	Self-regulatory	Yes	Code of practice
ASA (B)	Broadcast advertising	Co-regulatory	Yes	Established 2005– Ofcom has backstop powers
ATVOD	On demand services	Self-regulatory	Yes	Code of practice
BBC	Broadcast	Self-regulatory/	Guide lines	Impartiality and accuracy
		Statutory	Yes	Other areas via Ofcom Programme Code
BBFC	Cinema/films	Co-regulatory (with local authorities)/ Statutory	Guide lines	
	Video/DVD	Statutory		
	Video Games	Co-regulatory (with PEGI)/ statutory for non-exempt games		
DMA	Direct marketing	Industry assoc.	Yes	
ELSPA-ISFE (Europe)	Electronic games	Industry assoc.		Uses Europe-wide rating system (PEGI)
ICO	Data protection issues	Advisory	Yes	Advises on breaches of data protection law
ICRA	Internet	Self-regulatory		International ratings system for websites
Phonepay Plus	Premium rate telephony services	Co-regulatory	Yes	Code of practice for promotion powers and content. Ofcom as backstop
IMCB	Mobile content	Self-regulatory	Yes	Code of practice and classification framework for content rating
ISPA Euro ISPA	Internet service providers	Industry body	Yes	Code of practice
IWF-INHOPE	Hotline for illegal Internet content	Advisory	Yes	Operates a hotline for reports of illegal content

Ofcom	Telecoms and broadcasting	Statutory	Yes	Licensing and regulation of broadcast content. Internet only through media literacy.
OFT		Statutory		OFT will prosecute breaches of the law; e.g. ASA referrals
PCC	Press	Self-regulatory	Yes	Code of practice
VSC	Video content	Self-regulatory	Yes	Code of practice

Increasingly, regulatory bodies (such as the BBFC and a number of European content regulators) are taking account of other areas such as the portrayal of antisocial behaviour or vandalism in their regulatory processes, or the fear or distress that may be caused to young people by the depiction of certain material.[11] For example, responding to its own research, the BBFC recently added the following issues to the range of classification concerns, some being new and others having increased in emphasis: incitement to racial hatred or violence; expletives with a racial association; language which offends vulnerable minorities; suicide and self-harm; emphasis on easily accessible weapons; sexual violence and rape; and promotion or glamorization of smoking, alcohol abuse or substance misuse.

A number of systems have been put in place to help protect or forewarn users of media from material that may be considered 'inappropriate'.[12] In many cases, 'Codes of Practice' or guidelines back up these systems of forewarning and content suppliers or providers sign up to them, often as a key element within their membership of a regulatory framework. Shearer (1998) outlines what some of the basic principles of such a code might be, addressing the Internet in particular. These include:

■ Maintenance of interconnectivity.

■ Freely accessible 'public good' information.

■ Authentification of information.

■ Privacy of communications.

■ Freedom of speech within the Internet (with the proviso that the best interests of children are protected in information delivery).

The regulatory processes vary by media. A key consideration is how readily accessible the content is, especially to children. The systems also vary by audience type (whether designed to protect children or adults or other potentially vulnerable groups, such as disabled people (Institute for Communication Studies, 1997). For example:

■ Broadcasting uses scheduling systems, based loosely on the probable age of children in the audience. (Unlike in the United Kingdom, some European countries have an explicit graduated age-based scheduling system.)

■ Pre-transmission information is used widely to forewarn members of the audience about content that may be offensive.

■ Other non free-to-air services delivered through the television screen use labelling systems which give information about age-appropriateness.

■ In the on-demand world, where content is actively requested by the user, and in some other areas of broadcasting (such as-pay-per view), access management systems such as Personal Identification Numbers are used.

■ Film uses access control systems such as age verification (at point of sale) and labelling.

■ Music uses packaging information to warn of explicit material at point of sale.

■ The Internet has filtering devices and 'walled gardens' available, based on age-appropriateness or type of content.

■ Mobile telephony systems that provide audio-visual content or access to the Internet have age verification systems in place.

■ The press, in particular press catering to niche markets such as magazines, *de facto* tend to attract particular audiences.

The effectiveness of these various systems, especially with the development of technologies, is being challenged. The principle of a family viewing time on television, defined by the watershed at 9 p.m. in the UK, is being contested by broadcasting systems which allow viewing at any time – although usually after additional access management systems have been implemented. Similarly questions are being asked of the effectiveness of filtering systems or the efficiency of search engines in aiding child protection (Machill et al., 2003).

In the United States and Canada the V-chip has been introduced in all television sets (Roberts and Storke, 1997). This reads a 'label' attached to each programme and the adult (presumed to be the parent) sets a threshold level for sexual content, offensive and obscene language and violence.[13] Studies have been undertaken however, that challenge the adequacy of these systems, either because of lack of parental understanding or ineffective rating of programmes (Kaiser Family Foundation, 2001; Kunkel, Farinola, Donnerstein, Biely, and Zwarun, 2002). The evidence in America suggests that parents value content rating systems more than age ratings, but do not always understand these systems (Helsper, 2005). Bushman and Cantor (2003) found that age and content ratings work better for under eights than for older children, arguing that for teens, such ratings increase children's motivation to watch such programmes (Sneegas and Plank, 1998).

Television programmes in Australia are also classified (Aisbett, 2000) and Australian children were found to be highly aware of, though also critical of, content rating schemes (Nightingale, 2000). Not only do children claim to evade age-based restrictions and see 'adult material' but also they are positively motivated to do so. Classification systems are used by children as benchmarks of their progression to adulthood. There is a shift between adults monitoring children's media viewing and children maturing into monitoring it themselves. Children seek out adult content to learn more about adult life and test themselves to see if they could 'cope with' adult material (p. 13).

The United Kingdom has rejected a uniform content classification system to date, recognizing the different relationships that viewers have with content through various delivery platforms. The broadcasting content regulator, Ofcom, has suggested that the possibility of a cross-media common labelling system should be considered, and it proposed as part of its media literacy remit (Ofcom, 2005):

> a study to test the feasibility of a common labelling scheme for content across all broadcast and interactive platforms, and whether this will equip people to make more informed choices.

The interactive games industry has developed a pan-European age-based rating system, the Pan European Games Information (PEGI) system.[14] Although developed by the trade body for the European games industry (the Interactive Software Federation of Europe), it is administered by a non-governmental organization in the Netherlands (NICAM). In the United Kingdom, the Video Standards Council acts as an agent for NICAM. The BBFC classifies all games that have 'gross violence, criminal or sexual activity, human genitals, certain bodily functions, or games with linear film content' – in effect this means that all games likely to receive an 18 classification are classified by the BBFC. While the PEGI system is voluntary, console manufacturers do not allow games to be played on their system if they have not been rated by either body. Further, the vast majority of UK retailers will not stock games without one of these ratings, thus ensuring that games generally go through one or other of the ratings processes (Byron, 2008). The Byron Review has suggested that there is considerable consumer confusion about the classification system (especially among parents, who sometimes misunderstand the PEGI ratings as corresponding to 'ability' or 'skill' ratings). She therefore recommends that future reforms of the classification system incorporate an extension of the statutory basis to include video-games which would otherwise receive a 12+ PEGI rating and that the industry works towards a single classification system.

In addition to these systems of regulation, all these bodies have complaints procedures in place. These allow users to make known their views on the content they have consumed, or to correct any inaccuracies. The FCC in the United States has just introduced an online complaints system for people to complain about 'indecent' programming on television and radio (Federal Communications Commission, n.d.). Some of the bodies also conduct research into satisfaction with such procedures to ensure they remain relevant to customers (New Zealand Broadcasting Standards Authority, 2004). Nonetheless, some continue to argue against the development of self-regulatory mechanisms, most recently with regard to the Internet, and for greater responsibility to be taken by individuals; according to Akdeniz (2001):

If a 'light regulatory touch' with an emphasis on self-regulatory or co-regulatory initiatives represent the (UK) government's vision, then 'self' should mean individuals rather than self-regulation by the internet industry without the involvement of individuals and internet users.

AUDIENCE RIGHTS AND RESPONSIBILITIES

Each medium brings with it different expectations and this is recognized in regulatory practice, as noted above. The differences in the nature of the relationship between radio listeners and television viewers has been well-documented, for example, with the essentially private relationship between the radio and its listener acknowledged in comparison with the more public communication generally offered by television (Millwood Hargrave, 2000b). There are differences also in the way that different types of television services are received and interacted with. Numbers of complaints about subscription services are far smaller than complaints about free-to-air programming because of the nature of the 'contract' with the viewer. In the case of subscription services, viewers pay for the material they watch and this gives them a greater sense of control over the management of the service they receive (Goldberg, Prosser, and Verhulst, 1998).

This degree of control felt by the audience or user is important. There is a financial relationship in place with subscription television services. In addition, there are a variety of access control systems for many media delivery platforms. For satellite television, this may be access via personal identification (PIN) codes. In the cinema there may be entry restrictions based on (apparent) age. In the mobile telephony world, access may be based on age verification at the point of purchase of a telephone. However, the blurring of these traditional boundaries may occur as content is delivered via more or less 'public' access systems, such as radio over the Internet, radio via mobile telephony or radio via television (Ofcom, 2006).

FREEDOM OF EXPRESSION AND RIGHTS AND RESPONSIBILITIES

The Human Rights Act 1998 also impinges upon the communications industry, along with legal instruments (see Annex II), statutory processes and self-regulatory Codes (Lord Chancellor's Dept, 2002).

> (The) Human Rights Act…refers mainly to the responsibilities of public bodies when making determinations about people's rights. Importantly the Act (and the Convention) are seen as dynamic tools, adapting to societal change.[15]

The Human Rights Act, derived from the European Convention on Human Rights (ECHR), is described as a 'living instrument', which must be interpreted in the light of present-day conditions. Societies and values change and the court takes account of these changes when interpreting the ECHR.

There are key articles that are particularly relevant in the context of this review. They are:

- ■ Article 8: Private Life and Family: This allows for freedom from intrusion by the media. However, a public authority can interfere with these rights if the aim of the interference was, among other things, the protection of health or morals or the protection of the rights or freedoms of others.

■ Article 9: Freedom of Belief.

■ Article 10: Free Expression: This allows for the holding and expressing of views or opinions and the freedom to receive information 'so you possess expression rights as a speaker and as a member of an audience. You can express yourself in ways that other people will not like or may even find offensive or shocking. However, offensive language insulting to particular racial or ethnic groups would be an example of where a lawful restriction of expression might be imposed'.

In 2004, the Government passed the Children Act and published its paper *Every Child Matters: Change for Children*, the aims of which include the right of a child, whatever their background or their circumstances, to have the support they need to be healthy, stay safe, enjoy and achieve, make a positive contribution, and achieve economic well-being (Department for Children, Schools and Families [DCSF], n.d.). This has been formalized into the 'Children's Plan'. One part of this commitment includes consultation with young people and children, which will be discussed in terms of the research reviewed here, together with suggestions for further work.[16]

While the concern of regulators is with harm, much of the research reviewed here deals with the risk of harm – by measuring incidence of exposure to risk, risky behaviour, or the use of certain media contents which may be harmful to some. Some of the evidence does demonstrate a link from exposure to 'actual' ill effect, although this is generally measured either experimentally in the short-term or by using correlational methods which cannot rule out all confounding factors (see Annex I). However, we note that the above definition of harm includes both potential and actual ill effects, and thus we discuss harm largely in terms of possible influences on behaviour and attitudes.

NOTES

1. http://www.dfes.gov.uk/byronreview/
2. http://www.everychildmatters.gov.uk/socialcare/safeguarding/internetsafety/
3. http://www.homeoffice.gov.uk/documents/violent-crime-action-plan-08/violent-crime-action-plan-180208
4. http://police.homeoffice.gov.uk/news-and-publications/publication/operational-policing/social-networking-guidance
5. http://www.bsigroup.com/en/ProductServices/Kitemark-for-Child-Safety-Online/
6. http://ec.europa.eu/avpolicy/reg/avms/index_en.htm
7. http://europa.eu/rapid/pressReleasesAction.do?reference=IP/07/1970&format=HTML&aged=0&language=EN&guiLanguage=en
8. http://europa.eu/scadplus/leg/en/lvb/l24030a.htm
9. http://ec.europa.eu/information_society/activities/sip/programme/index_en.htm
10. www.parliament.the-stationery-office.co.uk/pa/cm200405/cmhansrd/vo050125/debtext/50125-40.htm
11. See the guidelines for the Consell de l'Audiovisual de Catalunya for example. http://www.cac.cat/
12. Intriguingly, research suggests not only that graphic violence is capable of inducing immediate as well as enduring stress reactions but also that, as predicted by cognitive theories of emotion, forewarning of the content allows individuals to reappraise situations presented to them and thereby increases their level of suspense (De Wied,

Hoffman, and Roskos-Ewoldsen, 1997). So, in an experiment, respondents (especially women) who were told that the film clip they were about to see contained graphic violence experienced significantly more distress on viewing than did respondents who were told that graphic violent content had been cut out of the clip (in fact, the violence had been cut, so it was the forewarning that resulted in the stress experienced). This suggests that forewarning can be more problematic than no warning (it may also be interpreted as questioning the validity of experiments which, for reasons of research ethics, forewarn participants about the content to be viewed).

13. For further information about US law and the mass media (see R. L. Moore, 1999). For a full description of the FCC policy regarding broadcast indecency, see the Policy Statement www.fcc.gov/Bureaus/Enforcement/ News_ Releases/2001/nren0109.html

14. Pan European Games Information http://www.pegi.info/en/index/

15. This and other references here to the ECHR are taken from www.dca.gov.uk/hract/pdf/act/act-studyguide.pdf. For legal discussion see Annex II.

16. http://www.dcsf.gov.uk/publications/childrensplan/

2

RESEARCHING MEDIA EFFECTS

THEORISING MEDIA EFFECTS

> The primary effects of media exposure are increased violent and aggressive behavior, increased high-risk behaviors including alcohol and tobacco use, and accelerated onset of sexual activity. (Villani, 2001)

> Little consensus exists...[and] research which has examined audiences is rarely able to demonstrate clear effects of the mass media. (Cumberbatch and Howitt, 1989)

> To agree that there are severe limitations of research design in the experimental literature is not tantamount to confirming that psychological research reveals 'absolutely nothing' about children's use of violent video games. (Kline, 2003a)

If social influence is 'any process whereby a person's attitudes, opinions, beliefs, or behaviour are altered or controlled by some form of social communication' (Coleman, 2001) then the question here is what kind of influence is exerted by the media? As befits the complex role of media and communications in today's society, theories of media influence or power abound, some identifying a particular process, some entailing almost a theory of society, some framed as macro-theories of power, others as micro-theories of attitude change (McQuail and Windahl, 1993). Consequently, there are many ways of thinking about harm and offence as these may result from exposure to specific media contents. Different approaches have each spawned a range of empirical investigations over past decades, and the field is now vast. Specific potential harms have attracted more or less attention, as have different audience groups. By far the greatest research effort has been devoted to the effects of media, especially television, on children, especially in relation to violence.

Despite its vast size, it is widely acknowledged that the body of available research is less than ideal. Many studies are designed to identify correlations not causes. Possible confounding factors tend to be examined where convenient to measure (e.g. age, gender) while key factors may be neglected (e.g. parental mediation, personality, social inequalities, peer norms). Restrictions on research funding are evident in the plethora of studies with small samples and simple measures, and in the paucity of longitudinal designs and the lack of good replications. On the positive side, much of the research has been funded by public bodies, conducted by independent researchers, and published in peer-reviewed journals available in the public domain.

McQuail observes that 'the entire study of mass communication is based on the premise that there are effects from the media, yet it seems to be the issue on which there is least certainty and least agreement' (1987: 251). By contrast, home, school and peers are all readily acknowledged as major influences on children's development, though the theories and methods designed to investigate them are complex, diverse and often contested. In the contentious field of media effects too, the research questions asked are remarkably similar to those asked in the fields of education, sociology and psychology regarding the many other potential socializing influences. As in those fields, the media effects literature is divided on questions of methodology (what counts as evidence) and politics (why are certain research questions asked), resulting in confusing messages to policy-makers. Yet it seems that straightforward answers are more often expected, in relation to media influence.

Beyond simple effects

One problem endemic to these debates is the markedly simple, even simplistic nature of the questions often asked about the effects of the media in both public and academic discussion (e.g. Is television bad for children? Do video-games make boys violent?; Gauntlett, 1998).[1] Yet if we set aside the media coverage that often accompanies new findings – admittedly often sought and sanctioned by the researchers – and instead examine the peer-reviewed published articles, we find that, by and large, effects researchers do not claim simply that, for instance, children copy what they see on television. Rather they tend to claim, carefully, that certain media contents increase the likelihood that some children, depending on their cognitive and social make-up, may copy what they see, provided they have interpreted the content in a particular way (this in turn depending on its textual framing – e.g. an association between violence and reward) and if their circumstances encourage such behaviour (e.g. playground norms) and – here a long list may follow, identifying a variety of contingent factors. Such qualified and contingent answers do not make life easy for industry or regulators; nonetheless, when dealing with complex social phenomena (violence, aggression, sexuality, prejudice, etc.), many factors – including but not solely the media – must be expected to play a role.

There are, arguably, rhetorical advantages to posing questions in a form that makes them 'impossible' to answer, and this points us to a further problem, namely the highly polemic nature of the debate, pushing opponents to extreme, polarized positions. These opposing views often, though not always, draw on psychological versus cultural studies traditions of studying the media.[2] In their volume, Alexander and Hanson (2003) pit opposing sides directly, showing the theoretical and methodological disputes at stake. Asking, for example, whether television is harmful to children, Potter (2003) takes a psychological perspective, pointing to the extensive body of research pointing to harmful effects, while Fowles (2003), from a cultural studies perspective, identifies a series of methodological issues (artificial experiments, small effect sizes, inconclusive fieldwork) that undermine claims for effects. Potter concludes that media violence has become a public-health problem; Fowles is concerned that this represents a scapegoating of the media that distracts politicians from addressing the main causes of violence in everyday life.

On reading the advocates of the pro-effects and null-effects camps, we suggest that the rhetoric of their reviews is perhaps as persuasive (or unpersuasive) as their content. Each side notes the methodological inadequacies of opposing evidence, not applying the same critique to the evidence that supports their case. Each side presents their supporting evidence second, as the 'answer'. Psychological researchers tend to ignore their critics; cultural researchers tend to deride the experimental research uniformly. However, although posed as alternative positions, we will suggest that it is possible to reconcile them, by concluding that the evidence points to modest harmful effects for certain groups, these effects being perhaps smaller than the many other causes of violence that may, in turn, merit greater public policy interventions but they are not, nonetheless, either insignificant or unsusceptible to intervention.

In undertaking the present literature review, we attempt to sidestep the over-simplifying and polarizing approaches to the question of media influence, neither recapping old debates nor categorizing findings into pro- and anti- camps, for this field has been reviewed more than many.[3] Nor is our focus on the degree to which research evidence can or should inform policy-development (see Barker and Petley, 2001; Kunkel, 1990; Linz, Malamuth, and Beckett, 1992; Rowland, 1983), though it will be apparent that our preference is for a balanced, non-partisan approach that seeks a precautionary and proportionate response to questions of media harm and offence.

SHORT AND LONG TERM EFFECTS

Many theories exist regarding the nature of media effects (see Anderson et al., 2003; Bryant and Zillman, 2002; MacBeth, 1996; McQuail, 2005; Signorelli and Morgan, 1990). The literature may be divided theoretically into research focusing on short-term cognitive, affective (or emotional) and behavioural effects on individuals and research focusing on long-term effects, these each being theorized at different levels of analysis (effects on individuals, social groups and society as a whole). There is also, separately, a considerable psychological literature on child development, on attitude formation and persuasion, on identity and social behaviour, much of which informs theories of media effects. Although this review is not the place for an elaborated theoretical discussion, certain key points may be made regarding research of different kinds.

Effects research is so-called because it positions the media as a cause and the individual's behaviour as an effect of that cause. However, most theories do not pose mechanistic explanations parallel with physical processes; rather they develop models of psychological processes, combined with statistical (i.e. probabilistic) testing of directional (a ➜ b) hypotheses derived from those models. Further, many theorists acknowledge the bi-directional nature of social influence (e.g. media exposure ➜ aggression but also aggression ➜ media exposure choices). Media effects are generally identified through statistical comparisons (in experiments, between experimental and control groups; in surveys, between high and low exposure groups), a statistically significant finding meaning that the measured difference between the groups would not be expected by chance. The findings are thus probabilistic, and do not imply that each individual in the group is affected equally or even at all.

Most empirical research measures short-term effects, though they are often hypothesized to accumulate so as to result in long-term effects. Thus, the evidence usually pertains to short-term effects (e.g. measurements of effects over a matter of minutes or days following media exposure), but theoretically, long-term effects are postulated through the repetition and reinforcement of the short-term effect, this resulting in a more fundamental alteration to the individual (e.g. personality, emotions, thoughts, self-perception, habitual behaviours) or society (see below). Many different kinds of effects have been examined over the years – cognitive, affective or emotional and behavioural effects (e.g. encouraging racist stereotypes, engendering fear reactions, increasing the likelihood of aggressive behaviour).

Some theories link these different effects together: for example, media content ➔ cognitive effects ➔ emotional effects ➔ behavioural effects. Other theories propose multiple steps: for example, media content ➔ priming of attitudes ➔ increased availability of attitudes for subsequent recall ➔ behaviour. In relation to media violence, Browne and Pennell (2000) identify the following possible outcomes: (i) disinhibition – violence becomes seen as normal, reducing social inhibitions to act aggressively; (ii) desensitization – familiarity with violent images makes the observer more accepting of violence, so that more extreme violence can be tolerated; (iii) social learning (imitation) – through repeated viewing of rewarded violent acts, observers learn to associate violent behaviour with being rewarded; (iv) priming – violent images prime already present aggressive thoughts, feelings and actions, strengthening associations and making violent effects more likely.

As for short-term effects, long-term effects may be theorized as purely individual effects (e.g. an early fear response which has long-term effects on anxiety or nightmares; or the interaction between childhood abuse and early exposure to pornography in the aetiology of an adult abuser). They may also be theorized as long-term aggregate effects (e.g. the 'drip-drip' effect of stereotypical portrayals that contributes to normative prejudices among the majority): as cultivation theorists observe, television is 'telling most of the stories to most of the people most of the time' (Gerbner, Gross, Morgan and Signorielli, 1986: 18).[4] While most concern centres on unintentional effects of this kind, some may be deliberately planned, as in media or information campaigns (advertising, fund-raising, political campaigns, public information, propaganda); theories of persuasion make little distinction based on intentionality.

Further theories propose effects not at the aggregate but at the collective or societal level (e.g. television's role in a growing social tolerance to homosexuality, or the press' role in a growing intolerance to immigrants in society). These may be termed 'reality-defining' effects (McQuail, 1987), namely the systematic tendencies of the media, through the repetition of many similar messages, to affirm and reinforce the particular cognitions that fit one version of social reality (e.g. stereotyping or exclusion of certain groups or experiences); for children, these effects are part of socialization. It is here that researchers explore the possibility that media content shapes the social construction of reality (irrespective of whether or not the content also reflects that reality).

Others propose long-term collective effects which are mediated by personal or social influences (e.g. the influence of the news agenda is perpetuated by being taken seriously by opinion leaders who then repeat and perpetuate that agenda; or the way that the teen peer group takes up and then exerts pressure on the group to continue to favour the latest fashion brand or food product). Different again, mainstreaming theories propose a collective and long-term effect not in terms of content but by excluding (through social pressure) the expression of non-standard, 'extreme' or critical voices, thereby reinforcing (i.e. preventing change to) the moral *status quo*.

DIRECT AND INDIRECT EFFECTS

Although research generally examines the effect of media exposure on an outcome, theoretically it is recognized that multiple other factors are likely to affect the outcome also; the media thus represent one causal factor in a multi-factorial framework (e.g. advertising ➜ children's food choice, but so too does parental diet ➜ food choice). Since these multiple factors themselves are likely to interact or mutually influence each other, this further complicates the study of indirect effects (e.g. advertising ➜ parental food choice ➜ children's food choice ➜ selective viewing of advertising). Note that, importantly, effects theories are neutral regarding the harmful or pro-social nature of the effect. In other words, the same processes of persuasion are assumed to underlie effects judged positive (e.g. encouraging helping) or negative (e.g. encouraging aggression), though often the former effects are deliberate (as in public-health campaigns) and the latter unintentional. As noted earlier, we do not here review the also-sizeable research literature on the potentially beneficial effects of exposure to media content, including educational benefits, though many of the same conclusions apply there also.

Many of these theories, being concerned with long-term social change, must contend with many confounding variables and problems of inference in relating evidence to theory, this making the demonstration of media effects more difficult. Often they rely on the demonstration of short-term effects consistent with their long-term claims, longitudinal studies being in short supply. However, proponents of such theories can establish that evidence is (or is not) consistent with their hypotheses, and/or that the evidence supports one theory better than another. They are at their weakest when establishing the underlying mechanisms by which they propose media effects to work in the long-term.

As with short-term effects, most long-term media effects are proposed to operate in tandem with other factors, so that outcomes (e.g. social norms, behaviours, beliefs) are multiply caused by factors themselves likely to interact with each other. Long-term effects are, indeed, more likely to be indirect (mediated by, interacting with, other factors) than are short-term effects demonstrated under controlled conditions. As with short-term effects too, the hypothesis for a long-term media effect makes no necessary assumption regarding the agency of individuals or groups. Particularly, the assumption of social (or media) influence is taken as an inevitable and essential part of social life, not as a denial of the individual's choice or responsibility.

To clarify the distinction between direct and indirect effects, it must first be acknowledged that, leaving aside the simplistic claims noted earlier, the media represent one source of influence among others. Only thus may the relations among these multiple influences be addressed. One may hypothesize:

■ Direct effects, in which one or many factors independently influence attitudes or behaviour. If many factors, each may exert a greater or lesser influence, and each contributes separately and additively to the consequences.

■ Indirect effects, in which the many factors interact, so that one factor influences another when working through one or more intervening variables. It may take several factors working together to bring about the effect. One of them may alter the effectiveness of another. One may provide the background conditions under which another has its effect. Indirect relations between media exposure and measures of effect are thus conditional on other factors and so these latter must be included in research.

■ Consequently, 'the total effect of one variable on another is the sum of its direct and indirect effects' (Holbert and Stephenson, 2003: 557).

Once we acknowledge that social outcomes are multiply caused, we must also acknowledge multiple possible paths of influence and, therefore, numerous possible processes of persuasion. However, since indirect effects bring together different factors in the social environment, including forms of face-to-face and institutional influence as well as media influence, the outcomes are harder to conceptualize theoretically and harder to track methodologically.

For example, many believe that 'research generally affirms that through language people can establish, maintain, legitimize and change the *status quo* or essentially construct a social reality' (Leets, 2001: 298). So, if language thus creates a negative stereotype of a social group, this can, many argue, constitute harm. However, the chain from media to social exclusion is so indirect as to challenge any research methodology. As Holbert and Stephenson (2003) comment, worryingly few empirical studies consider the importance of the media's indirect effects.

THE POLITICS OF MEDIA EFFECTS RESEARCH

Academic critics of media effects research are not only concerned about possible theoretical or methodological inadequacies of the findings. Indeed, the methodological disputes over samples, experimental controls, measurement and validity provide a means, a language, through which a more theoretical and political, even philosophical debate is being held regarding not only the nature of harm and offence but also why questions about these are being asked: this surely provides one reason why the scientific debate seems to run and run.

For example, there has been longstanding concern over the use of social science research as a justification for film regulation (e.g. Barker, Arthurs, and Harindranath, 2001; Gilbert, 1988; Mathews, 1994), not least because of the history of film censorship (e.g. Park, 2002) and media censorship more generally (Heins, 2001). There seems, in public discussion, often very little distance between 'regulation' and 'censorship', especially in relation to film, video and DVD content where a greater diversity of genres, aesthetic experimentation and catering for niche interests is evident than for a more 'mainstream' medium like television. Intriguingly, it has also been argued that moral panics are in the economic interests of and may be encouraged by certain sectors of the industry to create a niche or cult market outside the mainstream (Jancovich, 2002).

Others argue that 'violence' as an area of public concern is socially and historically constructed to achieve certain forms of political control while masking other forms of societal violence (particularly those committed by established authorities); 'violence' is by no means a natural category of behaviour (Barker, 2004). When cultural critics attempt to take on the censorship argument in relation to children, their case is unconvincing and inconclusive (e.g. McGuigan, 1996).[5]

In general, the position adopted by critics of media effects is itself complex and multi-dimensional. Broadly, it raises concerns over the moral and political role of social scientists in responding to an 'administrative' policy agenda (Lazarsfeld, 1941). In brief, critics of effects research are concerned that this body of research is:

■ Motivated by moral panics (amplified by the popular media) which accompany each new medium (preceding television, games or the Internet and back to the introduction of cinema, comics, and even earlier), channelling and appeasing public anxieties about economic and technological change.

■ A scapegoating of the media, distracting public and policy attention from the real ills of society (and the real causes of crime/violence/family breakdown, etc. – most notably, poverty and inequality).

■ A middle-class critique of working-class pleasures (in which the working-class are construed by effects research as irrational masses, undisciplined media consumers and so blamed for social unrest and disorderliness).

■ A denial of the agency, choice and wisdom of ordinary people who, if asked, have more nuanced, subtle and complex judgements to offer about media content, who do not react in simple and automatic ways to media content, and whose critical media literacy should be recognized and valued.

■ An unfortunate, even improper collaboration between supposedly objective social scientists and supposedly public-spirited policy-makers, the former gaining funding and reputation, the latter gaining justification for repressive and censorious but popular regulation.

■ A normative justification for ensuring public support ('manufacturing consent') for the establishment and the capitalist *status quo* by excluding the public expression (and mobilization) of diverse views, critical voices, niche interests or alternative perspectives.

■ A covert justification for strengthening a populist/moral/religious agenda that is against the enlightenment principles of the rights to freedom of expression.

Many of these arguments have widespread public and academic support (Barker and Petley, 2001; Drotner, 1992; Pearson, 1983; Rowland, 1983; Winston, 1996). They draw on recognized social values – freedom of speech, criticism of institutional censors, concern for the rights of the individual, including respecting the validity of people's own experiences, scepticism about academic funding decisions, concern to avoid moral or media-created panics, determination to avoid being distracted from more fundamental social ills, and so forth. Ironically, those advocating the critical position also believe the media to be a powerful and often malign influence on society, but they tend to frame that influence at a societal level (focusing on media influence over institutions, culture, society) rather than at an individual level.

From the point of view of the evidence base, one consequence has been the development of an alternative body of evidence – mainly using qualitative social research methods and asking different, more critical and contextual questions, according to a different, more culturally-oriented research agenda. Some of the often qualitative research that is emerging – typically based on exploratory or interpretative interviews and discussions with the public – provides a valuable counter to the otherwise dominant quantitative approach to media harms and offence. Where these studies pertain, even if indirectly, to questions of harm and offence, we have included them in what follows, in the interests of constructing a more balanced and multi-dimensional approach to the question of media harm than is often the case, particularly in psychologically-oriented literature reviews.

DETRIMENT, PROPORTIONALITY AND RISK

In translating the above theoretical, methodological and political considerations into the policy arena, a key question is what regulatory weight should be attached to evidence of risk? One approach is to estimate what statisticians term the 'size of the effect'. For example, Hearold (1986) conducted a meta-analysis of the findings reported in 230 studies of television violence, encompassing some 100,000 subjects over the past 60 years.[6] In general, the correlations between viewing and effect vary between 0.1 and 0.3. These are small effects, but one should note that statistically significant findings are not necessarily significant in social or policy terms. In other words, it is a matter of judgement (by policy-makers as well as researchers) whether effects which, as in this case, account for some 5 per cent of the variation in behaviour, are important or not, or whether they are more or less important than other factors.[7]

A satisfactory explanation of social phenomena, such as violence, stereotypes, consumerism or prejudice, will involve understanding the combined and interactive effects of multiple factors, of which television may be one such factor, although probably not a major one. For example, in a study that, unusually, compared the effect size for television with that for other influential factors, television was found to play only a small role: this particular study was in the field of television advertising, and found that viewing television advertising accounted for 2 per cent of the variation in children's food choice, compared with 9 per cent for the influence of parental diet on children's diet (Bolton, 1983). In this context, we can interpret the research findings for media harm as 'modest' in their effect size. In another example, in his work on electronic games, Anderson (2003) calculates the correlation across 32 independent samples studied to be r = 0.20 (confidence interval, 0.17– 0.22); this suggests that playing violent video-games accounts for 4 per cent of the variation in aggressive behaviour (Anderson and Murphy, 2003),[8] a figure that is broadly in line with meta-analyses for television violence (Hearold, 1986).[9]

What is generally lacking in this literature is a wider consideration of other factors that also influence aggression (although see Southwell and Doyle, 2004). However, Anderson, Gentile, and Buckley (2007: 143) compile a table comparing effect sizes for a wide range of factors associated with adolescent violence, as reproduced below. This suggests video-game and media violence play a substantial role, although the effect sizes they report here are higher than those found in several other studies:

Table 2.1 Longitudinal effect sizes of several empirically identified long-term risk factors for aggressive and violent behaviour.

Risk factor	Effect size	Variance accounted for (%)
Gang membership	.31	9.6 per cent
Video-game violence*	**.30**	**8.8 per cent**
Psychological condition	.19	3.6 per cent
Poor parent-child relations	.19	3.6 per cent
Being male	.19	3.6 per cent
Prior physical violence	.18	3.2 per cent
Media violence**	**.17**	**2.9 per cent**
Antisocial parents	.16	2.6 per cent
Low IQ	.11	1.2 per cent
Broken home	.10	1.0 per cent
Poverty	.10	1.0 per cent
Risk-taking	.09	0.8 per cent
Abusive parents	.09	0.8 per cent
Substance use	.06	0.4 per cent

Adapted from US Department of Health and Human Services (2001) *Youth Violence: A Report of the Surgeon General*. Rockville, MD: US Government Printing Office.
* From Study Three, with sex statistically controlled.
** From Anderson and Bushman (200).

Seeking to link such findings to policy decisions, Kline (2003b) offers a risk-based view of what accounting for 10 per cent of the variance explained (as cited by Freedman, 2002) really means in practice. He points out that:

The Youth Risk Behavior Surveillance data for 2001 of over 1,300 teenagers finds that 33 % report getting in a fight during the last year. Since 16% of the US population of 276 million is between 12–20 we can estimate that .16 x .33 x 276 = 14, 572, 800 fights take place each year. Using Freedman's estimate that 10% of those fights can be accounted for by the statistical relationship between violent media consumption and aggression, we can estimate that about 1.45 million more fights take place every year than would happen by chance, or for other reasons.

As he goes on to add, drawing on Popper's epistemology of falsification:

No experiment can ever prove media violence affects behavior, but rather only weaken our belief that there are no consequences from persistent exposure to media violence. That is generally the conclusion reached by the American Psychological Association.

In short, Kline seeks to move the debate from one of debating causality (yes or no), a debate that becomes polarized between freedom of expression and censorship positions, or that takes a reductionist approach to research evidence (can research show that child x will respond in a predictable manner to image y?). Instead, he advocates debating and weighing risk factors within a multi-factorial account. Arguing, in this case, about the potentially harmful effects of computer games, he observes that:

> Given the diversity in children's circumstances, there is little reason to expect uniform behavioral responses to violent entertainment among children whose circumstances and experiences are diverse. This is also why most contemporary effects researchers do not predict that a majority of children will be negatively influenced by media violence. It is only by factoring in environmental factors numerically that social psychological researchers will be able to explain why not all heavy consumers of violent entertainment grow up in some situations to be aggressive and antisocial while non-gamers become serial killers.

Quoting the American Surgeon General's review of evidence for media harm in 2001, Kline adds:

> The Surgeon General's media risk model does not predict that young people will uniformly commit aggressive acts immediately after watching because media effects interact with other risk factors experienced within peer groups, schools, families, communities. Weighing up the available evidence according to well established epidemiological criteria for studying causality in multiple and interacting determinacy relations…, he recommends a precautionary rather than panglossian principle stating that 'Research to date justifies sustained efforts to curb the adverse effects of media violence on youths. Although our knowledge is incomplete, it is sufficient to develop a coherent public health approach to violence prevention that builds upon what is known, even as more research is under way'.

What follows from the risk model is the hypothesis that altering risk factors will alter outcomes. Kline thus criticises those who assume:

> …that violence has always been with us throughout history and is so pervasive in our culture that there is nothing we can do about it. A recent natural experiment conducted by Tom Robinson in San Jose suggests otherwise. Robinson (2001, 2000) reasoned that if the amount of media use really is a factor in the violence effect (because of increased exposure) then reducing that media consumption should reduce the risk. He tested this causal hypothesis, finding that schools that participated in the media education program not only reduced their media consumption by 25% but also enjoyed in a significant reduction in playground aggression and had more children with a lower rate of increase of body fat.

Unfortunately, as already noted, while much evidence has examined individual risk factors – such as media exposure – little if any has compared risk factors, examining their combined influence on the outcome of interest (e.g. aggressive behaviour). Given the paucity of such evidence, the precautionary principle has generally been applied, policy dictating that it is always better to err on the side of caution:

The precautionary principle is not merely confined to the spheres of health and science. In today's risk-averse world, just about every sphere of life, from business and politics to parenting and health, is increasingly organised around the notion that it is better to be safe than sorry. (Guldberg, 2003)

In such circumstances, the burden of proof is said to lie with those who downplay the risk of disaster, rather than with those who argue that the risks are real, even if they might be quite small (Runciman, 2004).[10] Hence, the precautionary principle:

…should be considered within a structured approach to the analysis of risk which comprises three elements: risk assessment, risk management, risk communication. The precautionary principle is particularly relevant to the management of risk. (Van der haegen, 2003: 3)

Notes

1. Society does not ask, for example, whether or not parents have 'an effect' on their children or whether friends are positive or negative in their effects. Yet it persistently asks (and expects researchers to ask) such questions of the media, as if a single answer could be forthcoming. Nor, when it is shown that parents do have an influence on children do we conclude that this implies children are passive 'cultural dopes', or that parental influence is to be understood as a 'hypodermic syringe', as so often stated of media effects. Nor, on the other hand, when research shows that parental influence can be harmful to children, do we jump to the conclusion that children should be brought up without parents; rather we seek to mediate or, on occasion, to regulate.
2. The psychological tradition underpins classic 'effects' research, framing the media as a source of social influence that impacts on the individual, albeit as one of many influences. The cultural studies tradition is generally critical of effects research, focusing more broadly on media power in society (rather than on individuals) and critical of the ways in which such concepts as violence or sexuality are socially constructed by policy-makers and effects researchers.
3. For recent reviews, we would direct the reader to Cantor (2000), Perse (2001), Singer and Singer (2001), Villani (2001). For critical discussions of media effects research, see Barker and Petley (2001), Kline (2003b), Livingstone (1996), Cumberbatch and Howitt (1989).
4. In seeking analogies to explain long-term but gradual effects, Gerbner (1986) talks of the 'drip-drip effect' of water on a stone – a small effect that nonetheless wears away the stone; Potter (2003) uses the analogy of the orthodontist's brace exerting a weak but constant pressure that brings about a crucial realignment over time.
5. Cultural defences of challenging or controversial material (e.g. Barker, 2004; Gee, 2003) often stress that just such material is valued by people to stimulate their rethinking of normative or established views or roles, here drawing on a long tradition arguing for the cultural merits of diverse media. We note, however, that this defence is not generally offered in support of those in the audience who express pleasure in identifying with the aggressor or in viewing violence or suffering for its own sake (though such a defence is made of people's right to enjoy pornography for sexual pleasure). In other words, researchers (like the public) are inclined to treat violent content and sexual content rather differently.
6. 'Meta-analysis seeks to combine the analyses from all relevant individual studies into a single statistical analysis with an overall estimate and confidence interval for effect size' (Givens, Smith, and Tweedie, 1997: 221).
7. At best causal models usually account for only a proportion (usually no more than 20 or 30 per cent) of the variance in a dependent variable. For this reason causal models include a residual or error term to account for the variance left unexplained. There are, after all, many other social characteristics which affect how people behave, apart from those measured.
8. Though greater, according to Anderson, than the effect of condom use on decreased HIV risk or the effect of passive smoking on lung cancer.

9. Anderson (2002) follows statistical convention in describing such effect sizes as 'small to moderate', stressing that these are of considerable concern because of the repeated nature of video-game-playing in everyday life. Intriguingly, a 'best-practices meta-analysis' showed that studies that are better conducted (in terms of their reliability and validity) tend to show stronger effects of violent video-games on aggression and aggression-related variables than do less well-conducted studies (Anderson et al., 2003). A further meta-analysis of 25 studies suggests a slightly lower correlation between video-game-play and aggression at $r = 0.15$ (Sherry, 2001).

10. Tickner, Raffensperger, and Myers (1999) list the components of a precautionary approach, including taking precautionary action before scientific certainty of cause and effect; seeking out and evaluating alternatives, and shifting burdens of proof.

3

TELEVISION

INTRODUCTION

The continued pervasiveness of television viewing is well-documented (Ofcom, 2007; Roberts, 2000). It accounts for a significant proportion of media use in the United Kingdom, still mainly of the free-to-air channels although, for certain demographic groups, the niche channels are watched or used more. It is also used increasingly with other media, and the Internet has had the greatest impact on viewing (Livingstone, 2002; Livingstone and Bovill, 2001; Nie, Simpser, Stepanikova, and Zheng, 2004).

Recent research by Ofcom notes that for children of all ages in the United Kingdom (5–15 years old), television remains the medium that is most used (15.8 hours per week), although viewing is in decline (Ofcom, 2007). For older children (aged 12–15 years old) television viewing is even higher at 17.2 hours, as shown in the figure below.

The importance and perceived impact of television in people's lives have been long researched. Studies have been undertaken to understand how it affects people, how it shapes them and how

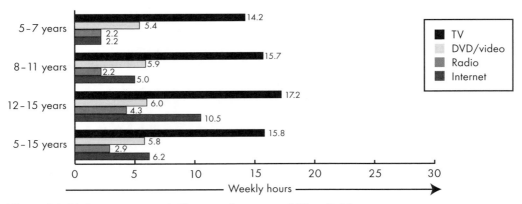

Figure 3.1 Media consumption (self-reported) – among children 5–15 years.

they respond to it. Certainly the audience has very clear views about broadcasting and is sophisticated, understanding the conventions of scheduling, for example, or the relevance of context in framing their perceptions of the appropriateness of material (Ramsay, 2003; Svennevig, 1998; Towler, 2001).

In their extensive review of media use and exposure among American children, Comstock and Scharrer (2007) observe that:

> The feature that distinguishes screen from interactive media is the content that is not open to alteration by the decisions of the user. (Comstock and Scharrer 2007: 12)

With the growth of the multi-channel environment, the traditional focus on television as equally available to everyone is shifting. First, audience fragmentation across multiple television channels is already fairly advanced (Webster, 2005), with some evidence also of polarization.[1] Second, it seems that audience choice is increasingly programme – rather than channel – based. Nearly all empirical research on harm and offence has addressed content broadcast on the main channels. There has been little or no published academic research which has addressed the changes in audience attitudes or behaviour that may be caused by developments in the nature of the television viewing experience. For example, there is research that shows how the experience of viewing a film on a small television screen is different from seeing it on a large screen at the cinema, but there is not yet research evidence that shows how viewing that content on a large screen with surround-sound, in one's home, may be different from the conventional television viewing experience.

Before reviewing the research evidence, it is worth reiterating that we will not consider either the positive effects of television viewing (where there is a large literature) or such potential harms as consumer detriment or physical health. Instead, our remit is to examine the research literature for evidence of the risk of harm and offence with regard to media-related content. It is also important to note that much of this literature has come from the United States, as will be indicated below where appropriate, as this has a different television regulatory environment from the United Kingdom. Last, we observe that research often examines the effects of exposure to media content which is not necessarily that intended for the age group researched. Particularly, since many children watch television content other than that specifically made for them, the research reported below investigates the effect on children of viewing content intended for a wider or older audience. Unfortunately, it is not always possible to determine, from the published research reports, exactly what kind of content was studied and nor, therefore, exactly how the particular research studies might be relevant to the UK audience.

The research effort in recent years has concentrated on:

- The way in which television might influence audience attitudes and behaviour.

- The effects of violent television content, especially on the young.

■ The effects of television content on the sexualization of the young and other development processes (such as attitudes towards body image or substance abuse).

■ The effects of reality-defining variables such as stereotypes on audiences.

■ The offence caused by, for example, the use of swearing and offensive language.

■ The way in which facts and information are presented – most notably, in the news.

Much of the debate about the potential influence or effects of broadcasting has rested on a debate about the child audience. The positive influences of children's broadcasting are recognized (although not discussed here) and studies have monitored closely the development and changes in the provision of programming targeted at children in the United Kingdom (Ofcom, 2007; Atwal, Millwood Hargrave, Sancho, Agyeman, and Karet, 2003; Davies and Corbett, 1997; Blumler, 1992). These argue that children should be able – and have a right – to experience a wide and diverse range of programming aimed at their particular interests. Patricia Edgar, the founder of the Australian Children's Television Foundation and a driving force in children's television production, wrote in 2005:[2]

> We know the importance of a child's early years. If children are not given the stimulation and support they need in those early years, they will grow up to become marginalised adults. Their health, literacy, and physical skills are all-important. But just as crucial for their social well-being is the development of their emotional and moral intelligences. Children require healthy bodies, educated minds, and an understanding of their social purpose…television can have a positive role to play.

While Comstock and Scharrer note that use of television (time spent viewing) is also high in the United States, their analysis of the research shows that relatively low levels of attention are given to much television viewing. It is when choices are being made between media and media content that more attention is paid to preferred types or genres of content. Their review looks at the way in which interest in the media develops and suggests that viewers start to use television images to form their own identities and vision of the 'outside' world and society from quite a young age. These potential socializing effects of the media are not only important when thinking of how perceptions of the outside world may be formed, but also in terms of the way in which people may feel marginalized or excluded: some people seldom see people like themselves on the screen.

Davies et al. argue, drawing on data gathered as part of a research project examining the changing nature of children's television culture, that those who seek to preserve children from 'poor' television are making judgements about children's tastes (Davies, Buckingham, and Kelley, 2000). In talking to children themselves, the researchers find that there are clear distinctions made by children between programming aimed at them and those made for adult audiences. Davies et al. discuss children's programming in terms of 'absences' – that is, children's programming does not contain offensive language, sex and so on, and children aspire to programmes targeted at an older audience. They suggest that children's assertions of their own tastes 'necessarily entail a form of "identity work"– a positioning of the "self" in terms of publicly available discourse and categories'. The view of children's programming through an adult's eyes is very likely to be different. Many of the studies identified within this review examine reactions to a range of programmes, not necessarily those made for a youth audience.

In coming to a conclusion about the role of television in children's lives and its possible effects and influences, Comstock and Scharrer note a sharp divide between content designed for young children and that made available to older children (from about 10 years of age):

> We are struck by the realisation that there are largely two different worlds of content – the protective, educational, and prosocial bubble provided by media for the very young (infants, preschoolers, and children of early elementary age) and the sometimes harsh and often sensationalised material of media for older children, teenagers and the general audience (music television, internet sites, primetime television, video games). The two exist with little buffer forcing an abrupt change when 'children's media' are no longer satisfying. (Comstock and Scharrer 2007: 117)

In the following sections, the research literature which has examined the potential for the impact of television is presented, for all segments of the audience as well as children and young people. Much of the research has considered the portrayal of violence and sex on television, in particular. However there have been other areas that have been researched, in particular for their ability to give offence – what Barnett calls an 'affective' notion of harm (Barnett and Thomson, 1996).

ISSUES OF GENERAL OFFENCE

The update of the literature, examining research evidence since 2005, concentrates on the evidence for harm, while the first edition had looked at the evidence for both harm and offence. It had found little academic research into offence caused by viewing television, with most research effort concentrated on harm. However, there was a substantial body of market or social research conducted by regulators and the industry which had looked at issues of offence. Ofcom's 2006 'Communications Market Report' shows that perceptions of standards on television have been fairly stable in the recent past. While almost half the sample (47 per cent) think standards have not changed over the previous year, 40 per cent think standards have declined. The proportion saying they have been offended by something on television has remained unchanged since 2004 at 32 per cent.

In the 2005 Communications Market Report, most respondents (84 per cent) had thought that material that might offend them personally could be shown, but after a clear pre-transmission warning. The 2006 Report explored the public's views towards children and their exposure to different media types. The figure below shows that there was most concern about the Internet, while post-watershed television programmes on terrestrial television were the second area of most general concern. Ofcom notes that these concerns were not affected by the parental status of the respondent.

As in previous years, most (71 per cent) thought that the primary reason for regulating television was to protect children and youth, with 25 per cent thinking that television should be regulated

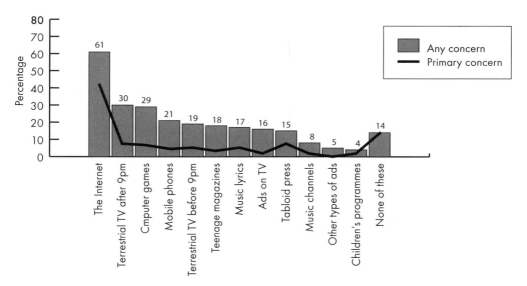

Figure 3.2 Concern over children's exposure to different types of media content.

'to protect the public at large'. Complaints statistics compiled by Ofcom for the calendar year 2004 bear out these concerns. They show a total of 9,297 complaints about television received (74 per cent of all television complaints) related to harm and offence. 61 per cent of these concerned general offence, 11 per cent were about language, 8 per cent religion and 8 per cent sexual portrayal, and 3 per cent were about depictions of violence. A further 282 complaints about radio related to harm and offence (54 per cent of all radio complaints). For radio, sexual portrayal and violence are of less concern, while language attracts a greater proportion of complaints.

Similar data have been found in other countries. In Australia, around one in three people consistently reported having seen material on broadcast television that they were 'offended by' or 'concerned' about (Cupitt, 2000). The top concerns are the portrayal of violence and the nature of news/current affairs programmes (e.g. intrusive images of suffering, violence, bias and inaccuracy). Further, half of the survey respondents agreed that news and current affairs programmes put unnecessary emphasis on personal characteristics (ethnicity, sexuality, disability etc.). The information used to prepare viewers for potentially distressing images is judged appropriate by four in five respondents. Concern is also expressed regarding the unrealistic nature of violence in televised films (e.g. violence presented without consequences, unnecessary graphic content, glamorization of violence).

However, recent research by the communications regulator in Australia (the ACMA, 2007) shows that, when asked to rate their level of concern about a range of possible issues, media and communication related concerns do not stand out from other issues. As in the United Kingdom, of the media and communication activities, the Internet gives rise to the most concern (two in five parents express some level of concern) while television viewing and gaming come next. Despite these concerns, parents recognize the benefits of these media and communication opportunities: almost all that 'the internet provides learning or educational opportunities for their children, while the main benefits of watching television are perceived to be its educational value and its contribution towards their children keeping in touch with the world around them'. The study also notes that the age of the child is the most influential factor in determining parental levels of concern about each technology type:

> Parents express concerns about television viewing more frequently in relation to younger children, whereas gaming concerns are more frequent in relation to 12–14 year olds. Concerns about internet use are more common for parents of 12–17 year olds, and mobile phone concerns are focused on the 13–17 year old age bracket…Parents of boys are more often concerned about video and computer games than parents of girls, but the reverse is evident for use of mobile phones.

Unlike both the United Kingdom and Australia, in New Zealand (2008) parents are more concerned about their children's exposure to television media content than the Internet (84 per cent and 48 per cent respectively). If concern is expressed, they are most commonly worried about violent content (51 per cent), sexual material (33 per cent), and inappropriate language (20 per cent). 22 per cent mention specific programmes – the news is mentioned by 15 per cent of concerned parents. The 9–13 year old children interviewed agree – content that they most commonly say bothers or upsets them relates to violence (29 per cent), sexual content/nudity (21 per cent) and scary/spooky things (20 per cent). Asked what they themselves think is not suitable for children of their age to see on television, half mentioned violence (51 per cent), while just over a third said bad language (36 per cent), sexual content/nudity (34 per cent) or 'adult' programmes with explicit sexual content (33 per cent). Their reasons centre on a perception of them as 'an undesirable influence on children's behaviour' (59 per cent). Younger children (6–8 years old) are more likely to talk about the negative effects, such as getting scared and having nightmares (47 per cent).

In 1998, the Independent Television Commission in the United Kingdom became the first broadcasting regulatory body to use citizens' juries to examine public attitudes towards the regulation of broadcasting (Independent Television Commission, 1998). This methodology had been developed with the political process in mind but has since been used successfully for examining attitudes to the media (including television and film) (Ramsay, 2003). The format of the citizens' jury brings together a group of randomly chosen people to deliberate on a particular issue, in this case, broadcast content regulation. In the two ITC juries, participants spent time collecting information and hearing presentations by 'witnesses' selected on the basis of their expertise. Trained moderators supervised the process and the jurors were able to cross-examine the witnesses. They then delivered a report on what they saw as the purposes and principles of such regulation, determining that the main thrust of regulation was to protect children and provide sufficient information for adults to regulate their own viewing. They identified six guidelines in particular for such content regulation:

■ The watershed should be maintained at around 9 p.m., before which material unsuitable for younger viewers should not be shown.

■ The use of strong language or scenes of sex or violence must be justified by the context of the programme, whether fact or fiction.

■ Warnings should be used with discretion where relevant, before or during the programme. There should be an indication of content and perhaps an agreed system of warning symbols in the television guides that appear in newspapers and magazines.

■ Broadcasters should be aware of individual and national sensitivities, and avoid intruding into private grief.

■ Pornographic material could be shown provided it was legal and limited to pay-per-view or subscription channels.

■ Advertisements should be truthful and not misleading.

The Broadcasting Standards Council (BSC)[3] commissioned a panel of monitors for some years to report on their television viewing and their opinions of the broadcasting standards issues within programmes, such as the amount of violence, swearing and offensive language or sexual explicitness. Panellists also had to say whether or not they thought such material was editorially justified. Each panel reported for two weeks and there were four reporting periods in a year. In 1999, the data from these panels were presented along with the results of a survey of public opinion about broadcasting, conducted among over 1,000 people (Broadcasting Standards Commission, 2000). That study found that half the sample (50 per cent) spontaneously expressed a concern about television, with age and gender as significant variables – female respondents and those who were older were considerably more likely to voice concerns (56 per cent of those who expressed concern were women and 72 per cent were over 65 years old).[4]

Nonetheless, when monitors were asked in detail about the issues they were concerned about, most said that the majority of incidents they noted (of violence, swearing and offensive language or depictions of sex) were justified within their editorial context. The conclusion drawn was that 'because respondents may think television covers an issue "too much", it does not necessarily follow that offence will be caused'. What is of prime importance is the context in which the issue is presented and the other expectations that viewers have built based on their prior knowledge of the way in which programmes are scheduled, for example, or the actors involved in the production.

Ofcom offers a definition of 'context' in Section 2.3 of the Broadcasting Code which illustrates the breadth of possible viewer expectations (Ofcom, 2005). Context includes (but is not limited to):

■ the editorial content of the programme, programmes or series;

■ the service on which the material is broadcast;

■ the time of broadcast;

■ what other programmes are scheduled before and after the programme or programmes concerned;

■ the degree of harm or offence likely to be caused by the inclusion of any particular sort of material in programmes generally or programmes of a particular description;

■ the likely size and composition of the potential audience and likely expectations of the audience;

■ the extent to which the nature of the content can be brought to the attention of the potential audience (for example by giving information) and

■ the effect of the material on viewers or listeners who may come across it unawares.

No research was found that discussed the effects of changes in any of these contextual variables that might be driven by recent technological change, such as the use of personal video recorders to cross the watershed for example. Hanley (1998b) described how audience expectations can be affected by new technology. In her study, respondents might have found content that shocked them when they first acquired cable or satellite television. Once they had learned how to navigate it and had understood its particular conventions (such as the scheduling differences from free-to-air television), they found little reason to complain.

VIOLENCE

Much of the research literature considering the possible negative effects of media content continues to focus on the medium of broadcast television, and on the depiction of violence, in particular. The audience of specific concern has been children, ranging from the very young to adolescents and – in terms of data collection – college students. Now, with increasing potential access to an ever-widening array of media content, there has been an increase in expressions of concern about the possible effect or influence of violent media content on children. In the foreword to the *Yearbook on Children and Media Violence*, Carlsson describes the genesis of the UNESCO International Clearinghouse on Children and Violence on the Screen, set up in the 1990s, to look at the research evidence for harm that may be caused to children viewing such content (Carlsson and Von Feilitzen, 1998). She describes how;

> Many discern a relationship between the rising level of violence and crime in everyday life, particularly violence committed by children, and the scenes of violence shown on television and video and simulated acts of violence in video and computer games.

To this list of media are now added the Internet and mobile communications. The Yearbooks have expanded to include all these forms of delivery, comprehensively collating the latest research on children and media content. The organization has now been renamed the International Clearinghouse for Children, Youth and Media (Nordicom, n.d.) to reflect this change.

Much of the research into children's attitudes towards violent media content is television-based. Television was the first widely available medium. Its rapid growth mirrored an interest – particularly in the United States – in behavioural psychology. This experimental, often laboratory-based, system of study has not been used as widely in other countries. For example, the United Kingdom, Australia or France (see Zann, 2000) tend to employ qualitative research techniques, often in conjunction with quantification, such as the administration of questionnaires. As Barker and Petley argue, these layered methodologies offer a more rounded picture of how the media and audiences interact than do the experimental studies from the United States (Barker and Petley, 2001):

> An array of methods of investigation has been developed in recent years which has been proving its usefulness, and offering insights and explanatory models which can transform our picture of these media, their audiences and their social, cultural and political implications.

All the research methods recognize that the media do not operate in a vacuum and, in general, that there are some effects on children. Where they differ is in terms of what those effects might be, how direct they are and if there is a causal link between viewing behaviour and subsequent (violent) behaviour. Back in the 1950s, Hilde Himmelweit had argued:

> Television can't alter a child's basic personality. It might change some of his opinions and attitudes but definitely not his character. There was no evidence in our study that the kind of personality the child has influences the type of programmes he chooses to watch. A child brings his personality to the set, not the other way round. (Himmelweit, Oppenheim, and Vince, 1958)

This review found most research in this area still comes from the United States, a different regulatory regime from that of the United Kingdom, especially in terms of programming made for, and available to, a child or youth audience. Further, the review found that much recent work, itself, consists of research reviews of projects that have been undertaken in the field of media effects research and media violence.[5] This review will look at those reviews but will highlight original contemporary research, where possible, and will draw out those projects in particular which are based in the current UK television viewing environment. The analysis of such research in this central area of discussion about the media and violent content is framed by the notion that the media create a response in children (not necessarily negative). The research evidence is considered in order to make a judgement as to whether or not the response is behavioural or attitudinal, if it is short-term or has long-lasting effects, and – finally – if it might be harmful to the child or to society. Potter and Mahood (2005) in the United States accept that:

> Many studies have been conducted to link particular elements in a treatment with particular behavioural outcomes, but we are not sure about the process that takes place inside a person's mind that is the linkage between the treatment and effect.

The chapter 'Researching media effects' describes the various methodologies used in the projects covered by this review. There is also a short, helpful summary of research methodologies used in the United States by Anderson and Bushman (2002; see also Singer and Singer, 2001).

TOWARDS A DEFINITION OF VIOLENCE ON-SCREEN

The wide-ranging and comprehensive 'Report of the Commission on Children and Violence', convened by the Gulbenkian Foundation in the United Kingdom, had defined violence as 'behaviour by people against people liable to cause physical or psychological harm' (Calouste Gulbenkian Foundation, 1995). The Commission looked at all kinds of violence to and by children and young people, including violence portrayed in the media. It did not find the place of the media significant, except as providing a window on the world – the report highlights as particularly important the way in which role models are portrayed on television (especially male role models and especially those involved in sports).

On-screen violence has been defined in a number of ways which have evolved as research has uncovered more and more nuances in the way in which viewers watch violent images. Morrison undertook a wide-ranging qualitative study of attitudes to violence on television on behalf of the content regulators and major broadcasting organizations in the United Kingdom (Morrison, 1999). 'Real-life' violence was defined by participants as 'actuality' material. Fictional violence, on the other hand, was categorized into three types:

- Playful violence: clearly unreal, with little significance beyond its entertainment value.

- Depicted violence: characterized by realism, has the potential to 'assault the sensibilities'.

- Authentic violence: violence set in a world that the viewer can recognize, such as domestic violence.

Within each category, Morrison identified two factors which determined how violent a scene was considered to be: (i) the nature and quality of the violence portrayed (the primary definer) and; (ii) the way in which it is portrayed (the secondary definer).

The Communications Research Group had undertaken content analyses of depictions of violence in the United Kingdom from 1992. In 2002, they revised the definition of violence used for the content analyses to encompass Morrison's findings (British Broadcasting Corporation, Broadcasting Standards Commission, and Independent Television Commission, 2002):

A violent act is any action of physical force, with or without a weapon, used against oneself or another person, where there is an intent to harm, whether carried through or merely attempted and whether the action caused injury or not.

In addition, within the content analysis, each violent act was coded into one of three categories, drawing explicitly on Morrison's work:

- Accidental violence: unintentional, such as accidents or natural disasters.

- Aggression: the intentional destruction of inanimate objects.

- Intentional interpersonal: violence against people.

While Morrison's work is essentially qualitative and is applied to a quantitative methodology (content analysis), Sander in Germany presents a dynamic-transactional perspective of audience perceptions of violence – that is, an analytical way of thinking that seeks to bridge the gap between the behaviourist 'effects' model and a social psychology based model that allows for active involvement by the viewer (Sander, 1997). This model 'conceptualises TV stimuli and viewers as interdependent phenomena'. To test this, over 300 participants were shown clips from programmes and completed questionnaires based on their reactions. Sander showed that physical violence was the most important dimension in defining violence but other dimensions such as psychological violence were also important. The study also showed that participants' own feelings of anxiety and aggression were the two major emotional factors affecting perceptions of violence. But she accepts that there will have been other variables affecting responses that were less clearly defined, and underlines the fact:

> It is little wonder that findings concerning influences of single (or a few) variables were equivocal considering how their influence can change with the introduction of other relevant but uncontrolled variables.

For example, Wied et al., in the United States, show the effect of empathetic reactions to the amount of reported distress felt by viewers watching scenes of violence, based on how they identified with the characters (Wied, Hoffman, and Roskos-Ewoldsen, 1997).

In the United States, a standard definition of violence, adopted by the Cultural Indicators Project in the 1960s, was that violence is 'the overt expression of physical force, with or without weapon, against self or other, compelling action against one's will on pain of being hurt or killed, or actually hurting or killing'. Researchers in the United States, as in the United Kingdom, have since sought to distinguish between overt violence and aggression.

The three-year National Television Violence Study (NTVS) in the United States was an extensive, and influential, review of research as well as a content analysis of violence in entertainment programmes (Anderson, Berkowitz, Donnerstein, Johnson, Linz, et al., 2003: 81). The project team defined violence as:

> Any overt depiction of a credible threat of physical force or the actual use of such force intended to physically harm an animate being or group of beings.

Using their research sources, the authors identified a range of 'contextual features that influence how audiences respond to television violence' and created a table to argue that the inclusion of a particular feature would increase or decrease the risk of harmful effects from that portrayal (Table 3.1).

Table 3.1 How contextual features affect the risks associated with TV violence.

Contextual features	Learning aggression	Fear	Desensitization
Attractive perpetrator	↑		
Attractive victim		↑	
justified violence	↑		
Unjustified violence	↑	↑	
Conventional weapons	↑		
Extensive/graphic violence	↑		↑
Realistic violence	↑	↑	
Rewards	↑ ↑	↑ ↑	
Punishments			
Pain/Harm cues	↑		↑
Humour	↑		

Note: Predicted effects are based on a comprehensive review of social science research on the different contextual features of violence. Blank spaces indicate that there is no relationship or inadequate research to make a prediction.

SUMMARY OF CONTEXTUAL FEATURES:

Looking across all the contextual features of violence, a portrayal that poses the greatest risk of learning of aggression contains:

■ An attractive perpetrator.

■ Morally justified reasons for engaging in aggression.

■ Repeated violence that seems realistic and involves a conventional weapon.

■ Violence that is rewarded or goes unpunished.

■ No visible harm or pain to the victim.

■ A humorous context.

As a comparison, a portrayal that poses the greatest risk for desensitization contains:

■ Repeated or extensive violent behaviour.

■ A *humorous* context.

Finally a portrayal that poses the greatest risk for audience fear involves:

■ Violence that is aimed at an *attractive victim*.

■ Violence that seems undeserved or *unjustified*.

■ Violence that is *repeated* and that seems *realistic*.

■ Violence that goes *unpunished*.

Source: Federman (1998).

By 'harmful effects', the authors of the NTVS study refer to:

■ Learning aggressive attitudes and behaviours.

■ Desensitization to violence.

■ Increased fear of becoming victimized by violence.

This last – the creation of fear – is further analysed by Potter and Smith (2000), using the NTVS sample. They use content analysis methodologies, and statistical analyses, to conclude that it is the fear effect that is more likely to be engendered by graphic portrayals of violence than either desensitization[6] or disinhibition.[7] However, it is difficult to understand how essentially subjective notions such as fear can be calculated from a content analysis of images.

LEVELS OF VIOLENCE

In order to measure the levels of violence on television, and in other media, content analyses have been used, although these are less frequently conducted now. In the United Kingdom the most recent such analysis was undertaken in 2002 (British Broadcasting Corporation, Broadcasting Standards Commission, and the Independent Television Commission, 2002). The data were part of a longitudinal series of nearly ten years. They found that the programme genre that contained the most depictions of violence as a proportion of its total output was film, with drama following most closely. However, television violence had increased over the ten years, with the biggest increase in the news in 2002, containing 24 per cent of all violence noted in the sample. The data collection period covered 11 September 2001, which accounted for most of this particular change. This exposes the difficulties of sampling to create an 'accurate' picture of television content output and the possible distortions that may occur in content analyses. It is a clear argument for monitoring such content over a period of time so that such peaks can be ironed out.

Firmstone reviews research on perceptions of violence in the United Kingdom, much of it commissioned by the Broadcasting Standards Commission (Firmstone, 2002). Her review showed that through the 1990s, viewers consistently judged there was 'too much' violence on television, although the proportion who said this had slowly declined from 67 per cent in 1991 to 59 per cent in 1999 (and it remains at that same level – 59 per cent – in 2004, Ofcom, 2005). Firmstone reports that Morrison's news editing studies (Morrison, 1992) elaborated viewers' dilemmas, for many considered both that violence in the news (e.g. of war or conflict) should be portrayed, because it is real, and yet that, at times, it is upsetting, even shocking – often more so than fictional violence (and, in this regard, adults concurred with children's perceptions of televised violence, finding real-life violence often more distressing than fiction).

As found elsewhere, context matters – wartime news was expected to be more violent than civilian news; audiences can prepare for documentaries and so these may be expected to contain more graphic images; events close to home were more upsetting than distant casualties and so forth. The editing methodology used by Morrison was interesting because viewers could demonstrate the subtlety of their judgements regarding particular frames or shots (see also Cumberbatch, 2002; Philo, 1993). As Firmstone also notes, there are overlaps between judgements made regarding the acceptability of factual and fictional violence, though in fictional violence viewers were concerned also about the nature of the perpetrator, the degree of realism, whether the consequences of violence are shown for the victim and the nature of the reward or punishment portrayed for the perpetrator.

The following studies reviewed here come from the United States. Signorielli (2003) conducted an analysis of a sample of nine years of peak time network programmes to update the work conducted by the NTVS and look at the portrayal of violence on television. She found little change in the levels of portrayal of violence across the sampling period, unlike the UK sample. However, she noted that there were fewer people involved with violence and they were more germane to the storyline. Although Signorielli does not make this point, this would suggest that the violence portrayed is becoming editorially more justified. She noted little change in the way in which the consequences of violence were portrayed, and questions the effect that such frequencies of depicted violent acts may have on the viewer and their attitudes towards society.

Scharrer, in a study which is indicative only because of the small sample, looked at the way in which police drama series portrayed 'hypermasculinity'[8] and aggression in the United States (Scharrer, 2001). She did this through content analysis, examining one week only of this television genre. The study reveals – perhaps obviously – that there is a relationship between depictions of hypermasculinity and aggression. It also shows how characters are drawn: those who might be considered the 'bad guys' are often compelled by emotion, while the 'good guys' show self-control and are often motivated by a desire to protect female characters in the plot. Such findings are interesting when one considers possible audience responses to different role models.

Based on the NTVS sample,[9] Wilson et al. looked at levels of violence in children's programmes (Wilson, Smith, Potter, Kunkel, Linz, Colvin, et al., 2002). They noted that children's programming contained more depictions of violence than other genres. They also looked at the way in which the violence was depicted, and how that differed between children's programming and programming not targeted at children. They found two key differences:

■ In children's programming, the perpetrators were more likely not to be human but to be anthropomorphized.

■ Perpetrators are more likely to be rewarded for their violence with material goods or praise.

■ The serious consequences of violence are less likely to be shown in children's programming – the use of guns and depictions of blood and gore were also less prevalent.

■ The violence is more likely to be presented with humour.

The researchers distinguished five categories of children's programmes with violence, including slapstick and superhero genres. These two they mention in particular because of their high frequency of violent incidents. Wilson et al. argue that the lack of consequences and the sanitization of violence may lead children to misunderstand the negative consequences of violent behaviour (though it should be noted that their study is not related back to children's perceptions).

THE EFFECT OF MEDIA VIOLENCE ON CHILDREN AND YOUNG PEOPLE: RESEARCH REVIEWS

Many of the research reviews examining violent media content draw on research conducted in the United States which does not operate under the same regulatory conventions for television as does the United Kingdom. Browne and Hamilton-Giachritsis (2005), based in the United Kingdom, look at such international research reviews from a public-health perspective. In their short, useful overview, highlighting the complexities of the research, they suggest there is consistent evidence that violent imagery in television, film, video/DVD, and computer games may have substantial short-term effects such as 'arousal, thoughts and emotions, increasing the likelihood of aggressive or fearful behaviour in younger children, especially in boys'. Nevertheless, they also say, as does Savage (2004), that there is only weak evidence that links media violence directly to crime.

While Browne and Hamilton-Giachritsis accept the association effect is small, it does have implications for public-health policy. They make a series of recommendations, including raising the importance of media awareness:

PUBLIC-HEALTH RECOMMENDATIONS TO REDUCE THE EFFECTS OF MEDIA VIOLENCE ON CHILDREN AND ADOLESCENTS

Parents should:

■ Be made aware of the risks associated with children viewing violent imagery as it promotes aggressive attitudes, antisocial behaviour, fear, and desensitization.

■ Review the nature, extent, and context of violence in media available to their children before viewing.

■ Assist children's understanding of violent imagery appropriate to their developmental level.

Professionals should:

■ Offer support and advice to parents who allow their children unsupervized access to inappropriate extreme violent imagery as this could be seen as a form of emotional abuse and neglect.

■ Educate all young people in critical film appraisal, in terms of realism, justification, and consequences.

■ Exercise greater control over access to inappropriate violent media entertainment for young people in secure institutions.

■ Use violent film material in anger management programmes under guidance.

Media producers should:

■ Reduce violent content and promote antiviolence themes and publicity campaigns.

■ Ensure that when violence is presented it is in context and associated with remorse, criticism, and penalty.

■ Ensure that violent action is not justified or its consequences understated.

Policy-makers:

■ Should monitor the nature, extent, and context of violence in all forms of media and implement appropriate guidelines, standards, and penalties.

■ Should ensure that education in media awareness is a priority and a part of the school curricula.

Source: Browne and Hamilton-Giachritsis (2005).

Kuntsche (2003) surveyed over 4,000 children (mean age 13.9 years) in Switzerland and found that while the use of the media (television and electronic game-playing) were not linked to real life violence, frequency of use was linked to aggressive attitudes and 'indirect violence' (such as bullying). In other countries, many groups of professionals and advocacy groups, including the Canadian Paediatric Society (2003), the Media Awareness Network (Josephson, 1995), and the Australian Institute of Criminology (Brown, 1996), have turned their attention to the potential for risk from exposure to media violence. In 1996, the American Medical Association issued the *Physician Guide to Media Violence*, reviewing the American research literature (American Medical Association, 1996). The guide offers specific recommendations 'about reducing the deleterious effects of media violence for physicians to use themselves as well as to pass on to parents.' These include noting a patient's media use as part of their medical history, educating parents and children into the possible effects of television use and, as 'concerned citizens', advocating, among other things, heightened media literacy.

In July 2000 the American Association of Paediatrics (AAP) issued a Joint Statement on the Impact of Entertainment Violence on Children, based on reviews of the research (AAP, 2000). (See also the AAP's recommendations in this area (2001) and further suggestions for research (Hogan, 2000)). The AAP said:

■ The effect of entertainment violence on children is complex and variable. Some children will be affected more than others. But while duration, intensity, and extent of the impact may vary, there are several measurable negative effects of children's exposure to violent entertainment. These effects take several forms.

■ Children who see a lot of violence are more likely to view violence as an effective way of settling conflicts. Children exposed to violence are more likely to assume that acts of violence are acceptable behaviour. Viewing violence can lead to emotional desensitization towards violence in real life. It can decrease the likelihood that one will take action on behalf of a victim when violence occurs. Entertainment violence feeds a perception that the world is a violent and mean place.

■ Viewing violence increases fear of becoming a victim of violence, with a resultant increase in self-protective behaviours and a mistrust of others. Viewing violence may lead to real life violence. Children exposed to violent programming at a young age have a higher tendency for violent and aggressive behaviour later in life than children who are not so exposed.

Many subsequent reviews of the literature have echoed elements of this statement or have sought to amplify segments, by concentrating on particular effects. However, the research evidence remains open to question, because of the often experimental nature of the studies on which these are based which decontextualizes the content, and because of the (generally) short-term effects that can be recorded. It is not clear how these short-term effects carry forward to become longer-term attitudes or behaviour. The AAP statement also recognizes that there are some groups of children and young people who may be more 'affected' by media violence than others. Again, it is important to note the different regulatory environment in which US television operates in comparison with the United Kingdom.

More recently, the US Federal Communications Commission (2007) considered the impact of violent television programming on children. In its report, the FCC drew extensively on the empirical research outlined above, agreeing that it shows a correlation between viewing such content and aggressive or violent behaviour. While violent content, unlike indecency, is protected under the First Amendment in the United States, the report suggests there are 'government interests' at stake which would allow for such content to be regulated (as for indecency and this includes the protection of children). It also reviewed some further studies that either develop or extend the work previously noted, discussed here.

Bushman and Huesmann (2006) undertook a meta-analysis of 431 studies that had been conducted in the United States to test whether the data are consistent in finding short-term and long-term media effects for aggressive behaviour. They considered all visual media (television, film, video-games, music, and comic books). Their analysis shows greater short-term effects of violent media for adults than for children, in terms of aggressive behaviour, attitudes and other negative arousal levels. For children there appear to be greater long-term effects, and the researchers argue that reported exposure to violent images should be guarded against. It is important to note that these studies purporting to show such long-term effects do not carry forward these measures of effect into adulthood so a true longitudinal outcome is not known. The researchers also point out that many meta-analyses are based on publicly available data, which may in itself create a bias (see Ferguson, 2007):

> In a meta-analysis, it is difficult to find unpublished studies. Studies with non-significant effects are often not published; they end up in file drawers rather than in peer-reviewed journals. If studies in file drawers had been published, the average correlation would be smaller. (Bushman and Huesmann 2006: 350)

Anderson et al. (2003) had conducted an extensive review of the American research. They argue there is 'unequivocal evidence' that media violence increases the likelihood of aggressive and violent behaviour in both immediate and long-term contexts across all media – television, films, video-games and music. They argue that, while the effects are more pronounced for milder forms of aggression, the effects on severe forms are as significant as 'other violence risk factors or medical effects deemed important by the medical community (e.g. effect of aspirin on heart attacks)'. The authors identify a number of areas that should be researched further in the United States:

- They point to recent longitudinal studies which, they say, provide converging evidence linking frequent exposure to violent media in childhood with aggression later in life. However, they accept that it will be necessary to have large-scale longitudinal studies to develop evidence for the role of exposure to violent media in childhood in extreme violent criminal behaviour.

- The authors link the level of viewing violent media with the amount of violence in the media. They argue that while 'it is clear that reducing exposure to media violence will reduce aggression and violence, it is less clear what sorts of interventions will produce a reduction in exposure'. The research literature suggests that parental mediation may be beneficial, but, they state, 'media literacy interventions by themselves are unsuccessful'.

- The authors also argue that more work needs to be undertaken on the underlying psychological processes involved in the viewing of violent media content, accepting that different characteristics (within viewers and within the content) may interact differently for different types of people.

The evolution of research in these areas, they argue, will allow appropriate policy decisions to be formulated.

Villani (2001), also in the United States, reviews media effects studies and content analyses from the 1990s, focusing primarily but not exclusively on television, and including film, music and music videos, advertising, video-games, the computer and the Internet. She argues that the studies show that children internalize the messages from the media they consume, which are not defined in most of these studies, but might be assumed to be material not targeted at a child or youth audience. This internalization in turn, she suggests, affects how children behave. She says that exposure to 'excessive media use, particularly where the content is violent, gender-stereotyped, sexually explicit, drug- or alcohol-influenced, or filled with human tragedy, skews the child's world-view, increases high risk behaviours, and alters his/her capacity for successful sustained relationships'.

The implication of this view, that potentially harmful behaviours may be based on changed attitudes, is a call for media literacy and a requirement that health professionals monitor media use as part of their work. Importantly, while Villani offers a brief overview of all media content in the United States, she does not discuss how the different media interact with one another or how the audience receives them as a whole, except to say they are widely used by young people. Nor does she look at the evidence which shows that certain forms of media delivery bring different expectations.

In summary, the reviews of the research literature rest upon a body of evidence drawn from the American academic literature. These generally suggest that there may be some influence of violent media content upon young viewers but the conclusions in relation to any particular effect are not clear.

LONGITUDINAL RESEARCH
As noted above, there have been many calls for longitudinal research in this area, but only a few such studies have been conducted.

In a rare opportunity for a before and after study, Gunter, Charlton, Coles, and Panting (2000) measured levels of social behaviour among a sample of children before and after the introduction of broadcast television on the island of St Helena. The children in the post-television sample also completed a media use diary, which was merged with a content analysis of violent television content. The findings showed that the boys in the sample had watched nearly twice as much violent material as the girls over the sampling period, but there were no differences in terms of antisocial behaviour measures between the pre- and post-television samples or between viewers and non-viewers of violent content. While the researchers accept that the sample is small and that the data should be taken as indicative rather than conclusive, the effects of violent media content were not demonstrated.

In contrast, a longitudinal study predicting aggressive behaviour as a result of watching television violence was published in the United States by Huesmann, Moise, Podolski, and Eron (2003). They examined the relationship between reported viewing of violent television content at ages 6–10 (not necessarily programming aimed at that target age group) and adult aggressive behaviour fifteen years later, using interview data. Each data collection period lasted two years. They argue, from their findings, that significant childhood exposure to media violence predicts young adult aggressive behaviour for both males and females. Identification with aggressive television characters and the perceived realism of the television violence also predict later aggression. They suggest that these relationships exist even when other factors such as socio-economic status, intellectual ability, and parenting factors are controlled for. There were some gender differences which are interesting in the study, although the overall findings applied to both males and females:

- While early television violence viewing correlated with adult physical aggression for both males and females, it correlated with adult indirect aggression only for female participants.

- Male participants who identified most closely with male aggressive television characters or who perceived such imagery as 'true to life' were considered most at risk for later adult aggression.

- Females who displayed aggressive tendencies were more likely to view violent television content.

The researchers argue these findings show the importance of children's exposure to television violence, rather than that of adults. They also disagree with the suggestion that only 'vulnerable' children are at risk from the effects of viewing such content. Finally, Huesmann et al. point to the 'contextual factors' of the sort that had been delineated in the NTVS, suggesting that different types of violent scenes have different messages for viewers. The study is valuable because it provides data over time. However, it would be interesting to have more regular snapshots of behaviour and attitudes to understand better the relationships between all the factors that operate in young people's lives as they grow to adulthood. The study has also, it should be noted, been strongly criticized by some (Cumberbatch, 2004).

A further longitudinal study, also in the United States, by Johnson, Cohen, Smailes, Kasen, and Brook (2002), assessed television viewing and aggressive behaviour over a seventeen year interval in a community sample of 707 families. The sample was interviewed four times over the period of the study. It found that:

> There was a significant association between the amount of time spent watching television during adolescence and early adulthood and the likelihood of subsequent aggressive acts against others (interpersonal aggression). This association remained significant after previous aggressive behaviour, childhood neglect, family income, neighborhood violence, parental education, and psychiatric disorders were controlled statistically.

The study used self-reported viewing measures, both in terms of time spent viewing and the sort of programmes watched. Johnson used content analyses to estimate how much violence the participants would have been exposed to. It is the link between time spent viewing and subsequent behaviour that Johnson et al. find most important, drawing inferences about the incremental risk of offending or aggressive behaviour based on estimated measures of watching violent television (as defined by the findings from content analyses). In a subsequent exchange of letters with critics, Johnson et al. (2002) expand by saying:

Youths who spend a great deal of time watching television are less likely to spend time engaging in interpersonal activities that promote social interaction skills. Such youths with relatively poor social skills may tend to have difficulty resolving interpersonal conflicts in a non-aggressive manner.

Of these three studies, the first (Gunter) finds no effects, the second (Huesmann) finds effects of viewing violence but has been much criticized methodologically, and the third (Johnson) finds effects but draws stronger conclusions about the consequences of heavy television viewing in general rather than viewing violent content specifically. One is tempted to conclude that longitudinal studies, desirable though they are, are no more conclusive than short-term studies.

THE IMPORTANCE OF CONTEXT

In the United Kingdom research has shown consistently that context, by which we mean the portrayed context within the programme, is key to the way in which audiences consider content (see also Ofcom's set of contextual variables, Ofcom, 2005). If a violent scene is thought to be editorially justified and appropriate to the scene, or appropriate to the genre, then the audience is far less likely to take offence to that scene, as opinion polls and other qualitative social research show. Context is also frequently stressed in research on children and media harm, with researchers being most concerned when violent actions are portrayed as detached from their consequences, or celebrated, or perpetrated by heroes rather than victims. This is also true in the American research tradition.

In a study employing group discussions among children in the United Kingdom aged 9–13 and using age-appropriate television and film clips as prompts, Millwood Hargrave argued that children have a more textured approach to violence than many adults, looking beyond what is seen as physical action to the consequences and moral status of the action. Crucially, they refer the content to their own lives. They can be sophisticated (i.e. media literate) in the way they deconstruct images and understand the way in which certain production techniques are used to heighten or to lessen dramatic effect. Importantly (see also Buckingham, 1996), this sample found real-life events far more frightening and violent than some of the clips they were shown – the unfolding of events from 11 September 2001 where many children said, the 'most violent' content they had ever seen, particularly because of the known and real consequences. Lastly, the study found that fictional violence that approximated children's own experience was upsetting – especially scenes involving children being attacked or hurt, echoing findings from the study by the Australian Broadcasting Authority, above.

Thus, research finds that children are more upset by violence embedded within a realistic context, including a context (or with characters) that resembles their own lives (Gatfield and Millwood Hargrave, 2003).[10] One of the key contextual factors found in many studies is the principle of 'justified violence' (Millwood Hargrave, 1993; Morrison, 1999, as well as the NTVS). This, it is suggested, minimizes the impact of violence for the adult as well as the child viewer. Potter and Mahood (2005) examined how people determine whether violent acts in stories are justified. They asked 475 college students in the United States to read one of three stories in which the characters (perpetrators and victims) were changed.[11] Respondents completed a questionnaire that measured their reaction to the degree of justification for the violence in the story, their reactions to contextual cues, and characteristics about themselves (gender, ethnic background, and television viewing patterns). The findings suggest that the greater the empathy or identification with a character, the higher the level of justification offered.

VULNERABLE AUDIENCE SUBGROUPS

Women

Most of the research which has looked at vulnerable television audience subgroups other than children has been conducted in the United States. This review found no such recent research in the United Kingdom except that which examined the responses of women to television and film violence. In this in-depth qualitative study of women's responses to depictions of violence against women (in television and film), Schlesinger, Dobash, Dobash, and Weaver (1992) found that those who had themselves experienced violence in real life (just over half of the sample) were more sensitive to television violence than were those who had not experienced actual violence, offering more complex interpretations and being more concerned about the possible effects. The researchers suggest that audiences' vulnerability to portrayed violence depends on the level of their fears about becoming a victim of such violence themselves (e.g. rape, domestic violence, murder) (see also Cantor, 2002). A follow-up study of men, half of whom similarly had been victims of violence (though interestingly, they were less likely to categorize themselves as 'victims'), found them to be less involved with dramatized violence, showing less interest in identifying the motives of those portrayed, expressing little sympathy for the characters and ambivalence for rape scenes in the films viewed, and less questioning about whether the sex portrayed was consensual (in *Basic Instinct*, for example). The responses of gay men in the sample were an exception to this, for they showed a greater likelihood to empathize with victims.

Kahlor and Morrison (2007), also in the United States, investigate the role of television viewing among a small sample of young women (N = 96) as contributing to an acceptance of rape myths (defined here as 'false beliefs and stereotypes regarding forced or attempted sexual intercourse and the victims and perpetrators of such acts'). They suggest that content analyses of television programmes in the United States support such myths. They find a significant positive relationship between television use and rape myth acceptance and perceptions that rape accusations are false. They do not find a relationship between television use and an estimation of the prevalence of rape in US society so the hypothesis that depictions may increase fear of rape was not proven. It is unclear from the research report how, and if, different genres affected these attitudes (the study covered television entertainment, television news, and music).

Coyne and Archer (2005), in the United Kingdom, examined gender differences in the use of indirect aggression, and the effect that viewing such content may have. Indirect aggression is defined as:

> a manipulative and covert way of harming others by using the social structure as a way to exclude, ostracize, and harm others…Indirect aggression can take many forms including gossiping, destroying friendships, spreading rumours, and breaking confidences. This type of

aggression is particularly effective as a way of harming females, as they place great value on relationships and social standing, the very facets of life that indirect aggression targets to harm. (Coyne and Archer 2005: 234)

They asked a sample of 347 adolescents (aged 11–14 years old) in the United Kingdom to list their five favourite television programmes (which were analysed for the amount and type of aggression they contained). Students were required to nominate fellow students who were considered to be aggressive, either directly (using physical aggression) or indirectly. Coyne and Archer found that peer-nominated indirectly aggressive girls, in particular, watch more indirect aggression on television than any other group. Peer-nominated physical aggression was predicted by other aggressive behaviours, but not by televised physical or indirect aggression (see also Coyne, Archer and Eslea, 2006).

Ostrov, Gentile, and Crick (2006) undertook a two year study of a small sample (N = 78) of American pre-school children and considered their media exposure, the type of content viewed and measures of aggression (as well as pro-social behaviour). They found that parental reports of media exposure are associated with relational (or indirect) aggression for girls and physical aggression for boys at school.

Other vulnerable adult groups
Zillmann and Weaver (2007) in the United States noted that, in an experiment in which men had to increase the pressure of cuffs on another person's arm, those men that scored high on measures of hostility used aggression more frequently than men scoring low on that trait. Further exposure to a violent film segment resulted in more frequent use of aggressive responses among men who scored higher in terms of physical aggression than exposure to a non-violent film segment.

Boyson and Smith (2005), also in the United States, seek to provide a conceptual framework for homicidal thinking, including building a model of traits that link to a disposition to such thinking. They conducted a two-part survey with 195 college students. It consisted of an inventory or questionnaire of homicidal thoughts as well as retrospective reports and questions about media use. They found that aggression as a trait was the strongest and most consistent predictor of homicidal thoughts. They also say the data suggest that 'media violence is most closely related to reactive thoughts, generated under conditions of negative affect and for whom attention to homicide in the mass media is most likely'. That is, the study argues for media effects but allows for different effects on different people, depending on their circumstances at the time. The study also accepts that it is not able to draw inferences from homicidal thought to homicidal behaviour.

Hoffner, Plotkin, Buchanan, Anderson, Kamigaki, Hubbs et al. (2001) used telephone interviewing in the United States to examine the 'third-person effect' (the belief that others are more affected by media messages than oneself). They found respondents were more likely to consider that television violence affected aggression in other communities and those who were more geographically distant. Such third-person effects are noted frequently in research, including among children who feel themselves less vulnerable to influences than, for example, those younger than they are (Millwood Hargrave, 2003; Office of Communications, 2005a).

Eyal and Rubin (2003), in an experimental study, examined how viewers' perceptions of characters interacted with their personal aggressive tendencies. They looked at the particular characteristics of homophily, identification and parasocial relationships.[12] Using American college students with an average age of 20, data on a variety of measures was collected. The researchers argue that their findings suggest that identification was greater among those who displayed aggression but was not significant either with homophily or with parasocial interactions. They suggest that 'aggressive characters might reinforce the aggressive dispositions of viewers'; however, the research only looked at identification with aggressive characters and not with non-aggressive characters. Why do some people choose violent media content? An American survey of young teens (average age 14 years old) found that gender (boys), sensation seeking and aggression all play a role in the choice of violent Internet content, with alienation from school and family playing a smaller role (Slater, 2003).

In the United Kingdom, Guy, Mohan, and Taylor (2003) conducted a study – using semi-structured interviews – of viewing preferences among men with a history of schizophrenia and violent crime (N = 20) and compared their findings with a group of men with schizophrenia but no history of violence (N = 20) and another group of men who were orthopaedic patients, without either history (N = 20). Their aim was to:

- Determine how much screen violence was watched, both pre- and post- hospital admissions.

- Note viewing preferences.

- Document positive and negative emotional responses to screen violence.

- Examine identification with screen characters.

They found that the group with both schizophrenia and a history of violent crime did not watch more screen violence than the other groups but they did display different emotional responses to the images, expressing greater preference for violent content, reporting more pleasure in viewing and identifying more closely with violent characters on-screen. The researchers recognize the difficulty with the size of the sample, and suggest viewing preferences should be collected as part of patients' medical assessment.

Savage (2004) reviewed the literature in the United States on criminal aggression and the link with viewing media content, including an insightful examination of the methodological constructions of media effects projects. She accepts that the data show a correlation between exposure to violent programming and aggressive behaviour although she questions just which effects may be in play. She also recognizes the methodological difficulty of examining a relationship between exposure to such content and subsequent criminal behaviour. In her view, however, the research literature thus far is not convincing of a direct link. Importantly, Savage (2004: 124) asks:

> If the effect is limited to a few trait-aggressive or neglected individuals (and evidence of an intervention of this type is mounting) it may not be appropriate to focus policy on television violence, but on the causes of childhood aggression and parental neglect.

The data from the United States, both on children and other segments of the audience, suggest that there are influences on vulnerable or at-risk groups but that well-developed socialized young people do not seem to fall within this group, although there is more evidence that boys rather than girls are vulnerable to media violence – as in Johnson et al. (2002). Indeed, an interesting finding in Johnson et al.'s (2002) study was that boys are most 'vulnerable' in adolescence while women are in early adulthood. However, as the next section shows, research among children themselves suggests that they are not passive, but active, consumers of the media with well-developed understandings of the importance or relevance of what they are seeing, subject to their age and social-cognitive development.

CHILDREN'S ATTITUDES TO TELEVISION VIOLENCE

There is a far greater research literature in the United Kingdom which directly examines children's attitudes towards television violence. Most of the studies mentioned, largely from the United States, have addressed issues about television violence with children as their subject matter. Few have spoken to children themselves about their reactions to the material they see. Outside the United States, where most of the contemporary studies have come from, and especially in the United Kingdom, there is a tradition of using qualitative techniques with children as actice participants (Australian Broadcasting Authority, 1994; Buckingham, 1996; Millwood Hargrave, 2003; ACMA, 2007; Broadcasting Standards Authority, 2008).

Chambers, Karet, Samson, and Sancho-Aldridge (1998) conducted research amongst groups of children to examine the role cartoon viewing plays in their lives. They found that television is seen as something which helps children to relax and unwind, and cartoons have a particular role within children's television viewing. They are always distinguished from reality, are short, easy to dip in and out of, fun, funny and exciting. For some, the link with merchandizing is seen as positive (they enjoy collecting and playing with the characters). Parents had differing views, finding cartoons less appealing – in particular, the violence in some of the material. The research also found gender differences – girls in general, and older boys, do not particularly like action cartoons. Younger girls (5–6 years old) find some of the imagery frightening and 'noisy'. Older children (8–9 years old) sometimes feel uncomfortable or uneasy if the characters are too human, or if the storylines are to do with children being in danger. This research underlines the different reactions that age, gender and even being an adult can bring to a programme genre designed for a young audience. It also stresses, once again, that fear results from similarities between children's lives and those portrayed.

Buckingham's study of the way in which children and young people aged 6–16 years old 'define and make sense of' media images that may be distressing, used in-depth qualitative techniques, interviewing participants and then re-interviewing a sub-sample in greater detail (1996). While it may be argued that the use of adult moderators can affect responses and that young people may display attitudes that they do not feel, this type of research does not seek to claim effects but reveals how children are thinking – as far as they express themselves honestly. The initial sample of 72 may be thought limited, although it is large for qualitative research, but the re-interviewing technique allows for more information to be extracted than might be forthcoming in a larger group, or in a structured experimental setting. Buckingham found that all the children interviewed for his study admitted to having experienced some 'negative' response to 'difficult' content, which was not necessarily age-appropriate. But none of these was long lasting or severe. Importantly such responses could occur to different media and media genres, including books, melodramas, cartoons and advertisements. Thus, developing the point made about context, above, Buckingham was able to show that 'in both fact and fiction,(negative) responses appear to derive primarily from a fear of victimization, rather than any identification with the perpetrators of violence' and children develop 'coping strategies' to deal with the things they view. He also concluded that 'there is no evidence here that children are any less upset by real-life violence as a result of watching fictional violence.'

In-depth discussions with children aged 10–15 years old about media harm in Australia revealed the classic 'third person effect', namely that children (like adults) do not believe that they themselves are affected by the media, but they do believe that others are influenced (Nightingale, Dickenson, and Griff, 2000). Although one might question children's capacity to identify what harms them, children did admit to being scared of realistic images, especially those in the news about matters close to the child's own life (see also Millwood Hargrave, 2003). Fictional images were seen as less harmful. Rather than seeing children as 'innocent victims', Nightingale argues that children are 'active players' trying to take in and deal with the inevitable changes in society and the media and, as Davies, Buckingham, and Kelley (2000) show, developing their own tastes and aesthetic judgements in the process. It was clear from these focus groups that the children were seeing material that was inappropriate for their ages. They discussed the negative consequences of violent material (especially horror or supernatural themes), including the effects of feeling scared (nightmares, sleep disorders and, often the most scary, re-enactments of the scene by a father or brother, playful or otherwise).They reacted strongly also to screen depictions of real-life risks (drugs, alcohol, unwanted pregnancy, sexual harassment, bullying). Nightingale (2000) notes further that the violent media content that many of the boys said they enjoyed was also enjoyed by their fathers, with both girls and boys agreeing that it is 'natural' for boys to like violence and gore. One might argue that the often-greater effect of media violence on boys than girls is because it is more socially acceptable for boys to act in a boisterous or aggressive manner.

Valkenburg, Cantor, and Peeters (2000) interviewed a sample of children in the Netherlands by telephone to examine if they thought television could create fear in children. One in three children in the sample (31 per cent) said that something on television had 'frightened' them in the past year, including news items. The researchers also noted that children's fears and their coping strategies varied by age and gender. Similarly, a survey of television viewing by Australian primary school children found that over half had stopped viewing or left the room because something on television – most often violence – had upset them (girls more than boys) (Australian Broadcasting Authority, 1994). Sex/nudity was rarely reported as upsetting, though the majority did not wish to view this. News stories, especially about children or animals being hurt/killed could be upsetting, as could programmes about parents arguing/fighting. On the other hand, most children liked to watch action drama, with guns and car chases, and many liked scary programmes with monsters or ghosts.

The level and importance of 'active' interaction with the television screen was looked at in a study examining the relationship between perceptions of the world (in particular, perceptions of crime and violence in society) among Flemish television viewers and among video-game-players (Van Mierlo and van der Bulck, 2004). This study acts then, as an inter-media comparative study as well. However the sample is fairly small (at 322 young people aged either 15 or 18 years old) and is based on self-reporting – the results should be taken as indicative only and should be re-tested. It found that there were greater effects on the perceptions of the world among the sample of television viewers than there were among video-game-players. The authors suggest this may be due to the way in which gamers play, and the active role they have in selecting what they play which may offer a degree of abstraction and distance from the content of the game.

Peters and Blumberg (2002) review the evidence for the proposition that violence depicted in television programmes, particularly cartoons, has a negative impact on young children's behaviour. They look at the research conducted in the United States among those aged 3–5 years. This group has relatively high levels of television viewing (up to 30 hours per week) and the authors point to content analyses that show that cartoons contain some of the highest levels of violence in television – the NTVS points out that 70 per cent of cartoon violence rarely shows negative consequences such as pain or suffering. They conclude that this gives children the impression that real-life violence also does not lead to pain. Yet, having reviewed the levels of violence in children's television, definitions of violence and research on children's interpretation of violent content (including the morality of these acts), the authors conclude that such a hypothesis is not supported:

- If children of pre-school age can differentiate between the appropriateness of violent cartoon actions and real life actions, as their research suggests, then cartoon violence might not have as negative an effect as some think.

- Also, the studies that have shown children reacting violently after viewing cartoon violence may actually be more situation-specific rather than a long-term effect.

Both these conclusions the authors accept as controversial. This is partly because, as Livingstone and Helsper (2008) show, the widespread assumption that more media literate viewers are less influenced by television is not supported by research evidence. What is not controversial, Peters and Blumberg argue, is that parents act as important mediators in the viewing of media violence, especially to help them better understand cartoon violence and the difference between reality and fiction (see also Austin, 1993; Davies, 1997).

The tensions – or disparities – that exist between methodologies (a cultural/active audience approach compared with an experimental/behavioural one) may be found in research into television wrestling. In the United Kingdom, an extensive qualitative study was conducted of children's attitudes to televised wrestling (British Board of Film Classification, Independent Television Commission, and Broadcasting Standards Commission, 2001). A variety of methodologies were used – standard length group discussions (90 minutes); extended group discussions combined with observation of participants (120 minutes); individual interviews; and paired interviews (with two friends). This research showed that while participants created 'relationships' with their favourite wrestlers, this was related to the way in which wrestling was seen, as a drama rather than 'real-life': 'each broadcast is seen as developing an underlying story, somewhat like a soap'. This is because the wrestling has stars, production values and imaginative 'storylines'. For a few participants there is uncertainty about how much of the depicted pain is real, and the researchers do suggest that depictions of these sorts of violence need to be monitored, but they do not suggest that the material has any effect other than to interest the devotees of the genre.

On the other hand, a content analysis of programmes collected for the NTVS found that there is a great deal of verbal aggression in televised professional wrestling, particularly offensive language (Tamborini, Chory-Assad, Lachlan, Westerman, and Skalski, 2005). This, the researchers argue, may lead children to think that verbal aggression which has no apparent justification is acceptable.

The contrasting methodologies to examine the same genre, and the resulting differing interpretations, argue for the importance of ensuring the use of multi-faceted research methods and of exploring what it is that the audience understands from the material they view, and the contextual environments of programmes and their genres. In the United Kingdom, these environments are both regulated and well-established.

Krcmar and Hight (2007) undertook research among very young American children (aged between 33 months and five years old). They claim to show that exposure to even slight aggressive visual stimuli (such as an 'action' character) could create an aggressive response (in this case the way in which a story was ended by the respondent). They suggest this shows that a single exposure to an action cartoon could help establish a mental model for aggression. This finding echoes the observation about video-games that Anderson et al. (2007) make, suggesting that even cartoon violence can have an influence. (For a review of the literature on cartoon violence see Kirsh, 2006.)

Using physiological measures as a means of evaluating responses to television violence, Murray, Liotti, Ingmundson, Mayberg, Pu, Zamarripa, et al. (2006) examined children's brain activity while watching such content. While the data and methodology are interesting, many of the criticisms made about experimental studies, especially those that measure physiological responses to images of violence, are applicable here. Respondents (in this case, children) are put in an artificial space with intrusive measuring systems linked to them. Nonetheless, the findings are worth noting as they suggest that there are responses that may not be vocalized or even consciously registered. The American child sample was small – the researchers measured the brain activity of just eight children (aged 8–12 years old) viewing age-appropriate televised violent and non-violent video-sequences. They found that both types of sequences activated regions of the brain associated with visual motion, visual objects/scenes and auditory listening. However, television violence activated *transiently* those brain regions involved in the regulation of emotion, arousal/attention, episodic memory encoding and retrieval, and motor programming. The researchers hypothesize that this may explain findings of behavioural effects, 'especially the finding that children who are frequent viewers of TV violence are more likely to behave aggressively'.

This, the researchers suggest, may be because aggressive 'scripts' are stored in long-term memory and they might act subsequently as a guide for *overt social behaviour* (see also Anderson and Bushman, 2002).

Slater, Henry, Swaim, and Cardador (2004) argue that the way in which a young person is feeling affects the relationship between their use of violent media and how aggressive they feel. To examine this, they surveyed over 2,500 students in the United States (aged 12 at the start of the project) four times over a period of two years. The measures included use of violent media content and reported levels of aggressiveness, including feelings of aggression and aggressive behaviour. Their findings support their view that there is a link between watching a greater amount of violent content than 'normal' and heightened feelings of aggression and that this 'effect of violent media on aggression is more robust among students who report feelings of alienation from school and during times of increased peer victimization'. The researchers accept that those in their sample who were well-socialized did not show such associations. (The definition of normal levels of viewing is not made clear.) This study builds on the 'downward spiral model' hypothesized by these authors which suggests that aggressive youth seek out violent media and media violence, in turn, increases aggression (Slater, Henry, Anderson, and Swaim, 2003).

Buchanan, Gentile, Nelson, Walsh, and Hensel (2002) also looked at the link between 'relational aggression'[13] and exposure to violent media content. They surveyed 219 children aged 7–11 years, examining media habits, attitudes to the self-reported media they consumed and aggressive attitudes/behaviours. They argue their study shows a link between aggression and exposure to media violence based on the programmes and films that the children said they watched or computer/video-games that they played. They accept the subjective nature of the study – for example, children, when asked to judge the level of violence in content, may exaggerate or play down the violence. Importantly the researchers suggest this research may be important to 'inform future interventions with maladjusted children', suggesting these are a group that may be affected by certain media contents.

In the United States, Grimes and Bergen (2001) argue that the empirical evidence to support the notion that violent television programming can cause psychological abnormality among previously psychologically normal children has not been shown. They suggest, having reviewed the evidence, that there is no reason to accept there is a cause and effect relation between violent television and psychological illness among normal children, although they do think it affects psychologically abnormal children who are not able to position television in an appropriate part of their lives. The particular group they single out is those with Disruptive Behaviour Disorders (DBDs). These children they say have 'an enhanced susceptibility to stimuli that feed already distorted interpretations of incoming social cues'. It is these children, they argue, who should receive attention in relation to the effects of media violence. In further papers, they describe psycho-physiological responses to media violence which show how such television content may affect this group negatively (Grimes, Bergen, Nichols, Vernberg, and Fonagy, 2004; Grimes, Vernberg, and Cathers, 1997).

Zimmermann and Christakis (2005) used data from the National Longitudinal Survey of Youth in the United States to look at the role of parental influences and television viewing, among other factors, in subsequent bullying behaviour. They argue that each hour of television viewed per day at the age of 4 years was associated with a significant effect for subsequent bullying behaviour.

Each of these studies supports the claim that viewing violent television content may affect aggressive attitudes or behaviour, generally in the short-term. However, all these studies are open to contention, especially as many of them are laboratory-based and are not able to be considered within a 'real' home or other viewing environment. Longitudinal data to examine how any short-term effects noted may translate into long-term changes are much needed.

SEX

LEVELS OF SEXUAL PORTRAYALS ON TELEVISION

A number of studies have examined the amount and manner of portrayals of sexual activity on television. Buckingham and Bragg undertook a comprehensive review of the international research literature in 2002. The review provides data on attitudes towards sexual material, cultural theories, content analyses and effects research (Bragg and Buckingham, 2002). It illustrates what they call 'the outline of a productive alternative to mainstream "effects" research' and they emphasize the active role of audiences in making sense of the media, in particular, content that refers to sexual matters.

The Communications Research Group had conducted content analyses of television portrayals of sexual activity for the Broadcasting Standards Commission over a period of ten years (1991–2002). Data on depictions of sexual activity from peak time programmes broadcast on the free-to-air channels were collected, as were references to sexual activity (including direct and indirect references). Although this wide-ranging capture of information about sexual activity was queried by the media and the industry as being too broad, the purpose of content analyses is to examine all the constituents of a particular type of content and to see how prevalent it is. Without knowing how much discussion about sex there is, or how much simulated sexual intercourse is depicted in a schedule, or what proportion of overall sexual activity they represent, one cannot respond to claims that television is full of images of 'sex'.

The most recent such content analysis was published in 2003 (British Broadcasting Corporation, Broadcasting Standards Commission, and Independent Television Commission, 2003; Cumberbatch, Gauntlett, and Littlejohns, 2003). The sample of programmes was drawn from peak time programming to represent programmes most likely to be viewed across the five highest rating channels; the free-to-air channels. They were also drawn from composite weeks to remove possible distortions created by particular events. Such methodological considerations make these analyses less open to the criticism that the sampled programmes are not 'representative' of the programming output.

However, sampling distortions do occur and in the 2002 survey, a small number (five) of factual programmes (out of a total sample of 802 programmes surveyed) took sex as their theme and so accounted for 40 per cent of the sex acts shown. Nonetheless, as part of a trend dataset, the findings showed that while 21 per cent of programmes in the total sample contained some form of sexual activity, they were infrequent and mild, with 60 per cent involving kissing. The 9 p.m.watershed was effective in terms of restricting more explicit portrayals of sexual activity, and the portrayals shown were most often within established relationships. References to sex showed an increase across the ten-year period monitored, and they occurred twice as often after the watershed as before. Significantly, given current concern over content that links sex with violence, almost none of these portrayals included violence.

ADULTS' ATTITUDES TOWARDS SEXUAL MATERIAL

The communications regulator, Ofcom (2005c), found, as part of a longitudinal tracking study, that nearly half the sample of adults interviewed (48 per cent) said there was the 'right amount' of sexual activity depicted on television, while 42 per cent said there was 'too much'. This latter is considerably lower than the proportion that says there is 'too much' violence on television, for example, at 59 per cent of the sample. Similar findings are made in this study the following year with over half the sample saying there is 'too much violence on television (56 per cent) with 36 per cent (a further drop) saying the same about depictions of sex (Ofcom, 2006).

The 2005 tracking study also found that most respondents (75 per cent) think that people should be allowed to pay more to watch 'particularly sexually explicit programmes not available on other channels'. This more accepting attitude towards the depiction of sexual material was underscored by other research which showed that participants in qualitative research in the United Kingdom were more concerned about the use of swearing and offensive language than they were about sexual activity on-screen (Ofcom, 2005). There was some concern that the media might add to the premature sexualization of children but many participants talked of the positive benefits of a more 'open' attitude towards issues around sexual matters.

An earlier study in 1999 had also shown that parents did not display much concern about their children being influenced in terms of their sexual development (43 per cent of parents disagreed that on-screen depictions encourage early experimentation), but they did dislike the daytime confessional talk shows, which were thought to be preoccupied with sexual matters (47 per cent of all respondents said there was 'too much' sex in talk shows; Millwood Hargrave, 1999). This study used three methodologies – qualitative discussion groups and family interviews; a quantitative survey of 732 adults with a boosted sample of 83 young people aged between 13 and 15 years old(permission to conduct these interviews was sought from their parents); and a further sample of 261 adults who completed a multi-media interview, watching and commenting on clips from programmes.

The study was an update of a project conducted in 1992 (Millwood Hargrave, 1992) and it found a decrease in the level of concern about the portrayal of sex in broadcasting from 1992. This did not mean that respondents approved of it, but its presence was accepted. Context was of prime importance and over three quarters of the respondents (78 per cent) thought that the depiction of sexual activity should be justified by the storyline. For many, the definition of on-screen sex was a depiction of (simulated) intercourse and the events around it. However, it was apparent that 'talk about sex' was seen as part of the overall environment of sexual activity (70 per cent of respondents said there was more talk about sex than actual sex depicted on television). The content analyses also measured 'talk about sex and nudity' and, in 2002, had found a 28 per cent increase in such references since 1999. Advertising was an area about which respondents commented negatively, disliking the fact that sex was used to 'sell' products. One might usefully distinguish here the question of whether portrayal of explicit sexuality encourages early sexual experimentation among teens, which has been the focus of much of the research reviewed, from the question of whether sexualized images of children encourage gender stereotypes and gendered consumer preferences.

The biggest change between the two studies had come in attitudes towards the depiction of homosexual relationships with 58 per cent of the sample in 1999 saying it was acceptable to show homosexual relationships on-screen compared with 46 per cent in 1992. Barnett and Thomson (1996) had also found that the context in which a scene was set was key in the tolerance towards the depictions of sexual activity. Their study had examined attitudes towards homosexual depictions as well as heterosexual depictions, finding far less acceptance of homosexual activity among older respondents. They concluded that, in this case:

> It appears to be not so much the representation of the act in the media that many people object to as the act itself, and therefore its portrayal.

No more recent research evidence was found which examined the attitudes of homosexuals on the way in which they are portrayed on television. Of more concern to participants regarding the depiction of sexual imagery is the domestic context in which one is viewing. Parents admit to embarrassment when watching sexual content with their children and vice versa, teenagers admit to embarrassment when watching with younger people – but it tends not to be offence that is caused in the regulated UK television environment, just embarrassment.

ATTITUDES OF, AND INFLUENCE ON, YOUNG PEOPLE

Buckingham and Bragg (2003; see also Buckingham and Bragg, 2004) looked in some detail, both qualitatively and quantitatively, at the way in which 9–17 year olds 'use and interpret media in the context of their interpersonal relationships and how this relates to the formation of their social identities'. They found that children frequently encounter sexual material in the media they use. Indeed, many of them value the media as a way of gaining information. For example, girls in the samples used teen magazines as a way of finding out information they would not learn at school or would not want to ask their parents or peers. Nonetheless, young media consumers are generally quite sophisticated and do not always trust what they glean from the media: for example, they were not often willing to accept what they saw as some of the overtly moral messages in drama series. This finding, that children may reject or ignore explicitly negative consequences presented to them in programmes, was supported by research into children and young people's attitudes towards the depiction of illegal drug abuse (Cragg, 2000) (see below).

The benefit of drama series, however, is that they offer an opportunity to talk about issues that might not otherwise be discussed (Millwood Hargrave and Gatfield, 2002; Office of

Communications, 2005b). Respondents in research say that they are able to distinguish soap operas from 'real-life' and acknowledge that the storylines presented are created for dramatic effect, squeezing many issues into a short episode: such issues are not always taken 'seriously', but they offer a valued vehicle for discussion.

Buckingham and Bragg (2003) found some significant gender differences especially in relation to attitudes towards depictions of sexuality, including homosexuality – this last was more influenced, they suggest, by family and peer values than by the media. Importantly, this study also found that children frame their viewing of media depictions of sexual activity within a moral framework, much as has been found in the viewing of depictions of violence (Millwood Hargrave, 2003). From the qualitative stage of this study, the researchers conclude:

> Both children and parents wanted to be addressed as individuals who were capable of making their own choices, rather than as the recipients of moral instruction.

Some researchers, mainly in the United States, have expressed concern regarding the lack of pro-social messages in mass media, especially in the context of sexual matters: for example, Brown (2005; see also Brown, Halpern, and L'Engle, 2005) used content analysis to show that positive depictions of sexual health or contraception are rare in all media even though, as they also show, those in need of such information (here, early maturing girls) are more likely to turn to teen media such as music and magazines and could therefore benefit from such messages. Similarly, Farrar (2006) undertook a small scale study in the United States ($N = 188$) and noted that women who saw programmes featuring condoms had more positive attitudes to condom use than women who had not seen such material. Importantly however, the sample's own intentions to engage in safe sex were unaffected by any of the media conditions.

Much of the reason behind conducting content analyses is to help understand how children and young people may form views about sexual matters as they are depicted in the media. A report from the American Psychological Association (2007: 1 of Executive Summary) examined the impact of sexualized messages targeting girls across diverse media. It defines sexualization as that which occurs when:

- a person's value comes only from his or her sexual appeal or behaviour, to the exclusion of other characteristics;

- a person is held to a standard that equates physical attractiveness (narrowly defined) with being sexy;

- a person is sexually objectified – that is, made into a thing for others' sexual use, rather than seen as a person with the capacity for independent action and decision making and/or

- sexuality is inappropriately imposed upon a person.

The report identifies a series of risks associated with sexualization, including the media sexualisation of girls, cognitive underperformance, mental health and eating disorders, diminished sexual health, reduced self-esteem and negative attitudes from others.

Eyal, Kunkel, Biely, and Finnerty (2007) undertook a content analysis of the twenty most popular television programmes among teenagers in the United States, examining the sexual messages contained therein. They compared representations over two seasons, finding that a high percentage of programmes made reference to sexual content (70 per cent in 2004–05 compared with 83 per cent in 2001–02). However, much of this was in discussion and much of it was between adults (none between children under 13 years old). The research also looked at the discussion of risks and responsibilities associated with sexual relationships. As had been noted previously, there was little discussion of these risks although the research found that no programmes in 2004–05 depicted positive consequences of intercourse. 33 per cent showed no consequences at all and 67 per cent showed negative consequences (NB the relatively small sample of programmes). As with the British-based content analyses referred to above, the study found the sexual content in most programmes was 'mild' in nature and was often verbal, rather than a depiction.

Earlier, in a paper drawing together three studies from America on different aspects of what they all 'sexual socialization', Biely, Cope, and Kunkel (1999) say:

> Electronic media, and television in particular, provide a window to many parts of the world such as sexually-related behaviour, that would otherwise be shielded from young audiences…The effect of viewing sexual content on television is not thought to be direct and powerful, with a single exposure to a particular programme leading a viewer to think or act in any given way. Rather, the effects of televised messages about sex are conceptualised more as the product of a slow and cumulative process…It is the overall pattern of messages across the television landscape that is of primary interest for explaining the effects of long-term exposure.

Each of the studies Biely et al. consider use content analyses. One looked at the sexual content in peak time programming, including the discussion of sexual issues; one considered such content in programmes most viewed by adolescents and the third compared the sexual content 'rating' (the V-chip rating[14]) given to a sample of programmes. Again, as in the United Kingdom, Kunkel et al. and others found that 'talk about sex' was far more frequent than the depiction of sexual activity. They also found that about one in eight depictions of sexual activity were portrayals of simulated sexual intercourse. Additionally, around 10 per cent of the programmes most watched by teenagers contained some discussion of the risks associated with inappropriate sexual behaviour.

A re-analysis of data collected from the American National Longitudinal Study of Adolescent Health between 1994–96 by Ashby, Arcari, and Edmonson (2006) notes that there is an increased risk of respondents having had sexual intercourse within a year of the study if they are under 16 years old, watch television for two hours or more each day, have a family that disapproves of sex and where there is no parental mediation or regulation of television. However these data, while much used in the United States, would seem to have little to commend them in the United

Kingdom where research on such issues would take account of many other factors, including peer groups and socialization.

Similarly in a longitudinal study (over two years) of over 1,000 adolescents in the United States, Brown et al. (2006) found that the more their sample was exposed to sexual content in television, film, music, and magazines, the more likely they were to have sexual intercourse when 14–16 years old. This was true even after factors such as sexual behaviour at the start of the study were accounted for. This was particularly true for white adolescents while black teens in the study seem to be more influenced by how they perceive the expectations of their parents and peer groups than the media.

Collins, Elliott, Berry, Kanouse, Kunkel, Hunter, and Miu (2004) also linked viewing among over 1,500 adolescents to attitudes towards variables described as 'associated with adolescent sexual initiation'. They suggest that watching television predicts sexual activity among this group. Eyal and Kunkel (2005) examined the portrayal of consequences of sexual behaviour in an experimental study on the effects of such exposure on attitudes and moral judgements among 233 American students aged 18–25 years old. The three types of consequences portrayed were positive, negative or neutral, and a control group saw no sexual content. Positive consequences were outcomes from sexual intercourse such as improving a romantic relationship or increasing one's self-esteem, negative consequences included feelings of guilt or regret. Each set of consequences was taken from a transmitted drama series. The clearest finding was that the portrayal of negative consequences of sexual behaviour affected the measures of attitudes towards premarital sex immediately post-viewing, leading to a more negative view of such behaviour. The viewing of positive consequences, however, did not make the subjects' attitudes shift in this way. Similarly where neutral consequences were measured, there was no effect on such attitudes. From this the researchers conclude that the consequences of behaviour, except in a negative context, do not play as significant a role as cognitive theories might predict.

A study by Pardun, L'Engle, and Brown (2005) in the United States seeks to establish a relationship between the amount of sexual media content viewed with attitudes – and assumed behaviours – towards sexual matters. Over 3,000 children aged 12–14 years old filled in a questionnaire about media use and a subsample of 1,074 was interviewed about their sexual attitudes and behaviours. Based on the results of the media use survey, the top television shows, films, music, Internet sites, and newspapers were analysed for portrayals of or references to all forms of sexual activity, including nudity. The researchers sought to sample in a representative manner by creating 'units' of media with sexual content which could be measured across each medium under consideration. The analyses showed that, in total, 11 per cent of the media used by these young people contained sexual content, with music containing significantly more (at 40 per cent). Nudity in a variety of forms and relationships accounted for two-thirds of all sexual content coded. From the media use data and the content analyses, a measure called the Sexual Media Diet (SMD) was developed to assess each individual's exposure to sexual content. Separate SMD measures were created for each of the media under consideration. The researchers noted that 'the SMD measure showed a statistically significant association with adolescents' sexual activity and future intentions to be sexually active, with measures of movie and music exposure showing the strongest associations'.

The researchers see film and music – rather than television – as the main area of concern though it may be argued that these audiences bring with them different attitudes and expectations for these media, which may have, in turn, different impacts (see also Hanley, 1998a; Millwood Hargrave, 2003). For an overview of the international evidence about media sex and all aspects of it in terms of theory, policy and regulation, see Gunter (2002).

L'Engle, Brown, and Kenneavy (2006) used a postal survey linked with content analyses to reach similar conclusions about the influence of the mass media (television, music, film and magazines) in comparison with other influences (such as family, religion, school, and peers) on adolescent behaviour and attitudes in the United States. They suggest that adolescents who are exposed to sexual content and who perceive greater positive approval in the media for teen sexual behaviour express a greater intention to engage in sexual activity (than those who watch a limited amount of content with a sexual theme). The study does not follow through to note whether or not such behaviour occurred.

Kelley, Buckingham, and Davies (1999) used open-ended interviews among British children across two age bands, 6–7 and 10–11 years old, to look at how they interpreted and responded to the representations of sexual behaviour encountered on television. It also examined what children define as appropriate, both for themselves and for children in general. Their findings suggest that children have some understanding of the way in which programmes are targeted at different audiences (and age groups). It also revealed how children, especially when among peers, use their knowledge of the media to display their identities, including gendered identities. They expressed a wish to protect children younger than themselves from possible harmful effects, with the older children drawing on what the authors call 'moralistic discourses'. This way of thinking about how viewers watch television or consume other media, which suggests an active, thoughtful process, is not well-addressed by the experimental methods favoured in the United States as these cannot allow the exploration of measures or attitudes that have not been previously defined.

There was discussion in the United Kingdom about allowing R18 material (depicting explicit pornography) on television, although only behind appropriate access control systems. This material depicts explicit consensual sexual content, and is only available currently from licensed sex shops. As part of its consideration of this, the regulator (Ofcom) commissioned a review of the research literature on the impact of R18 material, or pornography (Helsper, 2005). The review was, of necessity, limited by the fact that attitudes to pornography are not researched among young people for ethical reasons. The overall conclusion of the review (see also the chapter on film) is that there is little empirical research demonstrating that exposure to such material impairs either the mental or physical development of minors.

Overall, the research suggests an association between television viewing and actual sexual behaviour. However, other research (already reported on, and particularly in the United Kingdom) suggests that young people have a more active relationship with the media and many factors contribute to the way in which they use the media to rehearse their sexual behaviour and express their sexuality. Much depends, therefore, on the nature of the portrayal and the interpretative response of children and young people.

OTHER CONTENT ISSUES

LANGUAGE

In many of the countries where English is the native language, there is a particular concern about the way in which swearing and offensive language are used (Australian Broadcasting Authority, 1994; Ofcom, 2005). It is seen by some in the United Kingdom as a symbol of the relaxation of standards in society (Kieran, Morrison, and Svennevig, 1997):

> Language (swearing)…is taken as a statement of moral decline and as a statement about the decline in respect for authority.

The use of offensive language on television is often the issue that respondents complain most about, although they express greatest concern about the depiction of violence (Ofcom, 2005c).[15] Indeed, there is a general view that the exposure of young children to even mild offensive language is not acceptable (Millwood Hargrave, 2000a). Research reported on by Millwood Hargrave (2003) used both qualitative and quantitative techniques to investigate attitudes towards the use of such language, both in the home and on television. It demonstrated how dynamic language is. While attitudes to the use of the 'most severe' swearwords on television had not changed, there was considerable movement in attitudes towards terms of abuse in comparison with two years previously. It also showed significant offence could be caused by the repeated use of swearing or of a particular word. This finding was supported by more recent research by Ofcom (cited above) which showed that terms of racial abuse, especially, were considered highly offensive.

In the United States, a detailed content analysis revealed that the use of 'offensive language' has increased in the four years since the introduction of age and content ratings in 1997 (Kaye and Sapolsky, 2004). Moreover, this increase was noted across all programmes, not just in those labelled for older teens/adults. Content labels were found to be a reliable indicator of profanities – indeed, the researchers suggest the 'L' rating has become a licence for producers of material to include such content. Yet al.though public surveys consistently show concern over swearing and offensive language, the harm this may produce remains unclear – Kaye and Sapolsky suggest that such language encourages profanity in everyday conversation and it is to be assumed from this comment that they think this is harmful to society.

More recently in the United States, the Federal Communications Commission (FCC), has fined broadcasters for allowing the transmission of expletives. The then Chairman of the FCC said:

> This sends a signal to the industry that the gratuitous use of such vulgar language on broadcast television will not be tolerated. ('US TV', 2004, *para.* 6)

While the evidence for harm is unclear in terms of the use of swearing and offensive language on television, there is a concern about it in the United Kingdom, and as such it constitutes a matter of considerable offence, especially when children may be exposed to it. Other research (Millwood Hargrave, 1998) had found that respondents were more concerned about others being offended through the use of terms of abuse than they were about being offended themselves.

BODY IMAGE

Comstock and Scharrer (2007) find evidence of stereotyping regarding body image, with 'thinness' aspired to. They note this in television programmes and also in video-games where, they say, female characters have very thin bodies yet are highly sexualized with large breasts and hips while men are portrayed as being very muscular. Tiggemann (2005) asked nearly 1,500 students (N = 1452) in Australia to fill in questionnaires which measured attitudes to eating disorders, ideals of physical appearance and uses of television. It was found that total television time was not related to any body image variable for either boys or girls; what is important is the type of material viewed and the motivations for watching it. Thus, the time spent watching soap operas is related to a drive for thinness in both boys and girls, while music videos are related to a desire for muscularity in boys. Dohnt and Tiggemann (2006), also in Australia, find that a desire for thinness is affected by peers for girls as young as 5 years old (N = 97) while media become more influential as they get older. They argue that:

> as early as school entry, girls appear to already live in a culture in which peers and the media transmit the thin ideal in a way that negatively influences the development of body image and self-esteem.

As the above suggest, most studies find that levels of television viewing *per se* have little impact. Indeed, much of the research suggests that other media may be more influential, in particular music videos (Borzekowski, Thomas N. Robinson, and Killen, 2000; Fouts and Vaughan, 2002). Holmstrom (2004) suggests that, while television images of thin women seem to have little or no effect on women's body image, images of overweight women may have a positive effect by increasing viewers' satisfaction with their own bodies. Other studies have found that the media can have a positive effect on how young people perceive themselves, by advocating healthy lifestyle images (Taveras, Rifas-Shiman, Field, Frazier, Colditz, and Gillman, 2004).

An interesting study was undertaken by Nathanson and Botta (2003) in the United States who looked at the way in which parental mediation may interact with adolescents' television viewing, together with any body image concerns the young people may have. In particular, they looked at 'the mediation of central content (i.e. messages about the plots or behaviours of main characters) and mediation of incidental content (i.e. messages about the thinness-depicting images)'. They did this by surveying students, their parents and, in some cases, siblings aged between 12 and 17 years old. They found that any comment about body image issues, even negative comments on incidental content, could affect young people's concerns about how they looked. While the research may be criticized for being retrospective in nature and based on parents' recollections of what happened, along with those of their college-going children, it is interesting that the researchers suggest all comment may have an influence of some sort, if not lead to actual behavioural change. Further research in this area would need to look more closely at the interrelationships between this and other forms of incidental content and, indeed, responses to images in other media.

SUBSTANCE ABUSE

A content analysis of the top ten most watched programmes by 10–15 year olds across a three-month period in 2004 in the United Kingdom showed that most depictions of the use of alcohol, smoking or drug use were by a minority of characters, although those who drank alcohol or smoked tended to have prominent roles (Cumberbatch and Gauntlett, 2005). For each of these types of depiction, the majority of scenes depicting such portrayals were neutral in the message they conveyed.

A small sample (40 participants) of 12–17 year olds was interviewed as part of the consultation by Ofcom on the then proposed Broadcasting Code (Office of Communications, 2005a). Attitudes to the portrayal of alcohol, illegal drugs and smoking were examined:

■ Alcohol: Respondents considered that the negative aspects of alcohol use were not presented in most televisual contexts, and that this could be harmful to younger people. It was also considered important to present these negative consequences for both young people and adults (this sample felt that the negative consequences of drinking for the latter group were rarely addressed).

■ Illegal drugs: The sample underlined public concern about the use of illegal drugs, considered to be potentially very damaging to users. There was a perception among respondents that drug culture was often presented on television as 'part of a glamorous sub-culture that is "outside normal life"'…In general participants reported valuing a more general and reasonable portrayal of drugs and drug culture as something that affects the mainstream, rather than just sub-cultures'. This mirrors earlier work which found that one of the prime criticisms of television portrayals of illegal drug abuse was that it was presented, unrealistically, in a negative light at all times (Cragg, 2000). In other words, respondents want realistic portrayals, neither too positive nor too negative.

■ Smoking: There was some comment that the anti-smoking health messages prevalent in the media are not mirrored in television fiction. However, some of the anti-smoking health messages themselves elicited a strong reaction from the sample 'as creating fear in a negative way'. By this the researchers meant it did not necessarily put these young people off smoking but created concerns among them about their parents' health, for example.

Will, Porter, Scott Geller, and DePasquale (2005) used content analyses to look at 'risky behaviours'. They examined a sample of episodes (242) from peak time television shows in America in 1997–98 to monitor the way in which the behaviour of characters was portrayed, including the behaviour of vehicle occupants, especially in relation to wearing seat belts; violence; risky sex; and the use of drugs, alcohol, and tobacco. Their findings showed that negative consequences of risky behaviour were rarely depicted. The researchers go on to discuss the public-health issues involved in such depictions. Gerbner (2001) also found that messages about drugs, smoking and alcohol use do not give sufficient weight to the likely negative consequences of misuse of such substances (see also Watson, Clarkson, Donovan, and Giles-Corti, 2003).

Also in the United States, Yanovitzsky and Stryker (2001) conducted an analysis of the possible interaction between media (press) messages and young people's binge drinking behaviour and policy-making regarding alcohol abuse. They suggest that the use of news and entertainment genres may be more effective, and thus might be used more effectively, both for getting public-health messages across and for alerting policy-makers to the fact that something may need to be done about an issue.

SUICIDE AND SELF HARM

Some researchers have examined the possible links between depictions of suicide and actual suicide, with the suggestion that there is greater evidence for the influence of reports in the news media than in fiction (De Lange and Neeleman, 2004; Gould, Jamieson, and Romer, 2003). Romer, Jamieson and Jamieson (2006) report on a four-month analysis of suicide news reporting in six US cities in 1993 and the incidence of deaths by suicide for three age groups (15–25, 25–44, and older than 44). They find that local television news is associated with an increased incidence of deaths by suicide among those aged under 25 years old, while newspaper reports are associated with such deaths for both this group and those aged over 44 years old. However, they also note that there is no such increase in the sample of 25–44 year olds and suggest that, for this group, media depiction may have inhibited suicide. In the United Kingdom there are guidelines in place for the way in which suicide is discussed and presented on television.

Slaven and Kisely (2002) in Australia and Gould, Jamieson and Romer (2003) in the United States call for the education of practitioners involved with the reporting of suicide issues – the paper by Gould et al. offers some guidelines that may be used. Other studies have looked at the media's impact on suicidal and self-harming behaviours. Based on their findings from a small-scale pilot study of twelve British patients, Zahl and Hawton suggest that the media have a role to play in such self-abusive behaviour, with four subjects saying that a storyline had prompted them to self-harm (Zahl and Hawton, 2004). They also found that, for some of the patients interviewed, the media – especially the Internet – played a positive role in giving them information about their condition. These data need to be treated with some caution as they are based on a small sample but such findings would again support the call elsewhere for the collection of appropriate (and verifiable) media use data to be collected as part of clinical assessments.

REALITY-DEFINING EFFECTS

McQuail (1987) defines 'reality defining effects' as the systematic tendencies of the media, through the repetition of many similar messages, to affirm and reinforce the particular cognitions that fit one version of social reality (e.g. stereotyping or exclusion of certain groups or experiences). For example, Hoffner and Buchanan (2005) asked just over 200 young American adults to complete questionnaires about their perceptions of, and responses to, their favourite fictional television characters, both male and female. They found that respondents most wanted to be like (wishful identification) same-gender characters and with characters who were similar to them in attitudes:

> men identified with male characters whom they perceived as successful, intelligent, and violent, whereas women identified with female characters whom they perceived as successful, intelligent, attractive, and admired.

Both male and female respondents identified more strongly with successful and admired characters of the other gender.

Stern, Russell and Russell (2007), considering an advertising and marketing effect, used an online survey of American respondents to examine how long-term exposure to negative role models in soap operas might have a negative effect on the fans of such content.

> The relationships (viewers had with the characters) are unhealthy not only because the characters are poor role models but also because the viewers can become addicted to soaps and substitute surrogate friends for real ones. The themes provide insight into the negative influence of damaged heroines on viewers who are repeatedly exposed to depictions of subordinate and victimised women whom viewers observe closely, accept as real and consider friends. (Stern et al., 2007: 20)

Similarly, Aubrey (2007) finds negative effects upon American women's perceptions of their own sexuality based on their consumption of soap operas and prime-time dramas. These findings are in contrast with research in the United Kingdom which finds positive effects from viewing soap operas, particularly by raising social issues and concerns (Henderson, 2007). This may reflect the distinctively realistic, 'gritty' style of UK soap operas, in which strong female characters are predominant.

Ferguson (2005) reports on an experiment in which participants in the United States were exposed to an episode of the *Jerry Springer Show*. The show had female guests who were involved in either promiscuous or non-promiscuous behaviour. The results show that those respondents exposed to the promiscuous female guests perceived a victim of sexual harassment as less traumatized and more responsible for the event than those who saw women who were not involved in promiscuous behaviour. Ferguson draws a number of conclusions, including:

■ The present findings demonstrated that the influence of exposure to images of promiscuous women on subsequent judgements of sexual aggression can be mediated by the extent that the promiscuous female stereotype is applied to the victim.

■ The findings also indicate that exposure to non-pornographic images of promiscuous women from 'easily accessible' media sources (i.e., a popular television programme) can have deleterious consequences.

■ The findings indicated that the impact of exposure to images of stereotypically sexual women in a popular television show was not moderated by the extent of previous exposure to that show.

REPRESENTATION OF MINORITY ETHNIC GROUPS

Many argue that genuine harm may be caused to the populace at large through the inappropriate representation of minority groups, both to people from those groups and to society. Comstock and Scharrer (2007) note in their review of the research literature that there have been increases in the representation in American television programming of people based on race and ethnicity (especially for African-Americans who are more widely seen) but they also note that stereotypes still exist in terms of the characters portrayed. They also remark on stereotypes based on age, disability and sexual orientation.

In a far reaching review of the evidence for changes to be made to the Communications Act then under consideration in the United Kingdom, James argued that to fulfil 'the government's declared vision of developing an equal, inclusive society where everyone is treated with respect and there is opportunity for all', the media must play a full role (James, 2003). His particular focus was ethnic diversity. In preparing his report, he reviewed the research literature as well as legislative measures and the report of the Commission for the Future for Multi-Ethnic Britain (2000). His review demonstrated that 'despite the positive efforts of broadcasters and regulators in the past, UK media organizations were still largely failing to reflect cultural diversity'. As a result of the review and other lobbying, the Communications Act 2003 was adjusted to make it an explicit duty of the regulator (Ofcom) to have regard to the interests 'of the different ethnic communities within the United Kingdom' (HMSO, 2003).[16]

Hargreaves and Thomas (2002), using interviews and a survey among people from minority ethnic groups in the United Kingdom, identified a mistrust of mainstream media news programming and the way in which minority communities were represented. As a result, many people from minority groups, especially young Asians, used a variety of media (including the Internet) to create a more 'relevant' view of the world for themselves. Hargreaves and Thomas also found that there were large proportions of people from these groups (especially black people) who said they knew nothing about national or local political structures or events. The researchers point to the potential harm this may cause society:

> There is (further) evidence…of a serious loss of contact between a minority, but a significant one, of UK citizens and the core information base which makes democratic societies able to function at the local, national and international level.

For further discussion of these issues, see the section on news programming, below.

Millwood Hargrave (2002) examined the findings of a study which looked at attitudes among viewers and the industry towards broadcasting and the representation of minority ethnic groups. The study involved the use of focus groups and depth interviews among people from minority ethnic groups and the majority white population, depth interviews and an email panel among representatives of the broadcasting industry, as well as content analyses. It found that there was no clear single definition of 'multicultural broadcasting' but there was a list of values to which such programming should aspire. These were:

■ To be relevant for the particular audiences being served.

■ To present a variety of voices and opinions.

■ To consider the manner in which portrayals are presented (there was concern expressed about the use of stereotypical indicators of cultural difference which lacked authenticity).

■ To be aware of the need to improve the 'off-screen' presence of minority ethnic groups, and their level of creative input to the broadcasting industry.

There was praise in this research for the increase in minorities on-screen (see also Broadcasting Standards Commission, 2003) but there was also a call for greater representation in a diverse range of mainstream (free-to-air) broadcasting. It was argued that this would help to foster a greater feeling of inclusion within society by minority ethnic groups and to increase an understanding of ethnic cultures within all parts of British society (minority and majority) (see also Australian Broadcasting Authority, 1993; Sreberny, 1999).

Mastro and Robinson (2000) analysed US peak time television police dramas from 1997. They found that police officers were more likely to use excessive force when the perpetrators of crime were from young minority ethnic groups. However, their analysis also suggests that, compared with real crime statistics, television portrayals of officers over-represent minority groups while portrayals of criminals under-represent these groups (perhaps an attempt at positive discrimination?). These data are now rather out of date and may not translate to the United Kingdom well; it would be beneficial to conduct an equivalent study in the United Kingdom.

REPRESENTATION OF DISABLED PEOPLE

A content analysis of the representation of people with disabilities on the five UK terrestrial television channels across a period of five years from 1997 to 2002 (Broadcasting Standards Commission, 2003) showed such representations are particularly low (see also Cumberbatch and Negrine, 1992). Portrayals involving mobility impairments are most often seen as, visually, they are most evident. Two years on, content analyses of a sample of programmes have found that there is still under-representation of people with disabilities on the analogue terrestrial television channels during peak time programming, and the most commonly represented disabilities are generally those that are most easily recognized (Ofcom, 2005).

Sancho conducted a wide-ranging study in the United Kingdom of attitudes towards the representation of people with disabilities (Sancho, 2003). Industry members were interviewed, as were people with disabilities and their carers, and a survey conducted of the 'general public'. The study defined five attitude types who came from both the disabled and non-disabled communities:

- ■ Issue driven people (14 per cent of this segment represented in society) – this group is vocal and focused on the existence of prejudice on television.

- ■ Transformers (9 per cent) – this group wants more normalization of portrayals of disability.

- ■ Progressives (36 per cent) – this group sees the role of television as normalizing and educating people about disability.

- ■ Followers (26 per cent) – this group is quite passive, with no specific interest in disability.

- ■ Traditionalists (15 per cent) – this group has the clearest perceptions of what is and is not deemed acceptable on-screen, and disabled people are seen in narrowly defined ways.

The study was controversial and its findings attracted debate as it looked at areas such as social acceptability (including physical attractiveness) and sexuality (including sexual behaviour). It was the conclusions that Sancho drew that caused the most controversy, suggesting, for example, that some programme-makers found certain characters 'untelevisual' and so difficult to accept. This was strongly refuted by the industry. The report also looked at conditions for offence, taking comedy as the genre on which to focus discussion (see also Pointon and Davies, 1997). In considering the views of the (small sample of) children interviewed who either were people with disabilities themselves or were carers, Sancho noted that:

> All the children interviewed…are searching for disabled role models on television, but it is likely that they are struggling to find many examples. It is vital that children are provided with positive portrayals of disability, particularly within the children's genre.

Diamond and Kensinger (2002) found that pre-school children in the United States have the beginnings of an understanding of those disabilities that involve the use of equipment, such as wheelchairs. However, they have little awareness of other disabilities such as Downs Syndrome which have less overt distinguishing characteristics. Their study used videotaped segments from the children's television show, *Sesame Street,* to examine reactions to a child who was a wheelchair user and another who had Downs Syndrome. They suggest that it may be important for children's television programmes to make explicit those differences that are not immediately apparent. They see the media's role in such learning as positive:

> Teaching about individual differences in children's television programs requires an explanation of the differences that are highlighted in the episode, not just exposure to those who are different. …The results of earlier work, along with the present study, suggest that it is important to examine the ways that we help children to understand what it means to have a disability, particularly a disability that may limit a child's participation but requires no specialized equipment.

Kolucki offers a brief overview of current research in the United States on the media and disability.[17] The Canadian Association of Broadcasters (CAB) also considered this area in some detail. They concluded that they:

> …believe that all media, and particularly television can play a strong role in changing public attitudes on social issues, and that greater visibility, more accurate depictions and positive messaging can strongly influence inclusive practices across society.

To examine how best they could deliver this, the CAB (Canadian Association of Broadcasters, 2005) commissioned a significant piece of qualitative research among stakeholders involving:

■ Depth interviews with representatives from disability non-government organizations, persons with disabilities within the broadcasting sector, government officials, senior managers in the broadcasting industry and representatives from the television production sector.

■ A Stakeholder Forum with industry and government representatives, including NGOs.

In addition an analysis of broadcasting industry initiatives in the United Kingdom, the United States and Canada was completed. There was no content analysis by agreement between the industry and the regulatory authority (the CRTC) 'because it was generally agreed that on-screen presence of persons with disabilities is very low, and on-screen counting would yield little in the way of useful results'. Among other findings, the research noted that:

■ There is general agreement that the presence of persons with disabilities both on-screen and behind the scenes is low, and that negative portrayals still take place.

■ There is widespread support for the business case for diversity in broadcasting and more specifically, the business case for the inclusion of persons with disabilities in television programming, both on-screen and behind the scenes.

Based on these findings, the CAB developed 'a toolkit' for broadcasters 'to assist its members in advancing the inclusion of persons with disabilities in the industry and addressing presence and portrayal issues on-screen'. Having identified the issues through research, the toolkit sets out the objectives that the industry should be aiming for, makes recommendations and suggests the means to achieve these objectives. It also includes an evaluation process (*Source:* Canadian Association of Broadcasters, 2005).

REPRESENTATION OF PEOPLE WITH MENTAL HEALTH ISSUES

The significance of the CAB project is that it illustrates how research can be used to inform and impact upon media policy-making. In a related domain, Corrigan (2004) argues that the media can be instrumental in changing attitudes towards mental illness.

Diefenbach and West (2007) undertook a content analysis of American television programmes and surveyed 419 respondents to examine the hypothesis that media stereotypes affect public attitudes towards mental health issues. They found that portrayals of mental health disorders are negative with the mentally disordered portrayed as ten times more likely to be a violent criminal as non-mentally disordered television characters. The survey also shows that as television viewing increases, so does a concern among viewers about personal danger from such people. Similarly Wahl et al. (2007) conducted a content analysis to show that children's television programming in the United States also contained negative representations or disrespectful language about those with mental health issues.

In contrast, Zoller and Worrell (2006) found in their study in the United States of the audience's interpretation of televised depictions of multiple sclerosis (MS) in the television drama *The West Wing* that participants related to the depictions variously depending on their own physical and social experiences with the illness:

> Participants expressed a desire to see more symptoms depicted, and they noted concern about the identities communicated to the public about people with MS and its influence on their daily, lived experience.

The study – although small in terms of sample size – is of interest because it employs a number of qualitative methods, including a focus group, individual interviews and the collection of electronic message board posts. Such research leads Salter (2003) to argue, from a psychiatrist's point of view, that there needs to be better communication between the medical and media professions.

THE REPRESENTATION OF RELIGIOUS BELIEFS

To inform the approach to religious programmes in the Ofcom Broadcasting Code (2005d), a series of focus groups was conducted with those of diverse religious views in the United Kingdom. While most expressed tolerant views and expected regulation to protect these, some content was clearly felt to be inappropriate, especially that which seeks to persuade people to join a particular faith or which exploits susceptible or vulnerable audiences.

The perceived vulnerability of audiences was also key in concerns expressed by participants in an extensive qualitative and quantitative research project reported on by Sancho (2001). This looked at attitudes towards the representation on television of alternative beliefs, as well as psychic and occult phenomena. While alternative beliefs (such as reiki or yoga or homeopathy) were accepted as almost 'mainstream' and there were few concerns about them, this was not the case for the other beliefs or practices examined.

In particular, respondents made clear distinctions between the occult and the psychic – the former was talked of in terms of having 'negative intent' and therefore possible negative consequences for vulnerable people. It was felt that occult practices were 'about exerting influence, rather than fostering personal development or enlightenment'. On the other hand, psychic practices were felt to be more benign, with references made to horoscopes, clairvoyance, and so forth. Where these strayed into areas which might affect the mental state of vulnerable viewers however, there was concern expressed. Vulnerable viewers were those who had, for example, experienced bereavement or other life-changing events. There were also concerns expressed about children coming across such material on television, so respondents were keen that programmes dealing with psychic practices should be placed on niche channels and behind scheduling restrictions, while occult practices should not be shown unless they were in a 'legitimate' factual programme.

THE PLACE OF TELEVISION NEWS

Data from the United Kingdom suggest that the public is drawing its news from an increasing variety of sources.[18] However, television remains the key source of information and news, as the figure below shows.

In a report examining audience attitudes to the coverage of political issues around the 2005 General Election in the United Kingdom, a telephone survey showed that respondents used a range of different sources to obtain information on political issues, but television was most widely used (84 per cent of the 1,433 adults interviewed after the Election) (Ofcom, 2005). Studies such as these telephone interviews are based on self-reported perceptions of behaviour or attitude, as are many studies, but their benefit is they form part of a longitudinal dataset which has looked at attitudes towards the media during elections over a number of years.[19]

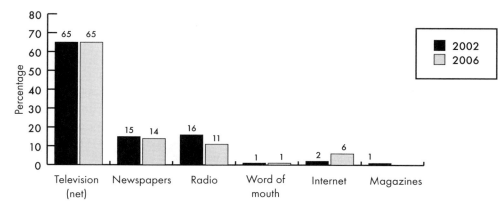

Figure 3.3 Main source of news identified by consumers. *Source:* Ofcom (2007) *New News, Future News.*

The news may be seen as a window into any particular culture, reflecting its preoccupations and its concerns. (For an overview of the debate about political communications within sociology, see Benson (2004)). Fowler (1991) argues that the way in which material is selected and presented reflects the shared experiences of the content/news producers and consumers.

> News is a representation of the world in language, because language is a semiotic code, it imposes a structure of values, social and economic in origin, on whatever is represented; and so inevitably news, like every discourse, constructively patterns that of which it speaks. News is a representation in this sense of construction; it is not a value-free reflection of facts.

There has been much debate in the United Kingdom about the quality of television news and whether it has been 'dumbed down'. 'Dumbing down' is a concept used by Graber (1994) to talk about the way in which network news in the United States was being edited to compete with local news stories which were faster in pace. The phrase has changed in popular meaning to include a perceived change in the quality of analysis (so that news analysis becomes more superficial) and a restriction in the diversity of news items. These changes, it is suggested, affect the public by giving them fewer opportunities to become knowledgeable about a variety of issues and thereby to play a full, informed part in civil society.

A comprehensive review of the balance between 'broadsheet' or 'serious' and 'tabloid'[20] news reporting was conducted by Barnett, Seymour and Gaber (2000). They sampled over 700 news bulletins from 25 days in each of six years, drawn from 25 years of programming (1975–1999). Domestic and international news bulletins were coded for content and format, noting the amount of time given to each story. Notwithstanding the limitations of content analysis, which cannot easily note the nuances or ambiguities of television presentation, Barnett et al. were able to show that – across time – the balance in news reporting had not changed and that national and international 'serious' news still outweighed entertainment stories ('tabloid' news). However, their study did note that most bulletins were moving towards an increasingly 'tabloid' feel and domestic agendas were on the rise, with a decline in coverage of political affairs. Barnett et al. also found evidence that different news bulletins catered to different groups within the audience. The researchers concluded (p. 13):

> Given the dire warnings about the damaging effect of channel proliferation and market competition, we tend to the conclusion that the UK has maintained a remarkably robust and broadly serious approach to television news…This broadly positive conclusion comes with a major qualification. The rise in sports and consumer stories, combined with the decline in political stories, gives some cause for concern. Given the impact of market pressures on other areas of television output, we are not wholly optimistic that 10 years from now television news will have maintained its current balanced and diversified approach.

Hargreaves and Thomas (2002) conducted a comprehensive study of attitudes in the United Kingdom towards news and the changing news environment. They used a series of datasets: a desk review of existing research into television news audiences; a quantitative survey of UK adults into their sources of news and viewing habits, with boosted samples drawn from ethnic minority groups; a qualitative focus group study; and a content analysis of UK television news output for a ten week period from May-July 2002.

As the election data above suggest, the research showed that television is the main news medium, used and respected by almost everyone. It is the only news medium capable of reaching across the whole of British society. Nevertheless, people are increasingly using a variety of sources, rather than relying upon a single source. These include 'new' forms of news, such as 24-hour television news, news on the Internet and also 'word of mouth' dissemination of the news. The researchers suggest these newer forms may be filling the gap left in information acquisition as viewing to the more traditional news genres declines. In some homes, such as those with multi-channel television or in households comprised of people from minority ethnic groups, people were making greater use of continuous news channels than previously thought. Indeed, the project found that many young Asians regarded the Internet as their main source of news. The area of greatest perceived attitude shift was in the decreased interest in, and knowledge about, political issues – this, it is suggested, is seen by respondents as more of a problem with politics than with the media.

Peter (2004), working in the Netherlands, showed how the media, working together and delivering similar messages, could act to create a particular point of view within society about an issue (in this case, greater European integration) in comparison with circumstances where the various media present different ('dissonant') views. That is, if the media in a particular country presented positive points of view about European integration, then people's support for such change was increased, while negative 'consonant' views decreased it. No effect of dissonant coverage was noted. Peter argues that this supports the claim for the effects of 'mass media'. Similarly, the importance of 'managing' media coverage to prevent so-called moral panics and potentially ill-informed policy responses is well-illustrated in an article by Ayre (2001). Ayre examined the contribution of the media to the creation of 'damaging distortions' in the child protection structure in England and Wales as a result of the responses by authorities, at both a local and national level, to media accusations of inadequate systems for the welfare of children in the 1970s–1990s.

Related to the concerns about the 'dumbing down' of the news, and the creation of a less informed citizenry, is the concern that 'soft' news or so-called infotainment (news events treated as dramatic items in order to gain viewers) will come to dominate the bulletins. Barnett's analysis of news items in 2000 did not support this hypothesis, at that time. Prior (2003: 150) tests the theory espoused by Baum in 2002 that:

> ...some people who would not otherwise watch any news at all pay attention to soft news coverage of wars and foreign crises. Some people do not watch hard news programmes because the opportunity costs from forfeiting payoffs from entertainment are too high. By focusing on the more entertaining, shocking, or scandalous aspects of politics, soft news offers these people an alternative that maximises their utility because it combines entertainment and information.

Prior used a web-based survey of over 2,300 adults in the United States to test this hypothesis. He found that while respondents did show a preference for soft news for its entertainment value, it was not as popular as either pure entertainment or hard news. Further, there was little evidence that respondents felt they acquired information from soft news stories. Should a move towards this style of news reporting be made, it will be important to monitor the balance of news as information against news as entertainment.

Grabe, Zhou, Lang, and Bolls (2000) also found that the soft news style did not improve recognition memory or delayed recall of information. However, this American study is rooted in the behavioural psychology tradition, using heart rate and skin conductance measures to examine which of the elements in a news item create arousal alongside self-evaluative tasks. This style of research is subject to considerable criticism about the artificial nature of the methodologies and the 'interference' there may be from other factors, such as respondent nervousness.

Koolstra (2007) undertook a small scale study in the Netherlands (N = 96) to examine the relationship between how the world is viewed and how that is affected by portrayals in fictional television programmes. Koolstra looks particularly at so-called 'fiction-to-news' confusion (i.e. viewers may remember fictional television stories as news). He finds that participants are often confused, even when they are exposed to 'relatively' many short television content extracts, especially if they contain threatening, violent events.

NATIONAL NEWS

Many recent studies have considered the way in which the news represents specific groups within society, minority ethnic groups in particular. The reasoning for this work, as Fowler suggests (1991), is that the news not only reflects society but also plays a role in the ways in which society is seen.

Surveys of the television audience examining minority ethnic attitudes to the news are infrequent (Hargreaves and Thomas, 2002; ITC, 1996). Noteworthy is a small-scale qualitative study that focused on Muslims in the United Kingdom after 11 September 2001 (Gillespie, 2002). This revealed a deep lack of trust in British and American TV news. The most common complaints included sensationalist reporting, limited or limiting perspectives and anti Arab and anti Muslim bias. It would be of interest to news producers and those who monitor news output to track such attitudes and see how they change or develop over time.

The representation of race is considered in many studies from the United States. Dixon (2006) noted that exposure to black suspects in American news programmes affected attitudes to assessments of culpability and perceptions of crime in society, among other factors (see also Dixon and Maddox, 2005). An earlier content analysis of American network news considered the presence of African Americans and whites in crime roles (Dixon, Azocar, and Casas, 2003). It found greater representations of whites in all crime roles (as perpetrator, victim and police officer) and also that African Americans were significantly less likely to be shown as victims than crime statistics would suggest. The authors question whether this signals a change in social attitudes as popular discourse suggests an over-representation of blacks as criminals. While the sample looked at four years of news programming alone, such a change would be an important shift and tracking of this development would be useful.

LOCAL NEWS

A number of studies have looked at the way in which local television news coverage has affected attitudes towards certain issues. In the United Kingdom viewing of local television news has been in decline, although scheduling decisions affect how the audience behaves (Ofcom, 2005c). Hargreaves et al. (2002) showed that audiences felt least well-informed about their localities. This is important as:

> This may point to an emerging crisis of local news infrastructures and could help explain why so many people find so much politics meaningless or difficult to engage with, because they are not able to judge its effects in their own communities.

Without adequate and objective information about one's own community, the effect on society may be significant. There have been a number of studies in the United States which have shown the way in which local television news coverage impacts on one's views (Romer, Jamieson, and Aday, 2003). The United States has a more clearly defined regional television structure so, while the studies are interesting in themselves because of the way in which they suggest the importance of television news, they may not be translatable directly to the United Kingdom.

Gilliam and Iyengar (2000) looked at the way in which exposure to the racial element in local television crime stories affected respondent attitudes towards people of different races and towards criminal punishment. This wide-ranging study included content analyses of over 3,000 television crime stories in Los Angeles across a year, comparisons with actual crime statistics and an experimental study with over 2,000 participants. The researchers divided the sample of participants into four groups. Each group was shown a television news broadcast in which one of four versions of a news item was placed. The broadcast either included an item about a murder in which the alleged perpetrator was African American, one in which the perpetrator was white, a third in which there were no clues given as to the identity of the perpetrator, and a control group had no crime news story within the broadcast. The content analysis found that the media disproportionately report violent crimes, while the audience study found that exposure to the race of the supposed perpetrator significantly affected attitudes both towards crime and race. This was especially true among white participants who had a more negative view of African Americans and supported more punitive crime policies if a black perpetrator was presented. The same result was not found among African American participants. Gilliam and Iyengar (2000: 572) say:

> The commercial realities of our time dictate that local news will continue to cultivate misperceptions and prejudice. Local television stations (in the US) reach huge audiences but face intense economic pressure. Crime dominates other news because its emphasis on vivid pictures and emotional personal accounts is believed to attract viewers. The news rarely presents non-racial attributes of criminal suspects. Information about race is conveyed automatically, due to the visual nature of the medium; other individuating characteristics are seemingly not newsworthy…the emergence of local news has made race an even more central component of American life.

Gilliam, Valentino, and Beckmann (2002) used experimental techniques in another study to show that exposure to the racial characteristics of a supposed crime suspect within a news story predicted attitudes towards punitive policies to address crime and (negative) stereotypic evaluations of, in particular, African Americans among white study participants. They also found an effect of 'neighbourhood'– that is, they were able to show that respondents who lived in a racially mixed environment reacted in a less hostile manner to the racial elements within a story than those who were in a predominantly white area. Hence:

> When exposed to racial stereotypes in the news, white respondents living in white homogeneous neighbourhoods endorsed more punitive policies to address crime, expressed more negative stereotypic evaluations of blacks, and felt more distant from blacks as a group. Whites from heterogeneous neighbourhoods were either unaffected or moved in the opposite direction, endorsing less punitive crime policies, less negative stereotypes, and feeling closer to blacks as a group as a result of exposure to the stereotypic coverage.

This study is of interest because it illustrates the point that the media are an element in a series of variables that affect attitudes and, possibly, behaviour.

THE EFFECT OF VIEWING THE NEWS

In the United Kingdom, research consistently finds a correlation between the amount of crime reported and fear of crime among the public. For example, one study found that, although reporting of crime by the press varies considerably, those papers that report most crime (especially violent crime) have readers with the highest levels of fear of crime (Williams and Dickinson, 1993). More generally, a number of studies have looked at the attitudes towards news and other factual television, with specific regard to depictions of violence. In the United Kingdom, studies have been conducted using quantitative questionnaire-based surveys of large samples as well as qualitative research, including group discussions and depth interviews, to amplify the numerical findings (Millwood Hargrave, 1993; Morrison, 1999; Schlesinger et al., 1992). The studies point to the effect that gender and age have on people's perceptions, with their own physical vulnerability making them more concerned about what they see in the news.

There has long been concern over the relation between levels of reported crime (especially media sensationalizing, or bias towards reporting violent crime) and levels of fear of crime among the general public (or, specific, vulnerable publics such as the elderly) (Gerbner, Gross, Morgan, and Signorielli, 1986; Sparks, 1992; Tumber, 1982). In 1993 Dennis, Lowry, Nio, and Leitner (2003) looked for statistically valid predictors for a substantial rise in public perceptions of crime as the most important problem facing the United States in 1994. The three-pronged study analysed survey results, the effects of three network television news predictor variables (the news item's length, emphasis and position in the broadcast) and two FBI predictor variables (the rate of violent crimes and the rate of other crimes). These variables were analysed to determine what accounted statistically for this dramatic increase in the perception of crime. The data showed that in 1994, the public perceived crime to have increased dramatically. The study demonstrated that this was affected by the way in which crime stories were reported (the television variables) significantly more than the actual crime rates.

The television variables, in particular the amount of time devoted to crime coverage, accounted for almost four times more variance in public perceptions of crime as the 'most important problem' than did actual crime rates. Further, local television news (in the United States) was found to be particularly effective in generating fear of crime, irrespective of actual crime statistics. The authors interpret this finding as supportive of Gerbner's 'cultivation hypothesis' which argues that the image of the world promoted by television gradually 'cultivates' public beliefs about the world, even against the evidence of daily experience.

An interesting study of differential anxiety responses to television coverage of national threat situations and terrorism was conducted in Israel (Slone, 2000). A total of 237 participants were divided into two groups. One was presented with the experimental condition which involved watching a television news item of terrorism and threats to national security. The second, or control, group watched news items which had no reference to national danger situations. The researchers found that women and those who were religious were more likely to express anxiety in the experimental group than in the control condition, though the researchers accept that they cannot determine how long-term these effects might be.

In an earlier study, Morrison (1992) had used both a questionnaire-based design and group discussions to investigate how the moral framing of war mediates reactions to visual images from that event. He explored attitudes towards images from the Gulf War (some of which had not been shown on British television as they were considered too graphic). He found that it was the apportioning of blame (to Saddam Hussein) that acted as the primary mediating factor in how explicit news items could be:

> Sensibilities are not free-floating but are anchored within a moral framework which makes acts more or less disturbing. At no point in any of the group discussions did viewers express a desire for the raw images of war to be kept off their screens. But the interesting finding is that throughout the group discussions viewers' sensibilities did appear to be buttressed against outright onslaught by their acceptance of the war as both just, and given the perceived intransigence of Saddam Hussein, inevitable...It was this framework of understanding and

judgement of the war that provided the adult viewer with an emotional shield against any harrowing scenes that they might have seen on television and also helped guard against general anxiety about the war.

Attitudes towards coverage of the war were assessed after the 2003 Iraq War, using a postal survey among panel respondents (Sancho and Glover, 2003). This was a comprehensive study, with a substantial sample of over 4,000 panellists, although the use of a panel always allows some criticism of habituation. The findings contrast with the (qualitative) findings of the Morrison study of the first Gulf War. In Morrison's study, participants had thought material acceptable because of the perceived moral status of the war. In the study by Sancho and Glover, there was less certainty among participants when it came to showing images of captured Allied prisoners of war and dead Allied soldiers. These respondents thought that the geographical closeness of the material made it more questionable, especially if the families of the soldiers might be watching. Nearly two-thirds (63 per cent) of the sample said the material should not be shown if the families would be upset.

Morrison used editing groups to great effect (Millwood Hargrave, 1993), pioneering an approach that split out components of an audio-visual image and allowed participants to reconstruct it, discussing their rationale as they did so. Television extracts, including news items, were seen intact by groups (who had been recruited based on age, gender and socio-economic group) and then the sound and visual images were edited to change the tone of the item, to make it more or less acceptable depending on the initial reaction to it. This methodology, with short discussions to consider each change agreed and made, allowed a clear understanding of the particular concerns that each group had. The researchers were able to demonstrate through this methodology that 'clichés about the primacy of the visual do not hold up to an audience response which very often centred on the words used in an individual report'. Different elements of the news impact in different ways, and the moral or emotional response can be heightened by the way in which the news is presented.

CHILDREN AND THE NEWS

In a survey in New Zealand of parents and children, 15 per cent of parents who expressed concern about television content mentioned the news (BSA, 2008). A survey of UK parents found that 32 per cent thought their child (aged 6–17 years old) was often upset by violence in the news and 22 per cent said the same for fictional television (Livingstone, Bovill, and Gaskell, 1999). Children's responses to news items and their potential to be affected by them means that the 'watershed'(at 9 p.m.) is applied for more graphic television news items. A number of studies have looked at the way in which children or young people respond to news items, often concentrating on their reactions towards violence in such images (Australian Broadcasting Authority, 1994; Millwood Hargrave, 2003; Morrison, 1999; Nightingale, 2000). All these studies have used group discussions or depth interviews as their data collection method.

They consistently show that the proximity to their own experience (or potential for experience) is what is most influential on the way in which a child responds to a news item. This is because they see such factual material as a potential for direct (personal) harm and require information for their safety, which might not be forthcoming. Buckingham used a two-part interview structure, re-interviewing children about particular programme types. He showed how moral understanding of factual news was not affected by viewing fictional material:

> While it was clear that watching fictional violence could enable viewers to become habituated to more fictional violence, there was no evidence that this translated to their perceptions of real-life violence, whether mediated by television or in their own experience.

A survey administered to 179 primary school children in the United States one month after the September 11 attack found that greater exposure to news reports was associated with higher levels of post-traumatic symptoms as measured on a Paediatric Emotional Distress Scale (Saylor, Cowart, Lipovsky, Jackson, and Finch, 2003). The authors noted that it may be that the children who were more likely to be upset sought out more news reports, rather than the news programmes themselves causing upset. Further, those who encountered the news on the Internet were more upset than those who saw it on television or in the newspapers, though the authors are uncertain why this occurred.

VULNERABLE GROUPS AND THE NEWS

The way in which news reporting can be considered to politicize society has been seen in the studies above, especially those which have looked at issues of race reporting. Other studies have looked more directly at links between news reporting and behaviour. De Lange and Neeleman (2004) considered the impact of the terrorist attacks of 11 September 2001 on suicidal behaviour in the Netherlands. They analysed time trends of suicide counts and deliberate self-harm (by gender, age, and date of death) over a four-year period (January 1997 to December 2001). While the researchers question the accuracy of the self-harm data, their findings showed that both suicide and deliberate self-harm increased in the Netherlands in the weeks following 11 September 2001, especially suicide (see also Phillips, 1986). However, the researchers concede it is not clear whether this trend was directly related to the psychological impact of the attacks or to other events during this time period. Further studies are required to replicate these findings and substantiate the notion that graphic news media coverage can affect viewers:

> Studies of other disasters suggest that reports of distant events can trigger stress reactions, especially among people who consider themselves to be similar to the victims, personalize the event, or see themselves as at risk.

Similarly Lightstone (2004) noted the role of health-directed media messages on increasing levels of anxiety in the United States, about bioterrorism in particular. In Australia, Pirkis, Francis, Blood, Burgess, Morley, Stewart et al. (2002) used a content analysis of newspaper, television and radio items on suicide to examine the way in which reporting occurred. They concluded that there was little information provided that directed the audience to help services, and around half of all the items examined were quite detailed in the amount of information they gave about the methods of harm used. They argue that both these elements suggest room for improvement in media reporting.

The possibility of direct effects caused by viewing material, in particular factual material on television, has been examined in other studies but they tend to be inconclusive. Veraldi and Veraldi argue that empirical research does not support the hypotheses that media content either causes its audience to behave violently or desensitizes them to violence. However, they suggest that media content can prompt violent behaviour among individuals with specific disorders, in this case, post-traumatic stress disorder, (PTSD) (Veraldi and Veraldi, 2000). Nevertheless, it is not easy to determine what sort of imagery can create these reactions – it would seem to range from violent to neutral imagery. The question they ask is, if violent behaviour may be prompted by media content among individuals with PTSD, where does the liability for producing such harm (defined as the consequences resulting from violent behaviour) lie? Coming from the United States, both the First Amendment and traditional concepts of liability, including identifying or preventing harm, argue against liability for media content that may trigger such violence. The researchers conclude that the focus for determining liability should remain on the stressors that cause PTSD in the first place, rather than on the role media content may play in triggering violent behaviour.

INFORMED CONSENT

The popularity of reality shows and television talk shows rests significantly on the fact that they deal with 'ordinary' people thrown into extraordinary situations of their own choosing. However, there is a question mark over how much participants in such programmes understand the potential outcome of the programmes they are taking part in. It is arguable that incomplete understanding can result in harm to the individual participant because of loss of reputation, for example. Or, in the case of children, because of embarrassment or distress at school or in later life if a programme is retransmitted.

When prompted, the majority of respondents (59 per cent) consider there is 'too much' intrusion by television into people's private lives (Ofcom, 2005c). Morrison and Svennevig (2002) had found that the viewing audience was quite robust about these issues, arguing that those who take part in such programmes have legitimate expectations of privacy but that these could be overtaken by the wider concept of 'public interest'. Both media professionals and participants in group discussions felt they had an instinctive understanding of the definition of the public interest, although neither could provide an exact definition. They were clear, however, that it is not the same as something that the public might find interesting, such as media stories about celebrities. The researchers themselves suggest that 'the public interest' refers to a concept which brings collective, social benefits:

> Where something might affect a single individual, it can be in the public interest if that effect involves some general principle that, in turn, has impact upon a wider population, such as the abuse of power or a serious crime.

Children, however, were thought to have an absolute right to privacy and intrusion into their lives was considered inadmissible, under almost all circumstances. Davies and Mosdell (2001) looked at the understanding of consent given for children in the United Kingdom taking part in non-fiction programmes. They found parents were often more eager to give their consent for their children to appear in programmes, than the children themselves were. The researchers were given access to the production of a children's game show as a case study, as well as interviewing families (not connected with the show) through depth interviews and via a questionnaire. This allowed them a clear view of the issues involved, and the inclusion of content production makes this study particularly interesting.

The Davies study complemented an earlier project by the Stirling Media Research Institute (2000) which examined the informed consent given by adults who took part in programmes. This found that adults did not always fully understand what they were consenting to, or that others gave their consent on their behalf (for example, in the workplace). To obviate any harm to the individual, the researchers suggested a 'plain text' consent form that should be completed by each individual appearing in a programme.

SUMMARY

- Significant research effort has been expended on this ubiquitous and accessible medium, and many studies of other media are based on those from television. Television is still an important medium, especially for young children. The research included here primarily concerns violence, sexualization and stereotypes, as these have attracted the most research attention. It also deals with the news and with reality-defining effects and argues that these are effects which could be damaging if not understood and addressed.

- Methodologically, the research evidence remains contested, especially that regarding the harm rather than the benefits of exposure, especially the experimental studies, and much of it derives from a specific cultural and regulatory environment (the United States). Thus the generalizability of research findings to everyday situations is not commonly demonstrated or discussed. There are also ethical reasons as to why research on harm cannot be conducted directly among children and it is these that constrain many of the studies.

- However, qualitative and social research techniques show it is valuable to talk to audience groups to understand their reasoning and reactions to content they view. Observing these issues, literature reviews in this field continue to debate the level of effect and the nature of the effect – is it just on short-term attitudes, does it last longer and is it converted into an effect on behaviour? Many but not all of the available literature reviews would argue that all those questions have a 'yes' answer.

- Recent research points to consistent, though not necessarily large, findings that support a case for media harms; these especially concern the short-term effects of violence, and a series of effects on attitudes. Thus it appears that, under certain circumstances, television can negatively influence attitudes in some areas, including those which may affect society (through the creation of prejudice) and those which may affect the individual (by making them unduly fearful, for example). It also seems that television plays a part in contributing to stereotypes, fear of crime and other reality-defining effects, although it remains unclear what other social influences also play a role, or how important television is by comparison with these other factors.

■ The primary subjects of research have been children and young people, as they are thought to be most vulnerable to negative influences which may, in turn, affect long-term attitudes or behaviour. Much of the evidence concerns exposure to programming that is not designed, or appropriate, for children or young people. In the United Kingdom in particular, such material is highly regulated, although still viewed.

■ There is also a growing body of evidence which suggests that there are also vulnerable groups of adults who may be negatively affected by certain types of media content; for example, people with particular personality disorders. The review showed clear audience differences based on gender (in particular, boys seem to be more influenced by violent content) and age; but also family settings, a predisposition for a particular programme genre, the way in which the content is used and other such variables all appear to play a part in the way content is viewed and assimilated.

■ The review showed the importance of contextual factors in guiding the audience in its task of making sense of or justifying a portrayed act. These include the context within which the act is set and the importance of identification and empathy with the protagonists. In some of the studies, identification may be based on fear and how realistic or possible the situation feels to the viewer. Identification and empathy with the protagonists is important to the way content is received, this helping to justify an act.

■ Further, there is evidence from studies in the United Kingdom that the audience is often 'sophisticated' or media literate in the ways that it views content; hence messages placed in programmes can lead to cynicism about the issue being discussed, as in storylines about the use of illegal drugs. Often the audience has a clear understanding of conventions within established media (such as free-to-air television) and uses variables such as scheduling to anticipate material they might view. This fits with the research trend, especially in relation to violent content, towards using broader rather than restrictive definitions that reflect the complex, context-dependent ways in which audiences react to content.

■ Note that the newer forms of television delivery are less well-researched although the evidence suggests that their conventions are understood. Note too that if the audience can make sense of, or justify, the act then it is more acceptable and less likely to be offensive; however, it may still be harmful, especially to children.

■ Much of the research has been unequivocal in demonstrating evidence of offence (such as with regard to offensive language, violence or the depiction of sexual activity). Again contextual and demographic variables are seen particularly to affect the levels of offence felt .Transmission time remains an important variable within audience attitudes towards current television content, with established conventions designed to reduce the potential for offence.

■ The view that television is a positive medium, offering a window on the world, is not questioned. However, the evidence for subtle and long-term reality-defining effects of television is suggestive, and there is a distinct lack of multi-factor studies that could locate television in a broader context. In other words, television seems to play a part, contributing to stereotypes, fear of crime and other reality-defining effects, but it remains unclear what other social influences also play a role, or how important television is by comparison with these other factors. Nonetheless, this points to significant responsibilities placed upon television, especially for the free-to-air channels.

■ The evidence also suggests that the viewing of fictional content does not diminish the distress that may be caused by violence in real-life. Further, significant concern – and research effort – has focused on examining the effects on children and young people, as they are thought to be most vulnerable and, in early years, the audience group least able to distinguish what is real and what is fictional. Even young people who view quite violent (and possibly not age-appropriate) television fiction were not less affected by real-life violence, even if it was not happening to them (although the level to which they could empathize with the real-life violence was a mediating factor).

■ No research was found that looked at the programming content on the niche channels which may be considered as more 'extreme' than programmes on generalist channels (for example, programmes which encourage imitative and potentially dangerous behaviour, these being often aimed at young adult men). It may be that such material could have negative effects on other groups, should they be in the audience. As the range of content available on multi-channel television becomes more diverse, research is needed to track the possible consequences of these changes.

Notes

1. Where appropriate, ages of research subjects have been given. However, it should be assumed that the term 'children' generally refers to primary school-age children and 'young people' to secondary school age children, though the latter sometimes includes young adults (i.e. students).

2. http://www.theage.com.au/news/Opinion/TV-violence-the-good-and-bad-for-our-children/2005/04/10/1113071849363.html

3. Subsequently the Broadcasting Standards Commission.

4. The particular susceptibilities of women, or those who are older, to a dislike of certain types of content is also noted elsewhere: reviewing a decade of community attitudes to broadcasting in New Zealand, Dickinson et al. note the consistency with which women and older viewers express concern regarding broadcast content, compared with men and younger viewers (Dickinson, Hill, and Zwaga, 2000).

5. See Abeles and Withey (1980), Anderson et al. (2003), Cantor (2000), Firmstone (2002), Murray (1994), Savage (2004), Simmons, Stalsworth, and Wentzel (1999), Villani (2001), von Feilitzen and Carlsson (2004), or reviews of the reviews (such as . Browne and Hamilton-Giachritsis, 2005). For a comprehensive review of the studies and research on media effects, in particular, media violence, see http://libertus.net/censor/studies.html.

6. Desensitization is the notion that heavy viewing of violent television over time conditions viewers to accept violence as normal, dulling their sensitivity to aggressive behaviour in everyday life.

7. Disinhibition suggests that television violence will result, in certain circumstances, in increased interpersonal aggression because it weakens inhibitions against such behaviour.

8. Hypermasculinity is defined as 'exaggerated, narrowly defined masculine qualities'.

9. We note that the quality of the NTVS sample is robust and much used. It draws on a significant sample of programmes and, importantly, looks beyond broadcast television to niche cable services, such as those aimed at children.

10. We are not, here, referring to the domestic context of viewing or using media, though this is equally important. Such issues we address under the heading of 'access conditions'.

11. They adjusted which character was the perpetrator, which was the victim, the motivation for the violence and the consequences of the violence.

12. *Homophily* defined as the degree to which people are alike; *identification* is the sharing of a character's perspective by the viewer; *parasocial interaction* is the level of 'empathy' felt for a character.

13. Relational aggression has been defined as behaviours that harm others through damage (or threat of damage) to relationships or feelings of acceptance, friendship, or group inclusion (Crick, 1996).

14. The V chip is a computer chip installed in a television to allow the user to control the display of certain programmes, especially of sexual or violent content – mandatory in new television sets in the United States.

15. see also Ofcom Broadcast Bulletins: http://www.ofcom.org.uk/tv/obb/

16. Racist and religious crimes, including the incitement to racial hatred, are prosecutable offences. For a description of this policy, see the Crown Prosecution Service: Racist and Religious Crime, 2003. http://www.cps.gov.uk/publications/docs/rrpbcrleaf.pdf

17. http://www.disabilityworld.org/06-08_03/arts/currentresearch.shtml

18. http://www.ofcom.org.uk/research/tv/reports/newnews/newnews.pdf

19. See the Independent Television Commission archive held at www.ofcom.org.uk.

20. The researchers were loathe to use the terms 'tabloid' and 'broadsheet' but gave their reasons for doing so and offered examples. Tabloid includes stories about crime, tragedy, royalty, showbiz, and the weather. Broadsheet includes politics, economics, business, EU issues etc. (see p. 4 of their report).

4

FILM, VIDEO AND DVD

In what follows, we overview evidence specific to film, video and DVD. Much of this research takes a similar approach to television, and the findings – as we shall show – resemble those found for other screen media. Our purpose in this chapter, as before, is to identify the kind of evidence for harm and offence that exists, together with criticisms of the research conducted where appropriate. The content that research has focused on has, however, been rather different, given the broader range of content available (according to different categories of restriction) on film/video/DVD than has been traditionally available on broadcast television.

Thus, in relation to harm and offence, much of the research has addressed pornography and sexualized violence.[1] Unlike for television, there has also been considerable academic discussion of the philosophical, legal and regulatory implications of the empirical research on pornography especially, this primarily linked to freedom of expression and human rights, though there are also long-standing feminist debates over the political and ethical status of pornography.

In relation to empirical research, our focus here, the research has encompassed adult as well as child audiences, both because concerns about harm have been raised in relation to all age groups and partly because young adults (typically college students) are often used in research as a proxy for teenagers, for reasons of research ethics.

REALITY-DEFINING EFFECTS
A main focus of research has been the role of film in cultivating gender and, to a lesser degree, racial stereotypes. Much of this work is content-based (rather than audience-based). For example, 21 movies released in the United States between 2000 and 2004 were analysed to explore messages that girls are receiving about the role and function of organizations and women's roles within them. The study found that many films present messages that reinforce traditional stereotypes, although others may challenge girls to think critically about gender roles (Hylmo, 2005).

Turning to audience-based research, across a range of media, including film/video/DVD, a major teen survey in the United States suggests that the mass media serve as a kind of 'super peer' for girls who enter puberty sooner than their age-mates; hence, earlier maturing girls report more interest than later maturing girls in seeing sexual content in the media, they are more likely to be listening to music and reading magazines with sexual content, more likely to see R-rated movies; and they are more likely to interpret the messages they see in the media as approving of teens having sexual intercourse, for they feel that the media portray sexual behaviour as normative and risk free (Brown, Halpern and L'Engle, 2005). Pardun, L'Engle and Brown (2005) found that the associations between 'Sexual Media Diet' and sexual attitudes are strongest for exposure to movies (and music; see the chapter on music) with sexual content.

EMOTIONAL RESPONSES

Fright responses among children to film, television and the news are, according to a number of researchers, 'quite common' (Cantor, 2002). Although some argue that 'there is growing evidence that media violence also engenders intense fear in children which often lasts days, months, and even years' (Cantor, 2000), it turns out that what children find scary or upsetting or fear-inducing can be difficult to predict as emotional reactions vary, depending on responses to specific genres (with fear reactions found not only for horror films but also soap operas and the news), on children's developing media literacy and on their parents' responses (Buckingham, 1996).

There are age differences in what children find frightening, dependent in part on a growing understanding of the distinction between fantasy and reality (see also Davies, 1997; Millwood Hargrave, 2003). Cantor (2002) also reviews evidence that adults remember intense fear responses to television and film many years later; in one of her studies, students recalled nightmares, sleep disturbance, avoidance of certain places (e.g. fear of swimming after *Jaws*), and so forth.

On the other hand, one strand of research examines the fascination of teens, especially teenage girls, with horror and slasher movies. This focuses on the merits of a safe and, often, playful exploration of otherwise taboo or frightening experiences (Hill, 1997; Jerslev, 2001), arguing that such an opportunity is important for teens (see also Buckingham, 1996).

PORNOGRAPHY

> Visual or aural material presenting erotic behaviour that is intended to be sexually stimulating, and is lacking in artistic or other forms of merit. It is often considered to be demeaning to both sexuality and to the body. (Philips, 2005)

Arguments that pornography is harmful come from diverse perspectives, including religious/moral objections that it corrupts societal values, feminist objections that it is in itself a form of sexual violence because it objectifies women and/or that it encourages male violence against women, and child welfare concerns that it harms children's sexual and emotional development.[2] While our focus is on the empirical evidence for harm, we draw on the range of kinds of harm identified within these philosophical, legal and political arguments. We also note that, as in several areas encompassed by the present review, major ethical considerations have restricted the kinds of research that has been conducted.

Exposure to pornography appears fairly widespread among teens and adults:

- An Australian survey reported that 73 per cent of 16–17 year old boys (and 11 per cent of girls) report having seen at least one X-rated film (i.e. containing real depictions of actual sexual intercourse),[3] with a small minority watching regularly (Flood and Hamilton, 2003a, 2003b). Peer pressure is suggested by the additional finding that 84 per cent believe that watching such videos is 'widespread' among boys.

- A Swedish survey of teens (average age, 18 years old) found that 98 per cent of men and 72 per cent of women had 'ever consumed pornography', and that those exposed to more pornography were more likely to be aroused by or try to perform acts seen in a pornography film (Häggström-Nordin, Hanson, and Tydén, 2005).

What effect does such exposure have? Itzin (2002) distinguishes evidence regarding pornography and harm in terms of categories of those harmed – the potential victims, including those involved in production, male consumers, society in general, and children in particular. We do not examine here her claim that pornography harms those women and children involved in its production, though we note that she cites evidence of the growing global trade and traffic in women and children. It is also worth noting that the UK legal framework makes the possession of child abuse images illegal precisely because possession is deemed to increase the demand for, and hence the production of, content which, generally, requires the commission of a crime; it could be suggested that the same argument applies to the possession (or viewing) of pornography portraying adults insofar as this creates a demand for content which may both portray abuse or violence to women and which may stimulate illegal traffic in or degrading treatment of the women portrayed.

A report by the ACMA (2007) points to comments made by policy-makers regarding the use of pornography and its link to violence in Aboriginal communities – both against women and children. However, as the report points out, and as the authors of this review found, it is not possible to find the research evidence to back these claims; the ACMA report suggests this is because of 'the political sensitivity of the issue' (p 262).

In what follows, we focus on the viewers of pornographic film (whether purposely or inadvertently) rather than its production.

MEN VIEWING PORNOGRAPHY
Does viewing pornography harm men through its effects on their attitudes, beliefs and behaviours? Itzin cites evidence from experimental research, clinical work with sex offenders, and accounts from victims of sexual abuse that suggests that pornography (particularly, sexual violence – cf. next section, on violence) plays a role in overcoming internal inhibitions against sexual abuse and/or providing 'triggers' to abuse for those already vulnerable to becoming offenders (in relation to the Internet, see Middleton, Elliot, Mandeville-Norden, and Beech, 2006; and for television see also Quayle and Taylor, 2001; Quayle and Taylor, 2002, 2003).

Another approach relates the availability of pornography with crime statistics. A literature review conducted for Ofcom (Helsper, 2005) found no relationship between the availability of pornography and an increase in sex crimes in other countries; indeed, when pornography was made more available, the incidence of sex crimes dropped in Denmark, while in Japan, where pornography is widely available, sex crimes are low. Further, research with adults indicates no relationship between the commission of sex crimes and use of pornography at an early age; again, there is evidence for the opposite effect. Such findings are often contested on methodological grounds (over time, procedures for collecting criminal statistics change, the moral climate influences readiness to report sexual crimes, etc.).

HARM TO SOCIETY IN GENERAL

Does pornography harm society by normalizing and mainstreaming misogyny through the pervasiveness of pornographic imagery (which may also be violent, racist, dehumanizing, paedophilic, etc.)? Itzin argues that we are witnessing a trend for what was once hard-core to become soft-core, there being – she suggests – a continuum in cultural representation between the shaved and beribboned 'little girl' look of top shelf magazines and child pornography, and between the sadism of *American Psycho* and hard-core videos.

The simplest approach here is to ask people. In an exploratory study of Canadian teens aged 14–19 years old, focus groups were asked to talk about dating (girl/boyfriend) relationships. The researchers found that violence was a common theme in their discussions of relationships, including conceptions of 'consensual violence' in which teens attribute part of the responsibility to victims (Lavoie, Robitaille, and Herbert, 2000). The teens themselves identified a range of sources for their conceptions of sexual relationships, including peer influence and pornography. In Swedish surveys of young people visiting family planning clinics, researchers found that one-third of young women (Rogala and Tydén, 2003) and half of young men (Tydén and Rogala, 2004) believed that pornography had influenced their sexual conduct. Hald and Malamuth (2007) conclude from their study of the perceptions of Danish adults (aged 18–30) that, on balance, pornography is considered generally beneficial to them.

More subtle and long-term effects of pornography on society are harder to track. We note the research cited above on the widespread sexualization of girls across the media, though this is not strictly pornographic. However, we also note that, among those for whom freedom of speech is the paramount principle at stake here, there is a well-developed liberal or even radical defence of pornography, in terms of its aesthetic merits, its political implications or, more simply, the pleasure of its viewers. Yet Allen (2001: 527) may speak for many in simultaneously recognizing but qualifying this position, acknowledging the material realities of the production and consumption of pornography:

> Insofar as pornography is empowering, it is a possible site for resistance, but insofar as the genre is structured to a large extent by relations of masculine dominance and feminine subordination, it is also a possible site of the application and articulation of oppression.

HARM TO CHILDREN

There is considerable interest in the possibility that pornography may harm those accidentally exposed to it, especially children. This is believed by clinicians to upset, disturb and damage children (Cragg, 2000) although, as Helsper (2005) notes, little research has directly tested this claim for harm, for ethical reasons (Thornburgh and Lin, 2002).

Indeed, due to ethical restrictions, there is a severe lack of research regarding the direct effects of exposure of children to pornography (Heins, 2001; Malamuth and Impett, 2000). Ofcom's recent review of the effects on minors of R18 material found only thirteen studies (out of 116 articles reviewed) that contained empirical information on minors, much of that retrospective (e.g. interviewing sex offenders about their media history) or conducted on older teenagers (or, indeed, university students) (Helsper, 2005). There is some, rather equivocal, evidence that indicates that sexual material influences the moral development of young people under the age of 18 years, so that through exposure to pornography young people may become more cynical about marriage, may alter their assessment of sex-related risks, and become sexually active at a younger age (Brown, 2005; Zillman, 2000), although the evidence is mixed, not least because many factors other than the media influence cultural attitudes and values. However, 'there is no conclusive empirical evidence for a causal relationship between exposure to R18 material and impairment of the mental, physical or moral development of minors' (Helsper, 2005).

Helsper's review of the academic literature updates an earlier report conducted for the BBFC (Cragg, 2000; see also Edwards, 2001) regarding experts' views of the potential harm which R18 videos pose to child audiences. Based on a series of interviews with child psychiatrists, clinical psychologists, family therapists, social workers and teachers, Cragg (2000) reports that most experts thought viewing pornography is harmful to children, though opinions varied as to the degree of harm, and some considered that little if any harm is likely. All agreed that the harm is greatest to already-vulnerable children. 'Harm' was considered to mean immediate shock and trauma, sexualization and possible re-enactment, and broader effects on perceptions of sexuality and relationships. There was little consensus on how many children may view pornography at home 'by accident', though again those children already at risk in other ways (including from sexual abuse) were considered to be most at risk of such exposure.

Interestingly, the report explored reasons why little evidence exists of such harm, although many believe pornography to be harmful: respondents considered that families (children and parents) would be unlikely to disclose the presence of pornography in the home while professionals (psychiatrists, social workers) would be attending to more pressing forms of neglect or abuse. Levine (2002), argues that more harmful is the way our society 'protects' children from positive images of sex and sexuality (see also Buckingham and Bragg, 2004).[4]

VIOLENCE, INCLUDING SEXUAL VIOLENCE

There is a literature examining the effects of film violence on viewers. The Video Standards Council asked Cumberbatch (2004) to review the evidence for harm resulting from violent videos. He observed that, although public concern persistently focuses on video violence, and although the majority of reviews of the empirical literature conclude that exposure to video violence has harmful effects, nonetheless the evidence is unconvincing (see also Freedman, 2002). The determination to find 'effects', he suggests, has resulted in review after review referring to the same body of evidence and drawing similar conclusions in response to the largely-American public policy agenda. Other researchers, especially American psychologists, would disagree strongly with Cumberbatch (cf. the chapter on media effects).

Nonetheless there is a body of research that considers the effects of violent entertainment. For example, an American survey of 9–10 year olds found that those exposed to more film violence had more proviolent attitudes (Funk, Baldacci, Pasold, and Baumgardner, 2004).[5] Most research on violence in film, however, is concerned with sexual violence – including pornographic violence and violence against women. This could equally well be reviewed under 'Pornography'. We prefer to discuss it here because the findings are very different. Emmers-Sommer, Pauley, Hanzal, and Triplett (2006) considered the film preferences of both men and women to different genres within film (love stories, suspense and sex and violence). They examined how the preferences impacted on their subjects' acceptance of the 'rape myth' (i.e. women are willing victims of rape).[6] They found that women preferred love stories and men preferred the film with sex and violence. The material that showed sexual violence was based on a true story and the researchers say they had expected this to impact on their findings, in contrast to sexual violence that was fictional. What they also found was that those who are more accepting of the rape myth were also more likely to prefer films with sex and violence, although women's attitudes were affected – they were less likely to accept the rape myth – when they knew the portrayal was based on a true story.

From this the researchers conclude that such filmic preferences should be considered when discussing the acceptance of violence such as the rape myth. While the research is of particular interest because it considers women as well as men, it should be noted that subjects were only exposed to a single exposure of the material and predictions about repeated exposure need to be treated with caution. As suggested, most research on violence, especially sexual violence, focuses on male attitudes to women. For example, Linz, Donnerstein and Penrod (1988) showed young men five slasher films over a two-week period, finding that after each film the men considered the film less violent or degrading to women. This, they argued, showed support for the 'desensitization' thesis.

Helsper (2005) reviews research that suggests both positive and negative effects of pornography. Positive effects include catharsis (lowering drive for sex crimes), while negative effects include addiction to pornography, deviant or criminal sexual behaviour, aggression and negative attitudes towards women. Most reviews conclude that it is explicitly violent sexual pornography (rather than consensual images of sex) that harms adults who view, increasing aggression and negative attitudes towards women, including desensitization to sexual violence towards women (Helsper, 2005; Villani, 2001). Some, therefore, conclude that it is violence rather than sexual content that is harmful. Note, last, that for the most part, these reviews are concerned with experimental findings, and so the question of generalizing to everyday circumstances remains unresolved.

Not all experiments on film use brief segments and short exposures. In one experiment, respondents were exposed to gratuitously violent or non-violent intact feature films on four consecutive days; and the following day they participated in ostensibly unrelated research on emotion recognition. As they performed a test, they were neutrally or abusively treated by a research assistant and were then put in a position to harm this assistant. Findings showed that 'prolonged exposure to gratuitously violent films is capable (a) of escalating hostile behaviour in provoked men and women, and (b) perhaps more importantly, of instigating such behaviour in unprovoked men and women' (Zillman and Weaver, 1999). As they go on to argue, while many experiments focus on short-lived effects (and so draw on cognitive theories that posit processes such as cognitive cueing and priming), in this study they draw conclusions about longer-term effects, arguing that non-immediate hostile behaviour is facilitated 'by repeated activation of aggressive constructs via prolonged exposure to media violence' (p. 148).

Zillman and Weaver's study illustrates the methodological challenges faced by experimental research. 93 undergraduate participants (53 males and 40 females) were recruited. An evaluation of various personality traits (i.e. extraversion, neuroticism, psychoticism, empathy) had been undertaken prior to this. Men and women were randomly assigned to one of two film conditions (i.e. innocuous vs. violent) and one of two treatment conditions (i.e. unprovoked vs. provoked). Participants were exposed to the film condition on four consecutive nights. On each occasion they were asked to rate the viability of the film in the video market. Following this participants were asked to participate in a supposedly unrelated study surrounding person perception. Performance feedback by an experimenter provided either the provoked or unprovoked treatment condition. Participants were then asked to rate the experimenter's performance. They were told that their evaluation would help determine whether the experimenter received study aid, this being the indicator of their hostility.

The strengths of this study are that it included:

- A sample of undergraduates that matches the youth focus of policy concerns.

- Careful controls for prior personality characteristics (to eliminate confounding factors).

- Random assignment to experimental and control conditions which eliminates problems of self-selecting samples typical of correlational/survey studies.

- Viewing of the whole film, in the evening, with some attempt to simulate normal viewing conditions.

- Provision of plausible pretexts given (viability for video market; should experimenter receive financial aid?).

On the other hand, the study also has some familiar weaknesses:

- A sample of undergraduates is not representative of the population (too educated/privileged).

- Film choices were made for the participants, as were the viewing conditions (not realistic).

■ Harsher judgements of the experimenter's performance is not necessarily indicative of hostility (could be a judgement of unprofessional approach, for example) and it is misleading subsequently to describe this as unprovoked hostile behaviour (many would image physical aggression from such a description).

Zillman's (2000) review of the literature also finds highly equivocal evidence for the effects of even violent pornography, but this leads him to conclude that attention should shift from effects on sexual/violent behaviour to the suggestion that 'sexual callousness' is increased. By this he means that an extended definition of pornography is needed that considers the way in which sexual access is sought and gained in media content. Earlier findings had shown an effect of sexual callousness (for example, those exposed to explicit sexual content experimentally were more likely to agree that 'a woman doesn't mean "no" unless she slaps you' (Zillmann and Bryant, 1982); yet when reviews collate findings across studies, failures to replicate are always in evidence. Even so, Malamuth, Addison and Koss (2000) conclude that there are 'reliable associations between pornography use and sexually aggressive behaviours, particularly for violent pornography and/or for frequent use of other types of pornography', though these are stronger for already-aggressive men. Vega and Malamuth (2007) found in their study of just over 100 male students that high consumption of printed pornographic literature (NB this study did not look at film) predicted sexual aggression among those with a predilection for such aggression. That is those who scored relatively highly on sexual aggression across other measures consumed significantly more pornography than others. Vega and Malamuth point to the limitations of their study but find it replicates other, larger-scale surveys.

Vulnerable groups

Psychologists recognize that individuals vary in many and subtle ways, these differences potentially mediating responses to media content, and so rendering some people more or less 'vulnerable' to harmful effects. Indeed, Browne and Pennell (2000) identify a commonsense midpoint between the extremes in the strongly polarized debate over the effects of film/video/DVD, in which 'the evidence of a link between violent media entertainment and violence may vary in strength depending on the vulnerability of the audience' (p. 152).

For many researchers, these individual differences help to account for the otherwise problematic variability in findings of media – here, film – effects. For example, Seto, Maric and Barbaree (2001) conclude:

From the existing evidence, we argue that individuals who are already predisposed to sexually offend are the most likely to show an effect of pornography exposure and are the most likely to show the strongest effects. Men who are not predisposed are unlikely to show an effect; if there actually is an effect, it is likely to be transient because these men would not normally seek violent pornography.

Focusing on a range of audience subgroups, a number of studies examine the nature and role of these individual or group differences within the population.

■ *Aggressive personality*. Kiewitz and Weaver (2001) showed people either a violent or non-violent movie, and asked them to report their perceptions of violent interpersonal incidents as described in four written scenarios. Findings revealed that respondents' prior aggressive dispositions and their gender mediated the impact of media violence on subsequent perceptions of violent, interpersonal conflicts. So, more aggressive individuals, especially men, 'displayed more callous and hostile tendencies in their perceptions of interpersonal conflicts' than did less aggressive individuals. However, the findings did not show that exposure to the violent movie had a negative impact on viewers, thus supporting the position that more aggressive people prefer more violent content (rather than vice versa). Also in support of this position, Bogaert (2001) surveyed 160 male undergraduates in the United States and found that those lower in intelligence and higher in aggressive or antisocial tendencies were more likely to prefer violent sexual material.

■ *Children with behaviour disorders*. One study examined the reaction of 8–12 year old children with a diagnosed disruptive behaviour disorder (DBD) to violent movie scenes, finding that the children process the antisocial messages in violent movies differently from children without a psychiatric disorder, so that 'an unabated diet of antisocial media could have harmful effects on children with a psychiatric illness' (Grimes, Vernberg, and Cathers, 1997).

■ *Young offenders*. Another examined the special case of young people who commit violent acts, finding that although their viewing habits are no different from the rest of the population, they have greater preferences for violent content and are more likely to identify with violent role models in films. The authors concluded cautiously that 'young offenders may like violent videos because of their aggressive background and behavioural tendencies. Whether such tastes reinforce violent behaviour and increase the frequency of aggressive acts and antisocial behaviour is open to question' (Hagell and Newburn, 1994; see also Pennell and Browne, 1999). However, Browne and Pennell's (1999) qualitative survey of young offenders' media use in the United Kingdom, assessing the reactions to violent videos by a group of 122 males aged 15–21 years old, obtained different findings. The sample included violent offenders, non-violent offenders and a control group of non-offending students. They found no differences in favourite film, 70 per cent of which were Certificate 18, even among the 15–17 year olds and even among those in secure accommodation. They suggested that 'both a history of family violence and offending behaviour are necessary preconditions for developing a significant preference for violent film action and role models'. They accepted that, while there was some evidence that young people imitate films, 'there is no firm evidence of the extent of such copycat behaviour'. Browne and Pennell also raised questions about the way in which material can be viewed in different situations, noting that the in-home experience seemed to be different for violent offenders, who sometimes replayed scenes of violence time and time again. Browne and Pennell (2000) argue further that the well-established link between poor social background and delinquent behaviour may be mediated by violent media, because this reinforces distorted cognitions and aggressive affect.

■ *Sexual offenders*. Consistent with Itzin's (2002) argument that pornography is an 'instrumental cause' in the aetiology of sexual offending, a study of 118 sexual aggressors against women found the following: 'a sexually inappropriate family environment, use of pornography during childhood and adolescence, and deviant sexual fantasies during childhood and adolescence are related to the development of deviant sexual preferences' (Beauregard, Lussier, and Prolux, 2004).

There is a small research literature that has looked at the influences of eating and drinking in film, especially on young adults. They suggest that such depictions may develop beliefs about what is 'normal' or appropriate behaviour (Bell, Berger, Cassady, and Townsend, 2005; Sargent et al., 2006). Cottone and Byrd-Bredbenner (2007) undertook a study which examined the effect of the film, *Super Size Me*, on the attitudes of young adults to fast food and other measures such as ideas of healthy weight. 80 young adults watched the film while a control group of 135 watched an unrelated film. Pre- and post-test measures were taken of both samples. The research found that the group that had watched *Super Size Me* was far more likely to have raised levels of awareness about the nutritional issues raised, than the control group.

There is a rather larger body of research which examines the effects of smoking depicted in films on young adults. Worth, Dal Cin, and Sargent (2006) note from a content analysis of characters who smoke, both adult and adolescent, that depictions are in decline, although the incidence of smoking is still higher than among the general population (see also Gale et al., 2006; Sargent et al., 2007). However, Sargent et al. (2005) suggest that exposure to smoking in films is a risk factor in encouraging smoking among young adults in the United States. Further, other research they conducted (2007) shows that such depictions reinforce smoking and help establish it as a habit. McCool et al. (2005) make a similar argument based on their research in New Zealand. Stern argues through an analysis of high-grossing American films aimed at the teenage market that substance abuse (smoking, drinking and drug use) is shown as common and 'mostly' risk free. Healton et al. (2006) use content analysis to argue that film trailers depicting smoking may reinforce normative perceptions. On the other hand Wills and colleagues (2007) argue that such effects are mediated through the influence of peers and other social factors. Smoking is not likely to be the cause of young adults starting to smoke.

A few studies were noted that considered the effectiveness of anti-smoking advertising placed before films that depict smoking. Edwards et al. (2007) in Australia suggest that placing such advertising before a film depicting smoking may be an effective antidote to seeing smoking as an acceptable practice. However the researchers caution that the type of advertising used must be carefully balanced as it could act as a call to smoke. This is rather a difficult balance for the industry (and the policy-maker) to strike.

OFFENCE

What do people find offensive in film, video and DVD? A national survey conducted in 2000 when revising the BBFC Guidelines[7] found that the most important classification issues for the public were (rating it very important):

■ Drugs and drug taking – 75 per cent.

■ Violence – 65 per cent.

- Sexual activity – 56 per cent.

- Swearing and offensive language – 49 per cent.

- Racial references – 46 per cent.

- Religious references – 34 per cent.

Focusing on sexual violence in film, Cumberbatch (2002) examined public attitudes towards graphic material on video in an in-depth qualitative and survey-based project commissioned by the BBFC. A small survey of video rental customers found that many believed video content was over-regulated, especially in relation to sexual content, though just over a half thought the amount of regulation 'about right'. Public attitudes towards sexual violence in videos was the least liberal, suggesting this area of content remains controversial and unacceptable to many. Men, and younger people, held more liberal attitudes towards content regulation. In the qualitative viewing panel, the research found 'surprising tolerance of sexual violence in film…so long as it was justified in the storyline and it was "in context"'. When contextual justification was lacking, respondents were more likely to consider cuts justified, especially among women.

An analysis of complaints to the ITC about broadcast content in relation to taste and decency compared responses to drama versus film shown on television suggested that public concern over the former was greater, with attitudes to films being more tolerant (Hanley, 1998a). Exploration of the reasons for this revealed that viewers are more likely to be offended by drama than film on television, because:

- Viewers believe films have already been regulated for cinema and video release.

- Watching films is 'a conscious and informed decision'.

- Films are accompanied by information, including information about content, and so there is less excuse for 'being surprised'.

- Films are one-offs, while it is more appropriate to complain about ongoing drama.

- Viewers feel they have more of a right to complain about a drama, made with 'their' money than about a film made originally for those who choose to see it in the cinema.

The study details the many and subtle considerations that guide viewers' expectations regarding content (perceived realism, understanding of the genre, importance of context, balancing offence against artistic merit, narrative honesty or the cultural importance of seeing challenging material; viewing conditions including whether children are likely to be present); these in turn guide their propensity to complain. The conclusions are worth quoting (p. 6):

> There is a need for a clear system of ratings and/or warnings to provide information, particularly for parents, about the content of programmes – especially drama, which is seen as

less predictable. Respondents show considerable respect for film makers' artistic integrity and feel that broadcasters and regulators should not tamper with their product through editing. They consider that, with appropriate scheduling and pre-transmission information, films should not need to be cut. This view was held especially by viewers in multichannel households.

Verhulst's (2002) survey for the BSC confirms that the public's main concern is protection for children, with only a minority concerned about content regulation to protect values and morals in society more generally. The exception, as so often, is sexual violence, where regulation is still expected. In general, it seems that people are often concerned about film / video / DVD content, at times finding it offensive, but overall they are both aware of and satisfied with existing systems of regulation and also they are tolerant of the rights of others to choose what films to watch. This situation of both concern and tolerance becomes clearer when we turn to the research on audience interpretation of film.

AUDIENCE INTERPRETATION

Why do people watch films, videos or DVDs containing potentially harmful or offensive content? There is a growing body of research on film audiences, much of it combining film studies with the cultural / interpretative approach of television audience reception studies (Livingstone, 1998). This examines the place of film in people's lives (e.g. Stacey's, 1994 account of women's long-standing fandom of glamorous stars), the routines of film going (e.g. Taylor, 1988), the use of film and video to sustain subcultures (e.g. Gillespie, 1995), audience fandom (e.g. Jenkins, 1992) and readings of particular genres (e.g. Wright, 1975) or controversial films (Barker and Petley, 2001) – in addition to the work already noted on teens' fascination with horror films.

Unlike typical research designs in effects studies, this approach draws on qualitative social research methods, focusing on the interpretative interaction between text and audience, showing how the text anticipates the audience (making assumptions about, leaving space for) and the audience expects what the text will be (based on knowledge of genres, on extra-textual commentary or peer discussion). Such qualitative research reveals that as 'lay critics', people can have thoughtful responses to media content (Stacey, 1994; Staiger, 2005). This has clear links to the public's understanding also of the regulatory framework and the difficult judgements involved in balancing, for example, freedom of expression with protection from harm and offence.

Particular interest attaches to non-mainstream or sub-cultural interpretations by audience subgroups, for example, gay readings of hyper-heterosexual characters or feminist readings of Hollywood narratives; curiously perhaps, the conclusions drawn tend to offer a defence of overtly stereotyped content precisely because audiences have been found to 'read against the grain'. For example, in his in-depth qualitative analysis of audiences' responses to Cronenberg's *Crash*, described by *The Daily Mail* as 'depraved' and 'sick', Barker (2004, 2001) found that such a 'moral panic' led respondents to expect a more violent film than they felt it to be and, moreover, some had gone to see the film 'to see what all the fuss was about'. In listening carefully to the justifications that viewers offer for describing the film as either violent or not violent, Barker uncovers a range of frameworks that viewers use to interpret films, implicitly drawing on a range of definitions of 'violence' that, he argues, are unhelpfully confused in 'media effects' research.

Thus his various respondents pointed to such matters as whether the film had artistic merit (rendering it, implicitly, not violent), how gory the violence was, whether the violence was associated with sexuality or pornography, whether they were personally shocked (i.e. violence shocks), whether the aggression appeared senseless (gratuitous aggression is violent), or justified by an interesting storyline, whether it demeans people's dignity (both on and in front of the screen; demeaning being violent), and so forth.

In response to the BBFC's refusal to permit the video release of Peckinpah's *Straw Dogs* until 2002 (on DVD) because of an extended rape scene, and noting that Cumberbatch's (2002) report for the BBFC found that viewers of this film were clear that it gives the message that 'women might enjoy being raped', Barker (2005) reports on empirical research with audiences regarding, in this case, what it means to watch a rape scene. He carefully uncovers a range of subtle interpretations and judgements from viewers, these not being focused on 'the message' of the film (as imagined, he argues, by Cumberbatch) but rather on puzzling out layers of meaning that draw both on the complexity of the film itself and, more importantly, on the complexity with which people think about society. A majority of his respondents enjoyed and admired the film, particularly the men, but – in normative terms – this did not lead them to draw the conclusion that women enjoy being raped; indeed, many of their responses were highly moral, and most found the rape scene disturbing or shocking, as in Cumberbatch's research (where, nonetheless, most were in favour of its distribution uncut).

Schlesinger et al. (1992) used qualitative research methods to examine the attitudes of women who had experienced violence, and those who had not, to a variety of scenes of violence in television programming (using an episode of a soap opera, a drama and a crime report series) as well as the film *The Accused,* which features a gang rape. The researchers found that the overwhelming reaction to the film and the rape scene was shock and significant proportions of the sample also found it 'offensive'. Women who had experienced violence were slightly more able than those who had not to relate to the rape victim and, more particularly, to the situations depicted around the rape. Schlesinger et al. demonstrated some cultural differences in attitude with women of Asian origin more likely to condemn the victim for the situation she found herself in.

> The responses evoked touched the emotional core of virtually all the women present. What was particularly striking – and this emerged in the course of group discussions much more clearly than from the quantitative data – was the universal identification with the situation of the rape victim, although many reservations and qualifications were forthcoming about her character…The worries were centred upon what 'men' were likely to make of this film. *The Accused* evoked extremely powerful feelings and sharp observations about the culture of male solidarity and its negative impact upon women.

Access conditions
The everyday context within which people watch film, video and DVD makes a difference. It has long been argued that film, by contrast with television (and, by extension, video) is experienced differently because of the dark, silent conditions casting a spell on the audience (Ellis, 1992).

Further, film – at the cinema or as broadcast – is linear, so violence must be watched in narrative context (either potentially increasing or decreasing any effects, depending on that context) while, by contrast, video may be watched in a number of ways, including fast-forwarding to (or away from) the violent scenes (Browne and Pennell, 2000).

Restricting the access of young people to films according to the age-appropriateness of the content is also managed differently in the cinema and at home. Indeed, the BBFC is obliged to consider a work afresh for video or DVD release even if it has already been classified for cinema distribution, because the Video Recordings Act 1984 requires that 'suitability for viewing in the home' and potential underage viewing is taken into account. Importantly the BBFC makes the argument about context in this regard (BBFC, 2005):

> In addition, video offers the possibility of freeze-frame, rewind, and frame-by-frame advance, thus allowing viewers to watch scenes out of context, while a cinema film can only be watched in the way originally intended.

In the cinema, a recent follow-up to its 2000 report, 'Marketing Violent Entertainment to Children' by the Federal Trade Commission (2000; 2004), found that self-regulation is beginning to work: advertisements for R-rated (restricted) movies are no longer directed towards under 17s, and ratings are routinely disclosed. In its undercover shopper survey, the percentage of 13–16 year olds who successfully purchased tickets for R-rated films had reduced to – a still substantial – 36 per cent. Of greater concern, 81 per cent of teen shoppers were able to buy R-rated DVDs on request.

In a small study which could be usefully replicated on a larger scale in the United Kingdom, Thompson and Skrypnek (2005; see also Thompson, 2003) examined the restricted media content accessed by 13–14 year olds in Canada. They found that two in three say they have no parental rules about movie choice, and that half consider that adults do not explain adequately why some movies are inappropriate for them, perhaps because mostly they think adults are concerned about sexual content (rather than, say, violence). On the other hand, a Dutch consumer survey conducted to inform the film rating system found that 70 per cent of parents said they would use a rating system to inform decisions regarding their children's media use – they wished for content ratings on violence, frightening content, sexual depictions, discrimination, drug abuse and coarse language (Valkenburg, 2002).

As found also for teens on the Internet (Livingstone and Bober, 2006), Thompson and Skrypnek also report a substantial gap between parental and teen understandings of (and communication about) domestic rules for media access. Interestingly, well over half reported attempting to rent – in Canada – adult-rated (18A or R) movies, often successfully, and over one-third have attempted to see restricted movies at the cinema: the difference here suggests that renting (and viewing) age-restricted movies at home is seen as easier than at the cinema.

Problematically, in an American study that could also usefully be replicated in the United Kingdom, parents were found to disagree with the industry in applying content ratings to movies, television and games: 'the amount of violent content and portrayals of violence are the primary markers for disagreement between parent raters and industry ratings' (Gentile, 1998; Walsh and Gentile, 2001). Generally, parents are more restrictive than the industry, especially when violent content is in a humorous context, when violence is glamourized or portrays harmful behaviour.

Particular attention has focused recently on whether home conditions permit children to view restricted content. Ofcom's (2005e) research found that, under current arrangements, some secondary school children (half of those who know their parents have a security system) say they know their parents'/guardian's PIN numbers, even though their parents think they do not. Of those who knew the number, slightly less than two-thirds claimed they had gained access to PINs with parental permission, but one-third had gained access by other means, though again their parents think they have not done so. Further, slightly less than half of those who say they know their parents'/guardian's PIN number say they have actually accessed PPV material without their parents' permission.

Summary

- The empirical research evidence for harm and offence in relation to film, video and DVD has been concerned primarily with 'adult' or relatively extreme sexual and violent content, such material being more available, though restricted by age, on film and video/DVD than – at present – on television.

- Although concerns are consistently raised regarding the reality-defining or stereotyping effects of film, we found little recent research on this, though a much longer history of research exists. The research on emotional responses to film, particularly fear, is relatively uncontentious, though whether this constitutes harm – particularly since some argue that people enjoy fear – is more difficult to determine, particularly given the absence of longitudinal research studies.

- Considerable attention has been paid to pornography, focusing variously on harm to those involved in production, to male consumers, to children, and to society (especially, attitudes towards women) more generally. The evidence for harm to men viewing non-violent (or consensual) pornography remains inconclusive or absent. However, the evidence for harm from viewing violent (non-consensual) pornography is rather stronger, resulting in more negative or aggressive attitudes and behaviours towards women as well as supporting the desire to watch more and more extreme content.

- Some argue that although the simple claim for causality cannot be 'proven', nonetheless the evidence suggests that media contents such as pornography do have causal effects (Itzin, 2002). This is not to say that pornography is a 'sole cause' of harm, for the causal process of becoming a sex offender is complex, takes place over years or decades, and is influenced by multiple factors. But nor does pornography play no role at all; on the contrary, she points to evidence to say that it plays a role in each step in the aetiology of becoming an offender, terming this an 'instrumental' cause.[8]

■ The evidence that viewing pornography harms children remains scarce, given ethical restrictions on the research, though many experts believe it to be harmful. Other vulnerable groups have been researched, however, with some evidence that the harmful effects of violent content especially are greater for those who are already aggressive, for children with behaviour disorders, for young offenders with a history of domestic violence and – for pornographic content – among sexual offenders.

■ Interestingly, throughout this literature it is often unclear whether the potential victims of portrayed violence or pornography are the individuals directly exposed to such content or those around them – if boys become more aggressive if they grow up with violent media, are they the victims or are the victims those they subsequently bully or act aggressively towards? Arguably, it is both.

■ Public attitudes to film content are, generally, more tolerant than for television. This is partly because the public is also aware of and supportive of, current levels of regulation in film, and partly because people understand the decision process behind choosing to watch violent or sexual content. Tolerance is lowest (or offence is greatest) for the portrayal of sexual violence. Studies of audience interpretation of potentially harmful or offensive content in film throw some light on the complex judgements made by the public in this area. Helping to elucidate the importance of narrative or generic context, qualitative social research reveals how people may draw out subtle or sensitive interpretations from overtly violent content. Nonetheless, the subtlety of their judgements does not mean they may not also be shocked or upset by such content.

■ We end this chapter by concluding that, particularly as the conditions for viewing film – both at home and in the cinema – are changing, too little is known, particularly in the United Kingdom, regarding the conditions under which people, especially children, may gain access to different kinds of potentially harmful content. More research is, therefore, needed.

Notes

1. The literature does not usually make the distinction flagged in the recent Home Office Consultation ('On the possession of extreme pornographic material') between 'serious violence in a sexual context' and 'serious sexual violence', though both kinds of content have been researched.

2. The long and complex arguments for and against pornography as a form of representation can be found in Attwood (2004), Allen (2001), Dworkin (1997), and Itzin (2002), among others.

3. The authors detail the typical practices depicted in X-rated videos as including anal intercourse, double penetration (vaginal and anal intercourse), men ejaculating onto women's faces, fisting, and intercourse with multiple partners.

4. The campaigning group Ofwatch (www.ofwatch.org.uk) argue that there is no evidence that children are harmed by viewing hardcore pornography and that, like other potentially or actually harmful substances kept at home (cleaning agents, matches, alcohol, etc.), parents must be responsible for keeping such material from their children. This, they point out, is the argument that permitted R18 material to be legally sold in UK shops since the BBFC case in 2000 (Edwards, 2001). They also point out that the market for restricted content is small, undermining the implicit argument that in regulatory debates the freedoms of the majority are being compromised by the protection of a minority. Moreover, we note an absence of empirical evidence regarding the oft-claimed desire of the majority to exercise their 'right' to view pornographic content. Rather, as we see under 'Offence',

below, opinion polls identify public support for the right of 'other people' to view such material (provided children cannot gain access), together with a variable degree of distaste or disgust when they themselves have viewed it.

5. This survey examined exposure to violent content across film, television, Internet and video-games, finding the strongest effects for video-games (see games chapter) and no effects for television or Internet.

6. Burt (1980) coined the term 'rape myth'. Rape myth acceptance (RMA) involves beliefs and values associated with sexual assault, the perpetrators, and the victims. One who adopts RMA beliefs believes that a woman who is victimized by rape is partially or completely responsible for the act.

7. These were further revised in February 2005, see http://www.bbfc.co.uk/.

8. Likening the argument to that of the evidence for a causal role of smoking in relation to lung cancer, she places more emphasis on the combination of a persistent correlation between pornography and offending (or smoking and cancer) combined with a theory that conceptualizes a mechanism that links cause and effect. To extend her analogy, just as several decades ago, it seemed plausible to the medical establishment to argue that lung cancer occurred irrespective of the presence of smoking, now she asks why does it seem plausible to argue that some people become sex offenders irrespective of the presence of pornography?

5

ELECTRONIC GAMES

As with research on other media, academic research on games (variously called computer games, electronic games or video-games) is divided among the following:

■ A sizeable body of psychologically-informed empirical evidence (experiments and surveys) examining hypotheses regarding the possible harms caused by electronic game-playing, with the main focus on violence.

■ A growing body of evidence of the potential for addiction to electronic games. This sits alongside a fairly small body of descriptive evidence charting the demographics and daily habits of game-playing as an activity (who, how much, when and why?), which is usually part of broader surveys on media use in everyday life (Entertainment Software Association, 2005).

■ A growing body of critical commentary, from a cultural studies perspective, examining the 'texts' of electronic games in context (i.e. their economics, production and cultural meanings), often taking the experience of fans/frequent players as primary.

■ Some policy-driven research considering the regulation of electronic game-playing, especially for young people, which is derived from research among carers and parents.

■ However, we have found little research specifically examining people's interpretations of electronic games (to parallel the sizeable body of research on interpretations of television programmes or films, for example). And other than in the general surveys cited elsewhere, we have not found a literature on whether the public finds games content offensive, notwithstanding considerable press coverage of this issue.

THE MARKET

The financial size of the electronic games market has expanded considerably in recent years, as has the proportion of the population that plays such games, and the amount of time they spend doing so. Particularly, that in the United States, games are now competing with the film industry in sales, and over 60 per cent of Americans play interactive games regularly (Williams and Skoric, 2005).

The Entertainment Software Association claims that 75 per cent of heads of households in the United States play computer or video-games, with an average age of thirty, 55 per cent of them men; on average, it also reports that they play for some seven hours per week, they have been playing for twelve years and they intend to continue playing in the years to come. Of 2004 computer and video-game sales, 16 per cent are rated 'mature'. Among top selling video-games for 2004, *Grand Theft Auto: San Andreas* is the top ranked, with *The Sims 2* as the top ranked computer game (Entertainment Software Association, 2005). In the United Kingdom, surveys show that many children and teens are also firm fans of electronic games (Buckingham, 2002; Livingstone, 2002), as in the United States (Kaiser Family Foundation, 2003), Canada (Kline, 2003a) and elsewhere.

A study conducted in Europe in 2007 by the market research firm, Nielsen, showed PCs are the most used platform for playing electronic games (72 per cent), followed by the PS2 (50 per cent). UK respondents were leading in the adoption of the newer consoles and handhelds (particularly the PSP, Xbox 360, and Nintendo Wii).[1–2] Boyle and Hibberd (2005) showed that the video-game market in the United Kingdom is the third largest market in the world (after Japan and the United States). Indeed the Nielsen survey (2007) found that the United Kingdom was second only to Latvia in terms of heavy users of electronic games (28 per cent of UK respondents said they played for 11+ hours were week, compared with 50 per cent of Latvian respondents). The research data on the demographics of gamers in Europe also show that gamers span a wide age demographic with a bias towards males: 27 per cent of those aged 16–24 in this survey were classified as heavy users (playing 10+ hours per week) in comparison with 20 per cent of those aged 25–64. 26 per

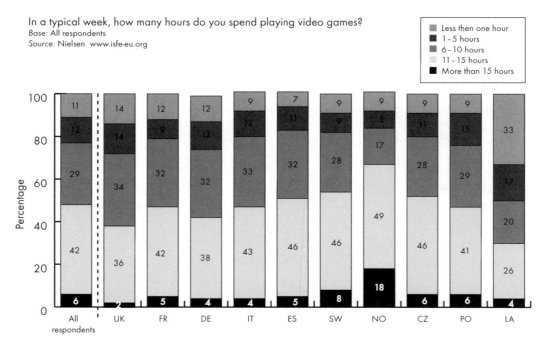

Figure 5.1 Total European gamers – breakdown by country. Columns may not total 100% due to rounding error.

cent of males said they played 10+ hours per week ('heavy users') compared with 13 per cent of females.

Data collected by Pew in 2005 showed that 81 per cent of Internet users aged 12–17 in the United States played games online in 2004 – a growth of 52 per cent in such users since 2000.[3] While electronic games are an old medium (30+ years), they can now be played online or on mobile platforms, with the associated difficulties of 'supervision' and risks.

> The location where computer games are played remains important; one of the major changes in the last two decades has been the movement out of the arcades (where some level of policing was able to take place) and into the home (where the responsibility shifts to the parents to police the domestic environment). Related to this is the extent to which the emerging digital landscape now finds games being played across a range of more diffuse often mobile media platforms, from mobile phones, pocket computers and the internet. (Boyle and Hibberd, 2005: 11–12)

In their major review of media use by American children, Comstock, Scharrer and Comstock (2007) point to the limited research on video-games:

> The inferential problem is that the quantity of consistent data is a small proportion of that for television and film. This is essentially an issue of reliability. We cannot have the same confidence that the results so far validly represent the possible universe of outcomes. (Comstock et al., 2007: 235)

Nonetheless, they argue, the evidence thus far suggests that playing violent electronic games can lead to aggressive behaviour, especially among males aged 10–14 years old. Indeed, it is widely asserted that electronic games are addictive and lead to social/behavioural and health problems; and that violence in electronic games leads to real-life aggression, as is argued about TV violence.

In the United Kingdom, the market research firm, Cragg Ross Dawson, found gender differences among gamers, with girls and women playing games that are less 'action' oriented, while boys and men are more likely to play games with significant action (such as so-called 'shoot-em-up' games) and sports games (Cragg, Taylor and Toombs, 2007). Similarly, Olson et al. (2007) looked at video and computer game-playing in the United States among adolescent boys and girls. They found that, among 1,254 seventh and eighth grade children, almost half (49 per cent) played at least one game rated as Mature (suitable for those aged 17 years old and over) regularly. Boys were far more likely to do so than girls (68 per cent of boys and 29 per cent of girls). They noted that playing such games (M-rated) correlated positively with being male, frequent game-play, playing with strangers over the Internet, having a game system and computer in one's bedroom, and using games to manage anger.

REALITY-DEFINING EFFECTS

A range of potential reality-defining effects can be identified. Much research focuses on stereotyping. A semiotic analysis of the implicit ideology in video-games suggests that 'video-games represent a powerful instrument of hegemony, eliciting ideological consent through a spectrum of white supremacist projects' (Leonard, 2003). In other words, by playing such video-games, it is claimed that one may end up repeating and reinforcing stereotypes and social inequalities in relation to ethnicity, though a similar case can be made in relation to gender. Levin and Carlsson-Paige (2003) add that since many programmes and games contain racial stereotypes, these 'present a special risk for children of color because of how racial messages are linked to violence'. A more straightforward content analysis of 60 best-selling games makes a similar case for gender – by comparison with male characters, female characters were found not only to be vastly under-represented but also to be more often partially nude, featuring an unrealistic body image, and wearing sexually revealing clothing (Downs and Smith, 2005).

In defence of these games, many laud the autonomy and interactivity that games allow, by comparison with 'passive' or 'linear' television. In criticizing such a celebratory view, Kline (2003b: 142) acidly summarises such a position as asserting that:

> gaming is endlessly enabling; making menued choices is the expression of creativity; any response to a simulated challenge is a strategic 'action'…; moving through virtual mazes is tantamount to exploring and mastering one's own imaginations; the fantastical settings are providing exposure to other perspectives…; and any kind of exchange between players entails the consolidation of the online player community.

It is also noteworthy that many who seek to promote an understanding of the cultural or experiential value of computer games do not deny that they also contain offensive content, acknowledging, but not dwelling on, the plethora of sexual, racial, and other stereotypes, for example (e.g. Gee, 2003).

VIOLENCE

CONTEXT
The arguments about the effect of playing violent electronic games on subsequent behaviour are as fraught with difficulty, as is the debate about the effects of viewing televisual violence. As with television, much of the argument centres on different research traditions and methodologies which suggest different outcomes. The more experimental approach, favoured by American psychologists, claims to show effects, usually short-term, as a result of viewing or – in this case – playing with violent content. The more cultural studies approach criticizes the experimental tradition, and instead examines the positive dimensions of media use. This debate, then, is taken into the argument about the effects of violent video-game-playing.

Over the past decade or more, considerable public anxiety has accompanied the growth in the market for electronic (video, computer, online) games, particularly in relation to children. In the United States, popular discussion frequently links violent games with the Columbine High School case, and other prominent cases of youth violence or delinquency. Certain games remain controversial – for example *Grand Theft Auto: San Andreas*, recently discovered to have hidden sex scenes in addition to considerable violence (Economist, 2005). Most research on electronic games, however, concerns violence rather than specifically sexual violence, leaving unresolved the question of whether the portrayal of sexual violence in games is widespread and, potentially, harmful.

Researchers often seek to contextualize the degree of violent content in electronic games in relation to game genres, narratives and other content features. Berger (2002) outlines, for example, *Mortal Kombat*, in which one character decapitates his victims while another rips out their hearts and a third tears off their heads to display the spinal cord attached to the bloody neck. Gee (2003) discusses some other troubling cases – the rash of post September 11 video-games featuring US soldiers killing Arabs and Muslims, for example, though others featured Palestinians expelling Israeli soldiers (and indeed, on the Internet there are numerous violent games with explicitly political/conflict themes, depending on one's view of who the 'goodies' and the 'baddies' are). Taking a cultural studies approach, he offers a defence, suggesting these games allow one to experience 'the other' from the inside, and encourage the player to reflect on political conflict in an interesting fashion. While Gee appears less tolerant of a game called *Ethnic Cleansing*, one of several produced by the known white supremacist hate group, the National Alliance, he raises the difficult case of player-designed games (or, player-customized games) – analogous to the question of harm or offence resulting from user-generated content (in talk shows, on mobile phones, etc.).

EVIDENCE

In her review of the evidence for the potential for harm to children caused by video-games, Byron (2008: 193) noted:

> Many gamers told me that it is not unusual for them to be exposed to inappropriate language, racist comments, or other verbal abuse when playing online, or for gamers to gang up on another gamer to prevent them progressing in a game. This is a point that is further illustrated by a recent poll of online gamers, where 87% of respondents said they had experienced conduct from other players (e.g. bad language or abusive comments) which they would deem inappropriate for children or young people under 18 to encounter, compared with 10% who said they had not...However, gamers also told me that it is usually the younger players who use bad language and threaten each other, whilst older players tend to use the mute options more and ignore the younger players.

However, most of the research evidence for possible harms caused by game-playing have concentrated on violent content within games, rather than the potentially harmful content created by users themselves, described by Byron above.

Gentile and Stone (2005) undertook a literature review of the effects research around violent electronic games. They looked at a variety of US studies and concluded that the results were unclear but that researchers needed to look at four dimensions:

■ Amount of time spent.

■ Content (i.e. violent content).

- Form (an understanding of the conventions of the medium as in television, such as realism).

- Mechanics (the types of devices required to play the games).

The same video-game could have both positive and negative effects, depending on which of these dimensions is being investigated:

> For example, playing the *Grand Theft Auto* series of games (in which one plays a criminal sociopath) a lot each day could hamper school performance (amount effect), increase aggressive thoughts and behaviors (content effect), improve visual attention skills (form effect), and improve driving skills if one plays with a driver's wheel and pedals or shooting skills if one plays using a gun input/output device (mechanics effects). (Gentile and Stone, 2005: 355–356)

Similarly Lee and Peng (2006) suggest that more research is needed on what the game-playing experience is. They draw parallels with other research in the United States from the 'television effects' tradition which found that components of a programme (what they call 'formal features' such as loud noises, unusual camera effects, fast action) had an influence on how children reported they were feeling.

Weber, Ritterfeld and Kostygina (2006) suggest that a direct effect between players and violent electronic games should not be expected. What may be important is the context in which the game is seen by the player. There may be positive effects of playing games, in particular they point to the social nature of game-playing:

> It is more promising to expect possible effects to be moderated by the way users interpret the game; for example they may interpret it as 'just a game' and an opportunity to socialize with friends, or as a simulation of reality and a way to prepare for social life. (Weber et al., 2006: 357)

Durkin (2006) argues that playing violent electronic games may be cathartic and that video-game-playing itself should be seen as part of normal development in contemporary society. Using research conducted previously among video-game-players, Durkin points to the social aspects of video-game-playing, as do Weber et al. above. Taylor (2006) suggests that those who consider themselves 'power gamers' are keen to act as helpers to those players who find themselves 'in trouble' during a game. Durkin (1995) also argues that there is evidence that educational games have cognitive benefits, and there are many studies that suggest the benefit of game-playing for improving student motivation (ACMA, 2007).

Williams (2006: 1) seeks to apply cultivation theory to video-game-playing – that is, to examine how such activities can affect a view of the world. He used experimental methodologies with a target group receiving a game to play while a control group did not. He suggests that 'participants in an online game changed their perceptions of real-world dangers. However, these dangers only corresponded to events and situations found in the game-world, not other real-world crimes'. Thus there was no proof that video-game-playing affects how respondents perceive real-life situations. As the previous review on the evidence for harm and offence showed, this has been found in other studies where television or filmic violence has been reacted to differently from violence in the 'real-world'.

On the other hand, in their chapter in Gentile's book (2003), Gentile and Anderson argue that game-playing violence may have a greater effect than television violence because identification with the aggressor can lead to imitation of the aggressor in a more involving way than television would. They also argue that if video technologies can be used to learn, why might it be thought that they could not teach negative aspects such as violence and violent or aggressive behaviour. Similarly, repetition increases learning and the practice of an entire sequence is more effective than practising just a part of it.

In a review of Scandinavian literature, Egenfeldt-Nielson and Heide Smith (2004) look at the competing literature in this area which comes from two models of aggression, themselves drawn from different traditions.

■ The first is the 'Active User' perspective – as with television, this model is predominantly European and argues that reactions to media content is context-dependent. Therefore in answer to the question about the possible effects of violent games, this model suggests that this is too simplistic a question.

■ The second (used more in the United States where a general aggression model based on behavioural psychology is generally used) is the 'Active Media' perspective which argues that violent games do have effects.

Egenfeldt-Nielson and Heide Smith themselves suggest that younger gamers may be susceptible to violent material but agree that there is little evidence for this.

The research programme established by Anderson and colleagues has investigated the hypothesized link between video-games and aggression. He acknowledges that the evidence from earlier studies has been mixed, providing little clear support for the 'pro-effects' case. However, he argues that researchers have not always properly compared violent and non-violent video-games nor instituted adequate controls on their experimental comparisons.

Anderson's 'General Affective Aggression Model' (Anderson et al., 2004; Anderson and Dill, 2000) draws on earlier effects models (social learning theory, socio-cognitive information-processing models, cultivation analysis, etc.). It proposes that individual (e.g. aggressive personality) and situational (e.g. violent video-game) factors influence a person's affect (e.g. hostility), cognitions (e.g. aggression scripts) and state of arousal (e.g. heart rate). These in turn influence the person's appraisal of their environment (e.g. feeling of threat, need for revenge), finally resulting in an increased likelihood of aggressive behaviour. These short-term effects then, he argues, initiate a new cycle by influencing the situation in which the person plays the next game. For example, in one experiment, participants played either a violent or non-violent video-game, and then they read ambiguous story items about potential interpersonal conflicts. When asked what the main character will do, say, think and feel as the story continues, the research found that people who played a violent video-game described the main character as behaving more aggressively, thinking more aggressive thoughts, and feeling more angry than did people who played a non-violent video-game (Bushman and Anderson, 2002). In the long-term, the theory argues that these patterns of cognition, affect and behaviour become over-learned and reinforced, thus influencing the individual's personality (and so, again, inputting into the aggressive cycle). However, the evidence for such long-term effects is lacking, being rarely tested in practice.

Key findings regarding the short-term effects researched are summarized below:

- A correlational (survey-based) study on college students found a correlation between realistic violent video-game-play (e.g. *Mortal Kombat*) and aggressive behaviour (e.g. threatening to hit/attacking someone/using force) and between video-game violence and aggressive personality (Anderson and Dill, 2000). However, analysis showed that the effect of video-game violence on aggression occurs primarily among already-aggressive individuals.

- Some research does suggest effects in the other direction (i.e. from game-playing to aggressive behaviour among the general population). To examine the question of causality, in one experiment students played a violent (or non-violent) video-game for three fifteen-minute sessions, each session being followed by one set of measures. These were affective (self-reported feelings), cognitive (word association) and behavioural (a competitive button-pushing reaction time task in which the participant delivers a noise blast of a variable intensity – chosen by the participant – to an opponent). Results showed little effect of game type on hostile affect or fear of crime/feeling of safety (although see Mierlo and Van den Bulck, 2004). Game type did affect accessibility of aggressive words, interpreted as 'priming aggressive thoughts' after playing a violent game, mainly among men. Last, a small effect on behaviour was found; those who played the violent game were found to be more aggressive to their opponent when they had been provoked by a noise blast (Anderson and Dill, 2000). Other researchers have found that those playing violent video-games have increased anxiety (self-reported and in terms of blood pressure measures) (Baldaro, Tuozzi, Codispoti, Barbagli, Trombini et al., 2004; see also Panee and Ballard, 2002).

- Interestingly, given that research often finds violence-related effects to be greater for boys and men (Bartholow and Anderson, 2002), a study on young women showed a similar effect of violent video-game-playing provided that they were motivated by revenge and provided they controlled a same-sex violent game character (Anderson and Murphy, 2003).

- Using similar methods to the above, in a further experiment participants played one of three versions of the same race car video-game: 1) all violence rewarded; 2) all violence punished; and 3) non-violent. Rewarding violent game actions increased hostile emotion, aggressive thinking, and later aggressive behaviour. Punishing violent actions increased hostile emotion, but did not increase aggressive thinking or aggressive behaviour. Results suggest that games which reward violent actions can increase aggressive behaviour by increasing aggressive thinking (Carnagey and Anderson, 2005; see also Anderson et al., 2004). In another experiment, those who played *Mortal Kombat* punished confederates more than those who played a non-violent game (Ballard and Lineberger, 1999); in a similar study (using *Doom*), those playing the violent game were more likely to exploit than cooperate with a partner in a subsequent task (Sheese and Graziano, 2005) or to learn an aggressive self-perception (though the findings in this study are mixed at best; Uhlmann and Swanson, 2004).

Meta-analyses (i.e. statistical analysis of findings across separate studies) suggest that, notwithstanding some variation depending on player characteristics, experiments demonstrate that violent video-games increase aggressive behaviour in children and young adults because they increase aggressive/hostile affect and cognitions (Anderson, 2004; Anderson and Bushman, 2001; Anderson and Murphy, 2003). Anderson and Bushman's (2001) meta-analysis also suggests that playing violent video-games decreases pro-social behaviour (e.g. helping others, being empathetic to others' needs).

Carnagey and Anderson (2005) conducted three experiments among participants in the United States which they said showed that rewarding violent behaviour in a game increased aggression and hostile emotion, while punishing such behaviour did not increase aggressive behaviour, although it did increase hostile emotion. All experiments used versions of *Carmegeddon 2*, as follows:[4]

■ Experiment 1: Used undergraduates (not children) and used physiological measures as well as subjective ratings of the game and completion of hostility questionnaires. Results showed that violence in a video-game increased feelings of hostility.

■ Experiment 2: Used (different) undergraduates and physiological measures as well as subjective ratings of the game and, instead of hostility questionnaires, used so-called 'word fragment' tasks. Results showed that when the violence was rewarded there was more aggressive 'thinking' or word choice than when violence was punished or where there was no violence in the game.

■ Experiment 3: Used (different) undergraduates to compete to press a button faster than an opponent – the result of failure was for the loser to receive a burst of white noise, the duration and intensity of it being chosen by the winner. The participants then played one of three versions of the game – violence was punished, or not punished, or there was no violence in the game. The findings showed that the rewarded violence in the game resulted in agressive effects, and also that prior exposure to such games is associated with self-reported aggression.

More recently, Anderson, Gentile and Buckley (2007) conducted three further experiments, also in the United States, this time among both college students and 9–12 year olds.

■ Study 1: Levels of 'punishment' (noise) imposed upon an opponent were measured. The hypotheses were that those who played violent electronic games were more likely to inflict more severe punishment and that repeated exposure to violent media would be associated with higher levels of violent behaviour. The findings showed that those who played electronic games with violent content displayed more aggressive behaviour in the laboratory. Players considered games that were rated as T (Teen – content that may be suitable for ages 13 and older) as more violent than children's electronic games. It was also found that even 'mild' violence as in cartoons had a (short-term) effect. The researchers argue that this shows that 'what seems to matter is whether the game includes aggressive content', not the realism itself.

■ Study 2: Here the researchers investigated emotional hostility measures among high school students and set that against exposure to violent media content (including electronic games). They found that those who played more violent electronic games did have more pro-violent attitudes, whether or not they measured as having more aggressive personalities at the outset. They also found no apparent difference between boys and girls. They suggest that the relation between violent behaviour and aggression may be stronger for violent electronic games than the other media. While they recognize the difficulties of comparing data across media, they claim that video-game violence exposure was 'more strongly and uniquely associated with violent behaviour and physical aggression' than violence in television or film (cinema) content.

■ Study 3: This tested school children to see how aggressive they were (and were perceived to be) and how they viewed the world. The study found that playing violent electronic games had a significant negative effect, and it is physical aggression that is more prominent as a result of violent video-game-playing (compared with the finding that television and film violence lead to increases in verbal aggression).

In concluding the authors argue that playing violent electronic games can have an effect on social development:

We have proposed that exposure to violent video-games is likely to result in rehearsal and learning of aggressive scripts, aggressive beliefs, and aggressive expectation schemata…These changes in turn lead to increases in aggressive personality and behaviors and decreases in pro-social behavior…It appears that no matter how many risk and protective factors the child already has, playing violent video-games still adds additional risk for future increased aggressive behavior. (Anderson et al. 2007: 140–141)

An experimental study by Arriaga, Esteves, Carneiro and Monteiro (2006) in Portugal, examining undergraduates' emotional reactions (measured on hostility, state anxiety and arousal), also showed that those participants who played violent computer games reported significantly higher hostility, which was exacerbated by an already aggressive personality.

We have already noted above that boys are found, in research, to play more action-oriented games than girls. Funk (2005) examined the literature that looks at the possible relationship between violent video-game-playing and desensitization to violence – the research is suggestive rather than definitive. However, she too, refers to the popularity of violent electronic games among both girls and boys – it is implied that this is a negative as the underlying assumption is that violent electronic games will have an effect on gamers.

Although Anderson's work has been widely cited, we note that it has attracted considerable criticism also, this focusing on its external validity – can the findings of these experiments be generalized to the everyday situations in which people play video-games? (Amici Curiae, 2001; Cumberbatch, 2004). Indeed, as with parallel experiments on television, some question the relevance of the experimental situation to real-life (see Bensley and Van Eenwyk, 2001). Problematically, only a brief period of game-playing is permitted, by contrast with the lengthy playing of familiar games in ordinary situations (Newman, 2004). The measures of aggressive affect, cognition and behaviour are unique to the experiment and their relation to everyday aggression is unclear (and, curiously, little discussed by experimental researchers). The laboratory, it has been fairly argued, bears little resemblance to the domestic living room (Amici Curiae, 2001).

The qualitative study undertaken for the BBFC in the United Kingdom in 2007 suggested that where violence is found in games there seem to be a number of reactions expressed by gamers (Cragg et al., 2007):

■ First, violence, in the sense of eliminating obstacles, is built into the structure of many games and it would be impossible to progress without it. Most gamers see eliminating enemies as another step in the game rather than something to savour for itself.

■ Second, violence contributes mightily to the tension in games not least because gamers are not just shooting, they are also vulnerable to being shot. Most gamers concentrate on their own survival rather than on the damage they inflict on others.

■ Third, the opportunity to be violent, without being vulnerable to consequences, clearly underscores the appeal of some games as escapist; the violence helps make the play exhilaratingly out of reach of ordinary life.

■ Fourth, gamers seem not to lose awareness that they are playing a game and do not mistake the game for real-life. (ibid.: 11–12)

The study goes on to say that video-gamers are 'virtually unanimous' in saying that they do not become desensitized to real-life violence, either to be violent or to care less about violence inflicted elsewhere. A criticism of such a study is that it is self-reported and has no longitudinal element to it so it is not possible to monitor whether or not an effect is noticed later on by these gamers.

Indeed, one of the criticisms of the research on electronic games made in Boyle and Hibberd (2005) is that there is little longitudinal research. Williams and Skoric (2005) conducted such a study online, lasting one month.

■ It was preceded by a participant observation study.

■ It used an online role-playing game (the most popular genre), in which multi-players interact.

■ Such games are not widely played by younger people and the researchers chose *Asheron's Call 2*,[5] described as a significantly more violent game than average.

■ The sample was made up of older people than has traditionally been examined (with a mean age of 27.7 years), and the researchers argue that the adult gamer is a neglected demographic.

■ It had one group who received the game (75) and a control group that did not (138).

Williams and Skoric found that game-play is not a significant predictor of aggression, when compared with the control group across a variety of measures, and they argue that traditional theories for aggression and media content may not be applicable to the interactive nature of game-playing, although the element of physical isolation may be important (although there is no evidential support).

In their third study, mentioned above, Anderson, Gentile and Buckley (2007) interviewed their subjects twice during the school year in the United States. They noted that gamers who played more violent electronic games changed how they perceived the world in terms of aggression. This attitude, they suggest, is shown to correlate, in other research, with an increase in hostile reactions to situations. This study, the researchers suggest, shows that both formerly aggressive and non-aggressive children are made more so after playing a violent video-game. They also accept this is just one study and more will need to be undertaken to prove their theory.

In a study measuring brain activity, Bartholow, Bushman and Sestir (2006) found evidence to show that certain types of brain activity associated with violence desensitization were reduced in those who played violent, rather than non-violent video-games. Further, they say that this neurological response predicted increased aggressive behaviour in a subsequent task.

It is interesting to note that the difficulties that effects researchers have in establishing their case for harm is similar for those concerned with positive effects: one review notes mixed evidence at best for the positive influence of home computer use (in terms of cognitive skills, educational performance, social development, etc.) (although see Gee, 2003; Subrahmanyam, Kraut, Greenfield, and Gross, 2000, for some thoughtful claims on the possible positive educational benefits). Another review notes the methodological difficulties with much research on violent video-games (see also Bensley and Van Eenwyk, 2001), resulting in inconsistent findings, but urges policy-intervention (in Australia) based on the precautionary principle (Unsworth and Ward, 2001).

At the same time, individual cases continue to challenge policy-making conceived for the population as a whole. In one case, a psychotic young man, admitted to a psychiatric facility after being arrested for stealing cars and assaulting people, was found to believe he was inside the game he had been playing obsessively. Forsyth, Harland and Edwards (2001) comment that,

in this report we are not suggesting that computer games can be the cause of psychosis; but it does seem likely that, with the growing use of computers for relaxation, game scenarios will be incorporated increasingly into delusional systems. A worrying aspect is that, in many of these games, points are scored for acting violently or even killing.

In a different view on the literature about the effects of violent electronic games on users, Ferguson (2007) conducted an analysis of possible publication bias in the types of material available for studies such as this update. Ferguson found that those studies (in the United States, of an experimental nature) that provide aggression of various forms are more likely to be published. In contrast, research in other areas, such as that which demonstrates pro-social behaviour, were less likely to be susceptible to publication bias.

EFFECTS ON CHILDREN

A survey among 9–10 year olds found that more exposure to violent games was associated with lower empathy and more pro-violent attitudes, suggesting a 'desensitization' effect (Funk et al., 2004). A survey of young teenagers revealed more overt behavioural effects, finding that those who played more violent video-games were more hostile, reported getting into more arguments and fights, and were doing less well in school. The authors conclude that those who play more become more hostile in general and, therefore, more aggressive when faced with difficult situations (Gentile, Lynch, Linder, and Walsh, 2004).

Funk, Jenks, Bechtoldt, and Buchman (2002) identify significant negative relationships between a preference for violent games and various outcome measures including self-perceptions of academic performance and behaviour. Since they find that such relationships are not found in every study, they propose that some children ('high risk' players) may be more susceptible to being affected by game-playing. Further, unsurprisingly, age makes a difference, with the effect of violent video-games hypothesized, but not always found, to be greatest in early adolescence (Kirsh, 2003). Gender also matters, as does personality (e.g. sensation-seeking; Slater, 2003) or other risk factors (Funk et al., 2004).

In a rare UK-based study, a survey of year eight comprehensive school pupils (aged 12 years old) found that more frequent game-playing was associated with lower self-esteem among boys (but not girls). By contrast with Anderson, who stresses that it is specifically violent content that is harmful, the survey found an association between aggression scores and overall amount of game-play but not with a preference for specifically violent games (Colwell and Payne, 2000). Similar results were obtained with German teenagers (more violent game-playing was associated with norms condoning physical aggression (Krahe and Moller, 2004) and with Swiss teenagers (Kuntsche, 2003). Although many researchers have called for longitudinal studies, few exist. One study of an online multi-player violent role-play game, that followed people randomly assigned either to play the game for one month or to a control group, found no effects on real-world aggression (measured in terms of aggressive cognitions, normative beliefs on aggression and aggressive behaviours) (Williams and Skoric, 2005).

Writing in *The Lancet*, Browne (2005; see also Kline, 2003a) draws the following, balanced conclusion regarding (American) evidence for effects across a range of violent media:

> There is consistent evidence that violent imagery in television, film and video, and computer games has substantial short-term effects on arousal, thoughts, and emotions, increasing the likelihood of aggressive or fearful behaviour in younger children, especially in boys. The

evidence becomes inconsistent when considering older children and teenagers, and long-term outcomes for all ages. The multifactorial nature of aggression is emphasised, together with the methodological difficulties of showing causation. Nevertheless, a small but significant association is shown in the research, with an effect size that has a substantial effect on public health. By contrast, only weak evidence from correlation studies links media violence directly to crime.

ADDICTION

Griffiths (2007) has written widely about addiction to electronic games as a phenomenon. He asks questions about the nature of addiction and suggests six criteria that would suggest addiction, including:

- Salience (the importance of video-game-playing in one's life).

- Mood modification.

- Tolerance (how much time is needed to achieve the mood modification referred to above).

- Withdrawal symptoms.

- Conflict (e.g. interpersonal conflict created by excessive playing).

- Relapse (how quickly after, for example, a period of abstinence, former levels of game-playing are resumed).

Griffiths suggests that such addiction does exist but it affects 'only a very small minority of players'. In previous research that he conducted (Griffiths and Hunt, 1998), Griffiths refers to 7 per cent of very heavy gamers in his sample (of 400 respondents in the United Kingdom aged 12–16 years old) – that is, they played 30+ hours per week. Further, he and Hunt found that nearly 20 per cent of gamers showed signs of dependence, against the factors above. Dependence was correlated too with gender, with males more likely to show such traits than females and with reported aggression as a result of direct game-playing. Thus he concludes that there does seem to be excessive game-playing among some gamers and suggests that addicted players are clinically monitored.

In an earlier survey of online gamers, Griffiths et al. (2004) found that teenage (12–16 year old) gamers (by contrast with adult players) were more likely to sacrifice education or work to game-playing and were more likely to enjoy the games' violence. Nonetheless, very few play 'excessively' (the survey found that 7 per cent play for 30+ hours per week) and playing is, for many, a sociable activity (with other online players) (Griffiths, Davies and Chappell, 2004). However, contrary to the notion that game-players are isolated or anxious individuals, an Australian survey of 16 year olds found that game-playing was associated with positive features of development (family closeness, positive school engagement, friendship network, etc.; Durkin and Barber, 2002).

In a study with Wood, Gupta, Deverensky, and Griffiths (2004), Griffiths had found that, among a sample of young people aged 10–17 years old in Canada, excessive video-game-playing may be linked with problem gambling behaviour. This link may be exacerbated, they argue, by online gambling which has many of the same elements as video-game-playing and makes gambling more accessible. Griffiths suggests, therefore, that excessive game-playing can be likened to online gambling although he is not suggesting that such gambling leads to excessive game-playing.

Although the present review concerns research published since 2000, it is worth noting that a substantial review conducted for the Australian Office of Film and Literature Classification in 1995 concluded that 'addictive involvement in computer games is quite rare' (Durkin, 1995). Durkin concludes further, that game-playing is generally sociable rather than solitary, and that there is little evidence that certain personalities or individuals are particularly and problematically drawn to game-playing, over and above the obvious gender differences (boys/men are far more involved in game-playing than girls/women).

Grusser, Thalemann and Griffiths (2007) asked over 7,000 gamers about their gaming behaviour (note this was a self-selecting sample drawn from members of an online gaming magazine). They found that nearly 12 per cent of those that responded fulfilled the diagnostic criteria of gaming addiction (see above), and that monetary reward was not crucial. They also found weak evidence (based on self-completion online questionnaires) that aggressive behaviour and excessive gaming are connected.

ACCESS CONDITIONS

Byron (2008) found it is difficult for parents and/or children to 'make a choice' about the appropriateness (on age or moral grounds) of playing certain games. Further, as everyday conventions within homes mean that parents pay little attention to game-playing by children, the role of parental mediation may be less than, for example, television viewing (which tends to be more a shared family activity).

In the United States, there is little reported parental supervision of children's video-game-playing, either in terms of time spent or use of age-ratings (Carnagey and Anderson, 2004). Some argue that straightforward restrictions on game-playing do not work, and that children should be themselves involved in decisions about media use (Chang, 2000). The difficulties for parents are exacerbated by having children of different ages – it is unknown how often games for older children are passed down to, or otherwise accessed by, younger children.

Taking a public-health approach, a US parent panel revealed that:

> When an entertainment industry rates a product as inappropriate for children, parent raters agree that it is inappropriate for children. However, parent raters disagree with industry usage of many of the ratings designating material suitable for children of different ages. Products rated as appropriate for adolescents are of the greatest concern. (Walsh and Gentile, 2001: 1302)

Based on a review of the empirical literature, the American Psychological Association recently adopted a resolution recommending that all violence be reduced in video-games and interactive media marketed to children and youth, and calling for the development of a content-based rating system for video-games and interactive media.[6] Key points stressed were:

- ■ Video-games routinely portray the perpetrators of violence going unpunished, thus teaching young people that violence is an effective means of resolving conflict.

- ■ Research finds that children who play more video-games are judged more hostile by their teachers, have more arguments with authority figures, are more likely to be involved in aggression with their peers, and perform less well academically; experiments find that after short exposure to violent games, children rate themselves as more aggressive and tend to imitate aggressive moves from the games when later playing with friends.

- ■ Research on learning suggests active participation may be more influential than passive observation: game-playing may be more harmful than television viewing because it involves attention, enactment, repetition, reinforcement (although, other research suggests an association between active participation and critical distance).

- ■ Media literacy is important for it teaches children a critical approach to media content, to distinguish fantasy and reality, potentially reducing identification with aggressive characters, understanding the consequences of violence to victims, and reducing fear reactions.

- ■ Parents/educators/healthcare providers can do more to mediate young people's game choices.

Summary

- ■ Research in this field, as for television, is framed very differently depending on its disciplinary origins. Although research on electronic games is relatively new, it is strongly polarized between the psychological/experimental approach that argues that electronic games have harmful effects, and the cultural/qualitative approach that defends games as engaging, pleasurable, and generally under the control of the player (though empirical evidence from game-players is sparse here).

- ■ Critics focus on familiar problems with the experimental method, contesting how far findings can be generalized to aggressive situations in everyday life (as discussed earlier); they also point to culturally-focused qualitative research that explores how game texts and the experience of game-playing is very different in the real-world to the short extracts encountered in the experimental situation. Nonetheless, it seems that the cultural approach implicitly gives ground in assuming certain kinds of effect (e.g. positive educational or identity effects) in a manner inconsistent with the denial of violent effects. Nor do critics agree among each other – for example, Berger (2002), from a cultural/semiotic perspective, concludes that video-games do have violent effects such as imitation, desensitization and altered attitudes or norms.

■ Within the psychological/effects approach, a growing body of research is accumulating which suggests harmful effects, especially in relation to aggression/violence (i.e. especially for games with violent content) and especially on boys or men who play them. Thus the research findings suggest that there are harmful short-term effects associated with playing games with violent content. There is some evidence to suggest the effects may be as much associated with games containing unrealistic or cartoon violence as they are with those employing realistic and sophisticated computer graphics. Indeed, outcomes, including harmful ones, depend on the type of game and the context in which it is played, though findings are not always consistent in identifying mediating factors of this kind.

■ As it is mainly boys and men who play violent electronic games, they are likely to be more affected (though some research suggests that, among those who play, there are no gender differences in effects). Gentile and Anderson (2006) claim that the studies they have undertaken show that violent video-game-playing has an effect on children, regardless of whether or not these children displayed aggressive traits before the study. There is also growing evidence about excessive game-playing, which some researchers suggest shows addictive behaviour among a minority of players (approximately 7 per cent).

■ It is unclear how much this evidence concerns media violence in general and how much it is video-game specific. Many researchers point to the specific nature of game-playing – Anderson argues for the immersive nature of video-game-playing that makes the player play the part of the attacker (or victim); for others, game-playing may be a social event (Weber et al.) and so may teach real-life skills. It has been argued that since electronic games require a more involved and attentive style of engagement – a 'first-person' rather than a 'third-person' experience (Skirrow, 1986) – this may make games more harmful.

■ More research is required to compare the effects of, for example, violent television and video-games. One empirical comparison across research studies found that the effect of violent video-games on aggression is smaller than that found for television violence. On the one hand, it has been argued that television imagery has hitherto been more graphic/realistic and hence more influential (although technical advances in video-game technology are allowing them to 'catch up'). Further, qualitative research (Cragg et al.) among gamers suggests that the importance of storylines was not as important as it is, say, in television or film; rather, what is important is the progression through the game and the acquisition of skills – gamers said that electronic games are 'distinctive' and are more involving because of the active nature of the participation.

NOTES

1. The sample comprised 4,000 respondents, based on 400 per territory (United Kingdom, France, Germany, Italy, Spain, Sweden, Norway, Czech Republic, Poland and Latvia).
2. Nielsen Interactive Europe, VIDEO GAMERS IN EUROPE – 2007, Interactive Software Federation of Europe 2007. http://www.isfe-eu.org/index.php?PHPSESSID=2re1u0uj0ctu5vqs0reehalib7&oidit=T001:662b 16536388a7260921599321365911.
3. Pew Internet and American Life Project, 2005 http://www.pewinternet.org/PPF/r/93/report_display.asp.

4. Ratings: ESRB (US) M — Mature: Contains content that is considered unsuitable for children under 17. ELSPA (Europe) 18.

5. Ratings: ESRB (US) M — Mature: Contains content that is considered unsuitable for children under 17. PEGI (Europe) 12+.

6. See http://www.apa.org/releases/videoviolence05.html (press release dated 17 August 2005).

6

INTERNET

INTRODUCTION

Despite the considerable difference between the Internet and other media in terms of the diversity and range of Internet content, relatively little empirical research exists that examines the potentially harmful impact of Internet content on the public, in contrast to the considerable volume of research on the harmful effects of more established mass media. There is, in short, a pressing need for more research in relation to the Internet. Nonetheless the body of research is growing. This update of the literature review sees many more research projects considering the potential for harm from content delivered via the Internet, but it continues to lag behind the dynamic way in which the Internet is used.

In its report of a public consultation on online technologies for children, the European Commission ('Safer Internet', 2007) tabulates the differences between Web 1.0 and Web 2.0 thus:

Web 1.0	**Web 2.0**
Downloading	Uploading
Consuming	Creating
Corporate	Personal
Separate media	Converging media
Static	Interactive

It is the interactive and creative elements of Web 2.0 that offer tremendous opportunities to use the world-wide-web, but these increase concerns about the vulnerability of users, especially children. The report suggests that research is structured into three 'Cs' (content, contact, conduct) while recognizing that a child using online services can fall into all three categories.

The commercialization of the Internet is also a concern, and children's vulnerability to persuasion or exploitation is still little researched (although see Fielder, Gardner, Nairn and Pitt, 2007, for evidence that children are unclear on the boundaries between paid for and non-commercial content online; for research in the United States on this issue, see also Moore 2006). Research increasingly charts the rising volume of online advertising, as well as the range of strategies employed (Boone, Secci and Gallant, 2007). But little is yet known of its effects, though research on the commercialized media environment in general occasions growing concern (see Nairn et al., 2007).

That the Internet is much used by those that have access to it is not in doubt. The Mediappro survey (2006) surveyed 7,393 young people aged 12–18 years old in nine European countries and Quebec, Canada. The project, funded by the European Union, used a common questionnaire administered to the entire sample. Based on the results from the questionnaire, 240 respondents were interviewed in person, again against an agreed moderator's text. The study found that uses of the Internet are based on the following activities:

Table 6.1 Activities on the Internet (per cent: sometimes/often/very often).

	Search engines	Email	Instant messenger	Chat rooms	Downloading
Belgium	95	74	81	28	58
Denmark	92	66	87	26	50
Estonia	90	69	88	33	73
France	94	97	69	32	49
Greece	81	46	39	41	65
Italy	86	59	49	33	59
Poland	91	62	75	34	67
Portugal	95	69	77	38	60
UK	98	81	78	20	60
Average	91	66	71	32	60

Source: Mediappro (2006).

At the time of the fieldwork (September 2005–March 2006), the use of search engines was almost ubiquitous, while instant messaging and email were used by over two-thirds of the sample. At that time creating content was far less common and this may well have changed in the intervening two years, especially if one considers social networking sites.

Some lines of research have looked at the impact of Internet use on literacy and other forms of social development but these are outside the remit of this study. However, there has been a significant amount written about Internet addiction (and also video-game addiction). That is, dependency on, and excessive use of, the Internet. Widyanto and Griffiths (2007) conducted a literature review of the evidence for Internet addiction, with Griffiths arguing that 'excessive Internet use' may be better terminology. Nonetheless Griffiths accepts that excessive use has negative effects (he cites neglect of work and social life, loss of control as examples from his UK-based research) that are comparable to addictions. His premise is that the addiction may not be to the Internet *per se*, but to the content available through that medium (such as online gambling). In an earlier study, Niemz, Griffiths, and Banyard (2005) had suggested that 18 per cent of a sample of just over 300 students in Britain were excessive Internet users – a significant proportion.

For the most part, attention has been paid to pornography available via the Internet. There is growing interest in the risks of peer-to-peer contact, including contact with strangers online, grooming by paedophiles, online bullying, sexual harassment and cyber-stalking, and the apparent growth of race hate content and contact online. Other areas remain to be substantially researched, including suicide websites, gory/violent websites, and the commercial exploitation of children.

A recent review by ECPAT International for the United Nations (Muir, 2005) brings together a considerable body of evidence regarding the threats to children from cyberspace. As the review points out, cyberspace provides multiple opportunities for adults to harm children, these risks made greater by the ways in which children (and parents) may fail to recognize the consequences of their actions online. The review specifically seeks to examine the relations among the various content-and contact-related factors that are generally researched (and so, here reviewed) separately – these include pornography, grooming, prostitution, bullying and self-harm.

PORNOGRAPHY

The amount and availability of sexually explicit material on the Internet has grown considerably in recent years, this spanning health-related and educational content as well as that commonly labelled pornographic (Barak and Fisher, 2003; Fisher and Barak, 2001). Further, 'pornography' on the Internet encompasses a considerable range of 'adult content', with no easy line to be drawn between sexual content, often experienced as pleasurable, liberating or therapeutic, and pornography, generally regarded as degrading and exploitative.[1] The range of pornography available on the Internet varies enormously, from the equivalent of top shelf magazine images to content that is otherwise highly restricted or, indeed, illegal.[2] Pornography also varies from images of consensual sexual activity to violent or non-consensual, including criminal, activity.

Distinguishing types or levels of pornography is highly contested, but the absence of such distinctions is equally problematic, resulting in a lack of clarity about what research has been done and how it can be applied, including confusion even in estimating the amount and availability of online pornography.

Using a random sample of web servers, Orr and Stack-Ferrigno (2001) found adult content accounts for 2.1 per cent of information on the Web. The majority of adult-oriented sites (about 74 per cent) were found to display adult content on the first page (accessible to anyone who visits the page), often through the display of sexually explicit banner advertisements to other sites. Nearly two-thirds (66 per cent) did not include a notice indicating the adult nature of the site, and only 11 per cent included such a notice and also did not have adult content on the first page. About 25 per cent employed practices that hindered the user from leaving the site (e.g., mousetrapping), and only 3 per cent required a credit card or other 'adult check' to proceed past the first page of the site (that is, most sites allow the user to take a 'free preview' in which some additional content is provided).

EFFECTS ON ADULTS

Many would argue that there is little new about the content of online pornography, it seems uncontentious to assert that 'what is most new about Internet sex is its unprecedented access'

(Waskul, 2004: 4). The many previous formal and informal access controls for pornography (from age-restricted access to the sex shop to the embarrassment of buying a top shelf magazine) have all changed now that a vast range of content can be accessed at home with anonymity. Such access, many argue, alters the market, expanding the potential for niche and specialized content addressing any and all sexual tastes. As Waskul puts it, 'the old and the new are reconfigured, sometimes in ways that are predictable and sometimes in ways that surprise' (p. 5). Some welcome this expansion, others deplore it. Hughes (2004) calls the increase in pornography markets across diverse media platforms the 'mainstreaming of pornography', as what was once hidden and, arguably, difficult to find, becomes commonplace, her primary concern being the process of production rather than reception, the latter fuelling the former. As she says, 'The mainstreaming of pornography is increasing the exploitation or abuse of women and children used in making pornography' (p. 110).

The arguments for harm following exposure to pornography on the Internet are reviewed by Thornburgh and Lin (2002) in a report conducted at the request of the US Congress. These arguments draw heavily on the research discussed under 'film' and 'television', for little empirical research exists for the Internet (Helsper, 2005). As they note, the literature is hampered by; (a) the difficulty of inferring cause from observed correlations; (b) the difficulty of extrapolating from studies on college students to the wider public (including to minors); (c) the difficulty of generalizing from experiments to everyday contexts, particularly over longer time scales; (d) the question of whether research on one form of content (e.g. violence) can be extended to sexual content; and (e) the question of whether studies conducted in one country apply in another. As Thornburgh and Lin also point out, impacts can be measured in different ways, and they vary according to gender, special needs, type of exposure, type of content, and so forth. In summary, they conclude that such evidence for harm as exists in relation to exposure to sexual content online remains contested and, many argue, inconclusive, although undoubtedly some of it offends the majority of the population.

Doering (2001) considers the arguments that cybersex is harmful (see also Goldberg, 2004), distinguishing 'pro' and 'anti' arguments thus:

> the victimization perspective interprets cybersex as a heterosexist practice, and focuses on how women and girls as individuals and as a group are harmed by online harassment, virtual rape, and cyberprostitution…The liberation perspective, in contrast, focuses on the options computer-mediated communication offers women and girls who actively seek sexual pleasure online…cybersex frees females to explore their sexualities more safely and to enjoy more sex, better sex, and different sex.

A version of the liberation argument is also made in relation to those with stigmatized identities – for example gay young people enabled to come out to family and friends because of online support. Siding more on the victimization perspective, though acknowledging that cyberspace may accord women in the sex trade greater control, Chatterjee (2005) expresses concern over women's rights, the question of their consent to participate in the cyber-sex trade and their protection from sexual exploitation in this new trans-border market (see also Itzin, 1993, 2002).

The use of the Internet for sexual purposes ('cyber-sex') has begun to get the attention of clinicians (Goldberg, 2004). However, little direct research exists on the potentially harmful effects on adults in general of viewing online pornography, though see the sections below on vulnerable groups.

VULNERABLE GROUPS

An in-depth study of 41 child abusers who worked with children professionally and who are now resident in the Lucy Faithfull Foundation's Wolvercote Clinic found that 51 per cent had themselves been sexually abused as children, and that 59 per cent were aware of their sexual arousal to young children before they were 16 years old. Further, 29 per cent had used the Internet for pornography and 10 per cent to contact children for abuse (Sullivan and Beech, 2004). Similar findings were obtained in the United States (Wolak, Finkelhor, and Mitchell, 2005). The study does not consider whether the Internet facilitated the abuse in any way, though it does suggest that the Internet has become part of the lifestyle of an abuser.

Another study, in which over 7,000 individuals responded to an American survey regarding online sexual activity, helped identify potential problem areas for online sexual compulsives and at-risk users, suggesting that certain activities could lead to problematic behaviour in three areas: obsession, compulsion, and consequences (Cooper, Delmonico, Griffin-Shelley, and Mathy, 2004). Although not specifically concerned with pornography, a much smaller sample of twenty self-identified Internet addicts (defined as uncontrollable, distressing, problematic or excessive users) were found to meet clinical criteria (DSM-IV) for 'impulse control disorder' (Shapira, Goldsmith, Keck Jr., Khosla, and McElroy, 2000). Other research suggests, however, that the main predictor of use of online pornography is the prior use of offline pornography (Fisher and Barak, 2001).

EFFECTS ON CHILDREN

One study mapping online pornography identified much that is upsetting or embarrassing for children (Feilitzen and Carlsson, 2000), although Sutter (2000) raises some questions about whether inappropriately sexual or pornographic websites are experienced as problematic for young people and their families. Across Europe, 18 per cent of parents/carers state that they believe their child has encountered harmful or illegal content on the Internet (Eurobarometer, 2006)[3] – the UK figure is 15 per cent. Ofcom's 'Media Literacy Audit' (on children – 2006) found that 16 per cent of 8–15 year olds have come across 'nasty, worrying or frightening' content online.

In the study of young people in the United States by Wolak, Mitchell and Finkelhor (2006), more than a third of the young people interviewed (34 per cent) say they have seen sexual material they had not sought out – this is a significant increase from the previous study in 1999 when one-quarter had said the same. Nearly one in ten of the sample (9 per cent) said they had been distressed by the material they had seen.

The UK Children Go Online Project (Livingstone and Bober, 2004; 2005) surveyed a national sample of 1,511 9–19 year olds in 2004, together with 906 of the parents of 9–17 year olds. Evidence of harm is difficult to ascertain in a self-report survey for methodological and ethical reasons. In focus groups, children and young people held some lively debates over whether pornography was welcome or why, for many, it was not. Annoyance and disgust seemed to be more frequent reactions than being upset, and girls had especially negative reactions to being sent it, or shown it, by boys they knew (for example, having it displayed on computers at school). In relation to potentially harmful and offensive content online, the children's survey found that:

- 57 per cent had come into contact with pornography online, mostly unintentionally through pop-ups (38 per cent), junk mail (25 per cent) or email from someone they know (9 per cent), though 10 per cent had visited pornographic websites on purpose. Age makes a sizeable difference – overall contact with pornography jumping from 21 per cent among 9–11 year olds to 58 per cent among 12–15 year olds, 76 per cent among 16–17 year olds and 80 per cent among 18–19 year olds. 12–19 year olds claimed to be much more likely to see pornography on the Internet than on television (52 per cent), video (30 per cent) or magazines (46 per cent).

- Further, 10 per cent of Internet users between 9 and 19 years old had sought out pornography on the Internet on purpose, this being only 1 per cent of the 9–11 year olds but 26 per cent of the 18–19 year olds and only 3 per cent of girls but 17 per cent of boys aged 9–19. A substantial minority of the older teens also circulate pornography among themselves or those they meet online. Again, more boys than girls do this: 14 per cent of 9–19 year old boys have been sent pornography from someone they know but only 3 per cent of girls.

- The survey respondents, asked in a private self-completion section of the questionnaire, reported mixed reactions to online pornography: of those Internet users who go online at least weekly and who have come into contact with pornography on the Internet 54 per cent claim not to be bothered by it, 14 per cent disliked what they saw and 20 per cent were 'disgusted', 8 per cent wished they had never seen it, though 7 per cent thought it was interesting and 7 per cent enjoyed it.[4]

- In short, half of those who see pornography online claimed not to be bothered by it, and a small minority even positively like seeing it. However, a significant minority did not like it, one-fifth claiming to have been disgusted. Girls and younger children were more likely to say this: 22 per cent of girls said they didn't like it (8 per cent of boys), and 35 per cent thought it was disgusting (10 per cent of boys). 18 per cent of 9–15 year olds didn't like encountering pornography online compared with 8–9 per cent of 16–19 year olds, and 25–28 per cent of 9–15 year olds thought it was disgusting compared with 12–16 per cent of 16–19 year olds.

- There might be reasons why children claim not to be bothered by pornography when in fact they are bothered. There might be reasons why children claim to be bothered when they are not. Wanting to be 'cool' would account for under-claiming, and so one might be sceptical that as many as 54 per cent claim not to think too much about encountering online pornography. On the other hand, it is even less likely that children would exaggerate their concern in a survey suggesting, therefore, that the disgusted one-quarter of 9–15 year olds (one-fifth of 9–19 year olds) represents something of an underestimate of the population about which one might be concerned and for which policy-initiatives may be required. Interestingly, nearly half (45 per cent) of the 18–19 year olds who have seen pornography (on any medium) consider that they were too young to have seen it when they first did. We may conclude that a sizeable minority of children and teens have seen an upsetting or disgusting image, although the majority have either not seen or not been concerned about what they saw online.

Earlier, in the United Kingdom, the Kids.net survey found that in 2000, up to a quarter of children aged 7–16 years old may have been upset by online materials and that few reported this to an adult (Wigley and Clarke, 2000). According to the Cyberspace Research Unit in 2003, 5 per cent of 8–11 year olds admitted to accessing porn sites often, 22 per cent sometimes, and 73 per cent said they never did this (O'Connell, 2003a; O'Connell, Price, and Barrow, 2004). In a small survey of secondary school pupils in 2001, Allbon and Williams (2002) found that 45 per cent (60 per cent of boys and 28 per cent of girls) had encountered unpleasant or offensive material on the Internet, though only 14 per cent said their parents had discussed possible online threats with them. Over half the children were unconcerned about such exposure, considering that adolescence is a fair time to find out about racism, violence and pornography.

Surveys in other countries have found a similar incidence of pornography exposure. A Canadian survey of parents by the Media Awareness Network suggested in 2000 that one in five children have found undesirable sexual material online (2000). The American Kaiser Family Foundation 2000 survey found that one in three 10–17 year olds have seen pornography online (2000), and 12 per cent of 12–19 year olds admitted looking at sexual content in the US 2003 Digital Future survey (UCLA, 2003).

The European SAFT survey in 2003 found between a quarter and a third of 9–16 year olds had accidentally seen violent, offensive, sexual or pornographic content in the previous year: 12 per cent had accidentally ended up on a pornographic website (20 per cent of 13–16 year olds, 19 per cent of boys), mostly through typing in the wrong address, though 9 per cent had visited such sites on purpose (16 per cent of 13–16 year olds, 16 per cent of boys) (SAFT, 2003). While girls aged 9–12 years old were mostly upset by it and wished they had never seen it, boys aged 13–16 years old said they did not think too much about it or thought it was funny. These figures are considerably greater than the 4 per cent of 8–13 year old Dutch children who have seen pornography on the Internet (Valkenburg and Soeters, 2001); this could be due to the younger age group, earlier survey year, or a culturally different definition of pornography in the latter study.

A survey of 300 Spanish youth (12–25 years old) and their parents (2006) found that 37 per cent had seen pornographic websites, mostly accidentally (Grupo para el Estudio de Tendecnias Sociales, 2006). The ICTS National survey of 1,561 teenagers (13–18 years old) and 1,080 of their parents in the Netherlands (2005–6) found that 46 per cent have seen sexual images online, 39 per cent violent images, and that girls are more bothered than boys (Duimel and de Haan, 2006). In Poland, an online survey of 2,559 12–17 year olds (2006) reported the highest figures found, suggesting that risks can be high in a country which has only recently acquired mass access to the Internet, and also suggesting the incidence that may pertain in the absence of widespread safety guidance.[5]

- 71 per cent of Internet users found pornographic websites, mostly by accident.

- 51 per cent had encountered violent content, again mostly by accident.

- 29 per cent encountered xenophobic or racist content.

The Irish Webwise survey (2006) found that 35 per cent of 9–16 year olds in 2006 had visited pornographic sites; 26 per cent had visited hateful sites (mostly boys).

A smaller but still significant study in the Netherlands of over 700 adolescents aged 13–18 years old found that 71 per cent of males and 40 per cent of females had been exposed to some sexually explicit material in the previous six months. The researchers, Peter and Valkenburg (2006) suggest that for boys this correlates with their desire for sexual experiences through other media, among other attributes. With girls, the more sexual experience they have, the less such content is sought. The research also suggests that exposure to sexually explicit online content affects recreational attitudes towards sex (respect for women, regarding sex as unrelated to love or relationships, estimation of 'normal' sexual behaviours, etc.), especially among male adolescents and especially if they think the perceived realism of the online communication is high.

In Sweden, Haggstrom-Nordin, Sandberg, Hanson, and Tyden (2006) conducted an in-depth study of eighteen participants, suggesting that respondents can differentiate between the sexualization of such content and the intimacy of actual relationships. On the other hand, Shim, Lee and Bryant (2007: 71) found that 'those who were high both in sexual and antisocial dispositions reported being more likely to expose themselves to unsolicited sexually explicit material than all others'. They also review research findings (among the adult population) regarding harmful effects of exposure to violent pornography (desensitization, callous attitudes towards women, compulsive/addictive sexual behaviour, etc) (see also Itzin, et al., 2007, which similarly concludes that those exposed to extreme pornography may be more at risk of developing pro-rape attitudes or even committing sexual offences).

In Australia, Flood (2007) found three-quarters of a sample of 200 Australian teenagers reported accidentally having seen either pornographic or sexually explicit material on websites. However, Flood acknowledges that there may have been problems in defining and distinguishing between pornographic and sexually explicit content and so the findings of the study cannot be analysed further. An earlier survey of 16–17 year olds (Flood and Hamilton, 2003b) had reported that 38 per cent of boys but only 2 per cent of girls have searched the Internet for sex sites, although 60 per cent of girls (and 84 per cent of boys had had accidental exposure to explicit sex on the Internet). The authors note strong concern from parents and they suggest, though do not directly examine, a range of possible consequences of such viewing, from distress and disgust to an increased sexual callousness or tolerance for non-consensual sexual activity. One review argues that online pornography can affect the development of sexuality: 'children and teens can and do develop compulsive sexual behaviour e.g. masturbation' (Freeman-Longo, 2000).

The Children's Digital Media Center concludes that American children live in an 'all-pervasive sexualized media environment' in which the Internet especially routinely exposes teenagers to adult/explicit sexual and pornographic content, both on websites and in teen chat rooms (Greenfield, 2004). As Nightingale (Nightingale et al., 2000: 55) put it:

> the expansion of internet access to children has considerably extended the range of explicit, formerly 'adults only' media materials in circulation. The past reliance by adolescent boys on magazines, videos and postcards to discover and share the mysteries of sex has been superseded by access to lurid internet images of pornography and bestiality.

The EU-commissioned Eurobarometer focus group study (2007), which interviewed children aged 9–10 and 12–14 years old in 29 countries, found that children worried more about viruses, cons and fraud than about harmful content or contact. However, inadvertent encounters with violent or pornographic websites were described as disturbing by a proportion of the children, and the report notes some ambivalence (including curiosity as well as worry or shock) among the children interviewed.

HARMFUL CONTACT

As with other media that permit user-generated content, harm may also arise through peer-to-peer communication on the Internet. Whether the content that is thus generated can be regulated along with mass-produced content, or whether it can be regulated in other ways, remains unresolved. In relation to the Internet, this is both a growing issue and a fast-changing one as the means by which individuals communicate on the Internet is continually shifting (e.g. with the emergence of news groups, chat rooms, blogs, personal websites, message boards, etc. Internet Crime Forum, 2000; IPPR, 2004; Williams, 2001). Some such content is malicious in intent, other content may be harmful through its unintended consequences.

MEETING STRANGERS ONLINE

In the context of growing concerns over paedophile contact, research has investigated children and teens' behaviour in relation to making friends online, particularly when they may go on to meet these 'friends' offline. The EU-commissioned Eurobarometer to conduct focus groups with children aged 9–10 and 12–14 years old in 29 countries (European Commission, 2007). The study, part of a continuing series of research funded by the European Union, suggests that older children feel themselves better equipped than younger ones to engage in risky behaviour (particularly regarding meeting in person strangers met online). The Mediappro study (2006) found that nearly half (47 per cent) of children surveyed say they never talk to people on the Internet that they do not know, and 22 per cent say they do so rarely (by implication, one in three do meet new people online). The Norwegian SAFT (Safety Awareness Facts and Tools) survey of 888 9–16 year olds (2006; see Livingstone, 2007) found that:

- 34 per cent of online chatters (22 per cent of all 9–16 year olds) have been invited to a face-to-face meeting with someone they met online.

- 22 per cent of online chatters (15 per cent of all 9–16 year olds) have met offline someone they first met online, an increase on the 2003 figure, and a behaviour more common among those dissatisfied with friends/school/family, and there is an increase in physical and psychological abuses related to these net meetings.

In the United States, market research conducted by Cox Communications (2007) found that almost seven in ten teenagers (69 per cent) receive personal messages from a stranger. However, 57 per cent say they would ignore messages from someone they did not know while under a third (31 per cent, still a significant proportion) say they would reply. This survey also found that 16 per cent of these teenagers say they would consider meeting someone in person that they had only met online, while 8 per cent say they have done so. We do not know whether sensible precautions were taken, though similar surveys suggest that often young people do not tell an adult when they go to such meetings, though they do often take or tell a friend and, in the vast majority of cases, there are few if any harmful consequences (Livingstone and Bober, 2004).

In Bulgaria, the 'Child in the Net' survey (800 12–17 year olds interviewed offline and 590 online; Mancheva, 2006), finding that:

■ 38 per cent of Internet users met in person somebody they got to know online (11 per cent often).

■ 12 per cent often experienced insistent, persistent and unwelcome attempts to communicate with them (often about sex), and 20 per cent have experienced this at least once.

■ Four in ten are unaware of the risks of meeting online contacts offline.

And in Poland, an online survey (Nobody's Children Foundation, 2006) of 1,779 12–17 year olds and 687 parents found that:

■ 68 per cent of Internet users had been invited to meetings with online friends – 44 per cent of those invited went to the meeting, half of them alone; one in four of those who went to the meeting described the behaviour of the other person as 'suspicious'.

■ Nearly 30 per cent of parents did not consider the Internet a threat to children.

Each of these studies suggests that, while there may be increasing awareness and understanding of the potential dangers of associating with strangers 'met' online, significantly high proportions of young people still do so, and many are confused about the relation between acquaintances, 'friends of friends' and strangers.

Reporting high figures of sexual activity online, the Remco Pijpers Foundation online survey of 10,900 teens under 18 years old in the Netherlands (Pardoen and Pijpers, 2006) focused on social networking. It found that:

■ 82 per cent of boys/73 per cent of girls had flirted online in past six months.

■ One in four boys/one in five girls had had cyber-sexual experiences.

- 72 per cent of boys/83 per cent of girls had received sexual questions.

- 40 per cent of boys/57 per cent of girls had been asked to undress on webcam; one in three boys/one in ten girls did.

- 47 per cent of girls had received an unwanted request for a sexual act on webcam; 2 per cent complied.

- 62 per cent of girls/13 per cent of boys dislike receiving sexual questions online.

- 35 per cent of girls/12 per cent of boys claim to have had a negative experience.

- 9 per cent of girls/3 per cent of boys had posted sexual photos and regretted it.

It is unclear whether this activity took place with strangers or among peers, though the implication is that mainly it was among peers ('friends' and 'friends of friends'). Notably, teens appeared aware of the risk of 'paedophiles' but were unclear about boundaries among teens.

The UK Children Go Online project (Livingstone and Bober, 2004; 2005) found that 30 per cent of 9–19 year olds have made an online acquaintance, and one in twelve (8 per cent) say they have met face-to-face with someone whom they first met on the Internet. Although 6 per cent said the person they met turned out to be different from what they had expected, the majority of these young people tell someone they are going to the meeting (89 per cent), take a friend with them (67 per cent), meet someone of their own age (65 per cent) and, they say, have a good time (91 per cent said the meeting was 'good' or 'okay'). Similarly, a survey among primary school children in England by the Cyberspace Research Unit in 2003 found 54 per cent have never been asked to meet someone they first met in a chat room (12 per cent sometimes, 34 per cent often), but only 3 per cent actually met the person afterwards (O'Connell, 2003b).

Such meetings occur more among older than younger children, and they may be less common in the United Kingdom than in some other European countries. The European SAFT survey of older children (9–16 year olds) in 2003 reported that 14 per cent had attended a meeting (8 per cent of 9–12 year olds, 18 per cent of 13–16 year olds). Only 4 per cent of parents are aware of this. Furthermore, 13–16 year olds pretended more about themselves online than other age groups. In the United States, 24 per cent of 12–17 year old teens have pretended to be someone else in a chat room according to Pew in 2000, 60 per cent have received and 50 per cent exchanged messages with a stranger; more than half (53 per cent) were not worried about this though (see also UCLA, 2000, 2001, 2003).

On the other hand, Peter, Valkenburg and Schouten (2006) conducted a survey among just over 400 teenagers in the Netherlands. They found that the younger respondents in the sample (aged 12–14 years old) were more likely than older adolescents to talk to strangers online. The research also found that those who engage in long chat sessions are more likely to engage with strangers than those who chat frequently for short periods. Thus it was a desire to meet new people and entertainment that was the driver for such interaction, and not that those who visit chat rooms find it difficult to make social contact offline.

Asking how children themselves understand the risks of harmful contact, Burn and Willett (2004) suggest that the chat room paedophile has, for many children, become the new version of the 'bogeyman' who has long served not only as a warning against risky behaviour but also as a means by which children can discuss risk and, thereby, understand the constraints adults impose on their activities. This does not make the risks unreal, though panicky media coverage may undermine the effectiveness of safety awareness messages.

CONTACT BY PAEDOPHILES
Recently, attention has been paid to the circumstances under which these online contacts may make children vulnerable to online grooming. In the United States, law enforcement at all levels made an estimated 2,577 arrests during a twelve-month period from 2000–1 for Internet sex crimes against minors, this being roughly 4 per cent of all sexual assaults against minors (Wolak, Mitchell, and Finkelhor, 2003). Wolak et al.(2005) reported that 40 per cent of arrested child pornography possessors were 'dual offenders' who sexually victimized children and possessed child pornography, with both crimes discovered in the same investigation.

Carr (2004) reviews several such reports of criminal statistics to argue that the incidence of such offences is increased by widespread access to the Internet, and recent UK-based cases are reported in Palmer and Stacey (2004). Eneman (2005) too is concerned that the Internet protects and so facilitates paedophile activity, identifying the regulatory and technological changes underway in relation to online child abuse images circulating within Europe.

Based on interviews by the National Center for Missing and Exploited Children with a nationally representative sample of 1,501 youth, ages 10–17 years old, who use the Internet regularly, the Youth Internet Safety Survey in the United States found that (Finkelhor, Mitchell, and Wolak, 2000):

- Approximately one in five received a sexual solicitation or approach over the Internet in the last year.

- One in 33 received an aggressive sexual solicitation, three-quarters from someone who asked to meet them somewhere, called them on the telephone, or sent them regular mail, money or gifts.

- One in four had an unwanted exposure to pictures of naked people or people having sex in the last year.

- One in seventeen was threatened or harassed.

- Approximately one-quarter of young people who reported these incidents were distressed by them.

■ Less than 10 per cent of sexual solicitations and only 3 per cent of unwanted exposure episodes were reported to authorities such as a law-enforcement agency, an Internet service provider, or a hotline.

■ About one quarter of the youth who encountered a sexual solicitation or approach told a parent. Almost 40 per cent of those reporting an unwanted exposure to sexual material told a parent.

■ Only 17 per cent of the youth and approximately 10 per cent of parents could name a specific authority (such as the FBI, CyberTipline, or an Internet service provider) to which they could make a report, although more said they had 'heard of' such places.

■ In households with home Internet access, one-third of parents said they had filtering or blocking software on their computer at the time they were interviewed.

A large-scale national survey in the United States (interviewing 1,500 young people aged 10–17 years old) conducted by Wolak et al. (2006) repeated a survey previously conducted in 1999. This later survey found that a smaller proportion of respondents say they have communicated online with people they do not know than had said the same in 1999 (34 per cent compared with 40 per cent in 1999), and had received slightly fewer unwanted sexual solicitations (13 per cent vs. 19 per cent). Unwanted solicitations were, however, growing from acquaintances while reducing from strangers. Wolak et al. (2008) have since reported that it is risky online behaviour that makes young people susceptible to inappropriate contact, rather than their use of social networking sites. That is, victims of inappropriate contact respond to overtures made and are thus 'groomed' via the Internet.

Similar research across Europe is now being conducted, revealing variable levels of online risk. A survey of 1,545 12–17 year olds and 1,852 parents in the Czech Republic (2006) found that 49 per cent of 12–17 year olds have made an online contact.[6] Of those:

■ 84 per cent (49 per cent of all teens) have given out their email address (and 73 per cent their picture, 60 per cent their phone number and 23 per cent their home address).

■ 62 per cent were invited to an offline meeting (30 per cent of all online teens); and of those, 66 per cent went to the meeting (20 per cent of all online teens have met an online contact offline), almost 70 per cent going alone.

■ 82% of parents say they inform their children about safe usage of the Internet, though only 39 per cent of children agree that they do.

The introduction of the grooming offence in the Sexual Offences Act 2003 begins to address these kinds of problem in the United Kingdom, although the debate continues over whether the Internet increases, or mediates, existing levels of paedophile activity. The distinction between the activities of paedophiles, and sexual or harassing communication among minors, is often unclear.

For most children and teens online, encountering the former is a rare but dangerous event, but encountering or participating in the latter, while milder in effect, is becoming commonplace. Indeed, further research is needed to track criminal statistics and victim-related data, so as to link this where appropriate to the nature of the victim's Internet (or mobile) use: for example, do grooming-related incidents occur through moderated or unmoderated chat rooms, email, text or instant messaging; what is the role of images – for example involving cameraphones; overall, what patterns may be discerned here, and how are these changing as technologies change and as awareness campaigns begin to impact on children and parents' knowledge of the risks?

In-school surveys in the United Kingdom conducted by the Child Exploitation and Online Protection Centre (CEOP) in 2006 suggest that 25 per cent of children and young people have met offline someone that they first contacted online. The report does not comment on the consequences of such meetings. It does note, however, that 'there is insufficient data to be able to accurately qualify and quantify the threat presented by sex offenders who target children in the online environment' (p. 5). The reports submitted to CEOP from the public suggest considerable concern over grooming, this being the most frequent reason for reporting. CEOP's most recent report comments that:

> it is consistently apparent from the reports that children and young people have often placed themselves at risk online by engaging in risky, cybersexual behaviour that may have incited, catalysed or otherwise facilitated the resulting abuse scenario. (CEOP, 2007: 12)

BULLYING AND OTHER FORMS OF HARASSMENT

An online survey of nearly 500 respondents suggests that online antisocial or 'bad' behaviour is a serious and pervasive problem in a variety of online social settings; respondents perceived that such 'bad' online behaviour occurs frequently and has a strong negative effect on online interactions; that the methods they use to combat bad behaviour are not very effective; and that this may be because a surprising amount is perpetrated by acquaintances (Davis, 2002). Another study found that women were more likely than men to find spam emails with sexual content to be offensive (Barak, 2005; Khoo and Senn, 2004).

A survey in the United Kingdom for NCH (2005) found that a total of 770 youngsters aged 11 to 19 years old were questioned. 20 per cent had been bullied 'digitally' (i.e. via the Internet or mobile phone). Specifically, 14 per cent had ever been bullied or threatened by mobile, 5 per cent in chat rooms and 4 per cent by email. Similarly, the UK Children Go Online project (Livingstone and Bober, 2004; 2005) found that one-third of 9–19 year olds report having received unwanted sexual (31 per cent) or nasty/bullying comments (33 per cent) via email, chat, instant message or text message.

Research is still needed to establish whether this form of bullying is more damaging than or different from face-to-face bullying. Further, nearly half (46 per cent) of children and young people say that they have given out personal information, such as their hobbies (27 per cent), email address (24 per cent), full name (17 per cent), age (17 per cent), name of their school (9 per cent) phone number (7 per cent) or sent a photograph (7 per cent), to someone that they met on the

Internet. In part, this is playful, though no less risky for it: 40 per cent say that they have pretended about themselves online – using, for example, a different name (27 per cent), changing their age (22 per cent), appearance (10 per cent) or gender (5 per cent). And though they often know the rules, a minority (7 per cent) admits to forgetting about safety guidelines online while 17 per cent enjoy being rude or silly on the Internet.

In an online experiment, participants were deliberately ostracized by those with whom they were, ostensibly, playing an online game. It was found that the more participants were ostracized, the more they reported feeling bad, having less control, and losing a sense of belonging (Williams, Cheung, and Choi, 2000). Indeed, Deboelpaep (2006) had found in a sample of young people in Flanders that nearly two-thirds of his sample (64 per cent) described cyber-bullying as a significant problem. In the United Kingdom, the 'MSN Cyberbullying Report' (2006, UK, N = 516) found that 11 per cent of 12–15 year olds had been bullied online (18 per cent girls, 7 per cent boys), 74 per cent told no-one; 62 per cent know someone who's been bullied online; one in twenty admit to bullying someone else online.[7] The NCH Mobile Bullying Survey (2005, N = 770 11–19 year olds) reported slightly higher figures:

■ 20 per cent had been bullied/via text/Internet/email; 73 per cent knew the person; for 26 per cent it was a stranger.

■ 10 per cent had a photo taken of them that made them uncomfortable/ embarrassed/ threatened; 17 per cent of those said it was sent to others.

■ 11 per cent said they had sent a bullying or threatening message to someone.

In Ireland, the Anchor Watch Your Space survey (a survey conducted by members of a youth centre among their peers) showed that 52 per cent of the 375 respondents aged 10–20 years old had encountered bullying on a social networking site, although they themselves had not necessarily been bullied (Anchor Youth Centre, 2007). These much higher figures are echoed in a small study by Li (2005), which cites a number of incidents of bullying through the electronic media. Administering a questionnaire to examine experiences of bullying and cyber-bullying among a sample of 177 students in Canada, Li finds relatively high levels of bullying overall, and of cyber-bullying (although the sample itself is small):

■ Over half of the students (54 per cent) have been victims of bullying and a quarter (25 per cent) have experienced cyber-bullying.

■ Just under a third of the sample (31 per cent) say they themselves have bullied others, and 14.5 per cent say they have used electronic means to do so.

■ 52 per cent of the sample said they knew someone being bullied.

Li asked about the provenance of the cyber-bullies. Of the victims, most (41 per cent) do not know who is bullying them while 32 per cent mention school friends (a further 11 per cent mention the bullies as people outside their schools and 16 per cent mention 'multiple sources'). Further, nearly one-half of bully victims are also bullies and 27 per cent are cyber-bully victims.

Social networking sites were not here highlighted as a means of electronic bullying, but the Anchor Watch Your Space survey specifically concerned bullying on social networking sites. It is unclear whether social networking increases the likelihood of bullying, and more likely adds to pre-existing means – 55 per cent of bullies in Li (2005) said they use 'multiple sources' (NB this was a small sample). Chat rooms are mentioned by over one-third (36 per cent) of this group, with email mentioned only by 9 per cent. Of course, chat rooms – like social networking sites – can offer the element of anonymity, of not knowing who the cyber-bully is, and this is a key issue when possible intervention is being considered.

Smith, Mahdavi, Carvalho, and Tippett (2006) also conducted a small scale study in the United Kingdom among 92 students aged 11–16 years old, administering a questionnaire covering aspects of cyber-bullying. While their study does not examine the issue from as many angles as does Li's, nor do they ask questions of would-be bullies, the trend in many of their findings is similar. That is, they found that:

- Just over one in five students (22 per cent) had experienced cyber-bullying, with girls more likely to be bullied in this way than boys.

- Nearly one half of the sample (46 per cent) say they know of cyber-bullying taking place through the use of pictures/video clips, 37 per cent mention phone calls and 29 per cent mention text messaging.

- Both the use of pictures/video clips and phone calls are felt by respondents to be more impactful on the victim than traditional forms of bullying.

- Much of the bullying comes from a few individuals within the same class or year group (Smith et al. did not examine cyber-bullying from anonymous sources).

The research evidence for cyber-bullying shows that it is a problem, but it is bullying itself that is a bigger problem. The National Bullying Survey (2006, UK, N = 4772) reported that 69 per cent of pupils were bullied in the past year (half of those were physically hurt), of whom only 7 per cent said they had received unpleasant or bullying emails/IM/text messages.[8]

Cyber-bullying is distinctive in that it offers a degree of anonymity to the bully, but a degree of publicity to the victim that is distressing, it affords the use of visual images, as well as hurtful text and words, the bullying message can be quickly spread among a peer group, and the messages may be read in the victim's private and supposedly safe places (their bedroom, on their phone, at home). One of the concerns too, is that personal information contained in chat rooms or social networking sites can be passed on or manipulated by bullies.

Attention is growing to online harassment or 'cyber-stalking', which Bocij argues is qualitatively different from offline stalking (Bocij and McFarlane, 2002). Among a sample of 235 US undergraduates, nearly one in three reported some form of 'unwanted pursuit' on the Internet (Spitzberg and Hoobler, 2002; see also Bocij, 2003; Bocij and McFarlane, 2003a; Bocij and McFarlane, 2003b, 2003c). The students were not always able to cope with these, including the minority who experienced more severe forms of online harassment or pursuit. This survey found a modest link also between online and offline stalking, leading the authors to call for greater awareness of the range of available coping strategies as people face online threats from other members of the public. Further, it appears that an unintended consequence of the design of user registration systems on certain websites (including weblogs) is the facilitation of the spread of personal information that individuals have chosen to make public without fully considering the potential audience.

Nightingale et al. (2000) note the use of online facilities to generate and modify images – for example, grafting a girlfriend's face onto the body of a pornographic model. These and other images generated both curiosity and disgust among the Australian children (10–15 years old) in her study and many had stories to tell of downloading and selling or circulating pornographic images at school, sometimes experienced by girls as harassment.

The SAFT (Safety Awareness Facts and Tools) survey of 848 9–16 year olds in Ireland (2006) found that 19 per cent of chatters were harassed/bothered/upset/threatened online (Webwise, 2006). The US study by Wolak et al. (2006) showed that some 9 per cent of the sample of 10–17 year olds had been subjected to online harassment. 13 per cent of respondents said they had received unwanted sexual solicitations, and 4 per cent had been asked for nude/sexually explicit photos of themselves (see also Mitchell Finkelhor and Wolak, 2007). However, 'close to half of the solicitations were relatively mild events that did not appear to be dangerous or frightening'. While victims are not to blame for such events, it does appear that certain online behaviour (making rude comments, embarrassing others, meeting new people, and talking about sex online with strangers) increases the risk of online interpersonal victimization, suggesting a clear role for targeted safety guidance (Ybarra, Mitchell, Finkelhor and Wolak, 2007).

VULNERABLE GROUPS

Further analysis of the major US survey conducted by the National Center for Missing and Exploited Children (aged 10–17 years old) found that those who reported major depressive-like symptoms were three and a half times more likely to also report an unwanted sexual solicitation online compared to youths with mild/no symptoms, and among youths reporting an Internet solicitation, youths with major depressive-like symptoms were twice as likely to report feeling emotionally distressed by the incident compared to youths with mild/no symptoms (Ybarra, 2004). Note that in this study, it seems likely that depression is both a predictor of unwanted sexual contact and it also exacerbates the distress experienced as a result of such contact.

Further, from the overall sample, 19 per cent were involved in online aggression: 3 per cent were aggressor/targets, 4 per cent reported being targets only, and 12 per cent reported being online aggressors only. Youth aggressors/targets reported characteristics similar to conventional bully/victim youths, including many commonalities with aggressor-only youths, and significant psycho-social challenge. The researchers concluded that youth aggressors and targets (victims) are intense users of the Internet who view themselves as capable Web users. Beyond this, however, these young victims report significant psycho-social challenges, including depressive symptoms, problem behaviour, and traditional bullying (Ybarra and Mitchell, 2004a). The aggressors were also facing multiple psycho-social difficulties, including poor relationships with their parents, substance use and delinquency (Ybarra and Mitchell, 2004b).

Those who engage more with online contact (harmful or otherwise) may be more prone to isolation or depression. A survey of the American public found that those who go online to meet people become more depressed, although those who go online for entertainment purposes become less depressed (Bessiere, Kiesler, Kraut, and Boneva, 2005). Further, an anonymous survey of 50,168 ninth-grade (14 year old) public school students, including over 40,000 with home Internet access and 19,511 who accessed chat rooms, was conducted by the Minnesota Student Survey (Beebe, Asche, Harrison, and Quinlan, 2004). This found that, for both boys and girls, use of Internet chat rooms was associated with psychological distress, a difficult living environment, and a higher likelihood of risky behaviours. Although most chat room users did not report serious problems, this group included a disproportionate number of troubled individuals. The authors conclude that, chat room use serves as an indicator of heightened vulnerability and risk-taking, parents and others need to be aware of potential dangers posed by online contact between strangers and youths. In other words, it is possible that young people who visit chat rooms may be those more inclined to take risks; more research is, once again, needed to understand risk-taking among teens in relation to the Internet and other new media.

It appears that the outcomes of research studies considering sites and forums that deal with suicide are often in conflict. Gilat and Shahar (2007), for example, compared support groups in Israel for potential suicide cases delivered through different electronic forms – telephone helplines, direct electronic communication, and communication through a chat room with other similar people. Their analysis suggests that the third option (the chat room an asynchronous communication process) may be the most beneficial to potential suicides.

> The group offers its participants an intense feeling of affiliation and an experience of emotional support from others. (Gilat and Shahar, 2007: 16)

Their finding is supported by the results of an online survey conducted in Germany by Winkel, Groen and Petermann (2005) which finds that the social support offered by Internet forums is high. However, they do underline the fact that such support is higher in those fora where methods of suicide are not discussed.

McKenna and Bargh (1998) note that the Internet can reinforce group membership among people who belong to concealable marginalized groups (potentially including suicide groups as well as anorexia groups etc.). The ease of online communication among those with unusual or niche interests seems likely to increase the 'support' (both beneficial and harmful) available to such individuals. So, while Alao, Soderberg, Pohl and Alao (2006) review the influence of the Internet on suicide and suggest that it can be a positive tool if used appropriately, they also point to the harms that may occur as the communication opportunities offered by the Internet cannot differentiate between different levels of distress or need.

Taking another approach to vulnerability, an analysis of reported suicide attempts among young people found that sexual orientation, behaviour and identity did not predict suicidal attempt status, but suicide attempters experienced higher levels of both generic life stressors (low self-esteem, substance use, victimization) and gay-related stressors, particularly those directly related to visible (femininity) and behavioural (gay sex) aspects of their sexual identity. Although those who participated in an online support-group were more likely to make suicide attempts, they also had greater life stressors, making the direction of causality difficult to establish (Savin-Williams and Ream, 2003).

Further, an examination of information about self-harming on the Internet revealed that a considerable amount of such information exists, including personal experiences, advice on how to stop, first-aid, and so forth (Prasad and Owens, 2001). Similarly, when searching for suicide-related information, they found a fair amount of advice and support on offer, but little direct information on how to commit suicide. In other words, it seems that for the most part, the information available is well-intentioned, if not always accurate or professional, coming from other users seeking to support the information-seeker rather than to encourage self-harm. Rajagopal (2004) disagrees, identifying an increasing number of websites providing graphic details of suicide methods, while clinicians report on psychiatric cases in which online information about methods of suicide has played a key role (Alao, Yolles, and Armenta, 1999).

Little other evidence on the potential influences and effects of pro-suicide sites was found. However, we note that Bardone-Cone and Cass (2007) examined the effects of viewing a pro-anorexia website. First, they developed a pro-anorexia website, which 'well represented common themes'. A sample of 235 female undergraduates in the United States was then randomly asked to view either that site, a site on home decor or a female fashion site. The researchers found that those viewing the pro-anorexia website displayed more negative attitudes towards themselves than did the two control groups.

From a very different starting point, Orgad (2006) examined the relationship of breast cancer sufferers in the United States, United Kingdom and Israel with Internet-delivered fora that dealt with the illness. While she too, found that sharing experiences could be empowering to patients, she also found that they were particularly lacking as a forum for a discussion of treatments or other objective considerations; for these, patients would have to go elsewhere.

Overall, the balance between the beneficial and harmful consequences of specialist online communities remains unclear. Leung (2007) finds in a study among 8–18 year olds in Hong Kong that the Internet is often used for 'mood management' and social compensation during stressful periods. Support offered both offline and online remains important and can be aided by the opportunities offered by the Internet.

Valkenburg and Peter (2007) hypothesized that their results would show that the Internet was negatively associated with the well-being of adolescents aged 10–19 years old in the Netherlands. What they found, however, was that it is communication with strangers that has a negative relationship with well-being, while communication with friends, especially positive communication, has a beneficial effect on the well-being of adolescents (see also Valkenburg, Peter and Schouten,

2006). They did not examine support groups in their study so those mechanisms of interaction are still unknown in relation to feelings of well-being. Thus Meads and Nouwen (2005) suggest that their review of emotional disclosure (not Internet specific) is not conclusive in terms of its perceived benefits.

Mishara and Weisstub (2007) review the legal and ethical difficulties of controlling sites that may be considered pro-suicide. They note that one of the key difficulties is the lack of absolute research evidence, although media reports proliferate:

> These case reports do not meet the requirements for scientific proof that internet sites cause suicide, but they suggest that a relationship may exist. (Mishara and Weisstub, 2007: 59)

In relation to Internet gambling, Griffiths (2003; Griffiths and Parke, 2002) argues that it is not simply that societal gambling has moved to the Internet, but rather that the widespread accessibility of the Internet, along with its affordability, anonymity and convenience increases the incidence of gambling and, hence, gambling-related problems such as addiction.

HATE CONTENT ONLINE

Much hate speech is produced by individuals or groups rather than being professionally produced. Since industry self-regulatory codes of practice seem not to apply to such speech, and since individuals appear less inhibited about online than offline communication, the potential for offensive content online appears unrestricted (whether or not it falls within the law). For example, Willard (2003) examines 'harmful' online speech (for example a student-created website, blog, email or bulletin board) produced by school pupils. By 'harmful', she includes speech which is defamatory, constitutes bullying, harassment, discrimination, discloses personal information, is offensive, vulgar, derogatory, and so forth. Case histories in the United States are reviewed, showing that although schools attempt to discipline pupils for such speech, even when it occurs away from school premises, the First Amendment protects pupils from such disciplinary action.

Several groups catalogue the proliferation of hate sites on the Internet (The Simon Wiesenthal Center and Hate Watch; see also Bronkhorst and Eissens, 2004a; Bronkhorst and Eissens, 2004b; Thiesmeyer, 1999). In the United States, hate activity online is protected by the First Amendment, although it is illegal in France, Germany, Sweden and Canada. Different countries take different approaches to protecting human rights in the face of the rise of hate speech over the Internet (Vick, 2005).

Some American scholars have asked whether such material can be regulated using obscenity legislation.[9] For this, three conditions must be met for material to be judged obscene:

> The average person, applying contemporary community standards 'would find that the work, taken as a whole, appeals to prurient interest?; 'the materials must depict or describe, in a "patently offensive" way, sexual conduct specifically defined by applicable state law'; and 'the work, taken as a whole, must lack serious literary, artistic, political or scientific value'. (Leets, 2001: 299)

Although it has been objected that, for the (global) Internet, no relevant community can be identified by which to establish community standards, Leets asks how ordinary people respond to such material and in relation to what community standards, if any. Further, since the US courts do accept a restriction on free speech if it incites 'imminent lawless action' (similar to the United Kingdom's incitement to racial hatred legislation), she also asks how ordinary people respond to inflammatory speech – do they see this as mere hyperbole or as an incitement to imminent lawless action?

She thus invited a sample of 266 people of mixed age, ethnicity and religion to read and evaluate one of eleven white supremacist web pages, examining both of these questions and also asking people how harmful they consider these sites to be. The findings showed that although people consider themselves to be more tolerant than they consider others in their community (consistent with the 'third-person effect'), they did consider the sites to lie outside community standards, seeing the hate pages to be 'moderately harmful to themselves' and to 'society at large' (this was the view more of non-white than white respondents) and, further, to be lacking literary, artistic, political or scientific value. However, they did not consider the sites directly to advocate lawless action, being more inclined to see them as expressive or cathartic. That they also considered that the sites might incite (though not advocate) lawless action shows how difficult it can be to relate public opinion data relating to harm and offence to the regulatory or legal frameworks designed to address these. Indeed, they considered that since they did not consider the sites persuasive to themselves (though they did think them persuasive to other people), they judged that the sites should be protected by the First Amendment.

In a second study with 108 teenagers (average age 16 years old), Lee and Leets (2002) found that hate content online was persuasive in changing inter-group attitudes under certain conditions (of narrative, explicitness, intensity, etc.). The UK Children Go Online survey of 9–19 year olds (Livingstone, Bober, and Helsper, 2005) found that 9 per cent had accidentally visited a website that is hateful to a group of people and 2 per cent had visited one on purpose, 11 per cent in all, these figures being higher among frequent Internet users. A further 31 per cent of 9–19 year olds who use the Internet at least once a week have seen violent or gruesome material online. As with online pornography, half claim not to have been bothered but 27 per cent were disgusted and 16 per cent disliked what they saw. In general, the younger children surveyed (9–11 year olds) are less likely to have encountered undesirable content, but more likely to be upset when they do.

Leets' research is interesting partly because the design of these studies of harm and offence has been tailored to ask questions that specifically address precise points of law or regulation at issue. This contrasts with the majority of the research reviewed here, where an inferential gap generally exists between the conception of harm and offence in the research (or the public mind) and the conception of harm and offence as defined by policy and regulation.

As in other domains of putative harm, some groups collect case evidence associating specific violent or criminal acts with particular media contents – for example, the association between racist Internet sites and specific cases (Bronkhorst and Eissens, 2004a, 2004b). Notwithstanding the disturbing nature of some of the content identified, the difficulty in these cases is; (1)

determining whether such content increases (or merely shifts the organization of) harmful or criminal actions offline and; (2) whether regulation is required for the media content itself, given that such harmful or criminal acts as ensue are already covered by law. Blazak (2001) argues that the Internet plays a key role in increasing hate group activity (though not necessarily hate crimes), this pointing to the growing problem of user-generated harmful and offensive content. The Internet is, arguably, neutral in this regard, for it can bring together marginalized groups, encouraging what has been termed 'identity demarginalization' (McKenna and Bargh, 1998), of many kinds (e.g. for gay individuals to 'come out' in a supportive group, or for those promulgating race hate to come together).

SOCIAL NETWORKING

IDENTITY

This is the area of the Internet that has been most researched in the years since the first edition of the literature review. Research on social networking sites has concentrated on the fixed Internet, although these are also available on mobile telephony as a delivery platform. There are differences in the principal sites used – in the United Kingdom, Bebo (and then MySpace[10]) is currently more popular while in the United States much of the research has looked at Facebook, among others, partly because of relative popularity and partly because US research tends to concentrate on university students (who use it). There is more research on the risk of harm associated with social networking sites (raising issues of privacy) than with content uploaded onto user-generated sites such as YouTube (NB these are increasingly populated by 'professionally' produced material).

The Joint Information Systems Committee in the United Kingdom commissioned the market research organization, MORI, to conduct an online survey among 500 16–18 year olds who hope to go to university, and a small qualitative project (IPSOS MORI on behalf of JISC, 2007). Among the research findings relating to the use of information and communication technologies as a learning tool, was the finding that:

- Only 5 per cent of this sample claim never to use social networking websites; 65 per cent use them regularly.

- Three-fifths (62 per cent) use wikis, blogs or online networks; 44 per cent maintain their own blog or website.

- Only a fifth (21 per cent) is part of an online community such as Second Life.

- The group thinks technology is very important to their social lives but not a substitute for face-to-face interaction.

A study by the UK communications regulator, Ofcom (2008), noted almost half of children aged 8–17 years old had set up their own profile – 27 per cent of 8–11 year olds say they have done so, despite the fact that the minimum age of entry to most such sites is 13 years (14 years on MySpace).

A survey in the United States conducted as part of the ongoing Pew Internet and American Life Project in late November 2006 (Lenhart and Madden, 2007) found that more than half of all teenagers in the United States who have access to the Internet use social networking sites. Of these most (66 per cent) say their site is restricted or 'private'. Frequency of use is high with nearly half of the sample (48 per cent saying they visit the site at least once a day. There is a clear gender bias with 70 per cent of older girls (15–17 year olds) more likely to have used a social networking site and created online profiles, while just over half of the boys have done so (54 per cent say they have used a social networking site while 57 per cent of boys say they have created an online profile).

As we will see echoed in other surveys, the Pew Internet survey finds that most young people (91 per cent) use social networking sites to stay in touch with their circle of friends; 82 per cent say they stay in touch with their wider circle.

Table 6.2 Teens and friends on social networking sites.

What are the different ways you use social networking sites? Do you ever use those sites to...?

	Yes (%)	No (%)
Stay in touch with friends you see a lot	91	9
Stay in touch with friends you rarely see in person	82	18
Make plans with your friends	72	28
Make new friends	49	50
Flirt with someone	17	83

Source: Pew (2007: 5).

Hargittai (2007) suggests that the choice of social networking site used may increase both digital and social inequality. Digital inequality is a consideration as those who do not have access to the Internet at a friend's or family members' home are far less likely to use such sites. Further, Hargittai finds that high and low social status users in the United States cluster together around certain sites.

Hinduja and Patchin (2007) undertook a content analysis of publicly available, but randomized, MySpace profile pages (N = 2423) produced by those under 18 years old. On average they found that teenage users of the profiles they surveyed have 65 friends. They also examined the frequency of visiting the sites and found that about one-third of users had not logged on in the three months prior to the coding period. Over a third (38 per cent) had logged on in the previous three days. The researchers question, therefore, the suggested high frequency of use of these sites as a staple for young people. In contrast with the Lenhart and Madden findings above, Hinduja and Patchin find that a smaller percentage of users, about 40 per cent, restrict access to their site.

In the Anchor Watch Your Space survey in Ireland, 82.5 per cent of the sample of 10–20 year olds say they have used social networking sites, and 36 per cent are daily users. The difference in gender found is a difference in the length of time of each session in the site, with girls more likely to spend more time on the sites. Within the sample 15 per cent say they have more than one profile. This survey found that 71 per cent of the respondents have not set their profiles to private – this is a higher proportion, the researchers say, than that found either in the United Kingdom or United States. They suggest this is a technical issue related to the complexities of the architecture of Bebo, the most popular social networking site in Ireland.

A search of the literature (Livingstone, 2008) shows certain trends in the way social networking sites are used:

■ Most contact on social networking sites is with people known to the user, or with whom there is a shared interest.

■ There is some evidence that while social networking sites are displacing certain forms of electronic communication such as emails and chat rooms, other forms of communication are being developed (such as instant messaging) although direct contact is still preferred.

■ The distinction between online and offline communications becomes less clear as technologies are increasingly incorporated into daily life.

■ For young people such as teenagers, social networking sites allow them to take 'safe' risks or to use the risks as opportunities to test various adolescent behaviours.

Livingstone (2008) interviewed a small number of British teenagers (sixteen teenagers aged 13–16 years old) in an ethnographic study exploring their use of and behaviour within social networking sites. She found that the technologies did not in fact sustain the needs and desires of these teenagers. They had a sophisticated gradation of friendship and this was poorly supported by the social networking sites they used, as these generally do not permit distinctions among levels of friendship or intimacy.

Mesch and Talmud (2007) in Israel found that relationships developed offline are stronger than those created online, again supporting the view that online interactions are not seen by respondents as replacements for offline relationships. Other research also suggests that these technologies are used to enable social relationships – and that the entire variety of devices available is used. Participants in Dwyer's study (2007) in the United States switched between devices and communication systems as they wished. Similarly, Ellison, Steinfield and Lampe (2007) show that social networking sites in the United States are used to develop social relationships and may be a positive force for those who otherwise have weak ties with people on the site they used (in this case the site studied was Facebook).

As this report is concerned mainly with harm, this is not explored further here but it does underline the finding that users of social networking sites tend to communicate and interact predominantly with those within their social circle, although the radius of that circle is rather wider than it might be in an offline world. In short, social networking sites have a definite place in the lexicon of social interaction by providing insights into, for example, one's own identity through the actual presentation of self and through the way in which the network of relationships (of which such sites are one node) is developed:

> Each profile gains its meaning from the network to which it is connected and these links provide the basis for trust. (Livingstone, 2008)

Livingstone finds that teenagers present themselves in different ways, based on their ages. Younger participants present 'a highly decorated, stylistically elaborate identity' while older participants aim to create 'a notion of identity lived through authentic relationships with others'. The creation of these identities, she argues, contains an element of risk which public policy may try and manage.

Boyd and Heer (2006) also conducted ethnographic studies on the profile segment of the social networking sites, Friendster. They found that the presentation of one's self is determined and given structure by the identities of those with whom one is connected.

The previously mentioned issues of verifiability and anonymity are also studied by Boyd (2004). She describes the growth of 'Fakester', a false set of 'friends' collected on Friendster sites, which grew out of frustrations with the site's technological difficulties. As a result it is often unclear who is and is not 'real' on Friendster, Boyd argues, which can lead to confusion at best.

The value of social networking sites is clear, both as an entertainment tool and as a way of creating and giving oneself identity. Importantly the identities and profiles presented are generally constrained by social expectations. However, teenagers will continue also to practice what Hope (2007) calls 'boundary performance' risk-taking activities to push normative boundaries, something that is often publicly performed rather than performed in secret, as part of the process of identity construction. Moreover, even when the potential misuse social rules or norms are quite well-understood, they are not always acted upon.

PRIVACY

Definitions of what it means to be private appear to have been changed by social networking sites. Certainly teenagers in Livingstone's (2008) research keep much of their personal information and communication private and their interactions are determined by social mores. Yet they nonetheless share what might be thought of as 'intimate' information with many hundreds of people that they know very casually, if at all. Barnes (2006) in a discursive article also refers to the potential exploitation of young people's privacy which they may have given up, unwittingly:

> Currently social responses to privacy in social networks do not tend to deal with the potential misuse of personal information. Instead the response is based on the protection of children against predators, which is only one aspect of the privacy paradox. Similarly, a legal response has been the proposal of a bill to protect underage children. The government and industry responses tend to focus on the issue of predators and this focus distracts from the actual privacy issue – the social behavior of teenagers on the internet and the use and misuse of their private information. (Barnes, 2006)[11]

A recent survey from Get Safe Online (2007) found that

> Over 10.8 million people across the UK are registered to a social networking site. Of these, one in four have posted confidential or personal information such as their phone number, address or email, on their online profile, making them vulnerable to identity fraud. The research also found that 13% of social networkers have posted information or photos of other people online without their consent. This trend is strongest amongst younger users, with 27% of 18–24 year-olds admitting that they have posted information, photos of other people without their consent online.

Similarly the Information Commissioner's Office in the United Kingdom launched a website on information rights, which includes advice for young people about how they should use social networking sites (2007). The advice follows survey research conducted by the Office that showed that over half the young people surveyed, aged between 14 and 21 years old, do not have privacy settings on their entire site so as to attract new people to their sites.

A large-scale online market opinion study (of nearly 2,500 adults) among potential employers and Internet users in the United Kingdom conducted by YouGov (2007) found that:

- 15 per cent of 18+ year olds say they have posted 'personal information' on MySpace, 7 per cent on Facebook, 3 per cent on Flickr, 6 per cent on YouTube, and 3 per cent on Wikipedia.

- There is a definite effect of age with a greater proportion of 18–24 year olds having posted such information – 45 per cent of 18–24 year olds say they have posted personal information on MySpace, 44 per cent on Facebook and 17 per cent on YouTube.

- 19 per cent of respondents have posted holiday pictures online.

- 19 per cent have a profile on a social or business social networking website.

- 11 per cent have written a personal online blog.

- 54 per cent of 18–24 year olds say images of them had been posted online without their consent.

Just fewer than one in five potential employers (18 per cent) say they have found information about job candidates that had not been volunteered. (The study did not ask if employers always or often searched for information about potential employees as a matter of course.) James (2008) refers to the potential damage that can be caused to the privacy of both the individual and companies through the careless exposure of information.

Ofcom (2008) points to a range of potentially risky behaviours, especially where personal privacy is concerned. These include:

■ Leaving privacy settings as default 'open' – 41 per cent of children aged 8–17 years old who had a visible profile had their profile set so that it was visible to anyone. 44 per cent of adults who had a current profile said their profile could be seen by anyone (this was more likely among those aged 18–24 years old).

■ Giving out sensitive personal information, photographs and other content – this included details such as their phone number, home address or email address. Younger adults are even more likely to do this, with 34 per cent of 16–24 year olds willingly posting this information.

■ Posting content (especially photos) that could be reputationally damaging.

■ Contacting people they didn't know (and/or didn't know well) online.

■ Accepting people they didn't know as 'friends'– 17 per cent of adult users said they talked to people on social networking sites that they didn't know and 35 per cent spoke to people who were 'friends of friends'.

Ofcom goes on to say:

> Our qualitative research indicates that some people are more likely than others to engage in potentially risky behaviour. This suggests that communications about the implications of potentially risky behaviour may need to be looked at in different ways for different groups of people.

Hinduja and Patchin (2007), cited above, sought to examine empirically what information young people are posting about themselves and if this justified the concerns about the increase of sexual predation on these sites, or other forms of victimization. The key finding was that a substantial minority of young people (almost 40 per cent) set their profiles to 'private' so that visitors to their sites had to be invited in initially. However, this leaves just under 60 per cent that did not do so. Within this majority the researchers outline the content of the profiles:

■ 81 per cent listed their city.

■ 28 per cent listed their city and school.

■ Under 9 per cent included their full name.

■ 57 per cent included a photograph of themselves.

■ 5 per cent of these were seen in a swimsuit or underwear.

■ 18 per cent admitted to use of alcohol.

■ 8 per cent admitted to using tobacco.

■ 2 per cent admitted to using marijuana.

While Hinduja and Patchin accept that these overall percentages might be lower than anecdote would suggest, they do say that '26 per cent of the youth in the sample listed the school they attend and included a picture of themselves. This information alone could easily be used to contact the individual offline'. (Hinduja and Patchin, 2007: 14). Alcohol, tobacco and marijuana use are just three of many possible behaviours mentioned online which might also be used to harm teenagers' reputations or career prospects in later life. They also accept, as we have seen above, that it is difficult to verify the accuracy or veracity of the profile pages – and this of course remains a prime concern of those involved in the consideration of the protection of (particularly) minors from harm.

INAPPROPRIATE CONTACT

Smith used the Pew Internet and American Life Project (as did Lenhart and Madden above) to look at the contacts made by subjects who create profiles on social networking sites (Smith, 2007). Smith found that 7 per cent of this American sample said they had been contacted 'by a stranger who made them feel scared or uncomfortable'. Teenage girls (the sample was aged 12–17 years old) are more likely than boys to say this (11 per cent and 4 per cent respectively). Further, those who have posted photographs are far more likely to experience this (10 per cent compared with 4 per cent who had not posted photographs) although the absolute proportions are small. The survey found that nearly a third of the sample have been contacted by a stranger; again girls are more likely to say this than boys (39 per cent and 24 per cent respectively). Smith does note that there appears to be no consistent association between stranger contact and the type of information posted (other than photographs) or between stranger contact and the public/private nature of the profile. It is also noted that teenagers who say they use social networking sites to flirt are more likely to be contacted by strangers – which is perhaps not surprising.

Boyd (2006) found that teenagers in the United States are aware of adults on their sites, but that they ignore them. Their attention is taken by those whom they 'know' and for whom they are trying to look cool: 'Having to simultaneously negotiate youth culture and adult surveillance is not desirable to most youths, but their response is typically to ignore the issue'. So these teenagers may post pictures of themselves scantily clad or drunk, but these are images designed for their peers, not for the adults who may happen upon them. These subjects in the research are not able to fast-forward to the possible regrets they may have about these images at a later date, as – Boyd suggests – adults might.

In a study of video blogging, Lange (2007) notes that women who share levels of intimacy through their video blogs feel they are connecting with other people and with other people's ideas. The video blogs allow communities to be formed and for experiences to be shared.

The research evidence shows that social networking sites are used widely and are used to support and maintain relationships, although not generally to create them. However, a significant proportion of young people communicate with strangers online and post material about themselves which may be considered 'private' in most circumstances. The ability to restrict access to sites is known about but not always used.

We note, finally, that a position paper recently released by ENISA (European Network and Information Security Agency, 2007) outlines a series of commercial, corporate and social/individual 'threats' raised by social networking sites. They describe the threats in technological terms and raise the issue of the difficulty of deleting entries, identity theft as well as cyber-stalking and cyber-bullying. Their recommendations to combat the effects of these potential threats include raising awareness and increasing the transparency of data handling practices so that users understand the way in which content is stored and may be used.

USER-GENERATED CONTENT

There is little currently in the research world on the use of user-generated content sites such as YouTube, and much of the data are anecdotal. However, such content is placed firmly within discussions of 'participatory culture' which surround the newer uses of the Internet, including social networking but also online multi-player gaming and other forms of interaction such as instant messaging. Some of the privacy risks for user-generated content sites resemble those of social networking, and are exacerbated by the facility to submit such content under a pseudonym.

Marwick (2007: 2) looks at the structure of YouTube as a form of 'democracy', which she says refers to 'increased participation or increased access to previously unavailable channels of communication'. Like Keen, above, she questions this democratization. While Keen questions the ability to verify information in the blogosphere and goes on to discuss the intellectual property rights of professional content creators, Marwick argues that most major user-generated content sites – YouTube in particular – are essentially commercial, offering advertisers new ways of reaching their target groups. Her content analysis of articles about YouTube in websites belonging to newspaper organizations offers an insight into some of the issues that affect the more negative types of material, citing examples of racist and misogynistic content available. Here she argues that the self-rating system of choosing or rejecting material has no power because 'utopian rhetoric about internet democracies falls apart when communities of practice are populated with people for whom bigotry is an acceptable practice' (Marwick, 2007: 25). This is clearly an area where further research is required.

Viegas (2005) surveyed online weblog (blog) authors, asking about their attitudes towards privacy. (Viegas accepts this is a self-selecting sample and may not be typical of bloggers as a population.) One of the key findings of this study is that while bloggers are increasingly creating their own guidelines about what is and is not acceptable, the fact that they have little or no control over their readership creates considerations of privacy. A number of respondents (36 per cent of the sample) reported having found themselves in difficulty as information in their blog became known. Of the 24 per cent of respondents who said they edited entries posted on their sites, most belonged to a blog system (LiveJournal) that has technological features to allow a degree of control over those that access the site.

The article is useful in defining the characteristics of blogging such as the fact that blogs are:

archive-oriented. Instead of substituting new materials for old ones, as is normally done on regular web pages, the idea with blogs is to add postings frequently, creating an ever-growing compilation of entries…The mounting compilation of postings serves as context for readers of blog sites. (Viegas, 2005: 3)

In his article on the psychology of sex, Noonan (2007) refers to the empowering nature of blog sites as information becomes available to many, rather than a select few. However, as with many online developments, more research is needed into the motivations and activities of young bloggers in relation to the potential for harm.

ACCESS CONDITIONS

In its consultation document on children's programming, Ofcom (2007) notes that time spent on the Internet increases with age, with 12–15 year olds spending an average of 10.5 hours per week online. The report notes that 'a comparison with Ofcom's "Media Literacy Audit" among children 8–15 years (2005) shows that time spent online has increased significantly from 1.8 hours to 5.0 hours per week for 8–11 year olds and from 4.6 to 10.5 hours among 12–15s'. Children who use the Internet at home were asked about the activities they undertake online, as the chart below shows.

The chart shows that the ways in which the Internet is used increases in range with age, and the 12–15 year olds in the sample have significantly higher levels of usage across all aspects than the 8–11 year olds.

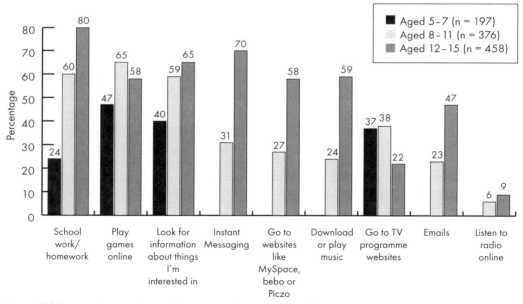

Base: Children aged 5–15 who use the internet at home. *Source:* Ofcom's Young Peope's Media Usage Survey, saville rossiter-base, April/May 2007.

Figure 6.1 Uses made of the Internet at home at least once a week, by age of child.

The 'Media Literacy Audit' (Ofcom, 2006) had found that about half of all parents with Internet access at home have put some kind of blocking or filtering in place on their computers to stop their children viewing certain types of websites. Of those who have not done so, the age of the child was the variable which drove such a decision, with parents of older children thinking they did not need to make such provision.

Mitchell, Finkelhor and Wolak's (2003) national survey of American teens aged 10–17 years old, cited above, found that 25 per cent had had unwanted exposure to sexual pictures on the Internet in the past year, and a quarter of these said they were very or extremely upset. The use of filtering and blocking software was associated with a modest reduction in unwanted exposure although research shows that parental attempts to reduce exposure through supervision or monitoring are not associated with any reduction in exposure, highlighting the difficulty of domestic regulation of potentially harmful media (Livingstone and Bober, 2006; Mitchell et al., 2003). This may be partly because the design of search engines permits exploitation by producers of pornographic content, making accidental exposure by minors commonplace (Machill, Neuberger, and Schindler, 2003).

Pew Internet research, in a survey of 1,100 12–17 year olds and their parents, found that more than half (54 per cent) of American families with teenagers use filters to limit access to potentially harmful online content, up from 41 per cent in 2000 (Lenhart, 2005). The filters tend to be used by parents who themselves are frequent users of the Internet and who have middle school-age children. Parents who have older children and who are less tech-savvy are less likely to use filters. Nonetheless, most teens and parents believe that teens do things on the Internet that their parents would not approve of: 81 per cent of parents of online teens say that teens are not careful enough when giving out information about themselves online and 79 per cent of online teens agree with this.

In the United Kingdom, a YouGov survey of 1,200 British parents for Comet/NCH in May 2004 found that 63 per cent say they have no parental control software on their home computer, and 64 per cent allow their child to use the Internet unattended. This is partly because children want privacy when using the Internet, and partly because they lack the technical expertise to install it (Livingstone and Bober, 2004; 2005). Further, blocking software has negative dimensions (Finkelstein, 2000) – the American Medical Association reports that on the most restrictive settings tested, 91 per cent of pornography, but also 24 per cent of health information was blocked (Richardson, Resnick, Hansen, Derry, and Rideout, 2002).

Indeed, even though adults are very concerned about the Internet as a threat to children's safety (Ofcom, 2005f), particularly by contrast with television (seen as both more familiar and safer), the UKCGO project found that many parents are unsure how to regulate their children's Internet access at home: 46 per cent claimed to have installed filtering software and 30 per cent monitoring software, but 18 per cent had not, and 23 per cent did not know. Indeed, only 15 per cent of parents claimed to be good at installing a filter. The survey asked both parents and children about domestic regulation, with parents claiming more rules and monitoring than appears to be recognized by their children. Taking the parents' responses, it seems that 81 per cent show an interest in what their child does online, 63 per cent keeping an eye on the screen, 57 per cent offering some help, 50 per cent staying in the same room, 41 per cent checking the computer later, 32 per cent sitting with the child, and 25 per cent checking their email. However, the children's survey found that two in three children valued their privacy online and so were concerned about their parents checking up on them, many of them taking some evasive action.

Children and parents do not see eye to eye, it seems, regarding Internet-related rules, children frequently not recognizing that their parents have established a rule, and one in five parents report getting annoyed about their child's Internet use. Reassuringly, 61 per cent of children say they would tell their parent(s) if something on the Internet made them uncomfortable, this including 71 per cent of 9–11 year olds (though a fair minority, by implication, would not). Of those who had received pornographic junk mail, however, only 8 per cent told either a parent or a teacher.

Looking internationally, a Eurobarometer survey (2004) surveyed over 16,000 people over 15 years old across the European Union in November-December 2003. It found that across Europe, 24 per cent of parents set rules for their child's (aged 0–17 years old) Internet use, compared with 42 per cent setting rules for television, and these rules include restricting sites they can visit (60 per cent of those who set rules), limiting time spent online (52 per cent), banning giving out personal information (49 per cent) or visiting chat rooms (32 per cent).

In Australia, a national telephone survey of 502 children (aged 8–13 years old) and their parents found that parents' main concern was with online pornography (40 per cent), while children were more concerned about security issues. Few parents (10 per cent) or children (1 per cent) reported a concern about violent material online (Australian Broadcasting Authority and NetAlert Ltd, 2005). Only one-third of parents, though nearly two-thirds of children, reported that children have encountered a 'negative experience' on the Internet, including 40 per cent who had accidentally visited a website their parents 'would prefer them not to see'.

There are many difficulties – in practice and in principle – with filtering technology. Esler (2005) stresses the dangers of embedding social choices (and prejudices) into filtering technology and the dangers of restricting children's access to the range of information online leading to a focus on normative/commercial culture. As Banks (2003) points out when comparing freedom of access to information in print and online, one key difference lies in the push/pull of conditions of access. Libraries do not generally subscribe to pornographic magazines (or neo-Nazi information, or pro-anorexia content) and nor is there a call for them to do so on the grounds of free speech. But when a deliberate intervention is required in order not to access pornography, as with filtering and blocking on the Internet, librarians must address the free speech argument. So too for parents at home: previously, they made choices about what to bring into the home (the same even applies for boys smuggling in pornographic magazines), but increasingly they must make choices about what not to bring home. Choice and censorship are not so easy to separate.

The consequences of mismanaging choices – failing to install a filter, lacking the competence to block a television channel, not noticing an age-warning – must also be considered and are, again, different in the new media environment. Before, consumer ignorance or confusion meant people might miss out on possible content, and they could (i.e. voluntarily) take action to discover and remedy this. Increasingly, consumer ignorance or confusion means people are faced with unexpected and possibly unwelcome content and contact, (i.e. the choice has been lost), and so they must take action to discover and remedy this if they intend to retain their choice over what comes into their home. In the first case, inertia means missing out (hence, concerns over digital or social inclusion and inequality). In the second case, inertia means unwanted inclusion in a culture not of one's choice. Both confusion and inertia are persistent features of consumers' daily lives.

Summary

- The widespread accessibility of the Internet, along with its affordability, anonymity and convenience is seen by many to increase the likelihood of media harm and offence. While some argue that there is little new about online content, familiar contents merely having moved online, others disagree, expressing concern about the accessibility of more extreme forms of content that are, potentially, harmful and offensive.

- Arguments regarding adult access to potentially harmful content are the least resolved. As many defend online pornography (mainly as regards adults) as suggest it to be harmful, though there is a growing body of research – though still small – suggesting such content to be particularly harmful for vulnerable groups, specifically people who are sexually compulsive and/or sexual abusers. Carr (2004) makes a similar argument in relation to child abuse, as does Hughes (2004) about pornography in relation to negative or hostile attitudes to women. Griffiths further argues that online gambling creates a sense of escape, or immersion and dissociation and, consequently, of disinhibition from everyday norms that proscribe gambling – again, a similar argument can be advanced in relation to engagement with online pornography.

- Methods for researching online content are still being developed. The lack of clear definitions of levels or types of pornography, violence, etc. on the Internet, where the range is considerable, impedes research, as do (necessarily) the ethical restrictions on researching the potentially harmful effects of online content, especially, but not only, on children. Thus there is little sound evidence demonstrating harm in relation to online content. The possible exception is research on vulnerable groups – specifically, people who are sexually compulsive and/or sexual abusers. While many researchers assume that effects similar to those noted in other chapters of this review will occur if the same material (from television, games or film) is encountered online, this is not a distinct line of empirical inquiry.

- For children, despite the lack of evidence (and the lack of research) on harm, there is a growing body of national and international research on children's distress when they accidentally come across unwelcome content online. This is high on parents' agenda in terms of their expectations of regulators, and they struggle to understand how to take preventative action themselves. Research on the potential harm from online content includes some studies on the effects of viewing pornography or violent content though, since the research is rarely experimental, it is unclear exactly what content is at issue. Some researchers are concerned that such content is more extreme than that generally available on other media. Since this raises ethical issues, particularly when researching the risk of harm to children, there are difficulties in calling for more research here.

■ Most research regarding potential Internet-related harm relates to risky contact rather than content, primarily that involving interaction with other Internet users. The research suggests that such contact may put users at risk of harm, either directly (as in meeting strangers in dangerous situations) or indirectly, from the consequences of their online behaviour. This includes everything from the school or workplace bully to the grooming of children by paedophiles. It has become evident that many children and adults experience some risky contact. Further, research shows that when people – adults and children – receive hostile, bullying or hateful messages, they are generally ill-equipped to respond appropriately or to cope with the emotional upset this causes. Similarly, parents are unclear as to how they can know about, or intervene in, risky behaviours undertaken – deliberately or inadvertently – by their children. As for online content, the consequences of exposure seem to be more harmful for those who are already vulnerable.

■ Some phenomena are very recent, especially regarding the uses of social networking sites. For social networking especially, the issue of verifiability and anonymity is a problem. A significant proportion of young people communicates with strangers online and post material about themselves which would be considered 'private' in most circumstances. The ability to restrict access to sites is known about but not always used. Thus, knowingly, some young people give away inappropriate (private) information publicly (allowing access to 'anyone'). However, it seems likely that many more also do so inadvertently, as a result of limitations in both Internet literacy and interface design. This leads to concerns about the possibility of underestimating the unanticipated or future consequences of making private information public, especially since it appears that many young people have an inadequate understanding of the long-term consequences of publishing such information.

■ The risk of inappropriate contact (especially in relation to sexual predation), harassment and bullying (including the easy dissemination of harassment or bullying content to others in the network) represent significant and growing policy-concerns when considering the regulation of the Internet. Research suggests young people may be aware of the risks, especially regarding social networking sites, but this awareness of these issues and problems is not always translated into action. Thus there is growing evidence that, notwithstanding their many advantages and pleasures, social networking sites permit young people to create profiles that expose the individual or that ridicule or harass others, that using such sites for extensive periods of time (as is common) may isolate users of these sites from contact with 'real' people, albeit only for a few, addicted users.

■ The picture for hateful content is rather different. Although people regard this as offensive, they are also inclined to be tolerant, on the grounds of freedom of expression. By and large, however, little is known about how recipients (rather than the general public) feel about such content – for example, how do the targeted groups (mainly, ethnic minorities, gay groups, etc.) respond?

■ In general, the case for further research seems clear, firstly in relation to the characteristics of vulnerable groups (including strategies for intervention) and secondly in relation to the ways in which the Internet seems to support or facilitate certain kinds of harmful peer-to-peer activity. Further, little or nothing is known about how young people respond to hateful content, especially in terms of how the targeted groups (mainly, ethnic minorities) respond. Nor is much known regarding the use of niche sites – such as those that promote suicide or anorexia, though research is beginning to accumulate here.

■ We note that most research on possible harm and offence occurs in the context of already regulated media. Research on television violence, for example, tests the influence of content produced and broadcast within a nationally-specific, highly regulated environment and an established culture of viewer expectations that also sets limits on what can be broadcast. To put the point another way, there is no evidence on the harm that television could give rise to in a differently regulated (or unregulated) environment, if very different kinds of content were to be broadcast.

■ For the Internet, things are very different. When asking about the harmful effects of exposure to Internet content, one is asking about the effects of any and all kinds of content that the human mind can construct. The same might be argued for print, with two exceptions. First, the Internet, unlike the print market, is not (yet) organized into mainstream and specialist outlets – a simple search may bring 'specialist' content to anyone, often by mistake. This point relates both to the different nature of the distribution systems and to the importance of media literacy on the part of the public in knowing what they are looking for and evaluating what they have found (see also the chapter on advertising below). Second, print is subject to national regulation through the law, something difficult to apply to Internet content since so much originates from other countries.

■ The EU consultation on online technologies for children discusses consumer detriment, and we found other references to, for example, infringement of privacy as data are collected from Internet traffic and used by advertisers or marketers but neither of these issues is considered in this update. The EU consultation also made a number of suggestions of areas for future research, suggestions with which we would agree:

☐ The importance of the broader context for the consequences of online communication and the need for longitudinal studies.

☐ To need to improve the understanding of risk in the relationship between online/offline worlds.

☐ The impact of online incidents: how the use of online communications complements abuse through traditional methods; more data on types, methods and rates; and tracking of online child abuse incidents.

☐ Identifying which types of websites attract both children and sexual predators.

☐ The (emerging) link between depression and grooming, in both abuser and abused.

☐ Risks evolving into actual harm to children; the precise nature of harmful consequences.

☐ Measuring the level of trust in trans-generational communication.

☐ Auditing online content aimed at children. (European Commission, 2007: 9)

NOTES

1. Although we do not here consider illegal content (particularly, child abuse images), there are some parallels in the arguments regarding the ease of access of potential or actual abusers to pornographic content that fuels and extends their interest and, therefore, likelihood to abuse; there are also parallel arguments regarding the relation between a market for images online and the stimulation of the activities, often abusive/criminal that lie behind the production of those images (Arnaldo, 2001; Eneman, 2005; Taylor and Quale, 2003).

2. For example: 'Tentacle hentai offers the telegenetic signs of the most perverse and debased sexualities. It opens for fantastic examination a sexuality that transgresses all "simulated" moralities of the "real" world where tentacle sex between nubile girl-women and cloned boy-men monsters are the order of the day – a monstrous sex feast of the most abnormal acts: pedophilic bestiality, sex with machines, sex with cyborgs. sex with dangerous protruding tentacles and. of course, an endless stream of the most debasing, brutal and humiliating rape images.' (Dahlquist and Vigilant, 2004: 99–100).

3. Eurobarometer Survey (May 2006) Safer Internet, Special Eurobarometer 250 / Wave 64.4, Brussels. Sample of adults reporting on a child (<18 years old) they are responsible for in the household (N = 7560).

4. Since respondents were permitted multiple responses to this question, these percentages do not add up to 100 per cent.

5. See http://www.childcentre.info/projects/internet/saferinternet/poland/dbaFile14112.pdf

6. Gemius (2006). *Children safety on the Internet. Final report for Czech Republic*. http://www.saferinternet.cz/data/articles/down_124.pdf.

7. MSN (2006) *MSN Cyberbullying report*: MSN. See http://www.msn.co.uk/customercare/protect/cyberbullying/Default.asp?MSPSA=1

8. Bullying Online (2006) *The National Bullying Survey 2006: The Results*. See http://www.bullying.co.uk/young_people/National_Bullying_Survey_2006/index.aspx

9. As the authors note, online pornography includes a wide range of explicit and violent material. They list websites offering images grouped in categories such as 'Ethnic black bitches', 'Fatties getting fucked', 'lolita', urination and defecation, rape-focused websites (usually depicting the use of restraints and images of pain), and so forth.

10. See www.nielsen-netratings.com/pr/PR_052306_UK.pdf.

11. Barnes, S.B. (2006) (ibid), also expresses concern about marketers' use of private information teens make public on such sites: 'Marketers who target teen consumers can use stated, personal information gathered from social networking sites for purposes other than what users intend. Today, the commoditization of information has made it necessary to consider the invasion of privacy by corporations.'

7

TELEPHONY

INTRODUCTION

Mobile telephony is the area of fastest growth within the scope of our review, at least in the public mind at present. Changes are wrought constantly, not just through technological developments instigated by the industry but also by users, taking up and extending the potential of the processes on offer. Ling's (2004) *The Mobile Connection* traces the history of the development of mobile telephony as well as the development of the fixed-line telephone and its functions. Our review of research did not find any projects that looked at the issue of harm and offence with regard to content delivered through the fixed-line environment. Indeed, there are increasing numbers of conferences and academic publications relating to the use of mobile telephony and its hypothetical or actual effect on society, but there is little empirical evidence about the impact of the technological advances being made.

Policy-makers and industry are turning their minds to the possibilities that developments in the mobile world might bring, without the benefit of evidence, but by hypothesizing from other industries – specifically, the Internet as the new mobile technologies offer access to the world-wide-web through the handset. In particular, concerns – and research – have centred on the protection of children. This review does not deal with the debates about the possible harm to the physical health of young people, but with issues of harm and offence created through access to content delivered in this way.

Research relating to mobile telephony overlaps with that on the Internet, raising issues connected to the social possibilities offered by the technology (3G+). Clearly, mobile telephony is now becoming part of pre-teen armoury, engaging far younger age groups than noted previously. This is likely to permit greater freedoms from parental restrictions and supervision, and raises new problems of cyber-bullying. However, there is little evidence to suggest that the Internet part of mobile telephony is being widely used (for reasons of cost as much as anything).

The Oxford Internet Survey 2007 noted that 88 per cent of Britons used a mobile in 2007, in comparison with 75 per cent in 2003, and almost all Internet users have a mobile (97 per cent) (Dutton and Helsper, 2007). Over two-thirds of non-users of the Internet (69 per cent) also have such a device. The survey found a significant increase in the percentage of mobile phone owners using the device to take photographs (60 per cent in 2007 compared with 38 per cent in 2005). Sending photographs was measured for the first time with 44 per cent of the sample doing so. Text messaging remains the most common use of the mobile telephone (after voice calls, not noted) at 83 per cent of this sample.

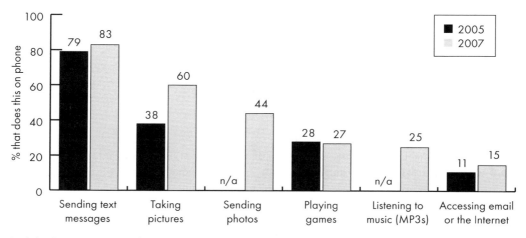

Mobile phone users – rest of text not clear.

Figure 7.1 Use of Features on Mobile Phones (QH18), Oxis survey.

Haddon undertook a review of the academic research for Vodafone. He noted that different studies lead to different conclusions about, for example, the prevalence of cyber-bullying by mobile telephone, although he does not dispute that such bullying is problematic. Indeed, he notes that 'in terms of perception there is some evidence about the specificities of cyberbullying, although the figures are not high' (Haddon, 2007: 16). Further, Haddon notes that use of the cameraphone is generally positive and leads to positive social interaction. However, he cites research that records some children's discomfort in having their photographs taken or sent. The report for the Anti-Bullying Alliance by Smith et al. (2006), cited above, noted too that bullying using phone pictures and video clips had more impact on the victim and was seen as more traumatic than traditional forms of bullying. What Haddon points out is that more research is required to be able to speak about the potential for harm from bullying via the mobile telephone, for example, in comparison with other forms of bullying: 'there is actually little systematic research to…check if different types of cyberbullying are actually experienced as being more pernicious than physical bullying or direct verbal bullying' (Haddon, 2007: 15).

The European Commission organized a Forum on 'Child Safety and Mobile Phones' to discuss the ways in which children and young people could be protected from harmful and illegal content. The Forum was called in the knowledge that the Commission would put forward proposed revisions to the TVWF Directive, extending it to cover all audio-visual content, including that delivered via 3G technologies. Some limited research was presented (primarily about usage) but the importance of the Forum – and the reason for mentioning it here – is that it set the agenda for the discussion of these issues. It also highlighted, therefore, areas for future research. Within the meeting, speakers spoke of the particular characteristics of mobile telephones, including:

■ Their high penetration levels, especially among the young.

■ The uniquely private relationship between the mobile telephone user and the device.

■ The levels and types of usage made of mobile telephones.

The Forum discussed some of the pre-emptive actions that can be taken (and have been in some countries) to ensure the protection of children from inappropriate or harmful content as well as unwanted contact with strangers. Discussion was held about:

■ The creation of industry-wide codes of practice.

■ Age verification processes.

■ Personal Identification Numbers (PINs) and other access control systems.

■ Content classification, being pursued in some countries.

■ Whether access to 'adult' content should be provided on an opt-in (as in the United Kingdom) or an 'opt-out' (as in several other EU countries) basis.

■ Contractual relationships between the mobile service provider and parents, for example, where permission is given for personal information about children to be held (as in location-based services).

The report from the European Union consultation on child safety and mobile phone services, which draws on the Forum quotes extensively from the responses received.[1] While not quoting the direct source, the report states that most child safety organizations mention the risks of grooming and sexual discussions through mobile and other Internet chat rooms and gaming, and provide examples of such cases:

> One child safety association mentions that 'the private and personal nature of the device has meant that it has featured in most, if not all, of the grooming cases in the UK as the technology used in the "last phase" of the grooming process'. The same association states 'there have been cases where the predator has sent the child credits for their phone (or indeed a handset itself) in order to maintain personal and secret communication'. (EU 2007: 5)

A number of other concerns, such as excessive use, or the downloading of pornographic material, are referred to but these have been covered in earlier parts of this report. There is relatively little research from the United States in this area as mobile telephony is not as widespread a phenomenon as it is in other parts of the world. In Australia the regulatory authorities have moved quickly in terms of providing information to parents and carers about cyber-bullying, as well as other forms of 'e-crime'.[2-3]

THE MARKET

Across the world, from just 11 million subscribers in 1990, the number of mobile cellular subscribers grew to 1.8 billion by the end of 2004; an annual average growth rate of 44 per cent compared to just 6 per cent for fixed telephone line subscribers. By 2002, there were more mobile subscribers than fixed-line subscribers. The market is still growing and in some countries more people have access to mobile telephones than fixed-line.[4] In the United Kingdom, 10 per cent of households were mobile-only households — that is the same proportion as are fixed-line-only households (Ofcom, 2007).

The 2005 'Mobile Youth' report suggested that one in three children under the age of 10 in the countries surveyed has a mobile telephone. In the United Kingdom the average age for acquiring a telephone has dropped to 8 years old; while in the United States it is 12 years old (World Wireless Forum, 2004). It is this young demographic that creates concern. Issues around child safety and the mobile telephone begin with the particularly private nature of the device and the fact that it is far more difficult to know what a child is doing with the handset and with whom they are talking or communicating. There is little way for a guardian to check what is happening. This situation has been more acute with the dominance of pre-pay in the market (estimated at 70 per cent of the market in the United Kingdom), which means that billing data are not available to the parent, for example, as would be the case in a contract-based model. However, mobile network operators are making it increasingly attractive to users to have contracts so this may change (Ofcom, 2006).

In addition, financial considerations come into play. There is some concern among observers about the development of premium subscription services that are particularly attractive to children and young people (Mayo, 2005). For example, the spend on ringtones in western Europe is estimated to be $478.0million in 2005, and a further $55.5million will be spent on mobile games (World Wireless Forum, 2004).

SOCIAL IDENTITY AND SOCIAL INTERACTION

Most of the studies considered for this review (Ling, 2004; Ling and Yttri, 2002; Reid and Reid, 2004; Silverstone, 1994; Vincent, 2004; Wilska, 2003) have looked at the role mobile telephones play in constructing young people's identities, within their families and among their peers.

> Adolescence is a period during which individuals develop their identity and sense of self-esteem. In this context, it is possible to suggest that the adoption of the mobile telephone is not simply the action of an individual but, rather, of individuals aligning themselves with the peer culture in which they participate. This is perhaps more true of the mobile telephone than of other adolescent artefacts since the mobile phone is, in the first instance, an instrument for mediated communication. In addition, the cover, the type, and the functions are a symbolic form of communication. These dimensions indicate something about the owner. Finally, the very ownership of a mobile telephone indicates that the owner is socially connected. (Ling, 2004: 85)

Key to this level of 'social connection' is the use of texting, prevalent among young people. According to the Mobile Data Association (n.d.), UK mobile phone users sent 2.6 billion text messages in June 2005, 24 per cent higher than in the same period in 2004. In the first six months of 2005, over 15 billion person-to-person text messages were sent in the United Kingdom and the MDA expects 30 billion text messages to be sent during 2005, compared with 26.2 billion in 2004.

The popularity of text messaging is ascribed to 'the immediacy, mobility and perpetual accessibility' it offers (Reid and Reid, 2004). Some studies suggest that constant access to mobile telephones is breaking down social structures and norms (Berelowitz, 2004; Ling and Yttri, 2002), and may be interfering with interfamilial processes. Reid and Reid investigated the text use of nearly 1,000 respondents and found, using sociability and other psychological measures, that text may open new forms of communication and socializing to people who might not otherwise experience such forms of sociability. The study defined people as 'texters' and 'talkers' and noted that those who use text more often than talking face-to-face were more insular in terms of personality characteristics. However, texting offered them other ways of developing and maintaining relationships with those they sent texts to that were beneficial to them. The researchers suggest these were more 'profound' relationships than those experienced by 'talkers'.

For a discussion of the use of mobile telephones in another country and their role in maintaining social networks, see Horst and Miller (2005) on the use of mobile phones in Jamaica. They argue that the rapid uptake of mobile telephones among low income Jamaican households reflects the complementary nature of the technology with other prevalent forms of social networking.

CONTENT

Although a range of media content (e.g. games, music, 'adult'/pornographic content, advertising, etc.) is now being developed for the mobile telephone market, little or no research is yet available regarding the nature of its use or, especially, the possible harm or offence to which this may give rise. Currently, the only data available about these sectors of the mobile telephone market are market projections. There is some debate within the areas of music and advertising about consumer detriment, but these are not the subject of this research review into the evidence for content-related harm and offence.

It may be hypothesized that concerns may be raised in these sectors about the psychological effects of content delivered through mobile telephony. These concerns may relate to areas such as accidental access, or indeed inappropriate intentional access, to content that may be harmful, such as certain forms of Internet-delivered material. While there are no data currently available for such access through mobile phones, Livingstone and Bober (2005) found that over half of children and teenagers aged between 9 and 19 years old have viewed pornography on the Internet, in most cases, unintentionally.

SECURITY AND PERSONAL CONTACT

For many parents the main reason for giving their children mobile telephones is so that they and their children can keep in contact. It becomes emblematic of security (Ling, 2004). It should not be thought that this is the sole reason for purchase of mobile telephones – primary school children aged 10–11 years old in the United Kingdom suggested that the majority of them (80 per cent) had initiated the phone purchase (Davie, Panting, and Charlton, 2004). However, the private nature of the mobile telephone means that the risk of grooming by paedophiles migrating from chat rooms in the fixed-internet environment to contact through mobile telecommunications may become an issue.

In Japan more people access the Internet through mobile phones than through fixed- line Internet. There has been a significant expansion of dating sites, in particular, which often have a young demographic. There is a concern though, that young people underestimate the dangers that may occur through meeting with strangers. A study of junior high school students (aged 13–15 years old) in Japan (Benesse Educational Research Institute, 2002) noted that while a quarter of the sample of students were aware that it is 'very dangerous' to meet strangers contacted via the telephone or magazines, this awareness diminished with increasing age, presumably as children felt more able to 'look after themselves' when meeting with strangers.

Location-based capabilities may mean that it is possible to pinpoint the exact location of children and young people (Green, 2001). While this may be welcomed by parents keen to know where their child is at all times, it also presents risks of misuse. There is a danger that the technology can be circumvented for purposes such as tracking a child for inappropriate contact. To this end a self-regulatory Code of Practice has been developed which 'seeks to balance usability with safeguards in a proportionate and reasonable manner', allowing children to exercise rights to privacy and consent while protecting them from potential harm.

BULLYING AND OTHER FORMS OF ABUSE

The Children's Commissioner for England, Dr Aynsley-Green, stated in November 2005 that most children have been the subject of bullying at some time. Research conducted for the Department for Education and Skills in 2003 showed that 50 per cent of all primary school-age children and over 25 per cent of secondary school children said they had been bullied in the previous year (Oliver and Candappa, 2003).

The technical capabilities of 3G phones mean that young people may be sent inappropriate images or videos, or be encouraged to send back images or videos of themselves using integrated cameras. The integration of cameras within mobile phones may also result in photographs of children and young people being taken and circulated or posted on websites without their knowledge or permission. However, as with many facets of the mobile telephony arena, it is important to note that there is little academic research data available about aspects such as bullying and that such research will be relatively time-sensitive in that cameraphones are not yet ubiquitous.

Nonetheless, in certain countries, such as Norway, measures are being taken now by the industry against a severe form of abuse – images of the sexual assault of children. Access to websites known to contain such images is being 'blacklisted' or blocked. Other studies show harm – or discomfort – may be caused to children and young people through the inappropriate use of texts or cameraphones. Davie, Panting and Charlton's study of children aged 10–11 years old showed that

17 per cent said that they had received frightening messages while 7 per cent said they had received threatening messages and 4 per cent rude messages (see also Charlton, Panting, and Hannan, 2002; Davie et al., 2004). While the sample is small, it is clearly indicative of a trend of perceived risk.

Similarly, a market survey commissioned by the children's charity NCH and Tesco Mobile (2005) showed that 14 per cent of young people aged 11–19 years old had been the subject of text-bullying. In addition, the survey asked the sample if 'using their mobile phone camera, has anybody ever taken a photograph of you in a way that made you feel uncomfortable, embarrassed or threatened?' 10 per cent had had that experience, and, of that group 17 per cent feared that the photograph had been sent on to others. This phenomenon of sending on humiliating still or video images has recently been the subject of much debate and has been referred to as 'happy slapping', although charities have since denounced the term saying such misuse of the technology is a form of severe bullying and assault. Victims of such abuse are certainly harmed among their peer groups and in terms of their own self-esteem, and the industry and law enforcement agencies are working together to raise awareness of ways of combating mobile phone bullying.

A study in Norway showed that, in comparison to the United Kingdom, a smaller proportion of 14–15 year olds (5 per cent) had been photographed by mobile telephone in the shower or cloakroom at school. While boys had been photographed slightly more often than girls (5.5 per cent compared with 5 per cent), the pictures taken of girls were significantly more likely to be published on the Internet (26.5 per cent) compared with those of boys (6.5 per cent) (Auestad and Roland, 2005). The NCH/Tesco study also found that 11 per cent of the sample said they had sent a bullying or threatening message to someone else. In another study, nearly two in five respondents aged 11–21 years old said they would feel *comfortable* texting unkind things about other people (Haste, 2005). Similar results were found in New Zealand where 23 per cent of users said they had received an offensive, pornographic, abusive or threatening text or picture – and 34 per cent of this group did not tell anybody about this. 14 per cent of phone users say they have sent such texts or pictures themselves – and this rises to 46 per cent of those who have received such material (Netsafe, 2005).

In their paper, Strom and Strom argue that 'electronic bullies hide behind the mask of anonymity…because digital bullies lack face-to-face contact with their victims, they may not know the amount of suffering imposed and consequently not experience feelings of regret, sympathy or compassion' (Strom and Strom, 2004). Brin proposes a system for 'registered pseudonyms' so that users could, in general, retain anonymity but their identities could be determined 'in an emergency' (Brin, 1998). Strom and Strom go on to describe five other ways in which cyber-intimidation works, using case studies to illustrate their point:

■ The transmission of text and videos is particularly damaging to the victim. Auestad and Roland found that 27 per cent of respondents said they had a fear of being photographed by mobile camera phones (Auestad and Roland, 2005).

■ It is less easy to trace cyber-bullies.

■ There are issues of jurisdiction and enforcement – it is unclear what powers a school may have, for example, over a student who is texting threatening or inappropriate messages from outside the school to someone inside it.

■ Children are reluctant to divulge they are being subjected to such bullying. 28 per cent of those who had been subject to 'digital bullying' in the NCH study said they had not told anyone about it.

■ There is a concern that little can be done about such intimidation – in the United Kingdom it is now seen as a form of assault and can be reported to legal authorities, but this is a fairly new process (2005).

■ When asked in a marketing-focused research study what they did when they received text messages from an unknown person, nearly two in five (38 per cent) 14–17 year olds said they read the text and replied, while a further 31 per cent read but did not reply (QA Research, 2005). One in five (21 per cent) say they ignore the text and delete it straight away. While the report suggests texting is an efficient way to target this age group with marketing messages, it does raise issues about inappropriate or unwelcome contact from strangers.

SUMMARY

■ There is growing evidence that mobile telephony can cause harm through the creation of fear and humiliation by bullying, for example. Although it is evident that new communication technologies are being incorporated into practices of bullying, harassment and other forms of malicious peer-to-peer communication, it is not yet clear that these technologies are responsible for an increase in the incidence of such practices, partly because we lack sound historical data against which to make comparisons.

■ Research on the ways in which mobile phones are incorporated into everyday social interaction does, however, point to the relative convenience and ease of use which, combined with highly personalized, private and often anonymous conditions under which these technologies are used, does suggest that cyber-bullying and cyber-harassment may introduce new kinds of problems for users, as well as exacerbating old ones.

■ In some ways, it seems, online and offline communication work differently; but in key ways also, they work together, with, for example, online bullying or harassment continuing or extending offline, rather than remaining entirely distinct. Given the difficulties faced by parents in understanding how to manage the conditions of access to these forms of content and contact, the implications for regulation may be judged differently; in terms of balancing the responsibility for controlling access and exposure across the industry, regulators, parents and children.

■ There is little other substantive academic evidence for the harms or offences caused through access to the mobile content market, although inferences are being made about such possible effects from other media.

■ It is questionable whether mobile technologies are used in the same way as other media and if they should be considered in the same way as other, fixed, technologies. The research evidence suggests that the mobile telephone has many pro-social effects – encouraging young people who may not easily communicate to find new forms of social interaction. Indeed the benefits of mobile technology are many, (including economic); as a social tool; as a creative tool; as a form of security for parents/carers and children; as an entertainment source; and as a measure of one's social identity.

■ Some of the debate about mobile telephony rests on which regulatory models are the most appropriate and which will be the most effective at protecting children. This includes technological developments designed to restrict access to inappropriate content, such as PIN mechanisms, opt-in and opt-out systems and age verification processes. The EU Forum on Child Safety underlined the importance of public awareness-raising initiatives and of ensuring that there is informed decision making about mobile content, not a 'moral panic'.

NOTES

1. European Commission (2007) Summary of the results of the public consultation 'Child safety and mobile phone services'. http://ec.europa.eu/information_society/activities/sip/public_consultation/public_consultation_mob/index_en.htm
2. http://www.decs.sa.gov.au/docs/documents/1/CyberBullyingECrimeProtec.pdf
3. http://www.netalert.gov.au/home.html
4. www.vodafone.com/africa, for example.

8

RADIO AND MUSIC

The academic literature on radio is relatively sparse, most of it focuses on music listening, and it rarely touches on matters of harm and offence. Rather, other than analyses of the political economy of radio production and distribution, most attention is focused on the social and cultural place of radio in everyday life. There is, however, a fair amount of policy/regulator-originated literature on the regulation of radio. In many countries the importance of radio lies in its ability to bring otherwise diverse communities together, and the issue of 'localness' is much debated (Meadows, Forde, Ewart and Foxwell, 2007).

There has also been research examining content issues in relation to public attitudes and tastes, detailing content regulation, public complaints and their adjudication. In sum, as regards harm and offence, the research literature has focused on:

- Public perceptions of offensive content in general, including the perceptions of children.

- Talk shows/phone-ins.

- Standardization/reduction in diversity (particularly of concern in relation to music).

- Music lyrics.

- News (though there is little specific interest in radio news, so this is addressed under television news).

ACCESS CONDITIONS

Most research attention has sought to track the changing place of radio in everyday life, this providing some insights into the access conditions for radio listening. Radio has not, as some feared, been displaced by screen-based media, but it has undoubtedly shifted in its place in everyday life as newer forms of media become available (ACMA, 2007; Ofcom, 2007). Much radio use is based, as with all audio media, around music. In the United States, the Kaiser Family Foundation study (2005) into the media use of 8–18 year olds found that 85 per cent of their sample spend at least a few minutes each day listening to one of the audio media, and 44 per cent spend more than an hour. On average they spend 1.75 hours per day listening to music, with the time almost equally divided between radio and various recorded media (tapes, CDs, MP3s).

Qualitative research fills out a picture of a medium typically used as a secondary activity, in the background, accompanying many daily routines. Of the half of the population that listens to the radio daily, much of this is for music listening, as noted above, and there are few available figures for music viewing on television (unfortunately Ofcom's figures combine music with entertainment in tracking viewing by genre, although their figures do show that nearly all households contain one or, more often, multiple music media including 18 per cent owning an MP3 player or portable music device; Ofcom, 2005c). Hendy (2000) questions the assumption that sounds are less significant than images, arguing that aurality is central to people's cultural and emotional experience, that it is intensely sociable (in establishing shared experiences), and that its reliance on the imagination to fill out the message enhances its impact.

The Kaiser Family Foundation study (2005) noted that music media grow in importance as children become older. Of their sample, on any given day, 74 per cent of 8–10 year olds, 87 per cent of 11–14 year olds, and 90 per cent of 15–18 year olds spend at least a few minutes with audio media, with 60 per cent of the oldest group spending more than an hour daily with audio media (24 per cent listen in excess of three hours daily). The study also shows that gender is important with slightly higher proportions of girls than boys spending at least a few minutes each day with one of the audio media. In comparing the 2005 study with the previous such survey in 1999, the report says:

> The big constants, when it comes to kids and media, are TV and music. Over the past five years, there has been virtually no change in the amount of time children spend watching television or listening to music, nor has there been any diminution in those media's dominance over other activities such as computers or video games. On the other hand, there have been some changes in *how* kids watch TV or listen to music. More watch cable than broadcast TV, and they are starting to go online in conjunction with what they're watching as well as to download and listen to music through the internet. (Kaiser Family Foundation, 2005: 38/executive summary)

In relation to advertising, the ASA's Radio Code[1] applies[2] the legal framework on sexual and racial discrimination to radio broadcasting, that of consumer protection to advertising information on price and price comparisons and that of obscene publications to sexual content. It also adds some further content restrictions (e.g. banning appeals to superstition or fear), and restricts the advertising of tobacco, firearms, political messages, prescription medicines and so forth. In addition, it outlaws advertising that may harm or offend the audience (following the Broadcasting Act), including specific protections for child audiences. Similarly, the Ofcom Broadcasting Code applies to both radio and television equivalently.

REALITY-DEFINING EFFECTS

In reviewing research conducted during the 1990s, Hendy (2000) identifies a series of cultural (though not individual) threats or harms posed by radio, based on an analysis of shifting content and criticism over years or decades:

- Increasing niche segmentation ensures a diet of familiar and reassuring aural experiences to audience subgroups, rather than enhancing either a common experience or cultural hybridization.

- Increasing trend towards highly formatted, low risk, commercial output that standardizes the listening experience, rather than enhancing diversity or creativity.

- A powerful persuasive effect predominantly in those cultural contexts where the public is reliant on radio and where society is highly unstable (he uses the case of genocide broadcasts in Rwanda in 1994).

- A populist influence on democratic debate through the talk show (especially the 'shock-jock') genre, apparently facilitating diversity of participation but in practice reinforcing conservative opinions.

Nonetheless, little research directly examines, or provides support for these hypothesized harms, particularly in recent years. An earlier literature on talk shows supports Hendy's suggestion that, while the range of views expressed is supportive to (not harmful of) public debate, the most problematic aspect is not what those calling-in have to say but the normative framing of the debate by the host or radio station (Livingstone and Lunt, 1994; Verwey, 1990).

Regarding music in particular, a series of content analyses of popular music lyrics have been conducted in recent years, responding to public concerns over music lyrics and videos as well as to social science research showing tobacco, alcohol and drug use and sexual activity are rising among ever-younger teenagers. For the most part, these studies have been conscientiously conducted on large samples, using straightforward content categories. The arguments vary, with most research hypothesizing that music offers potentially harmful role models, associations (e.g. between alcohol and sexual attractiveness), beliefs or, for some, negative health outcomes (encouraging under age sex, smoking, drug abuse).

The findings are generally consistent in showing that music is a key source of messages regarding alcohol, tobacco, sexuality, sex-role stereotyping and violence for their often teenage audience (Gerbner, 2001). DuRant, Rome, Rich, Allred, Emans and Woods (1997) found that one-quarter of music videos portray tobacco use, with the lead performer most often the one smoking or drinking, and a similar proportion portray the use of alcohol, often in association with sexuality. Further, African Americans are disproportionately represented among those shown to smoke and drink. Do such portrayals have harmful effects? L'Engle et al. (2006) include music listening in the pan-media finding that teens exposed to more sexual content in the media report greater intentions to engage in sexual activity (here construed as a harm because of health risks associated with sexual activity at an early age), a finding which, like many, establishes a correlation but not the direction of effect.

However, Pardun et al. (2005) find that exposure to the 'sexual media diet' of music and film is particularly associated with intentions to be sexually active among early teens. Others also suggest that music may pose particular risks. Borzekowski, Robinson and Killen (2000) found that only time spent watching music videos (and not time spent with television, video or computer games) is associated with concerns about appearance and weight among teenage girls; however, in this study, the findings disappeared once the researchers controlled for BMI and ethnicity, suggesting instead that overweight girls and those from certain ethnic groups may both have more concerns about appearance and spend more time with music videos.

VIOLENCE, INCLUDING SEXUAL VIOLENCE

Again focusing on content rather than evidence for effects, Martin and Collins (2002) show that a fair proportion of music videos contain violence, this being most often violence against people while, interestingly, there are some consistent associations between violence and brands. Smith and Boyson (2002) draw on data from the United States' influential National Television Violence Study to assess the proportion of music videos containing violence as 15 per cent, while Pardun et al. (2005) find 11 per cent of the media (including music) used by teenagers contains sexual content. These figures are generally in line with (or less than) those obtained for other mass media.

Examining one key study in more detail, this based on a content analysis of a composite week of music video programming, a sample of nearly 2,000 (1,962) videos (236 hours), Smith and Boyson (2002) report that:

■ 53 per cent of music video programmes (and 15 per cent of individual music videos) feature violence.

■ The portrayal of violence is of the kind most likely to increase harmful effects (i.e. realistic settings, little portrayal of victim suffering, little punishment for violent actions, violence committed by heroic/celebrity figures).

■ Within a music video programme, 80 per cent contain a single violent interaction, 17 per cent contain two and 3 per cent contain three or more.

■ Both perpetrators and victims are more often black than white, male than female, unattractive than attractive.

■ 56 per cent of violent interactions showed no injury or incapacitation to the victims, 19 per cent showed mild harm, 10 per cent moderate harm and 16 per cent extreme harm.

■ For the most part, violence is portrayed as neither justified nor punished.

Considerable differences in violence portrayal occur across channels and music genres (e.g. one in four rap videos feature violence, violence in rap more often involves black perpetrators and victims, while in rock they are mostly white).

In all such studies, clearly, much depends on the definition of 'violence'.[3] The authors conclude that the risks of viewing such videos vary, being greater for black audiences, that the 'sanitized' nature of violence portrayals (no pain, no suffering, no punishment) is particularly of concern regarding viewing effects on teenagers.

Content analyses generally do not examine the nature of the portrayal of an issue. In this context, it is interesting that Markert (2001) agrees that drug abuse is a common theme in popular music but argues that, increasingly, such drug use is portrayed negatively (i.e. in the context of harmful consequences rather than pleasurable ones). The result, they suggest, is a prosocial rather than an antisocial message. More important, content analyses cannot reveal media effects, this requiring further research, but evidence regarding media content is a prerequisite to claims for harm or offence.

Nonetheless, UK adults regard music videos as contributing to declining standards of behaviour through their explicit sexual content (Ofcom, 2005f). Yet only a few, mainly American, experimental studies have examined the potentially harmful effects of violent music videos (see Smith and Boyson, 2002):

- Using self-report mood scales, young men were significantly more angry and frustrated after viewing violent non-erotic videos than those who viewed violent and erotic, erotic only, or non-violent/non-erotic videos (Peterson and Pfost, 1989).

- Black teenage boys (11–16 years old) who were shown violent rap videos reported attitudes that were significantly more likely to condone the use of violence as a means of social problem solving than were the control groups (Johnson, Jackson, and Gatto, 1995).

These findings are consistent with findings regarding violent content in other media. Wilson and Martin (2006) note a series of correlational and experimental studies which they summarize as follows (p. 192):

A modest amount of evidence links exposure to violent music with aggression. Even brief periods of listening to or watching violent material can increase aggression. Certain violent music, particularly that which is misogynistic in nature, can also increase aggression toward women.

Later in the article they also note that racist lyrics can 'prime racial stereotypes' (p. 196) but for these findings as for the others, the usual caveats apply for, as they then note, 'All of the studies have looked at short-term effects only, predominantly with college students'.

AUDIENCE INTERPRETATION

Little research has examined listeners' responses to music, this being a research gap. However, Wilson and Martin (2006) review a series of studies showing how children's comprehension of the content of music lyrics, including sexual or violent innuendos or implications, increases with age from childhood to adolescence.

Celious (2003) provides evidence that listeners' responses mediate harm: specifically, black women interpret hip hop lyrics as complex texts if they believe the artist to be female but they 'hear' them as debilitating to women if they believe the artist to be male. Gardstrom (1999) finds that male juvenile offenders choose rap as their preferred music genre, noting that they themselves do not consider it harmful; unfortunately the study does not compare this group with the general population to see if their choice is atypical.

Audience response represents a means of assessing the importance of context, since a range of factors mediate interpretation of music, as for other media. One important factor is textual or 'perceptual' context:

> Consumers do not view products in isolation…the behaviour of the performers, or circumstances in which the product appears can have an influence. (Martin and Collins, 2002: 866–567)

OFFENCE

Ofcom's 2006 'Communications Market Report' shows that 75 per cent have never found anything on radio to be offensive, and that of those who had been offended, half (53 per cent) felt the offensive material should not have been broadcast, while one in three felt that it should have been; those offended generally turned off the radio (44 per cent) or tuned to a different channel (29 per cent). However, the Listening 2000 survey found that 40 per cent of commercial radio listeners had been offended by radio content, particularly the treatment of callers by presenters (19 per cent), swearing/offensive language (14 per cent) and racism (14 per cent) (Millwood Hargrave, 2000b). Less common causes of offence include insensitivity (10 per cent), disrespect for moral/religious beliefs (9 per cent), sexual innuendo (6 per cent), song lyrics (5 per cent) and sexual explicitness (5 per cent). As a consequence, 31 per cent of those offended had turned off the radio, 31 per cent had changed the channel, and 6 per cent had taken some other action (Advertising Standards Authority, n.d.). (It is important to note that the national music channels generally play 'broadcast versions' of music, these lacking the more explicit lyrics available when music is bought over the counter.)

Radio, more than other mass media, contains a significant proportion of content generated by listeners who call in (see also the discussion of user-generated content in the chapter on the Internet). In cases where such content causes offence, listeners' judgements appear to depend on the response of the presenter or host – if these seek balance, or suggest some critical distance from the caller, listeners may be less concerned than when the presenter appears to let the comment pass or even to concur. Most concern regarding presenters could be construed as concern over presenters acting personally or informally in an offensive manner – i.e. when they resemble listeners rather than professional broadcasters. The BSC's 'Boundaries of Taste on Radio' report (BMRB Qualitative and Social Research Unit, 2000) draws on qualitative research to elaborate on these public attitudes towards taste and decency on radio, particularly parental concerns that children hear inappropriate, embarrassing or offensive content on the radio. In comparison with television, it appears that the public consider television both more regulated and yet al.so easier for parents to monitor than radio. On radio, determining what children do listen to, and what it is acceptable for them to listen to, is not a simple or straightforward matter for parents.

From a cultural studies or sociological perspective, there is a specialized literature examining the cultural value of music, this offering the grounds for some defence against the otherwise dominant critique of the harms occasioned by music over and above the sheer pleasure that most people gain from popular music. For example, Abramson (2002) analyses the role of music in constructing the public's understanding of national culture and identity, and Bennett (2002) offers a similar analysis of music in constructing local culture and, hence, local identity. It is worth noting that when a culturally positive outcome is mooted, cultural scholars have little difficulty in proposing that media have effects; note also, however, that such claims are based on an analysis of the text not the listeners. Whether for good or bad, Hendy (2000) is clear that radio shapes the listening tastes of its audience.

Rap music has received particular attention for its supposedly violent, racist and/or homophobic lyrics, although the empirical research base here is rather small. Fried (1999) finds the public prejudiced against rap, showing that lyrics are perceived to be more violent if attributed to rap than to country music; this finding casting some doubt on the coding process in content analyses of rap. Ogbar (1999) offers a different defence, namely that rap offers a channel for otherwise marginalized voices, and so suggests they should be 'read' not as offensive but as offering 'fresh analyses' of the 'culture wars' – an intriguing argument, though one which leaves open the question of how listeners actually do read these lyrics. Richardson and Scott (2002) offer a similar analysis, proposing 'rap music as a creative expression and metaphorical offspring of America's well-established culture of violence', a scapegoat for the important societal ills responsible for an angry and disaffected youth. Hence:

> Without doubt, the misogyny, debauchery, and antisocial hedonism of some lyrics deserve to be attacked. But what may appear to be a sincere concern for the well-being of America's youth is often a guise of a more sordid and insidious attack on Black youth culture and its ability to critique, analyze, and provide commentary on society. (Ogbar, 1999: 181)

This argument resembles that of the music industry: under the heading, 'Offensive Lyrics' (8/1/2003), the British Phonographic Industry website (http://www.bpi.co.uk/) reports a letter from BPI's executive chairman, Peter Jamieson, to the then Home Secretary, the Rt Hon David Blunkett that:

> ...explains the record industry's stance on censorship and our voluntary code for parental guidance stickers that alerts the consumer to potentially offensive content in recordings. A key point raised with the minister was the fact that rap songs are a reflection of the problems in society rather than a cause of them and that the music industry should not be made a scapegoat.

Research evidence regarding harm and offence in relation to music is scant and, given its widespread reach, particularly among the young, surely merits greater attention and funding. The argument for more research in this area is strengthened by the content analyses, reviewed above, showing the prominence of messages in popular music lyrics regarding sex, drugs, alcohol, offensive language and violence. More subtle reality-defining messages regarding gender, sexuality and ethnicity have received even less scrutiny.

One strand of research examines the nature and/or consequences of media use across a number of media, allowing the opportunity to see whether different media produce different findings. In some of the studies, music produces similar findings to other mass media (although occasionally it appears to be more influential). For example, Anderson et al. (2003) report equivalent findings for portrayed violence increasing the likelihood of aggressive and violent behaviour for television, films, video-games and music. This finding is of interest since, in terms of access conditions, video-games and perhaps films and music are regarded as more of a deliberate choice, especially by comparison with 'linear' or 'push' television. Unfortunately, there is little research from a cultural or critical perspective examining the motivations for and contexts of listeners' appreciation of music, to take forward an understanding of the nature of their choices to engage with certain music content. Anderson et al.'s argument, against which little critique has been forthcoming, is that, whatever the reasons for choosing to use these media, the process of harmful effects is the same: priming existing aggressive scripts and cognitions, increasing physiological arousal, triggering imitative behaviour, learning aggression-supporting beliefs and desensitization.[8]

In general, the UK public appears broadly accepting of the diversity of radio content, confident that they can select programmes/stations that suit their tastes, provided that content information is available to preclude offence and that difficult subjects are handled with sensitivity (Millwood Hargrave, 2000b). However, parents are not always aware of what their children listen to, finding their children's radio listening difficult to monitor and, moreover, not considering it solely their responsibility.

SUMMARY

- Despite being the background to so many people's lives, little recent research of radio was found in relation to questions of harm. Such concern as does arise is concentrated particularly on talk shows and similar programmes based on call-ins or user-generated content, and in relation to the lyrics of popular music.

- There is little research which examines harm and offence in relation to music. The research that exists is mainly content analytic rather than based on audience reactions, except for occasional opinion surveys, and is mainly focused on popular music lyrics.

- Research shows that radio is found to be offensive on occasion by a substantial minority of the audience – particularly in relation to the treatment of callers by presenters, offensive language and racism.

- These studies reveal consistent messages in music lyrics that may be considered harmful and are considered offensive by some – including messages promoting violence among boys/men, homophobic messages, or those encouraging early sexuality among young girls/women. Some argue that these are particularly damaging for ethnic minority audiences.

- There is a small body of experimental evidence suggesting that, as for other media, these messages can negatively influence the attitudes or emotions of their audience.

■ Despite a growing literature offering a cultural defence of music lyrics, especially rap music, these may give rise to offence among some audiences.

■ The relative lack of concern may be both because the radio is accessed as a secondary rather than a primary activity, and because the wide range of stations available means that listeners are always aware of their choice to listen to a particular station.

■ Further, television has traditionally been seen as 'public' because the television set is shared by all while radio has been seen as 'private' with listeners establishing a personal relationship with the medium (Millwood Hargrave, 2000b).

NOTES

1. A music video programme was defined as a show that schedules and airs multiple music videos.
2. Following the definition of the National Television Violence Study (Wilson et al., 1997), violence was defined as: 'any overt depiction of a credible threat of physical force or the actual use of such force intended to physically harm an animate being or group of beings. Violence also included certain depictions of physically harmful consequences against an animate being or group that result from unseen violent means' (Smith and Boyson, 2002: 66).
3. While the tenor of Anderson et al.'s argument would seem to suggest that violence in music media should be reduced (or, certain audiences should be protected from it), Martin and Collins (2002) instead argue that the negative consequences of violence should be portrayed also, thereby altering the message so as to undermine a harmful effect.

9

PRINT

Histories of the rise of the print media as mass media show that with their growth came concerns about harm and their influence. In many cases this led to censorship and, later, regulation (Richards, 1997). In the United Kingdom, print media of all kinds, including posters, now fall within self-regulatory systems (e.g. the Press Complaints Commission, the Periodical Publications Association, and the Advertising Standards Authority).

A *cause célèbre* in the world of censorship was the attempt to prosecute Penguin Books, publishers of *Lady Chatterley's Lover*, under the Obscene Publications Act. In her succinct review, Richards describes events leading up to the revision of this 1857 Act. She tells of four prosecutions for obscenity that were before the court in 1959. 'In each case the judge told the jury to read the books as a whole' – this was a significant precedent because it created the environment for recognizing the importance of context in the consideration of content. Context remains key in the evaluation of media contents and discussions about how audiences (for print, broadcasting or other media) understand these. Another enduring result of the *Lady Chatterley's Lover* prosecution was that the book was published at a price that allowed it to become a novel that 'all and sundry' could read. To this day, the affordability of media contents determines levels of access and the exclusion of some parts of the audience.

Park (2002) conducts an extensive review of the history behind the regulation of comic books in the United States. This is of interest in a discussion of harm and policy- making as Park refers to the inclusion of experts in arguments about the potentially harmful effects of violent comic books and illustrates the conflicting evidence from experts about harm and offence in the media.

Much of the research literature within the print media has focused on:

■ The way in which readers interact with the medium.

■ How public the medium is and how that affects attitudes.

■ The importance of print, especially newspapers, in forming and framing public discourse about matters important to society as a whole, as well as the individual.

VARIETIES OF PRINT MEDIA

Analyses of the print media genres are not common and the review of recent research revealed no new findings with regard to the potential for harm and offence in the media. However, this is an area where research continues, especially in the United States with reference to the way in which print media might affect attitudes towards various groups within society.

In the United Kingdom in 2000, a group of regulatory organizations (including the editorial policy-arm of the BBC) commissioned research to look at the use of swearing and offensive language in the media, including the public's reactions to the use of such language in print and on posters (Millwood Hargrave, 2000a). The key distinction that people made (as they do in broadcasting) is between what is seen as 'public' and available to all and what is seen as 'private'. In relation to print content a similar distinction is made. Posters (and poster advertising) were seen by survey respondents as the most public of the printed media: the majority (86 per cent) felt that offensive language on posters was not acceptable because 'you could not make a choice about what you saw'. There was a particular desire to protect children from seeing swearwords in such a public place – 95 per cent of respondents thought there needed to be strict controls on posters because children could see them. In addition to survey research, focus groups and depth discussions were undertaken. Again, the accessibility of posters to children (and hence the potential for offence) was reiterated:

> Really, you're just thinking about children aren't you, asking questions, 'What's that word' I've never heard that word before.' Especially kids who are learning to read because they want to read everything they see, don't they? (Depth 1, Irish family with young children, Manchester, 2000)

There was a greater acceptance of the use of swearwords and offensive language in newspapers because they are seen as a more 'private' form of communication, access to which can be controlled (although there were some concerns expressed about children picking up newspapers left lying around). The greatest tolerance however, was for magazines, especially those targeted at defined audiences. These were thought probably to be outside children's interests, and not easily affordable. Nevertheless, because of the potential for access (with inappropriate magazines left accessible to children), there was a general disquiet about the use of strong language, even in such media.

The particular relationship between the reader of comic books and that medium is little discussed now within academic circles, although a recent study by Kirsh and Olczak (2000) suggests violent comic books may affect attitudes towards the justification for the violence. Those who read the more violent comic books in their study reacted more negatively, in the research scenario (using short stories) which showed the cause of the violence to be ambiguous, than did those who read mildly violent comic books. However, their findings, based on questionnaire responses to hypothetical situations, also admit that what predicts such reactions are more likely to be personality variables than short-term exposure to violence in comic books. It is also worth noting that the mildly violent comic books used in this study would not generally be thought of as 'violent' in any sense in popular culture.

The authors of this review looked for evidence for harm and offence created through the reading of Japanese 'manga' comics (which have spawned the popular animé film culture). They have a bad press as pornographic, both sexually and in terms of violence. The review finds little academic research about its interaction with readers, either within Japan or in the West, where it is increasingly popular. The material that is available tends to look at the history of 'manga' and its place in Japanese society, rather than at the social or cultural role it plays (Fusanosuke, 2004; Gros, 1997). Nor do there seem to have been any studies examining the way such a culturally-specific print medium has crossed into other cultures.

Vega and Malamuth (2007) noted that high consumption of pornographic literature predicted sexual aggression among those with a predilection for such aggression. That is, those who scored highly on sexual aggression across other measures consumed significantly more pornography than others. Vega and Malamuth point to the limitations of their study – a sample of 102 male college students and the findings were correlational, rather than causal – but find it replicates other, larger-scale surveys.

PRESS AND THE PUBLIC DISCOURSE

A definition of 'harm' may incorporate social harms, that is; harm created by misinformation or misleading or partial information. A number of studies have looked at the role of the press and the other news media in informing public discourse. The studies suggest that the media can set the agenda and the boundaries for the discourse, often using sensationalist or inadequate reporting (Cassels, Hughes, Cole, Mintzes, Lexchin and McCormack, 2003; Hargreaves, Lewis, and Speers, 2003; Hochstetler, 2001; Innes, 2004; Rosta, 2003; Van Brunschot and Sydie, 2000). Equally the public (or audience) does not necessarily seek to inform itself or investigate in-depth (Hargreaves et al., 2003).

Three major scientific issues (the MMR vaccine, climate change and cloning/genetic medical research) were examined in Hargreaves' study. Its intention was to look at the link between the public's understanding of science and the way in which the media covered it, and to examine what the implications might be for public policy. The study used both content analyses of press and broadcasting coverage and large-scale quantitative surveys. It found that public understanding of scientific issues was patchy, and was built over time as ideas or facts were assimilated. It also found that people often mistook themes that the media were following as scientific fact, often not recognizing the subjective nature of media reporting. The authors say that scientific themes offered by the media are used 'as building blocks for people to make sense of an issue, and while this sometimes allows people to make informed guesses about those issues, it can lead to misunderstanding.' In the case of the MMR vaccine, it might be argued that misunderstood information risked leading to substantial harm as children were prevented by their parents from having the vaccine, threatening outbreaks of measles and such diseases.

The style of reporting, the choice of subject and the subsequent effect on public discourse and public policy is well-documented in Hochstetler's extensive analysis of the reporting of executions in American newspapers (2001). He found that the most sensational executions, sensational either because of the method of execution or because of the nature of the crime, were the ones that received the most coverage, measured across a number of variables. In terms of potential harm to society, he also found that the first execution in a state received maximum publicity while subsequent executions did not – unless they were 'sensational' for some other reason. Thus, he suggests, a different question of harm is raised – this is the harm caused to society by such reporting not being effective as it does not act as a restraint on would-be criminals. Neither does it present a balanced view of people on Death Row who are what he describes as 'relatively mundane murderers'. In his view, the debate about the rightness of the death penalty is not well-served by such reporting:

> Media coverage of the death penalty plays to multiple audiences but ultimately is biased by sensationalism. The death penalty simultaneously is sold to abolitionists as sloppy barbarianism exported from the periphery of the nation and to advocates as romanticized just desserts for the most vicious of crimes.

Goddard and Saunders (2000) found that the language used by the print media in describing child abuse can lead to the objectification of the child and, more seriously in terms of public discourse and harm, to a reduction in the perception of the seriousness of the offences. Jenkins (1999) has also examined what he calls 'drug panics', arguing that the mass communications media have spread panic in the United States by racializing the drug problem. It is argued that:

> Proponents of the war on drugs use synthetic panics to scapegoat society's minorities, thereby exacerbating racial, class and intergenerational conflict.

Some studies have examined the way in which the press and other media have covered issues of corporate responsibility (Burns and Orrick, 2002; Muggli, Hurt, and Becker, 2004). Burns and Orrick find that the press play down what they call 'white collar crime', concentrating on the sensational aspects of a story such as direct harm (deaths) rather than examining the culpability of those responsible for the incidents that cause such events. This study used a fire in a dance hall in Sweden as the example considered.

Muggli et al. look at the way in which a tobacco company used its influence with the media – and through public relations – to present a case against a report assessing the risk of environmental tobacco smoke. Using company documents and news stories as their data source, the authors conclude:

> On the topic of the health effects of secondhand smoke, more scrutiny is warranted from these (media) organizations for articles written by their members lest the public be misinformed and thus ill served.

FEAR OF CRIME AND THE MEDIA

Innes (2004) discusses how 'signal crimes' affect social reactions to crimes, including behaviour. He describes a signal crime as 'an incident that, because of how it is interpreted, functions as a warning signal to people about the distribution of risk throughout social space'. This analysis draws from many disciplines including sociology and criminology and argues there has been a shift from 'moral panics' to a more ambient sense of fear, driven in part by the availability of the media:

> Moral panics about crime issues are increasingly the exception rather than the rule, primarily because of the institutionalisation of a '24–7' media culture where stories of outrageous deviance are continually presented for consumption and consequently assume a status of being a normal feature of everyday life.

While not rooted in academic evidence, Innes's arguments that the media affect the public's perception of the world due in part to their widespread and constant availability, resonate and elaborate on the work conducted by Gerbner and others (1986; see also Nancy Signorielli and Morgan, 1990).

Schlesinger and Tumber (1994), conducting both qualitative research and content analyses of particular news stories, suggest the link between the presentation of crime in the media and fear of crime is 'inconclusive'. What they argue for is a greater reliance on evidence (in the form of crime statistics, for example) so that 'the public may exercise its democratic right to make judgements about the conduct of policy'. Yet as we have noted earlier, Lowry et al. (2003) found that television news has a greater potential to scare the public than has a change in real-life crime. Thus they argued that television 'sets the agenda' for public opinion, including fear reactions.

Nonetheless, Hargreaves, Innes and Schlesinger and Tumber are concerned, from a public policy point of view and on behalf of the public, about the potential (negative) effects of journalistic reporting. One study that covered all the media, examined attitudes to, and in some cases the effects of, crime reporting (Shearer, 1991). The research sample was made up of the 'general public' and survivors of crime or disasters. While the sample of survivors interviewed is small, the results are unambiguous. High levels of offence can be caused by intrusion into grief, the disregard for accuracy (in some cases) and misreporting. It is the lack of ownership of the event in which they were caught that survivors express in this research, an interesting comparison with the work of Innes (2004) and others who look at the way in which the police and the media work together or are co-dependent in many crime (or similar) news stories.

Sudak and Sudak (2005) in their review of the literature recommend that psychiatrists and health professionals familiarize themselves with the media guidelines available (press and other media) to prevent what they refer to as the 'contagion effects' of suicide reporting that might dramatize or romanticize such deaths.

REALITY-DEFINING EFFECTS

Some studies have looked at the way in which the media present images of gender (Durham, 2005; Knight and Giuliano, 2001), race (Bittle, 2002; Durham, 2005; Rada, 2000), and other forms of social identity (such as sexuality (Sender, 2001)). While based on a small sample, and therefore indicative only, Durham shows how magazine representations make race a homogenous consumer option, devoid of history or social meaning. While the study does not show evidence of harm or offence being caused to readers through this presentation, cultural discourse would query the validity of such a model.

A detailed discourse analysis of press reporting of ethnic and racial affairs concludes that coverage has 'gradually become less blatantly racist, but that stereotypes and the definition of minorities as a "problem" or even as a "threat" is still prevalent' (van Dijk, 1991: 245). Further:

> an empirical study among readers suggested that the reproduction of racism by the Press is largely effective, not so much because all readers always adopt the opinions of the Press, which they often do and sometimes do not, but rather because the Press manages to manufacture an ethnic consensus in which the very latitude of opinions and attitudes is quite strictly constrained. They not only set the agenda for public discussion (what people should think about) but, more important, they strongly suggest how the readers should think and talk about ethnic affairs. (van Dijk, 1991: 246)

Other studies (Henley, Miller, Beazley, Nguyen, Kaminsky and Sanders, 2002; Stryker, 2003) have used a mixture of content analysis and other methods to point to a relationship between newspaper reporting and behaviour or attitudes. Although based on an analysis of news stories in only two American papers, followed by an experiment using 'mock' news stories, Henley's study suggests that the biased use of language affects readers' perceptions of the severity of attacks on, in this case, the gay population in comparison with the straight population. The study does not investigate predispositions or attitudes towards the sexuality of participants but it does show an effect of language, and also of participant gender. While this is an experimental study using undergraduates, the direct read-across from the way language is structured and the way different readerships may be influenced, is interesting and would be worth replicating. A study finding similar results is described by Korner and Treloar which showed that information (about needle and syringe exchange programmes) as presented is far from value-free (Korner and Treloar, 2004).

Xiamong and Yunjuan's study (2005) is of a magazine designed for expatriate Chinese women. It examines whether the media are agents of social change or reinforcers of the *status quo*. Through a content analysis of the front covers of the magazine over time, Xiamong suggests that the magazine reflects periods in history but is not an approximation of the reality of most women in China at any given time. In this case the media act to reinforce prevailing (political) stereotypes.

The debate about the way in which exposure to sexual content may sexualize the young continues to be important (Buckingham and Bragg, 2003; Press, 2001; Romer and Jamieson, 2001). The studies offer contradictory results, and their methodological differences are significant. Pardun et al. (2005) use a mixture of questionnaire and interviews that lead to a positive correlation between an individual's exposure to sexual content in the media and the adolescent's sexual activity or intention to become sexually active.

Buckingham and Bragg's work, on the other hand, argues that the reader has a more proactive relationship with the press. They suggest that the consumers of mass media sexual content are generally 'media literate' and are significantly affected by the (familial) values around them. They conclude:

> The media do not have an autonomous ability either to sexually corrupt children or to sexually liberate them.

Teen magazines, their seeming preoccupation with sexual themes and a concern about the negative effect they may have on the sexual health of young people have been of interest to the academy and policy-makers in recent years (Buckingham and Bragg, 2003; Wellings, 1996). In 1996 there was an attempt by the MP, Peter Luff, to have age-suitability classifications put on such magazines, but this was subsequently withdrawn. Wellings' briefing document for the Periodical Publishers Association shows there is no evidence that these magazines are preoccupied with sex but there is evidence that the results of surveys about sex presented in these magazines distort reality. This may be because they are generally based on self-selecting readers of the publication. The author warns that coverage about 'results' from surveys may become *self-fulfilling* and:

> The evidence suggests that the interests of young women may not be best served by perpetuating the belief that early sexual activity is the norm. The temptation to publish the results of in-house surveys is understandable, since these have an immediacy that comes from their being based on the reports of actual readers. Yet there seems to be a strong case for avoiding presenting the results as representing the behaviour of all young people, and for making available to readers more accurate estimates of behaviour at the broader level.

There has been some evidence in recent years to suggest that teen magazines and the coverage they give to sexual matters may be of positive benefit, complementing formal education and parental discussion (Buckingham and Bragg, 2003; Thompson and Scott, 1992). Buckingham and Bragg's study consisted of an extensive literature review of material relating to young people and their interaction with the media and its influence on their perceptions of personal relationships, as well as interviewing children and conducting a survey. They found:

> The children were generally very critical of the sex education they received in school, and many also found it embarrassing to be taught about such matters by their parents. They preferred media such as teenage magazines and soap operas on the grounds that they were often more informative, less embarrassing to use and more attuned to their needs and concerns.

In 2003, the Sexual Offences Act (2003) was amended to preserve the right of agony aunts and other adults 'to give advice to young people about the emotional and physical impact of sexual relationships' (Teenage Magazine Arbitration Panel, 2003). Buckingham et al. had found that some respondents treated problem pages with scepticism while others found them useful. There was a degree of media literacy brought to the reading of such material but teen readers were not totally competent – 'the modern media offer mixed messages and often explicitly require consumers to make up their own minds about sexual issues'. As Welling also suggests, the media need to be aware of the possibility of confusion for young people and the possibilities of real harm in terms of their sexual health.

Summary

- The history of the print media and the precedents set in terms of policy-making have helped frame debates about other media and have also provided a framework for the way in which much media content is regulated (such as a consideration of the importance of context, for example, or accessibility). The print media, especially the press, also frame public discourse, and the importance of an informed public is widely accepted as crucial, especially as it affects social and public policy-making.

- The potential complicity of the media in misinformation is questioned in many studies reviewed here, and it has been argued that the subsequent harm that may occur not only affects the individual but also has broader harmful consequences for society.

- A number of the studies looked at the way in which the print media could affect attitudes, about the society in which the reader is living, for example, or attitudes towards certain groups within society. This argues for a responsible presentation of the facts so that harm – such as making people unreasonably fearful – may be avoided.

- The research literature rarely examines the way in which print media values are ascribed to print 'brands' that may be delivered elsewhere, for example online, and how these may affect attitudes.

- Research suggests the print media, especially the press, can frame public discourse, providing important civil information. The potential complicity of the media in misinformation is questioned in many studies reviewed here. It is argued that the potential for harm that may occur not only affects the individual but also has broader consequences for society.

- The importance of the public or private nature of different types of print media has not been widely researched but the evidence suggests that how strongly one is affected by print content is closely linked with this distinction.

10

ADVERTISING

INTRODUCTION

The potential harms arising from advertising take several forms:

- Unlike much of the research reviewed thus far, research on advertising is often concerned with the deliberate intent of advertising. Here the question is whether the product being advertised is potentially harmful (e.g. tobacco, alcohol), albeit possibly only under certain conditions (e.g. excessive consumption) or for certain groups (e.g. children). Advertising, in short, includes messages that intentionally seek to increase the likelihood of someone purchasing a potentially harmful product, though much advertising does not (and advertisers may argue that such harm is not intended by the advertiser, being the unintended consequence of the consumer using the advertised product to excess or of the advertisement being received by an unintended audience).

- A second kind of harm that may arise from advertising concerns behaviours that advertisements may intentionally encourage. These include excessive consumption (e.g. over-eating, over-spending) and pester-power.

- A third concern in relation to advertising is similar to that of television, film and other media. This concerns the consequences of incidental (rather than deliberate) messages – i.e. messages that are not directly product-related. Such messages may include potentially reality-defining or stereotyping effects of messages regarding gender, sexuality or ethnicity, for example. Such messages may or may not be harmful, irrespective of the question of the intended message. For, just as one would not argue that television broadcasters intend the result of viewing violent content to be an increased aggression among the audience, so too one would not argue that advertisers intend the result of viewing gender-stereotyped messages to be increased gender-stereotyping among the audience; rather, the intent is to sell soap powder or cars or perfume.

Most research is little concerned with imputing intent to advertisers, and it may not clearly distinguish among these kinds of potential harm. Further, only some of the research specifically considers the distinguishing characteristics of advertising. For example, some point out that the very brevity of an advertisement may mean that the stereotyping of certain groups (e.g. the elderly) is more extreme (for the message must be conveyed quickly and little contextual or genre-based justification can be developed). A few studies have examined the link between television programming and the marketing of related products. For example, Hamilton (1998) provides an economic analysis of the market forces that drive the marketing of violent content, illustrating the attractiveness of the potential audience for such material to the advertiser.

A further limitation is that most empirical studies on advertising focus on television, with attention only now beginning to turn to new media (Fielder et al., 2007) – hence, there is much yet to do here.

Since adults are generally considered advertising literate, research on adults is more concerned with offence than harm, while for children the reverse is the case. Children are a major target for advertisers: $15 billion per year is spent on marketing and advertising to under 12s in the United States, double the amount spent a decade before; the average child sees some 40,000 television advertisements per year; and collectively they influence $500 billion in annual spending on fast/junk food, toys, and so on (Children Now, 2005). However, this is not to say that adults are unaffected by the reality-defining effects or, indeed, the persuasive effects of advertising, as suggested by the huge sums spent on targeting them. Nonetheless, empirical academic research has focused mainly in certain areas (Gunter, Oates, and Blades, 2005; Kunkel et al., 2004; Leiss, Kline, and Jhally, 1990; Valkenburg, 2004).

Reality-defining effects
Several kinds of harm have been associated with advertising to children – first, stress on parent/child relationships (pester-power, conflict, etc.) and second, more importantly, harm to children's health by promoting favourable attitudes to and consumption of unhealthy food, alcohol, aggressive media contents and, in some countries (though not the United Kingdom), tobacco. Romer and Jamieson (2001) review the evidence that smoking influences adolescent smoking, showing that efforts to counter this influence with anti-smoking messages have little effect given the overwhelming presence of pro-smoking messages in advertising (see also Boots and Midford, 2001). Indeed, Dillon (1998) points out that it is widely accepted among workers in the drug and alcohol field that one barrier to harm reduction is misrepresentation in advertising and other media.

It can further be argued that while the use of stereotypes in advertisements represents a strategy to communicate quickly about a product, it potentially causes incidental harm or offence precisely by reinforcing such stereotypes. In other words, harm may arise not from the product itself but from the means adopted to promote it. For example, Hanley, Hayward, Sims and Jones (2000) identified a series of cases in which television advertisements were seen, generally anecdotally, to encourage copy-cat behaviour among children (see also Young, 1990, on the use of celebrities in advertising to encourage emulation by children).

Numerous content analyses have established systematic biases in the representation of characters in advertising, when compared with population or social statistics. For example, television advertisements aired during the 1990s, as in earlier decades, continue to show men as more authoritative than women, women as sex objects, African American men as aggressive, and white men as powerful (Coltrane and Messineo, 2000). Other biases in advertising content include stereotypical portrayals of older consumers (Carrigan and Szmigin, 1999).

A review of content analyses cross-nationally reveals considerable consistencies in gender-stereotyping over a 25 year period, notwithstanding social changes during that period (Furnham and Mak, 1999). Concern has long been expressed about the consequences for women's negative self-image and anxiety about their appearance (Berg and Rosencrans, 2000; Martin and Gentry, 2003). In one study, magazine advertisements were content-analysed in relation to stereotypes of women, showing that, while men are 'demurely dressed' four in five times, this is the case for women only one in three times. The authors conclude that women are much more likely to be portrayed as sexual objects than are men in advertising (Carpenter and Edison, 2005).

Some attention has also been paid, using content analysis, to the potential of advertising to objectify men's bodies, with the author of one study explicitly linking such eroticization and commodification of men's bodies to the growing evidence of psychological distress (increased male incidence of anorexia, for example) (Rohlinger, 2002). Indeed, in an experiment on men's gender role attitudes, Bodenhausen and Garst (1997) found that the images of men seen in advertisements influenced men's attitudes, particularly for men with less traditional attitudes, suggesting a mainstreaming effect of stereotypical portrayals in advertisements. Specifically, they showed magazine advertisements to male students that systematically varied the masculinity and age of the male model portrayed, before testing the respondents' perceptions of gender roles using a standardized gender attitude inventory.

Certain advertising strategies are worth noting. Alexander (2005) shows how the tobacco industry has particularly targeted gay and lesbian people, a group that is already more likely to smoke than heterosexuals. Frith (2005) found that global advertisers tend to use Caucasian models in the Mandarin Chinese editions of their magazines, often associating them with sexual poses and using them to sell clothing in particular, the unintended effects of concern being the perpetuation of racial stereotypes.

Many of these biases are more strongly present in advertising to children. Gender stereotypes are widespread in advertising directed at children (e.g. B. A. Browne, 1998), with boys appearing more often, being more dominant, active and aggressive than girls. Girls, by contrast, are portrayed as more shy, giggly and passive. Further, one-third of television advertisements that featured child characters in the United States were found to include some kind of aggression (Larson, 2003). This was especially the case for images of white boys, often portrayed being aggressive in relation to toys, games or people.

HEALTH EFFECTS
A range of health-related effects have been researched over past decades. These include investigations into the potential effects of tobacco advertising (Lancaster and Lancaster, 2003),

alcohol advertising (Andsager, Austin, and Pinkleton, 2001; Calfee, 1994), and the relation between advertising and eating disorders (Harrison and Cantor, 1997). Further, many of the regulations regarding advertising, together with the often contested debates over regulation, have focused on health issues (Alexander and Hanson, 2003; Ambler, 1996, 2004; De Stempel, 2005; Gunter et al., 2005; Rotfeld, Jevons, and Powell, 2004).

One such recent case is that of the potential harms caused to children's health by the advertising of products high in fat, salt or sugar. Hastings, Stead, McDermott, Forsyth, MacKintosh, Raynor, Godfrey, Caraher and Angus's (2003) systematic review of research evidence on the content and effects of food promotion, mainly television advertising, to children argued that the advertised diet differs significantly from the recommended diet, and that television advertising directly affects children's food knowledge, preferences and behaviour (Livingstone, 2005; Livingstone and Helsper, 2004, 2006). Here the issue is one of intended consequences (i.e. increasing people's intake of the advertised product), rather than of the possibility of incidental harm caused by stereotyping effects, as identified above.

Although most research in this field is American, there are indications of a similar problem in the United Kingdom also. For example, Lewis and Hill (1998) conducted a content analysis showing that food is the most advertised product category on children's television, and that confectionery, cereals and savoury snacks are the most advertised (see also Dibb and Castell, 1985). Hence, 60 per cent of food advertisements to children are for convenience foods, 6 per cent for fast food outlets, and the remainder for cereals and confectionery (c.f. Young, 2003).

According to Halford, Gillespie, Brown, Pontin and Dovey (2004), food advertising exacerbates already existing differences in food advertising recognition and related food consumption. Obese children are already more aware of food advertisements than those children of normal weight and the exposure to food cues in advertising induces a higher intake of food by these groups. However, many children appear sensitive to these advertising messages, whether or not they are already obese. An American content analysis found that, compared with advertisements featuring no black characters, those with black characters were more likely to sell convenience foods, especially fast foods, though these contained less sugar. Both types of advertisements tended to sell nutritionally unbalanced foods (Harrison, 2005).

Hitchings and Moynihan (1998) conducted a survey in private and state schools. They found that children recall cereals, confectionery, and soft drink advertisements more than any other type of advertisement. The strongest relationships between recall and consumption are for soft drinks, crisps, cakes and sweets. They also found that higher levels of television viewing are positively associated with the number of purchase requests made to parents. Indeed, a recent survey of UK parents conducted for the National Family and Parenting Institute (2003) shows that parents feel their children are 'bombarded' by advertising – to ever-younger children and across an ever-greater range of media platforms. They claim to be anxious, irritated and pressurized, not least because of the considerable domestic conflicts they claim that consumer demands from children result in within the family.

Although much attention in relation to obesity has focused on children, there are also concerns regarding possible harm to the general (adult) public, particularly in relation to the provision of comprehensive and comprehensible information. The American Dietetic Association has recently expressed concern over food and nutrition misinformation, noting that as consumers are required to take greater responsibility for their nutrition, such misinformation is particularly worrying (Ayoob, Duyff and Quagliani, 2002); similar concerns are now being expressed in the United Kingdom.

Worrell, Rosaen, Greenberg and Salmon (2005) conducted a content analysis of the presentation of food, drink, tobacco and drugs in adult television programming, using the top ten television programmes in 2002–2003. They found that there was little attempt made to change the type of consumption being portrayed, despite the increasing concerns about obesity. The study also found there was little representation in the programmes of drugs or tobacco, more representation of non-alcoholic beverages, and more drink than food. This may argue for greater synergy between programme-makers and advertisers or clearer guidelines across all areas of content.

CHILDREN'S ADVERTISING LITERACY AND VULNERABILITY TO PERSUASION

Many studies have examined children's developing understanding of advertising as a persuasive form of communication, these contributing to an account of advertising literacy. Thus it seems that before about 5 years old, children do not consistently distinguish advertising from programmess and so regard advertising as entertainment or as information about products rather than as persuasion (Blosser and Roberts, 1985; Buijzen and Valkenburg, 2003; Gunter et al., 2005; Nairn, Ormond and Bottomley, 2007; Wartella, 1980).

Specifically, by about 7 or 8 years old, children have learned to identify the persuasive intent of advertising, distinguishing it from information although, as Roedder (1981) added, they often do not use this knowledge spontaneously and must be prompted to do so (Brucks, Armstrong, and Goldberg, 1988; John, 1999; Moore, 2004). From about 12 years old, children can articulate a critical understanding of advertising and of the intentions of its producers (Martin, 1997; Peterson, 1988; Peterson, Jeffrey, Bridgwater, and Dawson, 1984), even becoming sceptical or distrustful of advertising (Boush, 2001; Dorr, 1986; van Evra, 1998). Particular concern is attached to the use of unfair or deceptive practices in advertising to children (for example, the use of disclosures that children do not understand – 'batteries are not included' being a common example (Kunkel, 1992; Martin, 1997).

Although it is widely assumed that younger children are more influenced by advertising than are older teens, a recent review of the literature challenges this assumption (Livingstone and Helsper, 2006). Indeed, Kunkel, Wilcox, Cantor, Palmer, Linn and Dowrick (2004) concluded their recent review for the American Psychological Association by noting that they could find no study that examined the statistical relation between children's understanding of advertising's persuasive intent and the impact of advertising and that, 'there is little evidence that media literacy interventions can effectively counteract the impact of advertising on children of any age, much less the younger ones who are most vulnerable to its influence'.

Instead, the evidence is consistent with the view that different processes of persuasion operate at different ages, precisely because literacy levels vary by age. In other words, the evidence for influence suggest that children of all ages could be, more or less equivalently, affected by advertising (as, after all, are adults also), but that the effects of advertising are dependent on advertising literacy. Thus, it may be that because younger children have lower media (or advertising) literacy, they are more likely to be persuaded by advertising that is based on celebrities, jingles, colourful images, and the attractive physical features of a product. Older children, especially teenagers, whose media literacy is greater, are more likely to be persuaded by advertising strategies based on argumentation, especially those that contain high quality arguments and responses to counter-arguments. These arguments concern influence, whether positive or negative in outcome, and much therefore depends on what is being advertised.

ADVERTISING AND NEW/ONLINE MEDIA

Interactive media introduce new marketing and advertising strategies designed to target children (and adults) (Seiter, 2005). The Center for Media Education identifies several new forms of online marketing practices targeted at children, and it expresses particular concern over the economic pressure towards alliances between civic sites and commercial ventures (Montgomery, 2001; Turow, 2001). New advertising strategies include:

- Branded environments designed to foster brand loyalty, for example through 'advergames' – online games featuring specific products; these may also collect consumer preference information from players.

- One to one or relational (or 'viral') marketing targets consumers with personalized advertisements, based on individual information derived from tracking individual media use.

- Product-placement, providing a seamless integration of programming and products (challenging the media literacy of the audience), potentially linked with personal data about media and demographic variables.

Complicating matters, regulation in new media appears more difficult to enforce than for traditional media. Carroll and Donovan (2002) show that national self-regulatory codes for advertising (in their case, in Australia) are breached on the Internet, with new opportunities online for alcohol marketing targeted at underage consumers.

Little research, however, has yet examined the user's perspective to discover how children and teens respond to such sites and whether they can recognize and/or distance themselves from commercial approaches, let al.one whether they are influenced by such advertising (though such influence is assumed in the framing of guidelines of online advertising (e.g. Austin and Reed, 1999)). It is not known, for example, whether people even recognize advertising on mobile phones, although early indications are that they are hostile to it (Tsang, Ho, and Liang, 2004). Nor is it clear whether people can determine 'misinformation' presented online in advertising (Graham and Metaxas, 2003). The influence of advertising – both intentional and incidental – in new media and communication environments must surely be a priority for future research, including but not restricted to attention to potentially vulnerable groups (children, new media novices, etc.).

OFFENCE

The literature on offence in advertising is primarily concerned with the adult population, there being little attention in general (i.e. across all media) paid to the possibility of offence among children. A wide-ranging report on the public's perceptions of advertising (Advertising Standards Authority, 2002) found the term 'advertising' to be used broadly to include all forms of marketing. Often regarded positively by the public – as informative, as entertaining, and as an inevitable part of business – nonetheless, some concerns emerged from the public. These centred on the truthfulness, or otherwise, of advertising, including concerns over the disclaimers (or small print), seen as protecting advertisers rather than consumers.

Recent trends suggest a growth in potentially offensive advertisements internationally and, in the United Kingdom, this is evident in the steady increase in formal complaints (Crosier and Erdogan, 2001). Since these typically come from a relatively homogeneous social group of potential opinion leaders living in the South-East, Crosier and Erdogan suggest that may represent just the tip of the iceberg in terms of levels of public offence. The recent Advertising Standards Authority's 'Annual Report (2004–2005)' reports a steady year-on-year increase in complaints about advertising, including a significant increase in complaints about broadcast advertising.

However, in 2001 the ASA reported a slight fall in the number of complaints about taste and decency specifically.

What gives rise to offence? Sancho and Wilson (2001) conducted a qualitative project in the United Kingdom for the ITC and found that:

■ Disabled viewers felt marginalized in advertising (Tuchman, 1981, described the systematic neglect of certain groups as 'symbolic annihilation').

■ Ethnic minority ethnic viewers were concerned both that they were under-represented and, when represented, with negative stereotypes.

■ Parents and older children were concerned about images that appeared to condone bullying (e.g. identifying characteristics of children that others might pick on them for).

■ There were a number of sensitivities regarding advertisements containing national stereotypes (e.g. German stereotypes) or stereotypes of people from particular parts of the United Kingdom.

We might call these stereotypes of omission (neglecting certain groups) as well as stereotypes of commission (narrow portrayals of certain groups). Both of these may, the authors acknowledge, be used by advertisers as a short-hand means of conveying a message; yet they may offend certain groups in the audience. For example, older people were found, in one study, to consider advertising stereotypes that portrayed older adults as being out of touch, objects of ridicule, difficult, and unattractive to be offensive (Robinson, Popovich, Gustafson, and Fraser, 2003).

A survey of over 2,000 adults conducted for the Advertising Standards Authority (2002) found that, for non-broadcast advertising:

- One-fifth of adults said they had been personally offended by advertising in the past year, with 'push' media such as posters and direct mail being most likely to cause offence, and Internet advertising being the most offensive among those who had seen it (this represents a slight reduction on the one in four offended by an advertisement in 1996).

- Women, older people, middle-class, and non-white ethnic minority respondents were more likely to have been offended, while men and young people were more likely to have been offended on behalf of others.

- The portrayal of children in advertising occasioned most concern, particularly the sexualization of children or the association of children with images or words judged unsuitable. The location and context of such advertising (are children likely to see it?) was also of particular concern (see also ITC, 1995).

- Age matters – young people are more sensitive to the portrayal of vulnerable or minority group; older people are more sensitive to sexual or violent images.

- The use of shocking images was considered more acceptable for 'good causes' than for commercial messages, and was least acceptable in generalist (rather than specialist) media.

Particular products may also, in themselves, offend the audience, and interviews with Australian broadcasters reveal that they may not air those advertisements considered a breach of taste (Rotfeld et al., 2004). One study compared students' responses to the advertising of controversial products across four different countries – Malaysia, New Zealand, Turkey and the United Kingdom (Waller, Fam, and Erdogan, 2005). Previous research had suggested that advertisements for contraceptives are most often considered unacceptable, though advertisements for feminine hygiene products are often considered in poor taste, especially by older women (Waller, 1999). The student survey found that products/services associated with racially extremist groups were considered offensive in all four countries. Respondents in Malaysia and Turkey, both with significant Muslim populations, objected to advertisements for gambling and, to a lesser degree, contraceptives, underwear and feminine hygiene products. Alcohol advertising was more offensive in Turkey, as were advertisements for funeral services. Respondents in New Zealand and the United Kingdom revealed some similar attitudes, being offended by racist and sexist images, religious subjects, and portrayals of antisocial behaviour. In Singapore, Phau and Prendergast (2001) show that advertisements relating to chat-line services and sexual diseases were considered particularly offensive. In all, culture and, particularly, religion clearly shape people's responses to potentially offensive advertising.

SUMMARY

- This chapter has revealed a moderate body of evidence pointing to the modest effects of both intentional (i.e. product-promoting) and incidental (i.e. product context) advertising messages. This suggests that advertising has some influence on product choice, and that the nature of its portrayals has some influence on the attitudes and beliefs of its audience.

- Specifically, a range of reality-defining effects have been examined – in relation to the stereotyping of population segments and, most recently, in relation to obesity and products with other health consequences. Research tends to show modest evidence for the harmful effects of advertising, particularly on children, although this remains contested. Since the influence of advertising is not large, according to the evidence, research is needed to determine what other factors also influence these harmful outcomes (stereotyping, obesity, smoking, etc.).

- The question of intent has implications for media literacy. In relation to advertising, the intent to persuade is generally considered acceptable provided the public recognizes this intent. In relation to children, considerable research exists on the development of 'advertising literacy' with age, though it has not been clearly shown that more media literate, or advertising literate, consumers are less affected by advertising (or other media), nor that interventions designed to increase literacy have the effect of reducing media harm.

- This issue has recently received renewed attention in relation to children regarding specific health problems – obesity most notably, but also conditions associated with alcohol and tobacco. It is also receiving growing attention in relation to all audiences regarding advertising in the new media, for it seems that adults as well as children may lack the literacy to determine which new media and online contents constitute advertising or marketing messages. Indeed, little is yet known of how all audiences – adults as well as children – recognise advertising, sponsorship, product-placement etc. in relation to the new media environment, and this remains a priority for future research.

- The regulation of advertising, at least for broadcasting, film and print, also recognizes the importance of deliberate persuasive intent. For example, the regulation of tobacco advertising is far more restrictive than is the regulation of programming content containing images of smoking (where responsible portrayals are recommended but where other criteria – the demands of the genre, realism, context etc. – also matter). Within Europe, the appropriate degree of restrictiveness has been contested, with Sweden, most notably, banning television advertising to children.

- Last, we note that there is also a fair body of research linking advertising to offence. This research reveals the considerable cultural variation, both within and across cultures, in what content is found offensive and by whom.

11

REGULATION IN THE HOME

ATTITUDES TO CONTENT REGULATION

Research has consistently shown that the main reason for regulation cited by users of different media forms is to protect children. In 2006, nearly three-quarters (71 per cent) of a sample of respondents said this is the reason for broadcast regulation (Ofcom, 2006). Interestingly, this is a decrease over previous years – the proportion saying the same in 2003 was 82 per cent and in previous years it had been higher (Broadcasting Standards Commission, 2001). This may be because audiences feel there are more provisions in place to help them regulate their own viewing or that current systems work well.

However, these data should be seen against the growing trend, first noted in 2005, that an increasing proportion of respondents (51 per cent) feel that parents and broadcasters share equal responsibility for protecting children from unsuitable material (Ofcom, 2006). In previous years, it has always been thought of as primarily the parents' responsibility. It will be important to track these data to see if this trend continues – towards a diminishing perception that regulation is needed to protect children, and the increasing – and perhaps contradictory – view that broadcasters must assume equal responsibility.

Just over one in ten (13 per cent) said that regulation is important to protect them, as viewers, while 25 per cent said that regulation is important to 'protect the public' more generally (Ofcom, 2006). Earlier research showed that 'participants thought as citizens and not just consumers when thinking about regulation' (Ofcom, 2005).

Such research points to a concern about community values, a theme that was examined in some detail in an extensive study reported upon by Verhulst (April 2001). The research was commissioned by the former Broadcasting Standards Commission as the UK government issued its 'Communications White Paper'. This outlined possible changes to the regulatory structure in order to respond to, and take advantage of, rapidly developing technological changes in the field of communications (which led eventually to the formation of Ofcom). The research was directed, therefore, towards being able to make an effective contribution to the debate about regulation. The project consisted of focus groups and a questionnaire. The composition of the groups reflected the main life stages at which attitudes towards broadcasting regulation might be expected to differ from each other:

1. Independent adults aged 21–29 years old (with no children);

2. Parents with children aged 8–14 years old;

3. The 45–64 years old age group (recruited as opinion formers/'influentials');

4. The 65–75 years old age group.

In each of these categories were two groups – recruited as 'modern' (i.e. people with a broadly liberal or progressive outlook), or as 'traditional' with more conservative views. The interim results of the research were presented during a half-day round table with leading experts within broadcasting, both from the regulatory field but also practitioners. In this way the implications for the regulatory debate and areas of policy- concern could be discussed and taken into consideration in the next, quantified, stage of the research.

The results showed that 'family' and 'community values' were predominant in the thinking about regulation of broadcast media. The research sought to understand the different interpretations and levels of importance of these concepts of 'values'. Although many respondents had difficulty articulating what specific concepts they associated with 'values' in relation to media, there were common themes:

> In particular, it was evident throughout the groups that, at least in the context of the media, 'values' were described as 'family values'…The older groups related the phrase to their actual family, of which they were the head, and took it to mean togetherness, security, respect and decency. The younger groups related it more to an extended family or community, and linked it with tolerance, fairness and reciprocity.

While the protection of minors was considered the prime reason for regulation, respondents also talked of wishing to be shown 'greater respect for viewer's intelligence and for privacy, especially in times of grief'. Many participants in the focus groups expressed a preference for self-regulation, but accepted that they perhaps needed more information about the regulatory structures to help them undertake this task effectively. However, this desire is not well reflected in the finding (above), that people want broadcasters to share responsibility for the protection of children equally with parents.

However, there are concerns about the effectiveness of self-regulation (see also the discussion in the chapter on film, above). For example, in a follow-up to its 2000 report, 'Marketing Violent Entertainment to Children' (Federal Trade Commission, 2000), the FTC (2004) found that self-regulation is least successful for music. Advertisements for parental-advisory-labelled music continue to be available to teen audiences, and the industry's compliance over labelling remains problematic. As regards music downloading, the FTC found that most services provide advisory information but only one-third accompany this with a parental control mechanism. Their undercover shopper survey found that 83 per cent of 13–16 year olds were able to purchase an explicit-content labelled recording. In the United Kingdom, the BPI implements the 'Voluntary Stickering Scheme', a self-regulatory measure for potentially offensive content in audio recordings, and those audio-visual recordings portraying sexual, violent or criminal content are regulated by the BBFC (and given an age-restricted classification) in accordance with the Video Recordings Act 1984.

The same FTC report (2004) had found that self-regulation was proving successful in the video-games market, with 'substantial, but not universal, compliance with industry standards limiting advert placements for M-rated (mature) games' to children under 17 years old. Rating information on product packaging was judged satisfactory. Nonetheless, the FTC's undercover teenage shoppers were able to buy M-rated games when unaccompanied in 69 per cent of cases. More recently (July 2005), a game (*Grand Theft Auto: San Andreas*) that had been rated in the United States as Mature 17+, and as MA15+ in Australia, was re-rated in the United States as suitable only for adults (18+) after it was found to contain erotic content in a 'locked' section of the game. A software modification meant this section could be unlocked. In Australia the game was withdrawn from sale altogether, while in the United Kingdom it had been rated as R18 from the outset.

Similarly, BBFC (2005) research found that people are broadly satisfied with film regulation. The percentages of people who think the BBFC Guidelines are 'about right' are:

- Sex – 58 per cent.

- Violence – 53 per cent.

- Language – 51 per cent.

- Drugs – 54 per cent.

Regulatory structures continue to change as technologies allow different possibilities for the transmission of content, with flexibility and a desire to remove the regulatory burden so that markets may flourish the prime motivators in any development. The revision of the Television Without Frontiers Directive, which extends the remit to include some regulation of audio-visual content, regardless of delivery mechanism, also allows for co-regulation (see Ballard, 1999, for some of the arguments for this change).

PARENTAL MEDIATION

In coming to a conclusion about the role of the media, especially television, in children's lives and its possible effects and influences, Comstock and Scharrer (2007: 117) note a sharp divide between content designed for young children and that made available to older children (from about 10 years of age):

We are struck by the realisation that there are largely two different worlds of content – the protective, educational, and prosocial bubble provided by media for the very young (infants, preschoolers, and children of early elementary age) and the sometimes harsh and often sensationalised material of media for older children, teenagers and the general audience (music television, internet sites, primetime television, video games). The two exist with little buffer forcing an abrupt change when 'children's media' are no longer satisfying.

This echoes the findings made by Ofcom (2007) in the United Kingdom that 'parents are relatively content with provision for pre-school and younger children, but want more drama and factual programming for older children and young teenagers'. See also Vandewater et al. (2007) for a discussion of media use among very young children in the United States. For Comstock and Scharrer (2007: 78) in the United States, the importance of parental mediation and the circumstances in the home are essential to the discussion about 'effects':

> Our own misgivings (about the possible negative influences of television) are based on foregone opportunities – the ability of parents by their comments to increase what is learned from television when it has educational value, to increase understanding of whatever has been presented, to temper fear and uneasiness when the medium presents frightening or threatening images and events, and occasionally to guide tastes and references in what the media offer.

In some countries, regulators seek to encourage the involvement of parents directly in their children's media use. The Media Development Authority in Singapore provides a range of advice pages for parents to help 'guide' their children's use of video-games and the Internet, pointing to the advantages of each medium as well as the potential disadvantages or risks.[1]

REGULATING CHILDREN'S MEDIA USE

There is a long tradition of research on parental mediation of children's television use. Nathanson (1999; 2001) draws together the research literature by proposing three broad strategies of parental regulation, namely active, restrictive, and co-viewing mediation. Valkenburg, Krcmar, Peeters, and Marseille (1999) similarly group mediation strategies for television into the categories of active or instructive mediation, rule-making or restrictive mediation, and parental modelling or co-viewing. These strategies may be stated in a more general form to apply to all media:

- ■ *Active mediation* consists of talking about media content while the child is engaging with (watching, reading, listening to) the medium (hence, this includes both positive/instructional and negative/critical forms of mediation);

- ■ *Restrictive mediation* involves setting rules that restrict use of the medium, including restrictions on time spent, location of use or content (e.g. restricting exposure to violent or sexual content), without necessarily discussing the meaning or effects of such content;

- ■ *Co-using* signifies that the parent remains present while the child is engaged with the medium (as for co-viewing), thus sharing in the experience but without commenting on the content or its effects.

Parents also report considerably more domestic regulation than do their children, making it difficult to determine just what role parents do play in mediating their children's access to media (Livingstone and Bovill, 1999). For example, three in four parents say they tell their child when they can and cannot watch television or videos, but only just over one in three children say that their parents do this (see also Livingstone and Bober, 2005, for equivalent findings in relation to the Internet).[2]

Hence, although the UK public feels that 'the best protection for children (from dangerous or unsuitable influences) was to have been brought up by parents who spent time 'instilling' the right values in their children' (Ofcom, 2005b), it remains unclear how much this occurs, and how effective it really is.

Borzekowski and Robinson (2007) review the literature on parental mediation of television and video viewing, also demonstrating the construct validity of three main scales in common use – 'instructive' (sometimes termed 'evaluative' or 'conversational'), 'restrictive', and 'social co-viewing' styles of parental mediation. This study did not find parental styles to be related to the amount or location of domestic media, but it was shown that parents using instructive and/or restrictive styles had children who spent longer viewing videos (possibly reflecting a parental control strategy). A restrictive parental style was associated with less television viewing, while the co-viewing style was associated with more viewing.

In relation to parental mediation of video-games, three similar types of strategies have been found – 'restrictive mediation', 'active mediation' and 'co-playing' (Nikken and Jansz, 2006). It is possible that parents are now extending these familiar strategies to the Internet. Alternatively, it seems plausible that they may also develop new strategies, given the highly-publicized array of online risks, and the greater range of safety tools available (including filtering, monitoring, etc). Some strategies developed for television (and even video-games) may work less well for the Internet. For example, it is difficult to make Internet use a shared activity (because of screen size, sitting position, reliance on the mouse, and common location in a small or private room). Also, online activities are less easily monitored with a casual glance at the screen, given multi-tasking across multiple open windows. Most importantly, online risks to children are greater than are television-related risks (regarding the extremes of violent or pornographic content, privacy or contact risks from strangers, etc), giving rise in turn to greater anxieties among parents (Wolak, Mitchell, and Finkelhor, 2007; Peter and Valkenburg, 2006).

In the graph below, the proportion of European parents/carers who have set rules for their child's television use is taken as an indication of parental willingness to regulate domestic media.[3] This is, in turn, likely to reflect cultural factors, possibly accounting for the considerable variation in these proportions – from fewer than one in three setting rules for their child's television use in Bulgaria, Estonia, Denmark and Czech Republic, to nearly half in Austria, France, Greece and Germany.

Most noticeable is the fact that the parental regulation of television in all cases exceeds that of the Internet, suggesting a willingness on parents' behalf to manage their children's media use for a familiar medium such as television. In other words, there is a 'regulation gap' in parental approaches to these two media. This is particularly striking in Germany, France, Greece, Austria, Spain, Bulgaria, Slovenia, Portugal and Poland – mainly, but not all, countries for whom the Internet is relatively new technology. In Bulgaria, for example, a survey of 21 secondary schools in 2003 identified a very low level of parental awareness regarding children's online risks: only 5 per cent of parents thought the Internet could be harmful for their children, and one in four claimed not to know what their child does online (National Center for Studying Public Opinion (NCSPO), 2003).

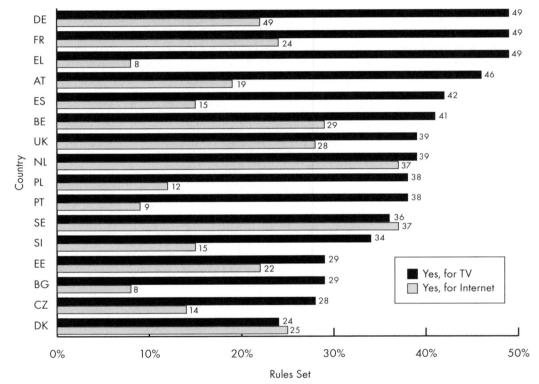

Source: Eurobarometer Survey (2006) Safer Internet, Special Eurobarometer 250 / Wave 64.4, Brussels. Question QC8: Sample is adults reporting on a child (<18 years old) they are responsible for in the household (N = 7560).

Figure 11.1 Have you set any rules for him/her about using any of the following either in your household or elsewhere?

In the above graph, the gap is smallest in Belgium, the United Kingdom, Estonia and, especially, Sweden, the Netherlands and Denmark – northern European countries in which the Internet is now well-established. Since parents seem willing to regulate media with which they are familiar (both television and the Internet), the low levels of Internet regulation by parents in some countries is likely to be a matter of low parental awareness, competence or understanding regarding safety issues online.

Overall, the recent Eurobarometer survey (2005–6) found that 38 per cent of parents or carers had set rules for their child regarding Internet use, and the figure was highest (48 per cent) for 10–13 year olds. Specific rules practiced across Europe, by the 38 per cent who do implement rules, are shown below (specific findings for the United Kingdom are not available):

Table 11.1 Rules applied by parents (by age of the child).

Rules	Aged 6 or younger	Aged 6–9	Aged 10–13	Aged 14–17
Not allowed to give out any personal information	14%	43%	54%	36%
Not allowed to visit some websites	28%	48%	63%	51%
Must tell if uncomfortable about something on the Internet	9%	34%	40%	18%
Not allowed to use rude language in emails or chat rooms	10%	27%	30%	18%
Not allowed to meet in person to someone only met on the Internet	10%	24%	45%	33%
Not allowed to copy document/pictures	5%	16%	10%	6%
Not allowed to go to chat rooms/talk to strangers in chat rooms	10%	34%	40%	23%
Not allowed to play games online	3%	17%	17%	11%
Not allowed to do online shopping	3%	33%	47%	38%
Not allowed to download music or films	1%	24%	24%	10%
Not allowed to download software	6%	28%	27%	16%
Rules regarding how much time child is allowed to spend on the Internet	42%	54%	55%	51%
Keeping phone lines free at certain times of the day	11%	8%	7%	3%
Ensuring that access to the Internet is shared fairly between family members	8%	22%	19%	18%
Other rules	46%	18%	16%	19%
Don't know	10%	5%	1%	2%

Source: Eurobarometer Survey (2006) Safer Internet

■ Most frequently mentioned
■ Second most frequently mentioned
▢ Third most frequently mentioned

However, the SAFT survey[4] reveals a sizeable gap between parental and children's accounts of online risk, suggesting that parents are unaware of the nature or extent of the risks of harm that their children encounter. It also reveals the converse gap, in which parents report a higher degree of regulation of their children than their children themselves recognize. Whether parents or children offer the more veridical account is a moot point, but the gap between them in perceptions of both risk and rules is notable.

Ofcom's (2006) Media Literacy Audit for children reports rather higher figures of parental mediation in the United Kingdom. For television, 85 per cent of parents report rules (mainly concerning content and time of day) for their 8–11 year old, dropping to 49 per cent for 12–15 year olds. For the Internet, rules are even more common, as shown below. In this figure, it is clear that even though children report somewhat less regulation than do their parents, the figures are still relatively high.

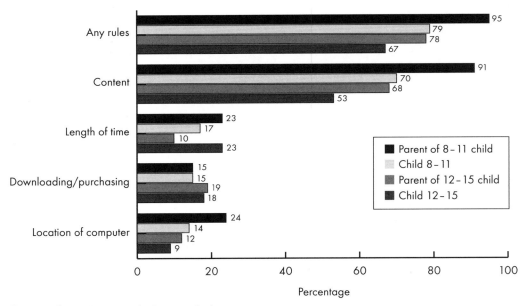

Source: Ofcom (2006) Media Literacy Audit.

Figure 11.2 Rules about access to the Internet as reported by parents and children.

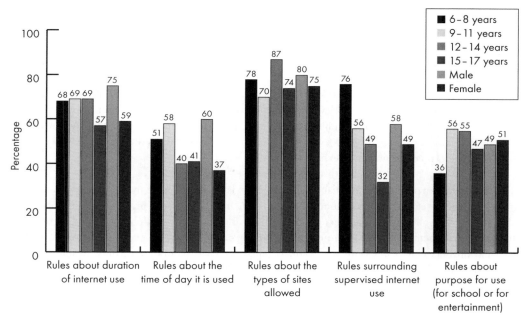

Source: Neilsen NetRatings (2007).

Figure 11.3 Rules for children's Internet use set by parents in Australia, by child's age and gender.

Also in Australia, Neilsen NetRatings (2007) found a recent increase in parents implementing rules regarding their children's Internet use, as shown in the figure below.

Nonetheless, there are still parents who do not implement rules, and little is known of the effectiveness of mediation when it is practiced. Qualitative work points to difficulties faced by parents in implementing rules, and they are also restricted by their own levels of media, or Internet, literacy (Livingstone and Bober, 2006). Vandewater et al. (2005), as do other previous researchers, report the strong association between parental mediation and parental education. Regarding 'television use among very young children (ages 0 to 6 years old), higher education level was related to rules regarding both amount of viewing time and specific content rules, whereas higher household income was related to having content (programme) rules'.

Even for television, Jordan, Hersey, McDivitt, and Heitzler (2006) identify a series of practical consideration that impede parents' ability to reduce their child's exposure to television (and, by implication, other media), including parents' need to use television as a safe and affordable distraction, parents' own heavy television viewing patterns, the role that television plays in the family's day-to-day routine, and a belief that children should spend their weekend leisure time as they wish' (p. e1303). In relation to the Internet, such practicalities may lie behind Rosen's (2006) observation that, 'Parents' high estimates of the dangers posed by online experiences were not matched by their low rates of setting limits and monitoring their teens'.

Crucially, the current indications are that parental regulation, even though widely practiced, is not always effective. For example, Buijzen et al. (2007) found, for a sample of 451 Dutch 8–12 year olds, active parental mediation (discussing the news with their child) reduced children's fear, worry and anger among the younger children only. Restrictive mediation had no or even the opposite effect. In Nikken and Jansz's (2007) survey of 1,115 Dutch families examining parental mediation of children's playing of restricted electronic games, they found that playing restricted games was predicted by certain characteristics of the child (younger children, boys, children inclined to violence and swearing, children who are enthusiastic about such games) and the parent (more play among those subject to more – not less – parental mediation, especially active discussion, social co-playing and verbal comments).

The somewhat surprising finding that more mediation is associated with more playing of restricted games led the researchers to conclude in favour of the 'forbidden fruit' argument (as theorized by the notion of psychological reactance). Alternatively, it may also be that children who already play more provoke their parents to comment unfavourably on their play, hence resulting in the positive correlation between restrictions and banned behaviour. Most important, only straightforward restrictions on playing electronic games (rather than playing with the child or discussing the games played) were found to reduce the amount of play in this study.

What of the Internet? It has not been established that parents who restrict or mediate their children's Internet use have children who encounter fewer risks. The UK Children Go Online project (Livingstone and Bober, 2005), which specifically sought to identify effective strategies of parental mediation, could find none such (unless parental interventions substantially reduce the child's Internet use altogether). Livingstone and Helsper (2006) found that the expectation that increasing mediation would reduce risks was not supported. As with findings for parental mediation and electronic games, it was found that parental restriction of online communication was associated with a significant reduction in the range of online risks encountered by 12–17 year olds.

However, neither active co-use (going online with your child, talking about the Internet, etc), though widely practiced, nor software-based strategies (filtering and monitoring) were found to be effective in reducing risk. This challenges future research to identify the benefits, if any, of such practices. It may be a matter of parental Internet literacy – the UK Children Go Online survey (2005) found that only 15 per cent of parents said they were good at installing a filter (Livingstone and Bober, 2005). But it may also reflect the sometimes difficult relations between parents and teenagers: findings regarding the Internet echo those for parental control and monitoring in relation to other areas of risk in adolescence (e.g. drug taking, alcohol use, etc.; Kerr and Stattin, 2000).

Fleming, Greentree, Cocotti-Muller, Elias and Morrison's (2006) survey of 692 Australian 13–16 year olds found significant differences in online safety practices such that younger teenagers (13–14 year olds) and those whose parents had not discussed Internet safety with them were less safety conscious. By implication, those whose parents had discussed safety issues with them, as well as those who were older, were more safety conscious. Moreover, Cho and Cheon (2005) found that parents' perceived control, obtained through shared Web activities and family cohesion, reduced children's exposure to negative Internet content. Further, Eastin, Greenberg and Hofshire (2006) found that parenting style (categorized as authoritative, authoritarian, permissive and neglectful) has a significant effect on almost all mediation techniques studied, whereas increased access only influences time online. Additionally, technological blocking as a restrictive mediation technique was found to be highest among authoritative parents, followed by authoritarian and neglectful styles of parenting.

While this shows an association between parenting style in general and parental strategies for mediating the Internet in particular, there was no direct measurement of online risky behaviours in this study: hence it cannot be concluded that parenting style reduces online risk. Although it is encouraging that research suggests restricting online interactions has some benefits, the costs in terms of reducing teenagers' freedom to interact with peers online must be weighed against the advantages in developing safety guidance directed at parents and teenagers. As noted in Livingstone and Helsper:

> There is a strong positive association between opportunities and risks. This points to the dilemma that parents and regulators face. Increasing opportunities increases the risks. Online opportunities, and online safety, bear a cost.

Cottrell, Branstetter, Cottrell, Rishel, and Stanton's (2007) review of the literature on parental mediation of Internet use summarizes recent research findings as follows:

- Child self-disclosure of risky activities is the main predictor of parental monitoring.

- Parents who use filtering/blocking software are more knowledgeable about their child's online activities.

- Open and supportive parent-child relations are associated with reduced online risk behaviour from teenagers, as is direct communication between parents and children about online risk behaviours.

Using data collected in 2005, Cottrell et al. used structural equation modelling to reveal that teenagers do recognize parental Internet monitoring activities and that this recognition works 'to modestly reduce current disapproved internet use behaviour' (p. 219). Further, parental monitoring knowledge (parents' knowledge of teenagers' risk behaviours) and parent-adolescent communication were also associated with a reduction in disapproved online behaviour. The authors concluded in favour of active parental strategies (put computer in an open area, set time limits, install blocking software, check Internet history) as well as open and direct communication between parents and teenagers. This raises the broader question of parenting skills and family communication patterns. This important question has, separately, occasioned a considerable body of empirical research, though rarely does this include questions of parental regulation of children's media use.

Nonetheless, some research does find parental mediation to be effective in relation to consumer socialization and media literacy (see Calvert, 1999; Singer and Singer, 2001). For example, in a field study of 627 children and 486 of their parents, Austin, Roberts and Nass (1990) examined the effects of family communication environment and parental mediation of television content on third, sixth and ninth graders' perceptions of the realism of television content, its similarity to real-life and their identification with television characters. Findings showed that effective interpersonal family communication helps children form the real-world perceptions which they then compare with their perceptions of the television-world so as to better assess realism.

Following up on such research, Nathanson has examined how different forms of mediation might mitigate the negative effects of viewing violent television content (Nathanson, 2001, 2004; Nathanson and Cantor, 2000). One of her studies looked at different approaches to mediating children's violent television viewing: 'factual mediation' which provides children with facts about a violent programme's production techniques and 'evaluative mediation' providing negative evaluations of the programme's characters. She split her sample between two age groups, 5–7 and 10–12 year old children, so that she could examine developmental differences. Children watched an edited episode of a children's action programme, with three blank ten second pauses inserted. During these pauses the mediation approach to be tested was introduced (a control group saw no mediation). The children then filled out a short questionnaire. Nathanson found that evaluative mediation was the most effective strategy for encouraging the children to reject the violence or the violent characters, particularly for younger children, while factual mediation had either no effect or increased some children's wish to be more engaged with the media violence they saw. This study was conducted in schools and Nathanson suggests it should be replicated to see how effective it might be in the home.

Another study by Nathanson looked at the importance of peer mediation, and found that both viewing and discussion of antisocial content occurred more frequently among adolescent peer groups (Nathanson, 2001). While this in itself is not surprising, the quantitative study – based on asking college students to think back to situations of viewing and emotions – also found that discussion of such material led to more positive views about aggression and even aggressive behaviour. The study also considered parental mediation and Nathanson found they functioned in different ways. Parental mediation acts as 'intervention' while peer mediation is a social interaction. Nathanson suggests it would be useful to create a study which can compare the two types of mediation directly.

Other studies have looked at different models of in-home mediation. Krcmar and Vieira surveyed parent-child dyads to look at the impact of exposure to television violence, family communication, and parents' moral reasoning on the moral reasoning of the child (2005). The children were aged between 5–12 years old and their moral reasoning was tested through presenting them with scenarios (stories) in which violence was either justified (violence used to protect another person or as restitution for harm done) or not justified. The data suggest that children who watch more fantasy violence are more likely to perceive unjustified violence as right, but also, importantly, that the way in which the family communicates impacts upon the amount of fantasy violence viewed. So that children who come from families that have 'better' communication watch less fantasy violence. The research did not find that parents' moral reasoning about justified violence was linked with their children's reasoning. The researchers conclude:

It appears that the way in which families communicate with their children – and not direct modeling *per se* – has the greater impact on the development of children's reasoning.

Similarly, Warren, Gerke and Kelly found (2002) that parental mediation may be dependent on the level of parent-child engagement in a variety of shared activities, regardless of the type of mediation used. The study was a telephone survey of self-reported involvement and media use, among other measures. It would be useful to find some way to develop this work to look more specifically at the way in which parental involvement works. Chang (2000) also found that the interactive nature of in-home communication was key to the way in which parental mediation worked most successfully – in this case, regarding the acquisition of toys associated with television programmes (see also Nathanson et al. to look at how mediation, based on active involvement with children, can affect gender-stereotypes in viewing; Nathanson, Wilson, McGee, and Sebastian, 2002).

Busselle (2003) surveyed 178 college age students and, independently, their parents about their crime-related viewing and their perceptions of crime prevalence. It found that there was a link between parental viewing and their children's views about crime prevalence. The data suggest that television viewing influences the frequency with which parents warn their children (when in high school) about the dangers of crime. However, parents and their children were being asked to think back up to four years previously and it may be worth trying to replicate the findings with current samples. Busselle also noted gender differences which warrant further research.

A study in the Netherlands equated the media preferences of parents with the educational achievement of their children (Elchardus and Siongers, 2003). It found that the more 'populist' the media content used, the less well the child performs. However, this quantitative study – drawing on cultural capital arguments – cannot take in to account influences outside the home that can impact on children's behaviour and it would seem to be unlikely that one can lay educational achievement solely at the door of parental viewing behaviour.

The way in which parents mediate children's viewing – and their difficulties in doing so – was examined by Ramsay (2003) in a study that used interactive workshops as the methodology, allowing an iterative discussion process. Eighteen workshops took place and larger sample survey data supplemented the findings. This methodology worked well in teasing out issues and developing them. Ramsay found that parents in the workshops expressed most concern about violent content, but the larger sample of panellists were more likely to mention depictions of sex or the use of offensive language as being more problematic for them. Workshop participants expressed most concern about regulating the viewing of children aged 8–12 years old as they were felt to be impressionable but less easy to monitor, especially around the watershed at 9 p.m. The panel included children aged 4–15 years old and these findings also showed that younger children were far more restricted in terms of what they could and could not see on television.

TOOLS AND STRATEGIES
In a review of the literature on parental mediation, Bellman (1999) observes that although parents can affect their children's television viewing, less than half of them do ban exposure to 'adult' or

'offensive' programmes, set bedtime limits on viewing or make comments on the nature of the content being viewed (though such comments do help children when viewing upsetting, scary or otherwise challenging content (Austin, 1993). He notes further that content ratings have been shown to produce a 'boomerang effect', with children avoiding the ratings but preferring the content rated too old for them. Indeed, a school-based survey in the United States found that 'those parents in the least need of mediation assistance are the ones most likely to be using the ratings information' (low/moderate viewers, high academic achievers, mainly women) – as Abelman (1999) puts it, content ratings are 'preaching to the choir'. This finding is consistent with knowledge gap research which more broadly shows that public campaigns are better at informing those already advantaged, motivated or informed than at reaching the less advantaged (who are dubbed, therefore, the 'hard to reach').

Many studies show that parents want the tools for parental mediation, pointing to a widespread unmet need in terms of parental awareness and support. For example, in an online survey of 765 parents, Nikken et al. (2007) found that parents are strongly in favour of content ratings regarding potentially harmful (violent, gory, pornographic, etc) electronic games; moreover, those parents concerned about the negative consequences of game-play were also shown to use these ratings in guiding their parental mediation.

Hanley (2002), in a qualitative study of parental mediation in the home, had found that there was little active mediation regarding television content. Instead parents relied on scheduling conventions or time-derived controls, such as limiting the amount of time spent viewing. Nonetheless parents say they would like more information about programme content, although it is unclear what they will do with such information. They also say that they make themselves available to discuss difficult content with their children, and are sometimes glad of the opportunity to do so being raised, especially in soap operas (see also Towler, 2001).

Byron (2008) in reviewing the evidence for the potential for harm to children from the Internet and video-games considers that parents need tools and strategies to help them cope, but that they need to understand what those tools are and how to operate them. For example, she points to uncertainty about filters or parental confusion in understanding what video-game classifications mean.

Media literacy

A prime purpose of parental (and other forms of adult) mediation is to enhance children's media literacy (von Feilitzen and Carlsson, 2004). Considerable attention has been paid to the question of media literacy, both through programmes of media education instituted and evaluated over many decades and, more recently, in response to the rapid expansion of new media technologies. Media literacy is, it should be noted, also a highly contested concept (Buckingham, 1989; Hobbs, 1998). One long-standing debate, relevant to our present considerations, is whether media literacy is primarily a means of reducing potential media harm or whether, instead, it is a means of enhancing potential media benefits.

The Gruenwald Declaration[5] states:

The role of communication and media in the process of development should not be under-estimated, nor the function of the media as instruments for the citizen's active participation in society. Political and educational systems need to recognise their obligations to promote in their citizens a critical understanding of the phenomena of communication.

The European Commission defines media literacy thus:

> Media Literacy may be defined as the ability to access, analyse and evaluate the power of images, sounds and messages which we are now being confronted with on a daily basis and are an important part of our contemporary culture, as well as to communicate competently in media available on a personal basis. Media literacy relates to all media, including television and film, radio and recorded music, print media, the internet and other new digital communication technologies. (European Commission Audiovisual and Media Policies, n.d.)

Although it notes the positive benefits of media literacy for citizenship, freedom of expression and personal choice, the primary thrust of this approach suggests that media literacy should be used as a barrier, namely as a means by which individuals may protect themselves from the harmful or problematic aspects of the new media and information environment (e.g. to evaluate the many messages that confront today's media consumer, to be aware of media filtering and bias, to help them become judicious consumers and to be aware of issues regarding intellectual property rights).

The research literature on media literacy has been reviewed in relation to children (Buckingham and others, 2004) and adults (Livingstone, van Couvering, and Thumim, 2005), as commissioned by Ofcom. These reviews reveal an uneven coverage in the literature, with most research concentrated on older rather than newer media. They also reveal a public – especially children – that is keen and motivated to become more media literate, gaining a range of skills and sophistication in their understanding of media content, this often being part of the pleasure of engaging with media. Yet a series of limitations on people's media literacy are also identified. This includes limitations on understanding across much of the public (e.g. in relation to the workings of media institutions and production processes) as well as among particular subgroups of the public (e.g. the elderly).

While many hopes are laid at the door of media literacy, two particular limitations on its potential especially to mediate (and undermine) harm should be noted. First, as the psychology of child development makes clear, age is a crucial factor in all aspects of children's relations with society and its influences. Too often in the research and policy-discussions, 'children' are treated as a homogeneous category irrespective of their cognitive and social development. Research on media literacy, however, emphasizes that how children understand the media (and the world) matters greatly (Potter, 2004; van Evra, 1998). There are, clearly, limits placed by age on what media literacy can be attained: put simply, below a certain age (which might vary somewhat from individual to individual), one cannot teach a child to distinguish, for example, fact from fiction, programmes from advertising or objectivity from bias. Notwithstanding the substantial theoretical debate over stage models of child development and their relation to age, most researchers would agree on some key milestones – that by the age of 7 or 8 years old, children can distinguish advertising from programming, they can link portrayed actions to their consequences, they can distinguish fact from fiction; and that from around 12 years old, they are becoming more critical and discerning media users, aware of bias, of moral implications, of more subtle persuasive and production techniques, and so forth.

Second, and curiously perhaps, the commonplace assumption that as children become more media literate they become less easily affected by the media is not supported by evidence (Livingstone and Helsper, 2006); indeed, if this were the case, one would suppose adults immune from media influence (again, this is contrary to the evidence for media effects on all audiences). Rather, it is likely that different forms of persuasion, different kinds of media influence, are effective at different ages, just as the media more generally have different effects on different audience subgroups. So, even if the public becomes more media literate, particularly for new media, research does not show that this would prevent the media causing harm or offence.

Further, one would expect the media – through their technologies, persuasive strategies and content design – to adjust to these new levels of literacy, thereby demanding yet further understanding and scepticism on the part of the public. For example, considerable efforts have gone into ensuring that the public, including children, can distinguish advertising from programming. At the time of writing, little or no such efforts have been devoted to ensuring the public can detect product placement or commercial sponsorship of content, these latter developments further ratcheting up the requirements on a media literate public. Indeed, the demands on the public to be media – and information – literate, are growing considerably as technologies and contents converge, new forms of content emerge, and as media and information contents become crucial not just for leisure but also for education, health, employment and civic participation.

The Internet especially raises many concerns regarding the anonymity of communication and the verifiability and veracity of content. In part, this is a media literacy issue, but media literacy relies on the availability of content features by which people may ordinarily discriminate public from commercial content, or professional from amateur content, or legal from illegal content. Within this debate one must not forget the self-regulatory features of many of the social networking and user-generated content sites which use self-reporting and self-regulatory measures to remove content that may be inappropriate or, indeed, illegal. These further challenges will be exacerbated by the introduction of Web 2.0. As one polemic commentator complains:

> In the digital world's never-ending stream of unfiltered user-generated content, things are indeed often not what they seem. Without editors, fact-checkers, administrators or regulators to monitor what is being pushed, we have no one to vouch for the reliability or credibility of the content we read…There are no gatekeepers to filter truth from fiction, genuine content from advertising, legitimate information from errors or outright deceit. Who is to point out the lies on the blogosphere that attempt to rewrite our history and spread rumour as fact? (Keen, 2007: 64–65)

Not only parents need guidance, but so too do young people. Overall, many young people are reasonably responsive to safety guidance, though nations vary. The Mediappro project concluded:

> There is also, importantly, wide evidence of self-regulation by young people. This includes awareness of violent and pornographic sites, sometimes in relation to concern about younger siblings, as in the Danish study; it may be that young people here replicate adult anxiety, adopting adult roles towards younger children. It also includes anxiety about chatrooms; and concern about viruses, spam, expense (buying ring tones, for instance), and hackers. However, awareness of risk and ability to deal with it varies considerably from country to country. In France, the young people were aware of a wide range of risks, and expressed sensible, cautious attitudes, which the French study attributed to extensive and successful public information campaigns and teacher training. Similarly, in Estonia, respondents were well aware of a wide variety of risks, from communicating with strangers to the dangers of internet shopping. By contrast, the Polish study found evidence that young people were sometimes too trusting of websites and in need of education to evaluate risk; while the Greek study found generally low awareness of risk. (Mediappro, 2006: 14)

In the Bulgarian survey referred to above, three in four pupils were unaware of online risks (though nearly half had experienced online pornography, violence, contact with strangers and even offers of virtual sex). However, in Slovenia, where 77 per cent of 12–19 year olds use the Internet, teenagers are more worried by spam, viruses and advertisements than they are by other harms; nonetheless, one in three teens worry about the safety of online information (RIS 2006), and one in two parents regulate their child's use of the Internet (Eurobarometer, 2006).

Not all concerns with media literacy concern the risk of inappropriate contact, and increasing interest focuses on people's (especially children's) judgements regarding appropriate or inappropriate content. For example, Eastin, Yang and Nathanson (2006) examined how children (on average, 9 years old) in the United States determined the credibility of online information. They found that most had trouble recalling online information when the text including advertising pop-ups in addition to plain text, that children tended to believe sites that included advertising and lacked a clear source (compared with those that provided a source or that lacked advertising). Similarly, Ofcom's (2006) Children's 'Media Literacy Audit' found that around one in three (31 per cent) of 12–15 year olds make some kind of check when visiting a new website (e.g. checking the date or source, or comparing across sites).

In general, research on media literacy (and other awareness-raising activities) shows that:

- Levels of media literacy vary considerably across populations, with those 'ahead' tending to sustain their relative advantage over others as the media environment develops;

- Lower levels of media literacy are associated with other forms of social exclusion and relative deprivation, thus adding to already-existing forms of disadvantage;

■ Critical media skills of interpretation and evaluation are not always implemented or practiced in real-life circumstances, reflecting a persistent knowledge/behaviour gap;

■ Greater levels of media literacy are assumed, but have not been shown convincingly, to reduce media-related risk of harm;

■ Initiatives to promote media literacy are generally more effective in reaching the information-rich than the information-poor (see Buckingham, 2005; Livingstone, Van Couvering, and Thumim, 2005).

Measuring media literacy and, particularly, measuring change in media literacy against relevant benchmarks is largely lacking on anything other than a project-by-project basis. The United Kingdom's establishment of a media literacy audit – measuring such variables as access to, attitudes towards, trust in and complaints or concerns about each of several media – is one way forward (see Ofcom, 2006). However, notwithstanding the growing number of initiatives underway to increase children's media literacy, resulting in increases in children's awareness of certain risks, it is not yet established that this translates into a reduction in actual harm. Indeed, more generally the commonplace assumption that as children become more media literate they become less readily influenced by media content, and thus are less at risk of harm, is not (yet) supported by evidence (Livingstone and Helsper, 2006).

There remains in most countries a considerable gap between the ambitions of those promoting media literacy and the delivery of an effective media literacy curriculum (see Hobbs, 1998). Media literacy principles are often articulated but less often translated into teaching resources. Moreover, they tend to be evaluated in their own terms (e.g. as teaching resources) more than they are assessed for their effectiveness in ameliorating the risk of harm. Other routes to media literacy (e.g. media campaigns, parenting guidance, online resources), like many awareness-raising campaigns, tend to reach the already-informed more than they do those who really need to know. Increasing resources, evaluating media literacy programmes, and equalizing competences so that all children may benefit remains a challenge for the future. As with the question of parental mediation, the importance of enhancing children's media literacy is widely supported and so merits further empirical investigation.

SUMMARY

■ Research shows that the public is generally accepting of some regulation of content – parents more so than groups at different life stages – and they have particular concern regarding, say, violence in the media, although these do not necessarily translate into complaints or any other active protest. In relation to television, for example, there are many more complaints about the use of offensive language.

■ Many parents have long employed various strategies for mediating their children's television use. Specifically, there are three main types of mediation activity practised – restrictive (limiting, banning), active (discussing, guiding) and co-use (sharing the activity). These and other strategies have been extended to electronic games and, more recently, to children's use of the Internet, but findings suggest that many parents feel far less confident regarding managing their children's internet use and may do little to intervene or discuss their use.

■ Indeed, research points to a range of practical, domestic and technical difficulties, especially but not only in managing their children's Internet use and, in consequence, some may do little to intervene in their child's online activities. For the Internet especially, there is a considerable gap between parental and child perceptions of the risks encountered by the child (i.e. parents underestimate risks as reported by the child). There is an equivalent, though reverse gap regarding reports of parental mediation activities (i.e. parents overestimate mediation as reported by the child). Notably, there is not yet much evidence that parental regulation effectively reduces the extent or nature of media-related risks, unless parents take a generally restrictive approach to their child's access to the medium altogether.

■ Crucially, there is as yet little evidence that parental regulation, even though widely practiced, is effective in reducing the extent or nature of risk or, indeed, in affecting how children respond to risk when encountered. Specifically, where there is some evidence that parental mediation is effective, this tends to be associated with restrictive strategies (i.e. those which reduce use of the medium altogether) rather than the often-favoured active and co-use strategies. Further, parental mediation can be more effective in homes where there is already a strong communications environment and that different forms of mediation work better for different groups, often depending on the age of the child. Overall, however, research has not found that parents who restrict or mediate their children's Internet/game use more have children who encounter fewer risks/harms.

■ Growing efforts are devoted to raising awareness among parents and children regarding the risks of media use, and there is evidence that both groups are generally aware of these risks. While evidence on specific practices remains sparse, especially in the United Kingdom, the academic work is generally of high quality. Among market research surveys on safety knowledge and practices, it is not always possible to obtain the full research report. Although research is growing on children's media literacy, as are the number of initiatives designed to increase this literacy, it is not yet established that increased media literacy either reduces children's exposure to risk or increases their ability to cope with risk. Hence more research is needed.

■ Some argue that risk should be managed not eliminated, both because a risk-free society would be highly restrictive and because children and teenagers need to encounter some degree of risk in order to develop their ability to cope. Such arguments point to the potential value of increasing children's media literacy in order to mitigate against the risk of harm. A growing number of initiatives are underway, and evaluations tend to show that children's awareness of certain risks is increasing. It is not yet established, however, that this translates into a reduction in actual risk. Since it appears counter-intuitive to conclude that neither parental mediation nor children's media literacy has a positive role to play in the management of media-related risks, more research is greatly needed.

NOTES

1. http://www.mda.gov.sg/wms.www/actualTransferrer.aspx?c=10.1.3.&sid=155&eid=-1&fid=-1

2 For example, in the UK Children Go Online survey, 77 per cent of parents but only 54 per cent of children say their child is/they are not allowed to buy anything online, and 62 per cent of parents but only 40 per cent of children say their child is/they are not allowed to chat online, and these discrepancies occur in relation to a range of specific uses of the Internet. However, in terms of general rules of use there was less discrepancy: 42 per cent of the children say that they have to follow rules about for how long and 35 per cent about when they can go online, and parents are broadly in agreement, with 43 per cent claiming to have set up rules for how much time their child can spend on the Internet.

3. *Source:* Eurobarometer Survey (May 2006) *Safer Internet*, Special Eurobarometer 250 / Wave 64.4, Brussels. Sample QC8: Adults reporting on a child (<18 years old) they are responsible for in the household (N = 7560). Country abbreviations op cit.

4. NCTE/SAFT (2003) *Executive summary: SAFT – Safety Awareness Fact and Tools.* Children's study – investigating online behaviour. May 2003. See http://www.ncte.ie/InternetSafety/Publications/d1736.PDF. Similar findings were obtained by *UK Children Go Online* (see www.children-go-online.net).

5. http://portal.unesco.org/ci/en/files/27310/12150121753MEDIA_E.pdf/MEDIA_E.pdf

12

CONCLUSIONS

This literature review was designed to examine the evidence that exists for the risk of harm and offence caused by media-delivered content. The review has been primarily organized by medium, and secondarily by types of material and/or groupings of audiences/users. It has addressed key questions currently facing regulators, industry, researchers and the public, bringing together findings across a range of different media, in relation to both harm and offence, and looking across a range of audience and user groups. As discussed at the outset, we first noted that the body of research on media harm especially, less so for offence, has long been subject to considerable contestation on theoretical, political and, particularly, methodological grounds. Our strategy in this review has been to incorporate, and balance against each other, the different kinds of findings, based on different methods and different perspectives on the debate over media harm and offence.

However, we promised no uncontentious summary of research findings, and nor can there be any simple answer to the question of media harm or any definitive empirical demonstration or 'proof'. But, while it is clear that more evidence is needed, especially for certain uses of the new media and for vulnerable groups, we note that the precautionary principle suggests that judgements may be reached assuming probable influence rather than postponing regulatory decisions to await the outcome of further research.

DISTINGUISHING HARM AND OFFENCE

In policy-discussions, 'harm and offence' have been used frequently as a single phrase. It is not clear, however, just what the difference between the terms is taken to be, nor how they differently relate to legal or regulatory frameworks. Similarly, harm and offence are often not clearly distinguished in terms of research evidence. Indeed, other than in relation to legal or philosophical discussions of the terms as used in regulation, we have not found the terms used very much at all in the academic literature.

While there is a large literature on harm (usually labelled 'effects'), we have found little recent academic research on offence. Our assumption is that this is because, on the one hand, experimental researchers are unimpressed by the self-report methods used, necessarily, to assess offence (i.e. they would identify problems of reliability in relation to offence), while on the other hand, cultural researchers fear that research on offence opens the door to a culture of censorship. Nor have we found any theory relating to 'offence' (though there are many for media influence), this also helping to explain the lack of research on offence.

From a regulatory or industry point of view, however, 'offence' provides a route to acknowledging and responding to audiences' or users' concerns about media content without necessarily framing this as 'harm'. These bodies have, therefore, conducted a fair amount of research, using both qualitative and quantitative methods, charting the extent and focus of 'offence' among the public, including some longitudinal tracking studies.

It follows that the distinction between harm and offence (or its relation to taste and decency) is not always clear. However:

- We suggest that harm is widely (though not necessarily) conceived in objective terms; harm, it seems, is taken to be observable by others (irrespective of whether harm is acknowledged by the individual concerned), and hence as measurable in a reliable fashion.

- By contrast, offence is widely (though not necessarily) conceived in subjective terms; offence, it seems, is taken to be that experienced by and reported on by the individual, and hence is difficult to measure reliably (and, equally, difficult to deny in the face of claimed offence).[1]

The terms vary in other ways:

- It may be argued that media harm can affect both the media user themselves and others around them. Harm may last for a short time or longer (though the evidence is largely lacking for the long-term effects frequently hypothesized by media effects theories). The risk of harm may apply at the level of the individual, group or society. Offence, by contrast, may be thought to affect only the media user themselves (or, perhaps, groups of individuals), and it is assumed to apply only in the moment (i.e. offence is not taken to last a long time, though it may be remembered).

- One implication is that it is potentially easier to demonstrate offence than harm; harm setting a high threshold in terms of evidence. Another is that the risk of harm merits greater attempts at prevention than does offence. A third is that the market may be assumed to address offence (since it damages the brand) while public intervention may be required additionally to prevent harm.

Each of these implications and assumptions can, of course, be contested: our point here is that the terms 'harm' and 'offence', although widely used, have attracted surprisingly little discussion or clarification. Since these terms are increasingly used in discussions of media content regulation, replacing the former term, 'taste and decency', we would recommend further consideration and, ideally, a degree of consensus, regarding the definition of both 'harm' and 'offence'.

Interestingly, harm and offence are generally discussed differently in relation to children and adults:

■ Harm is assumed to vary by vulnerability, being greater for children and for vulnerable adults. Considerable research attention has, therefore, gone into identifying the risk factors for harm, and most research is concentrated on the at-risk groups (typically, children).

■ By contrast, offence is not seen as related to vulnerability. Older people and women are generally found to find more media content offensive; yet this is not apparently related to vulnerability, except insofar as differential levels of media literacy may make it harder for these groups to control their exposure to certain contents.

■ Notably, there is little research on whether the media offend (rather than harm) children, and only recently is there some research on the response of marginal or low-status groups (adults and children) to the sometimes negative representations of them in the media (and whether this concerns harm or offence is unclear). This results in some inconsistencies when relating research findings to regulation: for example, if a child is upset by viewing violence, this is taken as evidence of harm; if an adult is upset by the same image, this is likely to be seen as offence.

On drawing conclusions

Drawing conclusions about offence is comparatively straightforward. Looking across all media, the research evidence shows a sizeable minority of the population find certain content offensive. This is especially the case for women and older people, though most are nonetheless tolerant of the rights of others to engage with the media of their choice. In particular, new forms of media occasion greater public concern and anxiety than do more familiar media. For these latter, the public is, in the main, supportive of the current regulatory framework. However, findings are mixed on whether people are satisfied with (or even aware of) the available processes for making a complaint about media content.

Drawing conclusions about harm, on the other hand, is more difficult and must take account of the limitations of the evidence base. This review has noted a range of theoretical, methodological and political difficulties in researching the possible harm and offence in relation to media content. In many respects, the evidence base is patchy and inconsistent (see also Annex I). Many questions remain difficult to research. Particularly, research can only offer evidence towards a judgement based on the balance of probabilities rather than on irrefutable proof. Persistent questions remain regarding:

■ How far the largely American findings in the published academic literature may be applicable to the UK situation, given differences in culture, in regulatory context and in the media content available (and researched).

■ How far the largely experimental research findings may be applicable to ordinary contexts of media use, given the often unnatural circumstances in which experiments expose people to media content, their measurement of effects, and the short-term nature of the studies. Reliance on correlational and/or social research methods poses equivalent problems of interpretation.

- How far the largely television-based (or mass communication-based) research may be applicable to other, especially newer and interactive media, given the likelihood that different expectations, knowledge and concerns attach to different kinds of media, each accessed under different conditions.

Understanding 'harm'

A wide range of definitions of harm are suggested in the research literature (McQuail and Windahl, 1993), including:

- Changed attitudes or beliefs affecting the individual (e.g. fear of crime) or society (e.g. stereotypes of the elderly).

- Changed behaviours, particularly the increased propensity to harm others (e.g. aggressive behaviour, this damaging both the perpetrator and his/her possible victims) or for self-harm (e.g. anorexia, obesity, suicide).

- Emotional responses, affecting both the self and others, including fear, upset and hate, which may lead to harm if they are long-term in effect. Such responses may, arguably, be more appropriately regarded instead as 'offence'.

Of these, we suggest that more attention is often paid to the first two than to the third, yet there are, perhaps unexpectedly, many studies showing that the media can have negative emotional consequences, often but not only in the short-term. It is clear that this is recognized in many policy-related decisions and we recommend that consideration is given to emotional responses in future research and policy regarding harm and offence.

Much of the debate about media harms starts from the argument that the negative influence on an individual will, in turn, create harm to society. This view of an inter-relationship between influences and effects has been taken up by the popular media – in reporting crimes, for example, which are linked to supposed (though not always established) media exposure. Those harms that are caused to the individual through the perpetuation of unfair or stereotypical depictions are not much discussed, except in the literature and within codes of practice. We suggest it would be valuable to distinguish:

- Risk of harm to the individual exposed to media content.

- Risk of harm to other people.

- Risk of harm to society in general.

Nevertheless it should be accepted that there may be inter-relationships between these possible harms. For example, to the extent that watching television violence encourages aggressive behaviour among boys, this risks, first, harm to those particular boys, second, harm to those against whom they might be aggressive (e.g. peers in the playground) and, third, harm to society (as aggression and fear of aggression become more widespread). However, the processes involved, the consequences, and the potential for intervention, differ for each kind of harm.

A RISK-BASED APPROACH

When television first arrived in American homes, the founding father of media effects research declared:

> …for some children, under some conditions, some television is harmful. For some children under the same conditions, or for the same children under other conditions, it may be beneficial. For most children, under most conditions, most television is probably neither particularly harmful nor particularly beneficial. (Schramm, Lyle, and Parker, 1961: 11)

We suggest that, after a vast amount of further research findings, on the basis of 'a balance of probabilities', this remains a fair summary of the evidence, even if much of that evidence has been collected under a differently regulated media environment. Hence, this review has argued that the search for simple and direct causal effects of the media is, for the most part, not appropriate. Rather, this should be replaced by an approach that seeks to identify the range of factors that directly, and indirectly through interactions with each other, combine to explain particular social phenomena. As research shows, each social problem of concern (e.g. aggression, prejudice, obesity, bullying, etc.) is associated with a distinct and complex array of putative causes.

The task for those concerned with media harm and offence is to identify and contextualize the role of the media within that array. The result will be a more complex explanation of what are, undoubtedly, complex social problems. This should, in turn, permit a balanced judgement of the role played by the media on a case by case basis. In some cases, this may reduce the focus on the media – for example, by bringing into view the many other factors that account for present levels of aggression in society. In other cases, it may increase the focus on the media – for example, in understanding the role played potentially by the Internet in facilitating paedophiles' access to children.

A risk-based approach seeks to take into account a wide range of relevant factors, as these establish the conditions under which any particular factor (such as media exposure) operates. Many such factors are culturally-specific, including national traditions of content regulation, approaches to parenting, and moral frames for judging content or determining offence. In addition to such factors, and to the important differences across the media and hence across media access conditions, we have also sought to stress that content does not affect all audiences equally. Research suggests that there can be greater negative influences on those who are 'vulnerable'. No standard academic definition of 'vulnerability' exists, but research findings do suggest that vulnerable audiences/users may include children and young people, especially boys, together with a range of other groups among the adult population (including psychologically disturbed individuals, people who are depressed, sexual offenders, young offenders, etc.).

CONTINGENT CONCLUSIONS

Conclusions must be drawn, we suggest, on a case-by-case basis, depending on the social problem at stake.

AGGRESSIVE CONTENT

There is a sizeable body of evidence that televised portrayals of aggression (typically, American action-adventure dramas intended for an older audience) may negatively influence the attitudes and behaviours of children, especially boys. Similar findings exist as regards aggressive content in film, video/DVD and, increasingly, electronic games. These media are, at present, all regulated through labelling and age-restrictions, although there is evidence that these regulatory processes may, in future, need to be simplified and/or strengthened.

It seems likely that the risk of harm will be greater when children view content inappropriate for their age (i.e. intended for those older than them), though unfortunately research does not always adequately link the effects of exposure to the specific nature or age-appropriateness of the content.

However, we suggest that at stake is the likelihood of risk rather than of inevitable harm, for, as the research also shows, not all in the audience are affected equally and many, it appears, are not affected. Broadcasters, regulators and parents must continue to make balanced judgements of the likely risk to some children, bearing in mind the conditions of access (e.g. scheduling, intended audience, narrative context) and conditions of mediation (e.g. role of parental discussion of content or restrictions on access).

ONLINE COMMUNICATION

Although there is mounting evidence that Internet-based and mobile communication technologies are being incorporated into practices of bullying, harassment and other forms of malicious peer-to-peer communication, it is not yet clear that these technologies are responsible for an increase in the incidence of such practices. This is partly because of a lack of sound data from, say, ten years ago, against which to compare present findings.

However, research on the conditions of access points to a relative convenience and ease of use which, combined with highly personalized, private and often anonymous conditions under which these technologies are used, suggests that cyber-bullying and cyber-harassment may introduce new kinds of problems for users, as well as exacerbating old ones. In some ways, it seems, online and offline communication work differently; but in key ways also, they work together, with, for example, offline bullying or harassment continuing or extending online, rather than remaining entirely distinct.

Given the difficulties faced by parents in understanding how to manage the conditions of access to these forms of content and contact, the implications for regulation may be judged differently, in terms of balancing the responsibility across the industry, regulators, parents and children for controlling access and exposure.

There is a fast growing body of further evidence regarding online communication and the evidence for online risk, especially in relation to inappropriate or hostile/exploitative contact, that is growing as the use of online communication – particularly on social networking sites – increases among teenagers. Issues of online privacy are also of potential concern.

There is still little research on areas such as user-generated content – the research agenda continues to lag behind the development of such rapidly evolving uses of the new media technologies.

OTHER HARMS

For some putative harms, the evidence is generally lacking. For example, despite widespread public concern over the exposure of children to adult or pornographic images, there remains little evidence that such exposure has harmful effects, with the notable exception of material that combines sexual and violent content. This lack of evidence partly reflects the methodological limitations of the evidence (one cannot ethically expose children to certain images, there is no agreed definition of pornography, it is difficult to measure long-term psychological disturbance, etc).

But it may also suggest that, at least in our present, largely regulated, content environment, the images available to children are not harmful, though they may be offensive or even briefly disturbing. If less regulated contents become more accessible to children (e.g. through the Internet), researchers will need to find a way to overcome these methodological difficulties, particularly given the apparent growth in material that does combine sexual and violent content.

For yet other putative harms, the cultural context is crucial. Researchers have long pointed to the media's role in relation to reality-defining effects, arguing that the media provide the frameworks or expectations with which the public understands the world around them. This has been, in various ways, considered harmful – potentially reinforcing stereotypes of marginalized groups, providing a biased account of current affairs, exacerbating a fear of crime, promoting a commercialized culture of childhood, encouraging the early sexualization of girls, and so forth.

However, the evidence is patchy and, by and large, neither recent nor UK-based. The difficulty here is that, as noted above, any effect of the media operates only in combination with many other social influences, and the effect is to be measured not in terms of an immediate impact on an individual but rather in terms of gradual shifts in social norms over years or decades. While few would suggest that the media play no role in socialization or cultural influence, it remains difficult to obtain convincing evidence that the media play a primary causal role. However, concerns regarding the sexualization of young girls continue, with some new evidence pertinent here.

Given the difficulties faced by parents in understanding how to manage the conditions of access to these forms of content and contact, the implications for regulation may be judged differently, in terms of balancing the responsibility across the industry, regulators, parents and children for controlling access and exposure.

OVER-ARCHING CONCLUSIONS

It will be observed that we have avoided over-arching conclusions being applied across all media and all segments of the public, for the evidence does not warrant such conclusions. To those who fear, then, that the media are responsible for a growing range of social problems, we would urge that the evidence base is carefully and critically scrutinized, for such findings as exist generally point to more modest, qualified and context-depending conclusions. To those who hope, however, that the media play little or no role in today's social problems, we would point to the complex and diverse ways in which different media are variably but crucially embedded in most or all aspects of our everyday lives, and that it seems implausible to suggest that they have no influence, whether positive or negative.

Overall, it seems that the research literature points to a range of modest effects, including effects on attitudes and beliefs, effects on emotions, and, more controversially, effects on behaviour (or the predisposition towards certain behaviours). Effects on emotions have, we suggest, received less attention than they should perhaps command, most attention focusing on attitudes and behaviours; yet running through the literature is a series of findings of people being made upset, fearful or anxious by the media. However, as we have also been at pains to point out, in each of these areas, there are some studies that find no effects, and many published studies have been contested in terms of their methodology and findings.

It is particularly difficult to be clear about the scale of these measured media effects since unfortunately these are rarely compared with other putative effects (e.g. of parenting style or social background). In other words, although it is widely argued that the effect of the media often depends on other factors also operating in the situation, the evidence here is generally weaker partly because there is no single theory of how indirect effects occur, partly because indirect effects are difficult to measure, and partly because indirect effects are often held to occur at the level of the culture not the individual (e.g. advertising ➔ peer pressure ➔ consumerism in society). Nonetheless, media effects appear to be one among many factors that account for the various ills in society (e.g. poverty, violence, fear of crime, stereotyping, etc.). Since unfortunately it is rare for research to identify or encompass these other factors within the same study, we cannot draw clear conclusions about which of these factors are more or less important.

Further, although effects are generally treated as direct (exposure to content ➔ effect), increasingly researchers assert indirect effects. Hence they seek to identify mediating factors (exposure ➔ mediating factor ➔ increased or decreased likelihood of effect); such mediating factors include personality,[2] age,[3] gender,[4] ethnicity,[5] parental influence, stage of cognitive development, viewing conditions, etc. This process of mediation renders the measured relation between exposure and effect to be indirect but no less significant. For example, Browne and Pennell (1999, 2000) report that while the evidence suggests that violent media ➔ aggression, it fits a more complex story better. This states that poor background ➔ choice of viewing violent media ➔ distorted cognitions ➔ aggressive behaviour. Note that this explanation is also more accurate than the simple claim that poor background ➔ aggressive behaviour. In other words, each intervening step, showing indirect as well as direct effects of the media and other factors, is important.

Consequently, we have recommended turning around the central question in this field and asking not, do the media have harmful effects, but rather, do the media contribute as one among several factors to the explanation of a social phenomenon (violence, racism, etc.). On a balance of probabilities, it seems less contentious to say 'yes' to the second question than to the first. But this also requires that any claims for media harms are contextualized in relation to the other factors contributing to the explanation. For example, to understand the role that television food advertising may play in children's diet, one must also examine the role of parental diet, school dinners, peer pressure, and so forth. To understand the role that television violence may play in levels of aggressive play among, say, primary school boys, one must also examine parental treatment of aggressive behaviour, the rewards and punishments operating in the playground situation, gender norms in the peer group, the difficulties experienced by some children at home, and so on.

WHICH GROUPS MAY BE MORE VULNERABLE?

Many research studies suggest that content does not affect all audiences equally, there being more negative influences on those who are 'vulnerable'. In most cases, this concept of vulnerability is applied to children and young people who are in the process of forming attitudes and behaviours for later life. But it is also applied to other groups of people who may be vulnerable, for example, because of specific personality traits or disorders (this includes research on psychologically disturbed individuals, people who are depressed, sexual offenders, young offenders, etc.).

Findings on specific vulnerable groups may be summarized as follows:

- There does seem to be evidence that young males may be more consistently affected by media content, and so they can be considered among the more vulnerable of the groups. They seem more likely to respond to violent media content with aggressive behaviour than girls, for example, and the data suggest they evince greater changes in attitude when presented with various potentially harmful contents (violence, stereotyping, pornography, etc.), though there are a fair number of studies where girls also seem to be influenced negatively.

- More attention has been paid to the reality-defining effects on girls of stereotyped or sexualized portrayals of gender; to the extent that these studies do show negative effects. However, they seem to occur for both genders.

- Reality-defining effects are sometimes shown particularly to affect minority or less socially valued groups (women, the elderly, etc.) – harm may thus be understood as encouraging negative attitudes both in the majority (e.g. racist stereotypes) and the affected minority (e.g. low self-esteem).

- Research has examined different hypothesized harms in relation to different age groups. For example, concerns about the harmful effects of advertising tend to be investigated in relation to young children. Similarly, the effects of violent content are examined across the range from young children to young adults, though for specific media, research tends to follow usage patterns (e.g. film and games are researched for teens/young adults, television among younger children). The risks of malicious or harmful peer-to-peer contact online or by mobile have mainly been researched among teens and adults, although attention is turning to younger children.

- Since different studies examine different age groups (often spanning very broad age ranges), evidence is sparse regarding developmental trends over the age range, making it difficult to pinpoint particularly vulnerable ages in relation to different media. It should also be noted that, for the most part, since research examines the effects of media on 'typical users', little is known about the effects on those who are not part of the typical or intended user group – further, ethical issues often preclude investigating the effects of exposure of younger children to material intended for older age groups.

IS THERE EVIDENCE THAT MEDIA CONTENTS MAY BE OFFENSIVE?

While academic research has focused on harms and the effects of the media, research into areas of offence has been conducted mainly by regulators and lobby or advocacy groups. Looking across all media, the research evidence suggests variable levels of offence. For example, in relation to television, around one in three have found something on television offensive, this more often being – as for most findings on offence – women and older people. This overlaps to some degree with our discussion of the risk of emotional effects or harms: recent research on self-reported emotional effects on being portrayed negatively as a marginalized group (women, the poor, gay and lesbian people, ethnic minorities, the elderly and children) suggests that these groups are often angry and upset at being so portrayed in the media. Further research is needed to track the concerns of marginalized and minority groups.

Intriguingly, little research has been conducted into the offence that might be caused to children, although in the United Kingdom there have been significant projects which have spoken to children about their attitudes to material. Most of the work on offence is focused on adults. While there may be ethical reasons for this disparity, the research evidence does show that children may be offended by certain depictions, in particular but not exclusively, of sexual activity.

Most research shows that, despite a substantial minority being offended, most people are tolerant of others' rights to view such material. The exception to this tends to be the combination of sex and violence (as in violent pornographic material), though even for such content, audiences seem to prefer to judge offence (and any regulatory responses that might follow) in relation to the narrative and aesthetic context of the portrayal. Generally, rather than calling for more restrictions on media content, the public is more inclined to call for better and more user-friendly access controls so that they can control what they see. Public support for content restrictions is highest in relation to the protection of children.

New forms of media are discussed more widely currently in relation to regulation than are the more established media for which, in many respects, the public is broadly supportive of the current regulatory framework. However, the findings are mixed on whether people are satisfied with (or even aware of) the available processes for making a complaint about media content.

COMPARING EVIDENCE ACROSS DIFFERENT MEDIA

This review has shown that much of the research undertaken has been technology-specific – in other words, applied to particular media. There is relatively little work that has looked at the overall consumption of a particular type of content across the media although some studies have sought to do that, particularly in areas such as sexual depictions and violence.

In recognition of this, many of the regulatory structures are set up with particular technologies in mind. Studies show that consumers of different media forms often approach the content on one platform differently from the way in which they approach similar content on another platform. Nonetheless, there is an avowed determination, in Europe certainly, to move towards technologically-neutral regulation. One of the principles behind this argues that the platform will become irrelevant to the consumer as the same or similar content is delivered across different platforms.

However, in a context of converging technologies and media content, we are particularly concerned at the lack of evidence providing a secure basis for making comparisons across media platforms. While audits of the media used by different segments of the population exist (for example, Ofcom, 2006; ACMA, 2007) and these provide cross-media information regarding use, none provides information about attitudes to content (e.g. violence) compared across a range of platforms. For the most part, then, in seeking evidence for harm and offence across media, we can only compare findings conducted for different media in different studies – this being the main purpose of the present review. Research has tended to extend the approach developed for television to video, games, Internet and so on – asking similar questions, and using similar methods, in relation to such potential harms as violence, sex, and stereotyping.

Where a research study has encompassed or compared across several media, the findings for effects tend to be inconsistent – some research finds the effects of television to be greater than for games; in other studies, the reverse is found. Therefore, we would question the argument that people respond to content irrespective of platform. Rather, the evidence suggests that people's response to media content is strongly shaped by the particularities of each medium, making it difficult to generalize across platforms, because:

■ Different access conditions and different public expectations (linear/non-linear, push/pull, chosen on purpose or accidentally, culturally familiar or novel) mean that audiences anticipate and self-regulate their media exposure in different ways.

■ Differently regulated content makes it particularly difficult to generalize from research on highly regulated content to content where there is no regulation (e.g. do the levels of violence on regulated, terrestrial television affect audiences in the same way, and to the same degree, as the levels of violence accessible through largely unregulated media such as the Internet?)

■ Broadcast (linear) media can be regulated in relation to the programming/scheduling context of particular portrayals (e.g. violence): this is important, since the context in which potentially harmful or offensive content is portrayed has often been shown to make a difference to media effects.[6] Yet both narrative/programming contexts and temporal/scheduling contexts are difficult to regulate for new (non-linear) media, especially where short extracts are likely to be viewed (e.g. Internet, mobile telephony): the consequence is a greater unpredictability of audience response.

■ Older media, in the main, comprise professionally produced, mass market content, and this too is different for new media, where a growing proportion of content is user-generated (peer-to-peer, spam, blogging, forms of self-representation), unregulated, niche-content that may be amateur in production and potentially extreme.

In short, there are many difficulties that remain with the premise of regulation that is technology-neutral, because the public does not treat different technologies as equivalent, and because the social and cognitive conditions of access also vary. Indeed, research on the conditions under which people access and use media in their daily lives in the United Kingdom makes it clear that many contextual variables are important in framing the ways in which people approach the media – prior familiarity and cultural expectations about a medium, the degree of choice or selection involved, the domestic and technological conditions of access, including media literacy (or technological competence and critical awareness), and the presence or absence of an interpretative context or frame (within the text) – all affect how people approach and respond to different media.

Since research persistently shows that many factors mediate between the media and the public, increasing or decreasing the possibility of media influence, for better or for worse, we must conclude that different kinds of harm and offence may result from different kinds of media contents and use. This is evidently the case even for older media – the findings for television, for example, differ from those for print. One might point to the power of the image, compared with the printed word. Others have argued that film is more potent than television, partly because of the conditions of viewing in the cinema, partly because of the power of a lengthy narrative. Others argue that the daily repetition of short messages on television or in computer games is more influential, or that the interactivity in computer gaming may make effects stronger. These arguments remain unresolved, and few research studies have directly compared the influence of (harmful or pro-social) messages across different media. For new forms of media, the differences are also considerable, and even less is known about them at present.

Regulation in the United Kingdom as currently implemented, draws on and is in many ways justified by reference to a complex base of media- and audience- specific research evidence. The balance to be struck between individuals (often, parents) and institutions (industry, regulators) in managing conditions of access should, we have suggested, vary for established and newer media. Clearly, as homes become more complex, multi-media environments, and as media technologies converge, it must be a priority to develop and extend the available evidence base, so that we sustain our understanding of the differences across, and relations among, the changing array of media and communication technologies. The challenge is to seek ways of minimizing risks, while also enabling the many benefits afforded by these technologies for our society and for the socialization of our children.

New media, new challenges

One purpose of the present review was to determine what lessons could be learned from research on older media to apply to new media, especially since there is relatively little research on new media as yet, by comparison especially with research on television. However, such evidence as has been produced suggests that new media may pose some new challenges. In consequence, empirical research on new media, and the evolving uses the technologies are put to, is now specifically required.

■ One of the main differences between many of the established media (television, radio, film, press and even advertising) is that of context (i.e., the framing of a portrayal within the text); when content is delivered in a linear way, it comes with a context that tells a story or establishes a framework of expectations that is recognized by and makes sense to the consumer. The research evidence suggests that this contextual setting affects how the content is received – and accepted – by the viewer. For example, the moral framework of a setting which contains violence will affect how 'justified' the violence is considered to be and, consequently, how it is received.

■ The newer technologies (including video but also the Internet and mobile communications) allow content to be seen out of context. One may see sets of trailers rather than the storyline in which to put the content. There is no research evidence to show how those trailers may be received, although some work on video has shown that certain groups (in this case violent offenders) choose to watch violent scenes repeatedly. Editorial context has always been important in content regulation guidelines (e.g. BBFC, Ofcom), but it may prove difficult to build into parallel guidelines for new media. However, it is clear from research on children's accidental exposure to pornography on the Internet, that unexpected and decontextualized content can be particularly upsetting. This poses a challenge for regulators.

■ It is difficult, therefore, to project forward the research evidence from one medium into another. There has been little research undertaken on specific areas within Internet use, especially areas thought to be harmful to the young such as pornography, anorexia sites or suicide sites. Many of the concerns raised by these studies (and popular discourse) are being applied to the mobile telephone. The evidence is not available to support this view, and it may be argued that the mobile telephone is a different technology, with particular characteristics. The chief of these is the personal and private nature of the mobile handset, quite different from a computer that may be shared or accessed by a number of people, or a fixed-line telephone.

■ While the content issues often remain the same (e.g. violence, pornography, stereotyping), the new media allow faster and more convenient access to these contents. They also allow access to more extreme content that would previously have been difficult to access; there are few effective controls available or in use to prevent such access, including by children.

■ The newer media offer greater opportunity to self-select. In terms of the way in which offence is caused there is some research evidence to show that self-selection makes a difference to the way in which content is perceived – people are far more likely to be offended by content on free-to-air channels than they are to content available on a niche channel that they themselves have selected, that is clearly signposted and that they are paying a subscription for. Similarly some of the research into video-games suggests that the self-selecting and active nature of playing may act as a distancing mechanism from the content in a way that passive viewing of television does not.

■ Similarly the newer media offer the opportunity to 'self-present', especially through social networking sites, some online games and user-generated content. Much of the research in this area – growing in volume – suggests that users do not always understand the consequences of the information they display about themselves to those outside their groups of selected contacts, assuming they create those boundaries.

■ Another key difference that the newer media bring is the ability to produce and widely disseminate user-generated content which has little or no regulation applied to it. The flexibility offered by camera telephones, with both production and diffusion capability, is quite different from hand-held video cameras. Similarly, the technologies can be linked so that images from mobile cameras can be downloaded on to the Internet and disseminated well beyond one's address book. However, there is little research into these areas as yet.

THE IMPORTANCE OF CONDITIONS OF ACCESS

■ Conditions of access strongly influence the research agenda. Television, generally the free-to-air services, is the most researched medium and has received such attention because of its ubiquity and accessibility, because it is a linear (i.e. push) medium, and because of its positive public potential (i.e. there is no real option for audiences to switch it off without missing out).

■ The Internet, the newest focus for research, partly merits research attention because of the ambition of ubiquity and public value – again, in an information society, it is increasingly not an option for people not to use it. As a largely unregulated medium, the Internet could provide access to a much greater range of potentially harmful and offensive content. This limits the applicability of findings from research on highly regulated media (such as television) to the Internet. However, the strictures of research ethics limit the potential to conduct research on this new medium.

■ Research on the Internet, unlike that for television, makes a fundamental distinction between potentially harmful material accessed accidentally and that which is sought deliberately. However, it is not clear whether this makes a difference to the degree of harm caused, though it does suggest different types of user or motivations for use (e.g. the child who seeks out pornography online may differ from the child who is upset because they found it accidentally: however, too little is known about user motivations or the consequences of different kinds of exposure).

■ For material accessed deliberately, attention has instead centred on the user's motivations, with evidence suggesting that the search for violent or pornographic contents may contribute to psychological disturbance for certain individuals. However, for both adults and children, some research suggests that, irrespective of whether content is found accidentally or deliberately, harm may still result (especially from violent pornography).

■ Similarly the paucity of research for mobile telephony rests in part on the relative novelty of the technology. This means that research from the Internet is being used to make assumptions about the possibility of harm and offence in this area; whether or not this is valid remains to be seen.

- At present, research finds that filters and other (physical) access control mechanisms are under-used by users or, in the case of children, children's guardians. This seems not to be because people are not concerned – it is evident that the Internet especially occasions the greatest concern of all media among the public. Rather, it is because people lack the knowledge and awareness of how to choose, install and use access controls or they feel such mechanisms are not necessary within their own families. This is not true of all new media however, and within the on-demand services, for example, the use of PIN codes and other access management systems are repeatedly advertised and marketed to the user.

- The evidence suggests that the children's responses to certain media contents can be lessened or heightened by the ways in which families interact and discuss what is seen. Evidence is lacking, however, for the claim that an increase in media literacy will reduce the potential for harm, although this is widely believed (and so should be the subject of future research).

- We have noted that the evidence for possible harm from violent content is stronger than that for sexual content (with the exception of violent pornography). This might explain why in response to portrayed violence, the public is more likely to call for content regulation, while for portrayed sex, people may or may not object personally but they tend to call for tolerance (respecting the rights of others to view diverse or niche content); the right to view violence appears more difficult to defend, it seems, than the right to view pornography. Given this, it is curious that most research on new media contents has addressed sexual content (especially pornography) rather than violence, there being particularly little on the potentially harmful effects of exposure to non-sexualized violence (this may reflect the ways in which public concern, rather than theory, sets the research agenda).

Looking to the future

The issue of common definitions remains. The concept of 'harm' is implicitly understood but rarely formally defined. Hence, it is not possible to provide clear advice or a check list to regulators or content providers about specific harms. However, the concept remains a valid one; it has a legal foundation and attempts should continue to be made to define and identify it. The concept of offence is more clearly understood. While there is little academic research into this area, there is a substantial body of work related to offence, reported on here, together with circumstantial evidence in the form of complaints and other participatory expressions.

The research evidence also suggests some links between offence and harm:

- In reality-defining effects, for example, on the one hand, opinion research (on offence) shows that certain groups resent their representation in the media; on the other hand, experimental and survey research (on harm) suggests that media representations perpetuate such stereotypes among the general population.

■ Another borderline area between offence and harm concerns user-generated content – racist or sexist messages are offensive to some and harmful to others in ways not yet well understood; nor is it yet understood how processes of offence and harm differ when the message source is a peer rather than, for example, a powerful broadcaster.

■ Some of the research also pointed to the crucial role of the media in creating an informed civil society and suggested that this role will need to be monitored, particularly as the information environment expands and innovates faster than the public's critical literacy (to determine reliability or authenticity of information) can keep up.

There is a growing call for arguments that go 'beyond cause and effect', as more and more commentators are frustrated by the simplistic polarization of censorship versus freedom of expression or regulation versus *laissez faire* (depending on one's position). Boyle (2000) argues, for example, that the pornography debate must be reoriented towards addressing male violence in society, rather than distracted by arguments over experimental methods. In a similar vein, Adams (2000) draws on philosophical as well as legal arguments to argue that the claim that pornography plays a causal role in rape does not, or should not, 'let the rapist off the hook'. Rather, multiple causes are at work, as they are in many domains of life, and the assertion that pornography plays a causal role does not in any way assume that pornography is the sole, or main, cause and nor that it works in the same way on all its consumers; consequently, 'evidence' for the effects of pornography need not be large or consistent.

Similar arguments have been advanced in other domains. For example, in relation to advertising of foods high in fat, sugar or salt to children, Livingstone (2005) argued that the problem with causal claims is not the question of causality *per se* but the nature of the question asked (see also Gauntlett, 1998). Instead of asking whether advertising causes children to make unhealthy food choices, the question should be turned around to ask: what are the influences on children's food choice and what role if any does advertising play in this multi-factorial explanation?[7] As we have seen, Kline (2003b) develops this approach through taking a public-health approach: 'rather than the causal hypothesis, the driving force behind the risk factors approach is the quest to understand what it all depends on'. Research should, therefore, focus more on establishing the range of relevant factors contributing to an outcome, identifying how important each is in explaining that outcome.

So, it is more useful, we have suggested, to turn the question around and ask not whether the media harm children but ask instead, of the many causes of particular social ills, what role do the media play? This more contextualized approach is increasingly adopted by those who are concerned with vulnerable groups, in particular, and argues for a more public-health facing approach, which advocates the examination of the media's role (and the amenability of media exposure to intervention) as part of a more complete picture of influences and effects (see, for example, Browne and Hamilton-Giachritsis, 2005; Kline, 2003b; Savage, 2004).

THE FUTURE RESEARCH AGENDA
A key aim of this review has been to pinpoint gaps in the existing evidence base. As a result, we identify the following priorities for future research: research on the range of marginalized and/or

vulnerable groups (including the elderly, gay, ethnic minorities, and those with psychological difficulties). Too often, the population is not adequately segmented. Beyond examining differences by age and gender, research must include ethnicity, sexuality, psychological variables, and so forth when investigating possible harm and offence; even for age, too little is known about the effects of media on different age groups as children develop.

■ Research on reality-defining/stereotyping effects that relates to recent changes especially in UK-originated media content, as well as imported content.

■ Longitudinal or long-term panel studies, to follow up the effects of short-term harm, to track changes in levels and kinds of offence, and to identify changing expectations and understandings of media (including the access conditions) among the public. At present, there are no examples of UK-based longitudinal studies of media influence, though there are tracking studies on media access and use. The lack of studies of media influence, incorporating content variables that allow replication over time, makes it difficult to examine in combination the matrix of content viewed (amount and type), media platform, personality traits, life stage and other demographic variables.

■ In the shorter term, there is strong evidence that triangulated methodologies, bringing together different data collection systems, may work most effectively to give an insight into the way in which the media and users interact, but these too, need to be combined more effectively with other variables, such as those affecting personality. Some methods have been particularly creative – the use of citizens' juries, for example, or the development of the news editing method – but these tend not to be reused, perhaps because they are more effortful or expensive; nonetheless, they reap dividends in terms of research insights.

■ Research on the under-researched media, particularly radio and music among the 'established' media and the Internet and mobile telephony among the newest delivery systems. For example, music attracts some concern over its lyrics, yet has barely been researched in this regard. As the content available even on familiar and well-researched media changes and diversifies, research must continue to track the possible consequences.

■ Research on the new issues arising from new media, particularly in relation to user-generated and malicious peer-to-peer content and contact. For example, research is beginning to accumulate on the harm and offence caused particularly by unwanted and unsought exposure to inappropriate material on the Internet: this agenda must now be extended to include mobile and other emerging digital platforms (research from the advertising literature suggests such effects not only occur but may be harder to defend against).

■ Similarly, little research has examined the effects of interactivity on the way in which content is chosen and received. Indeed it is not clear as yet that the active selection of content makes a difference to media effects. Further, research is needed on the commercial or promotional aspects of new media technologies (especially Internet, mobile, and other new and interactive devices) and new contents (interactive content, new forms of advertising and promotion, niche/extreme content).

■ Research that puts media effects in context, seeking to understand how the media play a role in a multi-factor explanation for particular social phenomena (e.g. violence, gender-stereotyping, etc.), this to include a comparative account of the relative size of effect for each factor (including the media) in order to enable regulatory decisions based on proportionality.

■ Research that directly compares the public's responses to the 'same' content when accessed on different media (e.g. violence on television, in film, in computer games, online) so as to understand whether and how the medium, or the conditions of access to a medium, including the regulatory environment, make a difference. Although it seems clear that the public brings different expectations to different platforms and technologies, as noted earlier, more research is needed on how they respond to the same content when delivered through different media platforms.

■ Research on the range of factors that potentially mediate (buffer or exacerbate) any effects of media exposure (e.g. level of media literacy, role of parental mediation, difference between accidental and deliberate exposure, etc.). Particularly, to inform the regulatory agenda, research is needed to produce a clearer understanding of how regulation can work with other mitigating or buffering processes (such as family mediation or communications literacy) to reduce any negative impact of inappropriate media content. Research on the range of possible mitigating factors remains patchy, being mainly focused on television, and must be updated as users (especially parents) continue to adjust to the changing media environment.

■ Similarly, users need to understand how, and when, they can use the self/in-home regulatory tools they are provided with by many of the new delivery systems, such as filters or PIN codes, and more research is needed on whether and when these are effectively used, and why they may not be.

■ It must be observed that calling for multi-method, long-term, cross-media, culturally-relevant research on a diverse range of audience/user groups is to call for expensive research. Just as regulation increasingly requires a multi-stakeholder approach, it may be that research also requires the cooperation of government, regulator and industry groups, together with the expertise of the academic research community. Finally, we would stress the importance, for evidence-based policy and academic knowledge, of sustaining a body of research that is relevant to the United Kingdom, that is up to date, that has undergone peer-review, and that is available in the public domain.

NOTES

1. To call these 'objective' and 'subjective' measures is perhaps too simple, for the judgements of observers are subject to biases (being a form of self report, and influenced most notably by the third-person effect), and the judgements of individuals concerned may be the only available method (how else can fear be assessed?). Of course, there are some studies that rely on self-report for evidence of harm, especially when the harm at issue is emotional, just as there are some studies of offence that rely on more objective measures (e.g. letters of complaint).

2. Several studies show greater media effects for already more aggressive participants. Others have shown greater effects of exposure to media violence among clinical populations (Browne and Pennell, 2000). Findings for offenders are more mixed: see Hagell and Newburn (1994) but also Browne and Pennell (2000) who argue that it is the violent backgrounds of young offenders that creates the vulnerability.

3. Among children and young people, the most studied groups, cognitive and social development accounts for different (and various) findings.

4. In many studies, especially of violence, the effects are found to be less, or even absent, for girls.

5. Many American studies show different (and various) results for participants of different ethnic backgrounds.

6. Perhaps curiously, both psychological and culturally-oriented researchers agree on the importance of textual (or programme) context, arguing that a violent or sexual act must be interpreted in relation to its narrative and genre context and, more importantly, that people indeed do interpret content in context, this affecting how they respond to content and whether it upsets or influences them.

7. For an influential illustration, in the field of children's food choice and obesity; see Story, Neumark-Sztainer and French (2002). In an approach that could be applied also in other domains, they suggest that the factors influencing food choice operate at four distinct levels. (1) Individual – psycho-social, biological and behavioural factors. (2) Interpersonal – family, friends and peer networks. (3) Community – accessibility, school food-policy and local facilities. (4) Societal – mass media and advertising, social and cultural norms, production and distribution systems and pricing policies.

ANNEX I: METHODOLOGICAL CONSIDERATIONS IN RESEARCHING HARM AND OFFENCE

Most empirical research on harm and offence, as reviewed in the present volume, falls into one of three groups – experimental research, survey research and qualitative social research. Different theories lend themselves to particular methodologies and it is the case that most short-term effects are examined using experiments and most long-term effects are examined using surveys, while qualitative social research is more often used to investigate offence and/or to explore the meanings and experiences associated with potentially harmful encounters. There is, in other words, an association that may occasion confusion between theory and method. Nonetheless, some experiments address long-term effects, some surveys examine short-term effects, and some qualitative social research reveals more subtle forms of effect.

Note, before proceding, that many questions asked by effects researchers raise serious ethical issues. For example, despite pressing policy-questions regarding the effects of pornography on children, one simply cannot ethically show pornography to children to see if it harms them (Helsper, 2005). The British Psychological Society's statement on research ethics[1] stresses the importance of informed consent and of avoiding harm, as 'Investigators have a primary responsibility to protect participants from physical and mental harm during the investigation. Normally, the risk of harm must be no greater than in ordinary life', and research should aim to 'eliminate all possibility of harmful after-effects'. The British Sociological Association stresses that 'sociologists have a responsibility to ensure that the physical, social and psychological well-being of research participants is not adversely affected by the research' and further, that 'research involving children requires particular care'.[2] Others add requirements for following up after the research, since research participation may have delayed consequences. In the United States, where much research on harm originates, 'human subjects' regulation has become highly restrictive in recent years, materially affecting the kinds of evidence that may be sought and, consequently, seriously limiting the potential for evidence-based policy.

EVALUATING RESEARCH

Quantitative research measures (used in both experiments and surveys) are evaluated by social scientists according to several agreed criteria (Calhoun, 2002):

■ Reliability refers to the ability to accurately repeat the results of an experiment or research project;

■ Validity refers to the appropriate fit of the indicator measured to the analytic variable or concept and to the appropriateness of the methods of measurement to the subject under study.

Studies may be accurately conducted with reliable results, yet the findings may be invalid if validity is low (in other words, if the measure used is judged a poor indicator of the effect one is interested in). Some of the debate over media effects concerns reliability – for results sometimes cannot be replicated. Some of it concerns validity – many ask whether pushing a 'hurt' button after watching a short violent excerpt is really a valid measure of aggressive behaviour in everyday life?

Psychologists further distinguish internal and external validity thus (Coleman, 2001):

■ Internal validity is 'the extent to which the conclusions of an empirical investigation are true within the limits of the research methods and subjects or participants used'.

■ External validity is 'the extent to which the conclusions of an empirical investigation remain true when different research methods and research participants or subjects are used'. This encompasses population validity – the extent to which findings from one study can be generalized to the population, and ecological validity, 'the confidence with which the conclusions of an empirical investigation can be generalised to naturally occurring situations in which the phenomenon under investigation occurs'.[3]

Using these definitions, we shall see that media effects research is contested in all these ways, but the question of ecological validity occasions most criticism.

Note too that standardized criteria by which to evaluate qualitative social research are less well-established, although the focus of considerable attention (Flick, 1998; Gaskell and Bauer, 2003; Schroder, Drotner, Kline, and Murray, 2003). Considerations of validity, quality and representativeness all apply, albeit in modified ways, together with other criteria (hermeneutic depth, reflexivity regarding the role of the researcher, ethic of care for participants, etc.).

Lincoln and Guba (1985) propose a set of alternative validation standards, which are analogous to conventional concepts of validity and reliability but which respect the interpretative or social constructivist tradition from which qualitative methods derive (see also Schwandt and Halpern, 1988, and Lobe, Livingstone and Haddon, 2007). These are as follows: (a) credibility is analogous to internal validity, for it asks whether findings and interpretations from a naturalistic inquiry are perceived as credible by the research respondents; (b) dependability is analogous to reliability, for it asks whether the process of inquiry is consistent, and whether it has been carefully documented and is auditable; (c) confirmability is analogous to objectivity, for it is concerned with the neutrality of the research process and its outcomes, thus examining how the interpretations are grounded in and consistent with the data, again something revealed through a process of auditing; (d) transferability replaces external validity, for it concerns the applicability of research findings from a sample to a population. Lincoln and Guba (1985: 316) propose that:

> the naturalist cannot specify the external validity of an inquiry; he or she can provide only a thick description necessary to enable someone interested in making a transfer [of findings] to reach a conclusion about whether transfer can be contemplated as possible.

Since each method used in studies of media influence has particular strengths and weaknesses, these are summarized below.

STRENGTHS AND WEAKNESSES OF EXPERIMENTS

Experiments can test causal claims or hypotheses, because they ensure; (a) random allocation of participants to experimental and control groups (so as to control for potentially confounding factors or 'third causes') and; (b) temporal ordering by which media exposure precedes measurement of outcomes or effects (Livingstone, 1996; Perse, 2001; Schroder, Drotner, Kline, and Murray, 2003). They include:

■ Laboratory experiments (conducted under controlled conditions away from the participants' everyday lives).[4]

■ Field experiments (conducted under controlled conditions as part of participants' everyday lives).

■ Naturalistic experiments (naturally arising groups retrospectively identified as experimental and control groups).[5]

However, experiments have some problems:

■ Laboratory experiments are 'unnatural'. The random allocation of participants to experimental or control groups, essential if the effects unknown/third causes are to be eliminated from the findings, is crucially different from the everyday conditions of viewing – based on motivation, selection and, generally, foreknowledge of the content. The experiment thus lacks ecological validity.

■ Not only is the setting different, but the key variables – media exposure and measured effect – do not match everyday circumstances. Thus typically, though not always, experiments expose people to just a segment of the programme or film, undermining the importance of seeing things in context, using the narrative to interpret portrayed violence, for example.

■ The measurement of effect often involves a simulated demonstration of violent (or other) thoughts, feelings or behaviours – as when loud noise blasts are delivered at another participant

(Anderson and Bushman, 2001) – whose relation to the real-life phenomenon (e.g. aggression in the playground) is often tangential or even implausible.

■ Crucially, a substantial meta-analysis found that the more an experiment achieves internal validity, the more it sacrifices external validity and vice versa (Hearold, 1986). Further, the question of whether experimental findings can be generalized to everyday life depends in part on one's conception of everyday life, a difficult matter in itself. For example, Borden argues that children only repeat aggressive behaviours after exposure because clearly the experimenter expects them to (Borden, 1975). Turner, Hesse and Peterson-Lewis (1986) agree, but argue that friends may also expect such behaviour repeated in the playground, so similar 'demand characteristics' occur in everyday life.

The findings themselves, and attempts to replicate them, are often inconsistent or even absent (Barker and Petley, 2001; Fowles, 2003; Freedman, 2002). Some are concerned that only the statistically significant findings are discussed (Amici Curiae, 2001; Rowland, 1983), others that the statistically insignificant findings are not even published (although Greenwald finds that such possible publication biases make little difference partly because, as some argue, experiments are already biased against finding effects; it is also the case that null findings could indicate methodological flaws in an experiment rather than an absence of an effect) (Greenwald, 1975).[6]

STRENGTHS AND WEAKNESSES OF SURVEYS

Large-scale surveys, particularly those that use representative sampling, provide valuable information regarding the scale and distribution of the phenomenon of interest within the population (Fowler, 2001; Oppenheim, 1992; Schroder et al., 2003). Since many questions can be asked of respondents, surveys also permit analysis of the phenomenon broken down by subgroups, compared across different circumstances, in relation to multiple other factors. Correlations between media exposure and possible effects can, therefore, be examined by demographic grouping, comparing across different media, in relation to personality or cultural indicators of many kinds. Surveys can also provide respondents with privacy and anonymity when answering questions, which may be important when asking sensitive questions about sex or violence. Also, since respondents can generally complete the survey in their own time, this allows them time to contemplate their answers. They include:

■ Detailed surveys of populations selected to be relevant to the hypothesis being tested.

■ Opinion polls – typically involving brief questioning of a large national sample.

■ Survey data collected for other purposes which may throw light on the issue at stake (e.g. criminal statistics).

However, surveys have some problems, even when conducted with large-scale, representative samples:

■ They cannot investigate causality, only correlation (i.e. association between two measures, with no assumption regarding the direction of effect). Nor are they strong on eliminating the possibility of a third cause that may, independently, account for variation in these two measures. Note, however, that establishing a correlation is a precursor to establishing causality (and that there is little point examining causality in the absence of a correlation). One exception is the use of the statistical technique of path (or causal) modelling of survey data to test causal hypotheses. Another is the use of longitudinal panel surveys in which statistical comparisons across groups can examine the effect of variable at time one, on another variable at time two.

■ There is a problem with the comparison (or control) group – especially for television. Since everyone is exposed to a greater or lesser degree, surveys may compare those who watch more or less but they cannot compare those who watch with those who do not.

■ Difficulties of measurement abound when examining subtle social processes. There are no simple and obvious measures and so little ready consensus over measurement for many of the variables at issue, including media exposure, aggressive behaviour, and social norms.

■ Heavy reliance on self-report measures – what is often described as an effect is, in reality, a self-rating of an effect, subject therefore to a range of response biases including that of social desirability. There is reason to be cautious in relation to self-report data in this field: as a rule, it is well established that people ordinarily deny that they are themselves influenced by the media, while believing that the media influence others. This 'third-person effect' (Davison, 1983) is taken to reflect a cultural preference for presenting oneself as autonomous and rational, rather than as an insightful account of media influence or its absence.

STRENGTHS AND WEAKNESSES OF QUALITATIVE SOCIAL RESEARCH

These methods encompass a range of different techniques (interviews, group discussions, observations, etc.) to obtain an in-depth, qualitative account of people's diverse responses to media content (Alasuutari, 1995; Gaskell and Bauer, 2003; Jensen and Jankowski, 1991; Schroder et al., 2003). Interestingly, it appears that these methods are more widely used in the United Kingdom, Europe, and in countries which share these research traditions (notably, Australia and Canada). The label here given to these methods includes the term 'social' because, at least in relation to media, the focus is not only on qualitative data but also on the social nature of responses to media: the purpose is thus not only to identify people's responses to media but also to pursue the differing circumstances under which they apply, the ways in which people themselves frame or evaluate their responses, and the relation between media response and people's social attitudes, values and practices.

Approaches include:

■ Depth interviews (e.g. retrospective life-history interviews with sex offenders).

■ Expert interviews (e.g. with psychiatrists regarding their patients' experiences).

■ Observations (e.g. observing child-parent interaction at home during advertising breaks).

■ Reception studies (e.g. how children discuss the reality or fantasy of a drama).

■ Ethnography (e.g. following everyday interactions in a nursery after a computer is introduced).

■ Focus groups (e.g. investigations into people's own beliefs about media harms or into the sources of offence).

These generally assume that people's responses are complex, often context-sensitive, occasionally incoherent or contradictory. The flexibility of the method permits the researcher to follow up specific or fruitful lines of inquiry within the interview/observation/discussion format itself, this resulting in a more thorough and careful analysis. They are also aware that the researcher him/herself plays a role in affecting the context of data collection, and so seek deliberately to build on this as a strength (or, avoid its dangers through anticipation). They assume also that people are able to reflect and report on their own responses or feelings which, given the 'invisible' nature of media response, is often a sensible starting point.

However, there are some limitations:

■ Qualitative research favours inductive forms of analysis, taking a lead from issues, terms or thoughts expressed by the participants rather than being mainly or only led by theory or policy. While often useful, especially in the early stages of research, the analysis may be more superficial (the collation of emergent themes, for instance, or the summary of main consensus reached) though it can be more detailed and interpretative.

■ More importantly, these methods are unable to offer causal evidence, or even sound evidence of association (or correlation), being better at confirming that certain phenomena occur (e.g. children's fear responses) than in demonstrating what causes them.

■ They are also unable to make claims about the distribution of a phenomenon throughout the population, although see the above discussion on alternative standards for qualitative research. Representativeness is thus generally sacrificed for depth of understanding, it being usually (though not always, for small but distinct populations – e.g. paedophiles) impractical to undertake in-depth qualitative work with large samples. Sampling is nonetheless a concern with qualitative work, though the standards applied differ: rather than sampling randomly from the population, for example, care is generally taken to identify all important sub-groupings or experiences, and to sample from them as widely as possible. Another principle is often to continue sampling until the findings begin to converge, throwing up little that is new. Moreover, they are vulnerable to the charge of social desirability – that the research context establishes certain expectations or norms which influence, more or less, the kind of data obtained, particularly when these data are dependent on self-report. In short, can people tell when they have been harmed? Especially, can children tell? Can their parents tell on their behalf?

TRIANGULATION: THE NEED FOR MULTIPLE METHODS

In addition to the various practical problems of sampling, measurement, and so on, some fundamental methodological issues are particularly salient in relation to the problem of media effects. Put simply, with purely correlational evidence, the direction of causality and the question of third causes cannot be resolved; with purely experimental evidence, the claim that findings can be generalized to the everyday lives of children cannot be sustained. Restating this more positively, a correlational study can demonstrate the existence of an association between exposure and behaviour under naturalistic conditions; an experiment can demonstrate the existence of a causal effect of exposure on behaviour under controlled conditions. Qualitative social research, as noted above, is better at seeking to understand the existence, nature and importance of a phenomenon (e.g. response of an audience subgroup to a particular media content) than it is at demonstrating either its causes or its distribution through the population.

Since no method permits the rigorous yet practical investigation of causality under natural conditions, researchers often try to combine multiple methods, triangulating findings (Flick, 1998) to show both the meaning of the phenomenon, an association between media exposure and audience response under everyday conditions, and also a causal effect under controlled conditions. It means, however, that academic conclusions, and possibly policy decisions, must be made in the absence of the single perfect test or the ideal experiment.[7]

As explained in Lobe et al. (2007), triangulation refers to a strategy (originally borrowed from trigonometry) for integrating multiple methods often, though not necessarily, across quantitative and qualitative research methods (Crano, 2000). The purpose is to reduce reliance on single-method measures by employing different independent measurement procedures to increase the validity of research results. Triangulation is not, however, without its own difficulties, as Bryman (1992) outlines. In contrast with triangulation, where different sets of data are expected to be consistent and congruent with each other, an alternative multi-method approach is that of complementarity. Here, the datasets are expected to diverge in order to capture a broader view of the phenomenon under study, for the basic idea is to use 'each approach in relation to a different research problem or different aspect of a research problem' (Brannen, 1992: 12). In this way:

> Results from one method can be extended by using another method. Quantitative methods focus inquiry on a discrete set of variables to address a specific research question or hypothesis. Qualitative inquiry opens up the field of investigation by recognising the broader but interconnected complexities of a situation. Thus, each type of method has advantages and can extend, in certain ways, our understanding of a researchable problem. (Lobe, et al., 2007: 15)

RESEARCHING 'OFFENCE'

As with 'harm', 'offence' is not easy to define. Nor is it always easy to distinguish from harm. Research charting the public's affective reactions to media content is often ambiguously positioned between harm and offence, it being unclear how to categorize negative reactions such as dislike, fear, disgust, upset, shock. Dislike is commonly considered 'offence', but 'fear' reactions (especially among children) are often judged in terms of harm. Yet, for the individual reporting on their responses to a researcher, there may be a continuum in strength of emotional reaction from dislike to fear, rather than these being experienced as quite different categories of response. To the extent that evidence for harm can only be obtained by asking people how they react to media, evidence for harm overlaps with evidence for offence, both raising questions about reliance on self-report and the limits of introspection. Most would consider, however, that offence concerns the immediate response to media content whereas harm – being theorized in terms of psychological development, or social identity, or societal relationships – is supposed to persist (although follow-up research tracking long-term consequences of short-term media harms is generally lacking).

Not only is it difficult to define, but offence is also difficult to measure. As Hill (2000) observes, different questions to the public result in different assessments of what offends them and how much. The very word 'offensive' puts some people off (implying they are prudish, for example), while others hesitate to claim that they 'disapprove' of certain contents. 'Disgusted', 'upset', 'nasty', 'complaint' – whatever term is used steers the public response in one direction or another. People would like to appear tolerant and open-minded, the result being an underestimation of levels of 'offence'.

Most empirical research on offence adopts either public opinion survey methods or qualitative social research. Further, most such research is conducted by industry and regulators rather than by academic researchers. This has various consequences. Such research is not always freely available in the public domain, and nor generally has it undergone a peer-review process. On the other hand, the survey samples used are often nationally-representative and may be conducted repeatedly over time, permitting an understanding of longitudinal trends. Moreover, in the United Kingdom, the regulators have established a strong record in the use of multi-method, qualitative and quantitative methods that seeks an in-depth understanding of the nature of offence with an attempt to map the extent of such offence across the population.

For the most part, academic research prefers to rely on external measures. For example, it is considered preferable to measure media exposure and fear of crime in a survey examining the data to see if there is a correlation between these two measures, than it is to ask people directly, 'does media violence make you fear that you yourself might be attacked?', this latter relying not only on a subjective insight but also on commonsense theories of media effects. However, the same distinction cannot so readily be drawn for research on offence. A person is, it seems, offended if they say they are offended, and not if they say not; an observer has no superior judgement here.[8]

As Hill also notes, the majority of complaints to broadcasters or regulators are from first-time complainants; this suggests, though does not establish, that the responses they receive do not encourage further complaints, again suggesting that the evidence merely reveals the tip of the iceberg. Overall, the rate of complaining is very low – in relation to advertising, just 1 per cent of adults in 1996, despite 25 per cent having been offended in the past year (Advertising Standards Authority, 1996).[9] Similarly, among those who say they have been offended by something seen on television, just 3 per cent said they had complained (Ofcom, 2005c).

Notes

1. http://www.bps.org.uk/downloadfile.cfm?file_uuid=5084A882-1143-DFD0-7E6C-F1938A65C242&ext=pdf
2. http://www.britsoc.co.uk/equality/Statement+Ethical+Practice.htm
3. Related but different, the 'ecological fallacy' is when one makes an inference about an individual based on the aggregate data for a group.
4. Note that the 'laboratory' may be a normal room, with no equipment or white coats (but since it is often not described, this can be hard to tell).
5. Although the two latter approaches may seem preferable to laboratory-based experiments, attempts to conduct naturalistic or field experiments typically encounter two difficulties. First, it is more difficult than in laboratory experiments to eliminate extraneous or confounding factors, reducing certainty when drawing conclusions that the observed effects are due to variation in the independent measure (message exposure). Second, if one seeks to expose children over the longer-term to hypothesized harmful exposure, one encounters serious ethical difficulties which make it unlikely that such an experiment would be permitted by a human subjects or ethics committee.
6. For example, Gerbner argues that experimental studies have difficulty finding effects or show only small effects because only the effects of exposure to a single programme can generally be tested against a control group who are not shown that programme. Yet the everyday lives of both experimental and control groups involve years of exposure to a similar television diet. Such a weak manipulation of exposure differences is likely to underestimate rather than overestimate effects. As they say, 'if as we argue, the messages are so stable, the medium is so ubiquitous, and accumulated total exposure is what counts, then almost everyone should be affected…It is clear, then, that the cards are stacked against finding evidence of effects' (Gerbner et al., 1986: 21).
7. Note that discussion of media effects frequently if implicitly refers to hopes of an ideal demonstration of effects – that if only we could resolve the methodological issues undermining research studies, we could determine for once and for all whether or not the media cause harm. Yet, as each new study is published, it too seems vulnerable to immediate and sometimes devastating critique. For example, Zillman and Weaver (1999) review the reviews critical of the relationship between media violence and aggression (supposedly that they are often 'intuitive', highlight inconsistencies in findings, and point toward negligible and short-lived effects). The authors accept that these criticisms are 'not without merit' (p. 146) but remind critics that their expectations are unrealistic for they demand 'research that in a free society simply cannot be conducted' (p. 147). Note too that theories cannot be 'proved'. Indeed, notwithstanding the preferences of those who write press releases, the research community generally follows the philosophy of science in eschewing naïve expectations of proof; research may seek to provide evidence consistent with a hypothesis or, better, to falsify a hypothesis; the lack of proof in this field is as much to be expected as in any other. The lack of consistency in the body of evidence, however, and the degree of theoretical confusion or lack of clarity, is indeed problematic.
8. For the most part, experiments and surveys used to measure harm rely on externally observable findings, though opinion surveys often rely on the individual's self-report. Although qualitative social research also relies on self-report, the strength of such methods is that they seek to identify, and deepen our understanding of, the context in which claims are meaningful, not simply 'collecting' decontextualized claims of harm or offence by individuals.
9. In Australia, Cupitt (2000) found that two in three complainants were dissatisfied with how their complaint was handled, and over half believed their complaint would not change broadcasting practice. In New Zealand, analysis of broadcasting complaints shows that more than half were first time complainants and that, while the process was generally considered clear and appropriate, many disagreed with the final decision (29 per cent thought it very fair or fair, 40 per cent thought it unfair and 20 per cent very unfair) (Colmar Brunton, 2004). UK research (Hanley, 1998b) suggested that cable and satellite subscribers are less likely to complain because they tend to feel more in control of the channels they receive, feeling less likely therefore to come across something accidentally that they object to. This is partly because cable/satellite subscribers are younger/less traditional in their views, and partly because viewers' expectations regarding terrestrial channels are for more traditional content that upholds certain standards. Lastly, the ASA (2004–2005) reports that a majority of those who complain about advertising are satisfied with the response of the Advertising Standards Authority.

ANNEX II: THE LEGAL FRAMEWORK OF ENGLISH LAW REGULATING MEDIA CONTENT

BROADCASTING ACT 1990

According to section 177 of this Act, as amended by the Communications Act 2003, the Secretary of State may make an order proscribing a foreign satellite service.

Section 177(2) stipulates that 'If OFCOM consider that the quality of any foreign satellite service which is brought to their attention is unacceptable and that the service should be the subject of an order under this section, they shall notify to the Secretary of State details of the service and their reasons why they consider such an order should be made'.

Section 177(3) states that 'OFCOM shall not consider a foreign satellite service to be unacceptable for the purposes of subsection (2) unless they are satisfied that there is repeatedly contained in programmes included in the service matter which offends against good taste or decency or is likely to encourage or incite to crime or to lead to disorder or to be offensive to public feeling'.

According to section 177(4), 'Where the Secretary of State has been notified under subsection (2), he shall not make an order under this section unless he is satisfied that the making of the order — (a) is in the public interest; and (b) is compatible with any international obligations of the United Kingdom'.

There are two leading cases regarding section 177: *R v Secretary of State for Culture, Media and Sport Ex p. Danish Satellite Television*[1] and *R v Secretary of State for National Heritage Ex p. Continental Television B V.*[2] Both of these cases concern decisions by the Secretary of State to prohibit the transmission of a pornographic satellite television channel.

CHILDREN AND YOUNG PERSONS (HARMFUL PUBLICATIONS) ACT 1955

This Act was passed to deal with 'horror comics'. When it was introduced, the Solicitor-General stated that it was designed to prevent 'the state of mind that might be induced in certain types of children by provoking a kind of morbid brooding or ghoulishness or mental ill-health'.[3] Section 1 of the Act states that the Act applies to 'any book, magazine or other like work which is of a kind likely to fall into the hands of children or young persons and consists wholly or mainly of stories told in pictures (with or without the addition of written matter), being stories portraying – (a) the commission of crimes; or (b) acts of violence or cruelty; or (c) incidents of a repulsive or horrible nature; in such a way that the work as a whole would tend to corrupt a child or young person into whose hands it might fall'. Section 2 states that 'a person who prints, publishes, sells or lets on hire a work to which this Act applies, or has any such work in his possession for the purpose of selling it or letting it on hire, shall be guilty of an offence'.

It has been stated that there has never been a successful prosecution under this Act.[4]

Cinematograph Films (Animals) Act 1937

This Act makes it illegal to show any scene if animals were treated cruelly in the making of that scene. According to section 1(1), 'No person shall exhibit to the public, or supply to any person for public exhibition…any cinematograph film…if in connection with the production of the film any scene represented in the film was organised or directed in such a way as to involve the cruel infliction of pain or terror on any animal or the cruel goading of any animal to fury'. Section 1(2) stipulates, 'In any proceedings brought under this Act in respect of any film, the court may (without prejudice to any other mode of proof) infer from the film as exhibited to the public or supplied for public exhibition, as the case may be, that a scene represented in the film as so exhibited or supplied was organised or directed in such a way as to involve the cruel infliction of pain or terror on an animal or the cruel goading of an animal to fury, but (whether the court draws such an inference or not) it shall be a defence for the defendant to prove that he believed, and had reasonable cause to believe, that no scene so represented was so organised or directed'. Section 4, as amended by the Animal Welfare Act 2006, states:

For the purposes of this Act ——

(a) a cinematograph film shall be deemed to be exhibited to the public when, and only when, it is exhibited in a place to which for the time being members of the general public as such have access, whether on payment of money or otherwise, and the expression 'public exhibition' shall be construed accordingly; and

(b) in relation to England and Wales, the expression 'animal' means a 'protected animal' within the meaning of the Animal Welfare Act 2006.

(c) in relation to Scotland, the expression 'animal' means a protected animal within the meaning of section 17 of the Animal Health and Welfare (Scotland) Act 2006.

For commentary on this Act, see M. Brooke, '1937 Cinematograph Films (Animals) Act', at http://www.screenonline.org.uk/film/id/592440/, noting:

Films that have caused problems under the Act include *Tom Jones* (d. Tony Richardson, 1963), whose stag hunt was modified after discussions with the RSPCA; various Italian cannibal films such as *Cannibal Ferox* (Italy, d. Umberto Lenzi, 1980), which were cut for unsimulated animal cruelty; and *The Abyss* (US, d. James Cameron, 1989), which lost a shot of a rat appearing to breathe underwater.

On the other hand, films that appear to feature considerable animal cruelty can be passed without cuts if the film-maker can prove that all the potentially contentious material was simulated...

Many other countries have similar attitudes towards animal cruelty in films, even if they are not enshrined in law. In general, most recent mainstream productions, particularly in the US, are supervised by organisations such as the American Humane Association to ensure that the welfare of animals is paramount during the film-making process.

The British Board of Film Classification (BBFC) has responsibilities under the 1937 Act. The BBFC is an independent, non-governmental body that classifies films, videos and digital media. It will not classify material that it believes to be in breach of the criminal law.[5] The BBFC has stated that it takes its responsibilities under the 1937 Act seriously: according to a 6 June 2001 press release,

The BBFC has required a cut to the cinema film *Before Night Falls* under the Cinematograph Films (Animals) Act 1937 which makes it illegal to show 'any scene...organised or directed in such a way as to involve the cruel infliction of pain and terror on any animal or the cruel goading to terror of any animal to fury'.

Before Night Falls is a drama about the life of the Cuban poet Reinaldo Arena. The scene which has been cut takes place in prison and involves the capture of a bird by one of the inmates. The bird seems to have been lassoed round the neck with a rope tied to the end of a stick. As it flaps, appearing to fight frantically for escape, it is pulled through a hole in the roof of the cellblock. The bird is evidently distressed.

The BBFC contacted the American Humane Association for further information about the film and the AHA expressed concern about that particular scene. The assurances from the trainer/handler of the bird about the way the scene had been filmed were not consistent with what appears on-screen. The BBFC, therefore, concluded that the scene should be cut before awarding the film a '15' certificate.

The BBFC takes its responsibilities under the Cinematograph Films (Animals) Act 1937 seriously and required cuts to twelve video works in 2000. These did, however, include some archive material being submitted on video for the first time. It has been several years since a feature film contained material which the Board considered to be in breach of the Act.[6]

For criticism of the BBFC's approach under the 1937 Act, see Animal Aid, 'Film Censor Under Attack for Defending Scenes of Animal Cruelty', at http://www.animalaid.org.uk/h/n/NEWS/pr_other/ALL/188//.

For newspapers articles about the BBFC's responsibilities in this context, see 'Feathers Fly As "Bird Cruelty" In Film Is Cut', at http://www.guardian.co.uk/uk/2001/jun/07/filmnews.filmcensorship, and 'Malkovich Battles Censors Over Exploding Chicken', at http://www.telegraph.co.uk/news/worldnews/northamerica/usa/1413103/Malkovich-battles-censors-over-exploding-chicken.html.[7]

COMMUNICATIONS ACT 2003

The Office of Communications (Ofcom) sets standards for the content of television and radio broadcasting. Under the Communications Act 2003 and the Broadcasting Act 1996, it is required to draw up a code for television and radio dealing with standards in programmes, sponsorship, fairness and privacy. Broadcasters are required by the terms of their Ofcom licence to observe this code. Observance of this code is also required in the case of the BBC by virtue of an agreement reached with the BBC ('the BBC Agreement') and, in the case of Sianel Pedwar Cymru, by statute. When a broadcaster breaches the Code, Ofcom may impose sanctions against it.

Section 319 of the Communications Act 2003 outlines the objectives that the Ofcom Broadcasting Code must seek to secure. These are:

(a) That persons under the age of 18 years old are protected;

(b) That material likely to encourage or to incite the commission of a crime or to lead to disorder is not included in television and radio services;

(c) That news included in television and radio services is reported with due impartiality;

(d) That news included in television and radio services is reported with due accuracy;

(e) That the proper degree of responsibility is exercised with respect to the content of programmes which are religious programmes;

(f) That generally accepted standards are applied to the contents of television and radio services so as to provide adequate protection for members of the public from the inclusion in such services of offensive and harmful material;

(g) That advertising that contravenes the prohibition on political advertising is not included in television or radio services;

(h) That the inclusion of advertising which may be misleading, harmful or offensive in television and radio services is prevented;

(i) That the international obligations of the United Kingdom with respect to advertising included in television and radio services are complied with;

(j) That the unsuitable sponsorship of programmes included in television and radio services is prevented;

(k) That there is no undue discrimination between advertisers who seek to have advertisements included in television and radio services; and

(l) That there is no use of techniques which exploit the possibility of conveying a message to viewers or listeners, or of otherwise influencing their minds, without their being aware, or fully aware, of what has occurred.

In drawing up the code now in force, Ofcom took into account the following which are set out in Section 319(4) of the Communications Act 2003:

(a) The degree of harm and offence likely to be caused by the inclusion of any particular sort of material in programmes generally or in programmes of a particular description;

(b) The likely size and composition of the potential audience for programmes included in television and radio services generally or in television and radio services of a particular description;

(c) The likely expectation of the audience as to the nature of a programme's content and the extent to which the nature of a programme's content can be brought to the attention of potential members of the audience;

(d) The likelihood of persons who are unaware of the nature of a programme's content being unintentionally exposed, by their own actions, to that content;

(e) The desirability of securing that the content of services identifies when there is a change affecting the nature of a service that is being watched or listened to and, in particular, a change that is relevant to the application of the standards set under this section; and

(f) The desirability of maintaining the independence of editorial control over programme content.[8]

For academic commentary on Ofcom's use of penalties against broadcasters who breach its code, see Kemmitt, H. (2004), 'United Kingdom: Telecommunications: Regulation' 10 *Computer and Telecommunications Law Review* N32, noting:

Ofcom has issued guidelines that it will follow in determining the amount of statutory penalties it may impose.

The Communications Act 2003 ('the Act') set out new powers for Ofcom to impose penalties in certain circumstances, for example for persistent misuse of an electronic communications network or service, for breach of conditions of entitlement, or for contravention of restrictions under the Communications Code. The Act sets a maximum amount for the relevant penalty (thus, for breach of a general condition, the maximum amount of any penalty imposed is 10 per cent of the turnover of the provider's relevant business for the relevant period), but up to that maximum it is for Ofcom to determine the amount of the penalty.

The statement does not cover penalties that may be imposed under the Competition Act, on which Ofcom will be producing separate guidelines.

GENERAL CRITERIA

The Act provides that the amount of any penalty must be appropriate and proportionate to the contravention in respect of which it is imposed. In addition, Ofcom must have regard to any representations made to them by the person in breach and any steps taken by the person to bring the contravention or misuse to an end and to remedy the consequences of the contravention or misuse.

The guidelines state that, in general, Ofcom is likely first to consider the following factors in determining the starting figure of any penalty:

■ The seriousness of the contravention;

■ Any precedents set by previous cases; and

■ The need to ensure that the threat of penalties will act as a sufficient incentive to comply.

SPECIFIC CRITERIA WHICH MAY BE RELEVANT DEPENDING ON THE CONTRAVENTION

Certain specific criteria may be relevant to adjust the starting figure of any penalty depending on the type of contravention. These may include:

■ Any gain (financial or otherwise) made by the person in breach (or any connected person);

■ The degree of harm caused, or increased cost incurred by consumers or other market participants;

■ Size and turnover of the regulated body;

■ The extent and nature of third-party responsibility for the breach; and

■ The duration of the contravention.

FACTORS TENDING TO LEAD TO AN INCREASE IN THE LEVEL OF ANY PENALTY

These may include:

■ Repeated contraventions by the same person;

■ Continuation of the contravention by the person concerned after either becoming aware of the contravention or being notified of an investigation by Ofcom;

■ The degree of wilfulness of the contravention;

- The complicity of senior management in any contravention; and

- The ineffectiveness or repeated failure of internal mechanisms or procedures intended to prevent contravention by the person concerned or other persons in the same group.

FACTORS TENDING TO DECREASE THE LEVEL OF ANY PENALTY

These may include:

- The extent and timeliness of any steps taken to comply with the contravention in question, and any steps taken for remedying the consequences of the contravention; and

- Cooperation with Ofcom's investigation.

CONSPIRACY TO CORRUPT PUBLIC MORALS

The law still contains several arcane offences that can be used to 'guard the moral welfare of the State against attacks which may be more insidious because they are novel and unprepared for'.[9] From the point of view of prosecutors, the potentially most useful offence is that of conspiracy to corrupt public morals, which could be used against any writing or broadcasting that a jury might hold to be destructive of the moral fabric of society. In practice, it is rarely used and is confined to publications advertising for the procurement of illegal sexual liaisons. The leading cases in this context are *Shaw v DPP (*ibid.*)* and *Knuller v DPP*.[10] According to Lord Morris in *Shaw v DPP*:

> There are certain manifestations of conduct which are an affront to and an attack upon recognised public standards of morals and decency, and which all well-disposed persons would stigmatise and condemn as deserving of punishment. The cases afford examples of the conduct of individuals which has been punished because it outraged public decency or because its tendency was to corrupt the public morals…Even if accepted public standards may to some extent vary from generation to generation, current standards are in the keeping of juries, who can be trusted to maintain the corporate good sense of the community and to discern attacks upon values that must be preserved. If there were prosecutions which were not genuinely and fairly warranted juries would be quick to perceive this. There could be no conviction unless twelve jurors were unanimous in thinking that the accused person or persons had combined to do acts which were calculated to corrupt public morals.[11]

CRIMINAL JUSTICE AND IMMIGRATION ACT 2008

Section 63(1) of the Criminal Justice and Immigration Act 2008 makes it an offence to be in possession of an 'extreme pornographic image'. According to section 63(3), an 'image is "pornographic" if it of such a nature that it must reasonably be assumed to have been produced solely or principally for the purpose of sexual arousal'. Section 63(6) defines an 'extreme image' as one that (a) falls within section 63(7), and (b) 'is grossly offensive, disgusting or otherwise of an obscene character'. Section 63(7) states:

An image falls within this subsection if it portrays, in an explicit and realistic way, any of the following:

(a) an act which threatens a person's life,

(b) an act which results, or is likely to result, in serious injury to a person's anus, breasts or genitals,

(c) an act which involves sexual interference with a human corpse, or

(d) a person performing an act of intercourse or oral sex with an animal (whether dead or alive), and a reasonable person looking at the image would think that any such person or animal was real.

Section 63 does not apply to 'excluded images'. Section 64(2) defines an 'excluded image' as 'an image which forms part of a series of images contained in a recording of the whole or part of a classified work'. Sections 65 and 66 provide defences to a charge under section 63(1).

For relevant academic commentary, see McGlynn, C. and Rackley, E. (2007), 'Striking a Balance: Arguments for the Criminal Regulation of Extreme Pornography', *Criminal Law Review,* 677.

CUSTOMS (CONSOLIDATION) ACT 1843
Section 42 of the Customs (Consolidation) Act 1843 prohibits the importation of 'indecent or obscene prints, paintings, photographs, books, cards, lithographic or other engravings, or any other indecent or obscene articles'. Attempting to evade this prohibition is a criminal offence under section 170(2) of the Customs and Excise Management Act 1979.

ELECTRONIC COMMERCE (EC DIRECTIVE) REGULATIONS 2002
'Articles 12 to 14 of the Electronic Commerce Directive 2001/31/EC contain limitations on the liability of providers of information society services where they act either as a mere conduit, in caching information or in hosting information. These articles are principally implemented in the United Kingdom by Regulations 17 – 22 of the Electronic Commerce (EC Directive) Regulations 2002'.[12] In *Bunt v Tilley*, Eady pointed out that '[t]he protection which these Regulations afford is not confined to the publication of defamatory material. They embrace other illegal material, such as child pornography or the infringement of intellectual property rights'.[13] However, Eady added that 'service providers may be obliged on occasion to act in order to prevent or stop unlawful activities'.[14] For a detailed explanation of this legislation, see Department of Trade and Industry, DTI Consultation Document on the Electronic Commerce Directive: 'The Liability of Hyperlinkers, Location Tool Services and Content Aggregators' (2005, chapter 3). For analysis of the pre-2002 law, see Pearson, H. (1995), 'Liability of Bulletin Board Operators' 1 *Computer and Telecommunications Law Review,* 54.

HUMAN RIGHTS ACT 1998
The Human Rights Act 1998 requires all legislation to be interpreted and given effect, so far as it is possible to do so, in a way that is compatible with the European Convention on Human Rights. Second, it makes it unlawful for a public authority to act in a way that is incompatible with a Convention right, and stipulates that proceedings may be brought in a court or tribunal against the

authority if it does so. Third, UK courts and tribunals must take account of Convention rights in all cases that they handle. This means, for example, that they must develop the common law (i.e. the rules of law created by the courts, as opposed to those created by legislation) compatibly with the Convention rights.[15]

According to Article 10 of the Convention, everyone has the right to freedom of expression. This article is relevant in relation to the regulation of media content. Thus, for example, Ofcom had to take it into account in drafting its Broadcasting Code:

> The Code has also been drafted in the light of the Human Rights Act 1998 and the European Convention on Human Rights (the Convention). In particular, the right to freedom of expression, as expressed in Article 10 of the Convention, encompasses the audience's right to receive creative material, information and ideas without interference but subject to restrictions proscribed by law and necessary in a democratic society.[16]

For an important case in this context, see *R (ProLife Alliance) v BBC*.[17] For analysis of this case, see Rowbottom, R. (2003), 'Article 10 and Election Broadcasts' 119 *Law Quarterly Review* 553, summarizing the dispute as follows:

> [T]he Prolife Alliance, a political party that opposes abortion, euthanasia and embryo research, qualified for a short party election broadcast in Wales in the 2001 General Election. The proposed broadcast was to feature images of the products of suction abortion, including foetuses in a mangled and mutilated state. The BBC, in agreement with other broadcasters, refused to screen the broadcast as it infringed standards of 'taste and decency', pursuant to the BBC's agreement with the Secretary of State…Later versions of the broadcast containing such images were rejected on similar grounds, so that on June 2, 2001, the Alliance's broadcast contained no images except the word 'censored' and a soundtrack. The Alliance complained that the broadcaster had infringed their expression rights under Art. 10 of the European Convention on Human Rights and at common law. Reversing the High Court's decision in favour of the BBC, the Court of Appeal concluded that little deference should be shown to the decision maker in political speech cases and that concerns of taste and decency could only justify a restriction in extreme circumstances. A majority of the House of Lords upheld the broadcaster's appeal, with Lord Scott of Foscote dissenting.

For further academic commentary on this case, see Barendt, E. (2003) 'Free Speech and Abortion', *Public Law,* 580.[18]

INDECENT DISPLAYS (CONTROL) ACT 1981

According to section 1(1) of this Act, 'If any indecent matter is publicly displayed the person making the display and any person causing or permitting the display to be made shall be guilty of an offence'.

For an explanation of this legislation, see *Blackstone's Criminal Practice 2007* (2006) (p. 898–899). For Home Office guidance on this Act, see Home Office Circular 083/1981. For relevant academic commentary, see Stone, R. (1982), 'Out of Sight, Out of Mind' The Indecent Displays (Controls) Act 1981', 45 *Modern Law Review*, 62.

'Indecent' is not defined by the Act. According to D. Ormerod, 'whether matter is indecent will no doubt be considered a matter of fact to be determined by applying the ordinary meaning of the word'.[19] In this context, it is worth noting that it was held in *Stanley*, a case decided under the Post Office Act 1953, that the words 'indecent or obscene' in relation to the 1953 Act 'convey one idea, namely offending against the recognised standards of propriety, indecent being at the lower end of the scale and obscene at the upper end of the scale...an indecent article is not necessarily obscene, whereas an obscene article must almost certainly be indecent'.[20] Prosecutions and convictions are rare under the 1981 Act; in 2006, for instance, there were no convictions under the Indecent Displays (Controls) Act 1981, and only one such prosecution.[21]

OBSCENE PUBLICATIONS ACT 1959

This Act makes it an offence to publish, whether for gain or not, any article whose effect, taken as a whole, is such, in the view of the court, to tend to 'deprave and corrupt' those likely to read, see or hear the matter contained or embodied in it. It also makes it an offence to have an obscene article for publication for gain. Section 1(2) of the 1959 Act provides, '[i]n this Act, "article" means any description or article containing or embodying matter to be read or looked at or both, any sound record, and any film or other record of a picture or pictures'. The Act covers forms of communication unknown in 1959, such as video cassettes and computer hard disks.[22] 'Publication' is a very broad term, and can include giving a book to a friend.[23]

Section 1(1) of the 1959 Act provides the test of 'obscenity': 'For the purposes of this Act an article shall be deemed to be obscene if its effect or (where the article comprises two or more distinct items) the effect of any one of its items is, if taken as a whole, such as to tend to deprave and corrupt persons who are likely, having regard to all relevant circumstances, to read, see or hear the matter contained or embodied in it'.

This definition requires proof of an actual tendency to deprave and corrupt.[24] In the well-known Lady Chatterley case, *R v Penguin Books Ltd*, Byrne said, 'to deprave means to make morally bad, to pervert, to debase or corrupt morally. To corrupt means to render morally unsound or rotten, to destroy the moral purity or chastity, to pervert or ruin a good quality, to debase or defile'.[25] This implies that the tendency must go much further than merely shocking or disgusting readers. Thus, the word 'obscene' in law has, at least in principle, a much stronger meaning than in colloquial language, and defendants have been acquitted because of this; for example, the Court of Appeal quashed the conviction in *Anderson* because the judge directed the jury that an item is obscene if it is 'repulsive', 'filthy', 'loathsome' or 'lewd'.[26] However, it is important to bear in mind that, according to Ormerod, 'whether the conduct to which the article tends amounts to depravity would seem to depend on how violently the judge (in deciding whether there was evidence of obscenity) and the jury (in deciding whether the article was obscene) disapproved of the conduct in question'.[27]

The principle that obscene material must have more serious effects than arousing feelings of revulsion leads to the doctrine that material that in fact shocks and disgusts may not be obscene, since its effect is to discourage readers from indulgence in the immorality so unappetizingly portrayed. This 'aversion' defence emphasizes the context and purpose of publication. Writing that sets out to seduce, to exhort and pressure the reader to indulge in immorality is to be distinguished from that which presents a balanced picture and does not overlook the pains that may attend new pleasures. An article would have no tendency to deprave if it were so revolting that it would put anyone off the kind of depraved activity depicted.[28]

As stated in section 1(1) of the 1959 Act, an article is only obscene if its effect is such as to tend to deprave and corrupt 'persons who are likely, having regard to all relevant circumstances, to read, see or hear the matter contained or embodied in it'. Section 2(6) provides that, in any prosecution for publishing an obscene article, 'the question whether an article is obscene shall be determined without regard to any publication by another person, unless it could reasonably have been expected that the publication by the other person would follow from the publication by the person charged'. In *R v O'Sullivan*, it was held that the jury must consider the impact not only on intended customers but on those to whom the customers could reasonably be expected to show or pass on the material, but not its impact on other persons who might, but could not reasonably be expected or be likely to, gain access to it as a result of the defendant's original act of publication.[29] The effect of this must be that if a child is corrupted by images in his father's pornographic magazine that has been carelessly left lying around the house, the publisher will not be responsible.

It is important to realise that the 1959 Act requires that the item have the effect of tending to deprave and corrupt 'persons', as opposed to a single individual. An article will not be obscene simply because it might tend to deprave and corrupt 'a minute lunatic fringe of readers',[30] but it is definitely obscene if it has a tendency to deprave a significant proportion of those likely to read or view it (ibid.), and it has been stated in the House of Lords that it is only when the number of persons likely to be affected is 'so small as to be negligible' that the article is not obscene.[31]

Depravity and corruption are not confined to sexual depravity and corruption; the courts have interpreted the statutory definition of 'obscene' to encompass arrangements to take dangerous drugs and to engage in violence.[32] However, the enforcement of obscenity laws is now directed mostly at hard-core pornography, concentrating not on the message of an article but instead on the physical incidents photographed or described. For example, stories may degrade women by depicting them as objects to be manipulated for fun and profit, without attracting a prosecution.

Section 4 of the 1959 Act provides for a 'public good' defence: although the work is obscene, its publication is nonetheless justified in the public interest. According to section 4(1), the ground upon which the defence may be made out is that publication is 'in the interests of science, literature, art or learning, or of other objects of general concern'. Effectively, any article that has a claim to literary merit could escape penalty under the 1959 Act. Since 1979,[33] the only books that have been prosecuted have either glorified illegal activities or have been hard-core pornography, lacking any literary pretensions or sociological interest. Section 4(1A) states that the section 4(1) defence 'shall not apply where the article in question is a moving picture film or soundtrack', but, in relation to such items, it creates a similar defence where 'the publication...is justified as being for the public good on the ground that it is in the interests of drama, opera, ballet or any other art, or of literature or learning'.

Section 2(5) provides a limited defence for defendants who are innocent disseminators of obscene material: '[a] person shall not be convicted of an offence against this section [the offence of publishing obscene material] if he proves that he had not examined the article in respect of which he is charged and had no reasonable cause to suspect that it was such that his publication of it would make him liable to be convicted of an offence against this section'. According to D. Ormerod, 'both conditions must be satisfied; so if D has examined the article, his failure to appreciate its tendency to deprave and corrupt is no defence under…[this section]'.[34] It is not clear how this defence would apply to Internet service providers (ISPs). One view is that:

> In contrast to providers who host Web pages or newsgroups, ISPs who simply provide a connection to the Internet are unlikely to be in a position to assess accurately the nature of even a fraction of the data that their systems carry, even if they wanted to. They are less likely to incur liability, even if some of their users use their systems as a conduit to access or distribute pornography, as they have no actual knowledge of the material carried.[35]

For academic commentary regarding the application of the 1959 Act to electronic bulletin board operators, see Pearson, H. (1995), 'Liability of Bulletin Board Operators' 1 *Computer and Telecommunications Law Review*, 54, p. 57, stating;

> The Obscene Publications Act 1959 covers material which has the effect such as to tend to deprave and corrupt. There has been a great deal of case law on what constitutes obscenity. One particular factor is the type of persons who may get hold of the material. Whereas conventional printed 'hard' pornography can only be obtained in general under very controlled circumstances, bulletin boards can be accessed by anybody with the right equipment, and it is notorious that teenage boys are very proficient at carrying out this sort of access. The prosecution should have no problem in convincing a jury that much of this type of material is obscene in those circumstances. An offence is committed if the defendant publishes an obscene article, even if not for gain, or has an obscene article for the purposes of publication for gain. Publication consists of any kind of distribution, sale or performance. There is no requirement under the Obscene Publications Act that the defendant must have actually have had an intent to deprave or corrupt, although it is a defence for the defendant to prove both that he had not examined the article and that he had no reasonable cause to suspect that it was of such a nature that his publication of it would constitute an offence under the Obscene Publications Act. As both these facts must be proved, it is not enough for a bulletin board operator simply to shut his eyes to what is going on his board; he must have no reasonable cause to suspect that pornography of any kind is being placed on his board. Given the open nature of most boards, particularly those connected to the Internet, it would seem that this condition could not be satisfied unless the operator did in fact inspect what was being placed on the board.

For further academic commentary regarding the 1959 Act, see in particular, Akdeniz, Y. (1997), 'Governance of Pornography and Child Pornography on the Global Internet: A Multi-

Layered Approach,' in L. Edwards and C. Waelde (eds), *Law and the Internet: Regulating Cyberspace*, 223, and Rowbottom, J. (2006), 'Obscenity Laws and the Internet: Targeting the Supply and Demand' , *Criminal Law Review,* 97.[36]

OUTRAGING PUBLIC DECENCY

A majority in the House of Lords in *Knuller v DPP* held that there is an offence of outraging public decency. In this case, Lord Simon stated;

> It should be emphasised that 'outrage', like 'corrupt', is a very strong word. 'Outraging public decency' goes considerably beyond offending the susceptibilities of, or even shocking, reasonable people. Moreover the offence is, in my view, concerned with recognised minimum standards of decency, which are likely to vary from time to time. Finally, notwithstanding that 'public' in the offence is used in a location sense, public decency must be viewed as a whole; and I think the jury should be invited, where appropriate, to remember that they live in a plural society, with a tradition of tolerance towards minorities, and that this atmosphere of toleration is itself part of public decency.[37]

In *R v Gibson*, Lord Lane added;

> [W]here the charge is one of outraging public decency, there is no requirement that the prosecution should prove an intention to outrage or...recklessness [in the sense of an appreciation on the part of the defendant that there was a risk of such outrage, coupled with a determination nevertheless to run that risk].[38]

The offence is not confined to sexual indecency; it applied in *R v Gibson*, where, in an art gallery, the defendant exhibited an article featuring freeze-dried human foetuses. Modern cases concerning the offence of outraging public decency include *R v May*,[39] *R v Rowley*,[40] *R v Lunderbuch*,[41] *R v Walker*[42] and *R v Hamilton*.[43] For academic commentary on *R v Gibson*, see Smith, J.C. (1990), 'Outraging Public Decency' *Crim LR,* 738. For a useful article on the offence in general, see Childs, M. (1991), 'Outraging Public Decency: The Offence of Offensiveness', *Public Law*, 20.

PROTECTION OF CHILDREN ACT 1978

Section 1 of this act, as amended by the Criminal Justice and Public Order Act 1994, the Sexual Offences Act 2003, and the Criminal Justice and Immigration Act 2008, creates various offences relating to indecent photographs or pseudo-photographs of a child under 18 years of age. According to section 1(1), it is an offence for a person;

(a) To take, or permit to be taken or to make, any indecent photograph or pseudo-photograph of a child; or

(b) To distribute or show such indecent photographs or pseudo-photographs; or

(c) To have in his possession such indecent photographs or pseudo-photographs, with a view to their being distributed or shown by himself or others; or

(d) To publish or cause to be published any advertisement likely to be understood as conveying that the advertiser distributes or shows such indecent photographs or pseudo-photographs, or intends to do so.

Section 39 of the Police and Justice Act 2006 and Schedule 11 to the Act amended the Protection of Children Act 1978 in relation to the forfeiture of indecent photographs and pseudo-photographs of children. For a summary of the consequences of the amendments, see Internet Watch Foundation, 'Police and Criminal Justice Act 2006 (Section 39 and Schedule 11)'.[44]

Section 45 of the Sexual Offences Act 2003 redefined a 'child' for the purposes of the Protection of Children Act 1978 as a person under 18, rather than 16, years of age. This change means that the offences under the 1978 Act will now also be applicable where the photographs or pseudo-photographs concerned are of children of 16 or 17 years of age. The same change applies to the offence of possessing an indecent photograph or pseudo-photograph of a child under section 160 of the Criminal Justice Act 1988 (section 160(4) applies the 1978 Act definition of 'child'). According to the Internet Watch Foundation, in this context, '[t]he word indecent should be taken at its dictionary meaning; as a guide, it means any images of children, apparently under 18 years of age, involved in sexual activity or posed to be sexually provocative'.[45]

According to section 1(4) of the 1978 Act:

Where a person is charged with an offence under subsection (1)(b) or (c), it shall be a defence for him to prove —

(a) That he had a legitimate reason for distributing or showing the photographs or pseudo-photographs or (as the case may be) having them in his possession or

(b) That he had not himself seen the photographs or pseudo-photographs and did not know, nor had any cause to suspect, them to be indecent.

The main function of the 1978 legislation is to close some potential gaps in the measures available to police and prosecutors; 'the Act particularly deals with the use of children in pornographic photography even where no other form of abuse had occurred'.[46]

G. Robertson and A. Nicol claim that the 1978 Act is effectively deployed against those who use computers to deliver child pornography:

Anyone who consciously downloads such an image from the internet 'makes' a photograph for the purposes of section 1(1)(a) and will be guilty if he deliberately prints them out, even if the internet site where they were uplinked is abroad…Providing a 'password' to access such data is a form of 'showing' it…The cases demonstrate that the courts will ignore technical or legislative distinctions in order to effectuate Parliament's intent to punish every new way in which sexual images of children may be exploited. These decisions prima facie breach Art. 8 of the European Convention, which guarantees respect for privacy, but the interference will probably be justified 'for the protection of health or morals, or for the protection of the rights and freedoms of others'.[47]

For academic commentary regarding the 1978 Act, see Jarvie, N. (2003), 'Control of Cybercrime – Is an end to our Privacy on the Internet a Price worth Paying? Part 1' 9 *Computer and Telecommunications Law Review*, 76, p. 80:

> Since 1997 there has been an enormous growth in the indiscriminate distribution of electronic mail messages offering access to pornographic images, often of children, sometimes via websites demanding credit card payments, before viewing is allowed. In most cases, the fact that the images or text are recorded and transmitted on digital material rather than on paper or videotape will not affect the determination of whether the contents are pornographic. While pornography is not itself illegal, where images of children are depicted, in terms of the Protection of Children Act 1978, an offence is committed by a person simply possessing an indecent photograph of a child.[48] In *R v Fellows and Arnold*, the question before the Court of Appeal was whether images stored on a computer disc could be classed as photographs within the meaning of the Act.[49] It held that the Act did not restrict the nature of the copy, and therefore the data represented the original photograph, albeit in another form. The court further held that knowingly holding photographs contained in an archive in digital form, where others could access them, amounted to active participation. As a result, the offence of distributing or showing photographs to others could be held to have been committed by the maintainers of the database. The offence extends to the possession or distribution of 'pseudo-photographs', where the impression created by the photograph is that the person shown is a child notwithstanding that some of the physical characteristics shown are those of an adult.[50] However, the offence does not extend to unintentional copying. In *Atkins v DPP*, the accused could not be convicted, as he could not be shown to have been aware of a cache of photographs in the first place.[51] This is disturbing news for law enforcement. Such a requirement places an even greater burden on those authorities for whom detecting and prosecuting paedophiles is already a difficult task.

Important cases in this area include *R v Owen*,[52] *R v Land*,[53] *R v T (Child Pornography)*,[54] *R v Bowden*,[55] *R v Smethurst*,[56] *R v Oliver*,[57] *R v Smith*,[58] *R v Collier*,[59] *R v Dooley*[60] and *R v Nicklass*.[61]

For academic commentary in this context, see Akdeniz, Y. (1997), 'Governance of Pornography and Child Pornography on the Global Internet: A Multi-Layered Approach,' in L. Edwards and C. Waelde (eds), *Law and the Internet: Regulating Cyberspace*, p. 223, and Selfe, D. (2007), 'Indecent Photographs of Children – The Scope of Indecency', 171 *Criminal Lawyer*, 3.[62]

PUBLIC ORDER ACT 1986

This Act creates various offences concerning the use of threatening, abusive or insulting words, written material or behaviour. It also covers incitement to racial hatred and acts intended to stir up religious hatred or hatred on the grounds of sexual orientation.

Section 17 defines racial hatred as being 'hatred against a group of persons...defined by reference to colour, race, nationality (including citizenship) or ethnic or national origins'.

Section 18(1) states that '[a] person who uses threatening, abusive or insulting words or behaviour, or displays any written material which is threatening, abusive or insulting, is guilty of an offence if (a) he intends thereby to stir up racial hatred, or (b) having regard to all the circumstances racial hatred is likely to be stirred up thereby'.

Section 18(1)(b) is subject to section 18(5), which states that 'a person who is not shown to have intended to stir up racial hatred is not guilty of an offence under this section if he did not intend his words or behaviour or the written material to be, and was not aware that it might be, threatening, abusive or insulting'.

Sections 19, 20, 21, 22, and 23 create related offences concerning acts intended or likely to stir up racial hatred.

Section 29A, as inserted by the Racial and Religious Hatred Act 2006, states that '"religious hatred" means hatred against a group of persons defined by reference to religious belief or lack of religious belief'. Section 29AB, as inserted by the Criminal Justice and Immigration Act 2008, states that '"hatred on the grounds of sexual orientation" means hatred against a group of persons defined by reference to sexual orientation (whether towards persons of the same sex, the opposite sex or both)'. Part IIIA of the Public Order Act 1986, as added by the Racial and Religious Hatred Act 2006 and amended by the Criminal Justice and Immigration Act 2008, creates offences involving stirring up hatred against persons on religious grounds or on the grounds of sexual orientation.

Section 5(1) of the Public Order Act 1986 states that a person is guilty of an offence if he:

Uses threatening, abusive or insulting words or behaviour, or disorderly behaviour, or displays any writing, sign or visible representation which is threatening, abusive or insulting, within the hearing or sight of a person likely to be caused harassment, alarm or distress thereby.

Section 6(4) states that a person 'is guilty of an offence under section 5 only if he intends his words or behaviour, or the writing, sign or other visible representation, to be threatening, abusive or insulting, or is aware that it may be threatening, abusive or insulting, or (as the case may be) he intends his behaviour to be or is aware that it is disorderly'.

For a recent case concerning the use of the Public Order Act 1986, see 'Abu Hamza Charged With Inciting Murders', at http://www.guardian.co.uk/uk_news/story/0,3604,1331204,00.html.[63]

For Crown Prosecution Service information relating to racist and religious crime, see http://www.cps.gov.uk/publications/prosecution/rrpbcrbook.html.[64]

For relevant academic commentary, see Goodall, K. (2007), 'Incitement to Religious Hatred: All Talk and No Substance?', 70 *Modern Law Review*, 89, and Wolffe, W. (1987), 'Values in Conflict: Incitement to Racial Hatred and the Public Order Act 1986', *Public Law,* 85.

Terrorism Act 2006

The explanatory notes relating to the Terrorism Act 2006 state:

> The purpose of this Act is to reform and extend previous counter-terrorist legislation to ensure that the UK law enforcement agencies have the necessary powers to counter the threat to the UK posed by terrorism…The Act creates a number of new offences. These new offences include the offence of encouragement of terrorism [and]…an offence relating to bookshops and other disseminators of terrorist publications.

For relevant academic commentary, see Hunt, A. (2007), 'Criminal Prohibitions on Direct and Indirect Encouragement of Terrorism', *Criminal Law Review*, 441.

Video Recordings Act 1984

According to the Home Office:

> In 1984, after increasing public and Parliamentary concern over the unregulated content of videos and, in particular, so-called 'video-nasties', the Video Recordings Act was introduced. The Act, which is applicable throughout the United Kingdom, established a statutory classification system which requires all video works, irrespective of the media on which they are carried (e.g. video-tape, Digital Versatile Disc etc.), apart from a small category of exempt works, to be submitted to the BBFC [British Board of Film Classification]. When considering the most appropriate classification certificate for a video work, the Act requires the BBFC to take into account the likelihood of works being viewed in the home. The Act draws no distinction between the Board's responsibilities in respect of R18 videos and other works. These general principles were supplemented by further statutory classification criteria set out in the Criminal Justice and Public Order Act 1994. Under the 1994 Act, the BBFC is required to have special regard to any harm that may be caused to those likely to view a video (including children), and any harm to society through the behaviour of those viewers afterwards, by the manner in which the video work deals with criminal behaviour, illegal drugs, violence, horror or human sexual activity. If the BBFC considers that a particular work is unacceptable for viewing, it can, and does, refuse to issue a classification certificate altogether. This has the effect of banning the video work concerned, as under the Video Recordings Act 1984 it is a criminal offence to supply, offer or possess for supply an unclassified video, or to supply a video in breach of the classification certificate issued by the BBFC.[65]

For further relevant information, see Video Standards Council, 'The Law', at http://www.video standards.org.uk/.

An overview of the current European law regulating media content

Audiovisual Media Services Directive (AVMSD)

Directive 2007/65/EC amended the Television Without Frontiers Directive and renamed it the 'Audiovisual Media Services Directive' (AVMSD).

According to EUROPA, the portal website of the European Union:

> AVMSD offers a comprehensive legal framework that covers all audiovisual media services (including on-demand audiovisual media services), provides less detailed and more flexible regulation and modernises rules on TV advertising to better finance audiovisual content.

> The new rules, which have been called for especially by the European Parliament, respond to technological developments and create a new level-playing field in Europe for emerging audiovisual media services.

> The new Directive reaffirms the pillars of Europe's audiovisual model, which are cultural diversity, protection of minors, consumer protection, media pluralism, and the fight against racial and religious hatred. In addition to that, the new Directive aims at ensuring the independence of national media regulators.[66]

CONVENTION ON CYBERCRIME

The Convention on Cybercrime entered into force in July 2004:

> [It] is the first international treaty on crimes committed via the Internet and other computer networks, dealing particularly with infringements of copyright, computer-related fraud, child pornography and violations of network security. It also contains a series of powers and procedures such as the search of computer networks and interception.

> Its main objective, set out in the preamble, is to pursue a common criminal policy aimed at the protection of society against cybercrime, especially by adopting appropriate legislation and fostering international co-operation.[67]

The Additional Protocol to the Convention extends the Cybercrime Convention's scope, 'including its substantive, procedural and international cooperation provisions, so as to cover also offences of racist and xenophobic propaganda'.[68]

DIRECTIVE 2000/31/EC (LIABILITY OF INTERMEDIARY SERVICE PROVIDERS)

> Articles 12 to 14 of the Electronic Commerce Directive 2001/31/EC contain limitations on the liability of providers of information society services where they act either as a mere conduit, in caching information or in hosting information. These articles are principally implemented in the United Kingdom by Regulations 17–22 of the Electronic Commerce (EC Directive) Regulations 2002.[69]

EUROPEAN CONVENTION ON HUMAN RIGHTS

The European Convention on Human Rights is an important international instrument. In 2006, the Department for Constitutional Affairs stated:

> The 1950 European Convention on Human Rights (ECHR) is a binding international agreement that the UK helped draft and has sought to comply with for half a century. The

Convention enshrines fundamental civil and political rights, but for many years it was not a full part of our own law. Using the Convention usually meant taking a case to the European Court of Human Rights in Strasbourg. This was often time-consuming and expensive.

Since coming into force on 2 October 2000, the Human Rights Act 1998 has made rights from the ECHR…enforceable in our own courts. This is much quicker and simpler than the old arrangement.[70]

In the United Kingdom, the Human Rights Act 1998 requires all legislation to be interpreted and given effect, so far as it is possible to do so, in a way that is compatible with the ECHR. Second, it makes it unlawful for a public authority to act in a way that is incompatible with a Convention right, and stipulates that proceedings may be brought in a court or tribunal against the authority if it does so. Third, UK courts and tribunals must take account of Convention rights in all cases that they handle. According to Article 10 of the Convention, everyone has the right to freedom of expression. This article is relevant in relation to the regulation of media content.

NOTES

1. (1999) 3 CMLR 919.
2. (1993) 3 CMLR 387.
3. Debs, H.C. (1955), *Hansard* Vol. 539, Col. 6063.
4. See e.g. Vincent, C. 'Briefing on Current UK Laws on Obscenity and Related Areas', at http://www.lawcf.org/index.asp?page=LCF%20briefing%20on%20obscenity%20laws.
5. For general information regarding the BBFC's history and role, see www.bbfc.co.uk and Answers.com, 'British Board of Film Classification', at http://www.answers.com/topic/british-board-of-film-classification.
6. BBFFC press release, June 6 2001, at http://www.bbfc.co.uk/news/pressnews.php.
7. We are unaware of any leading court decisions regarding the 1937 Act.
8. Ofcom, Ofcom Broadcasting Code (2005), 6.
9. *Shaw v DPP* (1962) AC 220.
10. (1972) 56 Cr App R 633.
11. (1962) AC 220, 292.
12. Department of Trade and Industry (DTI), DTI Consultation Document on the Electronic Commerce Directive: 'The Liability of Hyperlinkers, Location Tool Services and Content Aggregators? (2005), paragraph 3.1.
13. (2006) EWHC 407, (2007) 1 WLR 1243, at (38).
14. ibid, at (40).
15. For a comprehensive guide concerning the Human Rights Act, see the Department for Constitutional Affairs, *Study Guide: Human Rights Act 1998* (3rd ed., 2006).
16. Ofcom, Ofcom Broadcasting Code (2005), 3.
17. (2003) UKHL 23, (2004])1 AC 185.
18. See too Elvin, J. (2004), '*R v British Broadcasting Corporation ex parte ProLife Alliance*: The Right to Free Speech, Standards of Taste and Decency, and the "Truth" about Abortions', 1 *Web Journal of Current Legal Issues*; Jowell, J. (2003), 'Judicial Deference: Servility, Civility, or Institutional Capacity', *Public Law,* 592; and Macdonald, A. (2003), '*R (On the Application of ProLife Alliance) v British Broadcasting Corporation*: Political Speech and the Standard of Review', 6 *European Human Rights Law Review*, 651.
19. Ormerod, D. (2005), *Smith and Hogan: Criminal Law* (11th ed.), 965.
20. (1965) 2 QB 237.
21. House of Commons Library Research Paper 08/21 (February 2008), 20.

22. See, respectively, *A-G's Reference No 5 of 1980* (1980) 3 All ER 816 and *R v Fellows* (1997) Cr App R 244.

23. See section 1(3) of the 1959 Act.

24. *DPP v Whyte* (1972) 3 All ER 12, 18.

25. (1961) Crim LR 176, 177.

26. (1972) 1 QB 304.

27. Ormerod, D. (2005), *Smith and Hogan: Criminal Law* (11th ed.), 946.

28. *R v Calder & Boyars Ltd* (1969) 1 QB 151.

29. (1995) Cr App R 455.

30. *R v Calder & Boyars Ltd* (1969) 1 QB 151.

31. *DPP v Whyte* (1972) 3 All ER 12.

32. See, for example, *John Calder (Publications) Ltd v Powell* (1965) 1 QB 509, a case concerning a novel dealing with the life of a heroin addict.

33. The date of publication of the Williams Committee Report (*Committee on Obscenity and Film Censorship*) HMSO 1979 Cmnd 7772.

34. Ormerod, D. (2005), *Smith and Hogan: Criminal Law* (11th ed.), 955.

35. The Joint Information Systems Committee (JISC), 'New Developments in UK Internet Law (2000) (only available by contacting JISC Legal directly at info@jisclegal.ac.uk).

36. See too Cowan, V. (1992), 'Warrant Under Obscene Publications Act 1959, s 3 – Distinction Between Obscene and Sexually Explicit', *Crim LR* 57; Gringras, C. (1996), 'Computers – Internet' 2 *Computer and Telecommunications Law Review* T162; Edwards, S. (1998), 'On the Contemporary Application of the Obscene Publications Act 1959', *Crim LR*, 843; Manchester, C. (1995), 'Computer Pornography', *Crim LR*, 546; Ormerod, D. (1999), 'Obscenity – Whether Films Obscene "Taken as a Whole"', *Crim LR*, 670; Smith, J.C. (1996), 'Having An Obscene Article for Publication or Gain', *Crim LR*, 264; and Stone, R. (1986), 'Obscene Publications – The Problems Persist', *Crim LR*, 139.

37. (1972) 56 Cr App R 633, 698.

38. (1990) Cr App R 341, 349.

39. (1989) 91 Cr App R 157.

40. (1991) 1 WLR 1020.

41. (1991) Crim LR 784.

42. (1995) Crim LR 827.

43. (2007) EWCA Crim 2062, (2008) 2 WLR 107.

44. http://www.iwf.org.uk/police/page.22.504.htm.

45. Internet Watch Foundation, 'Protection of Children Act 1978 (England and Wales)', at http://www.iwf.org.uk/media/page.70.217.htm.

46. Akdeniz, Y. (1997), 'The Regulation of Pornography and Child Pornography on The Internet', 1 *Journal of Information, Law and Technology*, at http://www2.warwick.ac.uk/fac/soc/law/elj/jilt/1997_1/akdeniz1.

47. Roberston G. and Nicol, A, (2007), *Media Law* (5th ed.), 220.

48. Section 1(1)(c).

49. (1997) 2 All ER 484.

50. Protection of Children Act 1978, s 7(7).

51. (2000) 2 All ER 425.

52. (1987) 131 SJ 1696.

53. (1998) Crim LR 70.

54. (1999) Crim LR 749.

55. (2000) Crim LR 381.

56. (2001) EWCA Crim 772, (2001) Crim LR 657.

57. (2002) EWCA Crim 2766, (2003) Crim LR 127.

58. (2002) EWCA Crim 683, (2002) Crim LR 659.

59. (2004) EWCA Crim 1411, (2005) 1 WLR 843.

60. (2005) EWCA Crim 3093, (2006) 1 WLR 775.

61. (2006) EWCA Crim 2613.
62. See too 'Indecent Photographs of Children – No Direct Evidence of Age'[1998] *Crim LR,* 70; Akdeniz, Y. (1997), 'The Regulation of Pornography and Child Pornography on The Internet' 1 *Journal of Information, Law and Technology*, at http://www2.warwick.ac.uk/fac/soc/law/elj/jilt/1997_1/akdeniz1; Barsby, C. and Ormerod, D. (2001), 'Indecent Photographs of Children: Making An Indecent Photograph of a Child Whether Breach of European Convention on Human Rights, Articles 8 and 10', *Crim LR* 657; Gillespie, A. (2003), 'Sentences for Offences Involving Child Pornography', *Crim LR,* 81; Manchester, C. (1996) 'More About Computer Pornography', *Crim LR,* 645; Ormerod, D. (2000), 'Indecent Photographs of Children: Whether Downloading an Image Amounted to "Making" a Photograph', *Crim LR*, 381; Smith, J.C. (1999), 'Possessing Indecent Photographs' *Crim LR*, 749; Smith, J.C. (1988), 'Whether Photographs Indecent – Age of Child Relevant' *Crim LR,* 120; Rees, T. and Ormerod, D. (2004), 'Indecent Photograph: Possession of Indecent Pseudo-Photograph of Children', *Crim LR*, 1039; Thomas, D. (2003), 'Sentencing: Making Indecent Photographs or Pseudo-Photographs of Children – Sentencing Guidelines', *Crim LR*, 127; and Vencatachellum, G. and Ormerod, D. (2002), 'Indecent of Children', *Crim LR*, 659.
63. See too Crown Prosecution Service, 'CPS Decision on Article by Robert Kilroy-Silk', at http://www.cps.gov.uk/news/pressreleases/archive/2004/131_04.html.
64. For further official guidance in this context, see 'Public Order Act 1986 Racial Hatred ss 17–29', at http://www.crimereduction.gov.uk/toolkits/rh020506.htm.
65. Home Office, Consultation Paper on the Regulation of R18 Videos (2000), 8.
66. EUROPA, 'Regulatory Framework: The Future Framework: AVMSD', at http://ec.europa.eu/avpolicy/reg/avms/index_en.htm.
67. Council of Europe, 'Convention on Cybercrime', at http://conventions.coe.int/Treaty/en/Summaries/Html/185.htm.
68. Council of Europe, 'Additional Protocol to the Convention on Cybercrime', at http://conventions.coe.int/Treaty/en/Summaries/Html/189.htm.
69. Department of Trade and Industry (DTI), DTI Consultation Document on the Electronic Commerce Directive: The Liability of Hyperlinkers, Location Tool Services and Content Aggregators (2005), paragraph 3.1.
70. Department for Constitutional Affairs, *Study Guide: Human Rights Act 1998* (3rd ed., 2006), paragraphs 1.3 and 1.4.

BIBLIOGRAPHY

Abeles, R. and Withey, S. (1980), *Television and Social Behavior: Beyond Violence and Children: A Report of the Committee on Television and Social Behavior*. Hillsdale, New Jersey: Social Science Research Council, Lawrence Erlbaum Associates.

Abelman, R. (1999), 'Preaching to the choir: Profiling TV advisory ratings users', *Journal of Broadcasting and Electronic Media,* 43, p. 529–550.

Abramson, B. D. (2002), 'Country music and cultural industry; mediating structures in transnational media flow', *Media, Culture and Society,* 24(2), p. 255–274.

ACMA. (2007), *Media and Communication in Australian families*. Sydney: ACMA Available at http://www.acma.gov.au/WEB/STANDARD/pc=PC_310893

Adams, D. (2000), 'Can pornography cause rape?', *Journal of Social Philosophy,* 31(1), p. 1–43.

Advertising Standards Authority. (1996), *Weapons Advertising: A Survey of Standards in Advertisements for Weapons*. London.

Advertising Standards Authority. (2002), *The Public's Perception of Advertising in Today's Society: Report on the Findings from a Research Study*. London.

Advertising Standards Authority. (2004–2005), *Television Advertising Complaints Reports*. London.

Advertising Standards Authority. (n.d.), *The Radio Codes*. Retrieved March 1, 2008, from Advertising Standards Authority Web site: http://www.asa.org.uk/asa/codes/radio_code/

Aisbett, K. (2000), *20 Years of C – Children's Television and Program Regulation 1979–1999*. Sydney: Australian Broadcasting Authority, Australian Children's Television Foundation, Australian Film Finance Corporation.

Akdeniz, Y. (2001), 'Internet content regulation: UK government and the control of Internet content', *Computer Law & Security Report,* 17(5), p. 303.

Alao, A. O., Soderberg, M., Pohl, E. L. and Alao, A. L. (2006), 'Cybersuicide: Review of the Role of the Internet on Suicide', *Cyberpsychology & Behavior*, 9(4), p. 489–493.

Alao, A., Yolles, J. C. and Armenta, W. (1999), 'Cybersuicide: The Internet and suicide', *American Journal of Psychiatry,* 156(11).

Alasuutari, P. (1995), *Researching Culture: Qualitative Methods and Cultural Studies*. London: Sage.

Alexander, A., and Hanson, J. (2003), *Taking Sides: Clashing Views on Controversial Issues in Mass Media and Society*. Guilford, Conn.: McGraw-Hill/Dushkin.

Alexander, L. (2005), *A chronicle of tobacco's very active recruitment of gays and lesbians*. Paper presented at the 55th Annual Conference of the International Communication Association, New York.

Allbon, E. and Williams, P. (2002), 'Nasties in the Net: Children and censorship on the web', *New Library World,* 103(1172/1173), p. 30–38.

Allen, A. (2001), 'Pornography and power', *Journal of Social Philosophy,* 32(4), p. 512–531.

Ambler, T. (2004), *Does the UK promotion of food and drink to children contribute to their obesity?* (Centre for marketing working paper No. 04–901). London: London Business School.

Ambler, T. (1996), 'Can alcohol misuse be reduced by banning advertising?' *International Journal of Advertising,* 15, p. 167–174.

American Academy of Pediatrics. (2000), *Joint Statement on the Impact of Entertainment Violence on Children, Congressional Public Health Summit.* Retrieved February 24, 2008, from http://www.aap. org/advocacy/releases/jstmtevc.htm

American Academy of Pediatrics: Committee on Public Education. (2001), 'Children, adolescents and television', *Pediatrics,* 107(2).

American Medical Association. (1996), *Physician Guide to Media Violence.* Chicago, Illinois: American Medical Association.

Curiae, A. (2001), 'Effects of violent video games on aggressive behavior, aggressive cognition, aggressive affect, physiological arousal, and prosocial behavior: a meta-analytic review of the scientific literature', *Psychological Science,* 12(5), p. 353–359.

Anchor Youth Centre. (2007), *The Anchor Watch_Your_Space Survey: Survey of Irish Teenagers Use of Social Networking Websites.* Retrieved March 1, 2008 from http://www.watchyourspace.ie/article.aspx?id=7816

Anderson, C. A. and Bushman, B. J. (2002), 'Psychology: The effects of media violence on society', *Science,* 295(5564), p. 2377–2379.

Anderson, C. A. and Dill, K. E. (2000), 'Video games and aggressive thoughts, feelings, and behavior in the laboratory and in life', *Journal of Personality & Social Psychology,* 78(4), p. 772–790.

Anderson, C. A. and Murphy, C. R. (2003), 'Violent video games and aggressive behavior in young women', *Aggressive Behaviour,* 29, p. 423–429.

Anderson, C. A., Carnagey, N. L., Flanagan, M., Benjamin, A. J., Eubanks, J. and Valentine, J. C. (2004), 'Violent video games: specific effects of violent content on aggressive thoughts and behavior', *Advances in Experimental Social Psychology,* 36, p. 199–249.

Anderson, C., and Dill, K. E. (2000), 'Video games and aggressive thoughts, feelings, and behavior in the laboratory and in life', *Journal of Personality and Social Psychology,* 78, p. 772–790

Anderson, C., et al. (2003), 'The influence of media violence on youth', *Psychological Science in the Public Interest,* 4(3).

Anderson, C.A. (2004), 'An update on the effects of playing violent video games', *Journal of Adolescence,* 27(1), p. 113.

Anderson, C.A. and Bushman, B.J. (2001), 'Effects of violent video games on aggressive behavior, aggressive cognition, aggressive affect, physiological arousal, and prosocial behavior: A meta-analytic review of the scientific literature', *Psychological Science,* 12(5), p. 353–359.

Anderson, C.A., Berkowitz, L., Donnerstein, E., Huesmann, L. R., Johnson, J. D., Linz, D., et al. (2003), 'The influence of media violence on youth', *Psychological Science in the Public Interest,* 4(3), p. 81–110.

Anderson, C.A., Gentile, D.A. and Buckley, K.E. (2007), *Violent Video Game Effects on Children and Adolescents: Theory, Research, and Public Policy.* Oxford University Press.

Anderson, D. R. and Pempek, T. A. (2005), 'Television and Very Young Children', *American Behavioral Scientist,* 48 (5), p. 505–522.

Andsager, J. L., Austin, E.W. and Pinkleton, B.E. (2001), 'Questioning the value of realism: Young adults' processing of messages in alcohol-related public service announcements and advertising', *Journal of Communication,* 51(1), p. 121–142.

Arnaldo, C. A. (2001), *Child Abuse on the Internet: Ending the Silence.* Paris: Berghahn Books and UNESCO Publishing.

Arriaga, P., Esteves, F., Carneiro, P. and Monteiro, M. B. (2006), 'Violent Computer Games and Their Effects on State Hostility and Physiological Arousal', *Aggressive Behavior,* 32(4), p. 358–371.

Ashby, S. L., Arcari, C. M. and Edmonson, M. B. (2006), 'Television Viewing and Risk of Sexual Initiation by Young Adolescents', Archives of *Pediatrics &Adolescent Medicine,* 160 (4), p. 375–380.

Attwood, F. (2004), 'Pornography and objectification: Re-reading "the picture that divided Britain"', *Feminist Media Studies,* 4(1), p. 7–19.

Atwal, K., Millwood Hargrave, A., Sancho, J., Agyeman, L. and Karet, N. (2003), *What children watch: An analysis of children's programming provisions between 1997–2001.* London: BSC/ITC.

Aubrey, J. S. (2007), 'Does Television Exposure Influence College-Aged Women's Sexual Self-Concept?' *Media Psychology,* 10(2), p. 157–181.

Auestad, G. and Roland, E. (2005), 'Mobiltelefon og Mobbing (Mobile phone and Bullying)', *Tidsskrift for Spesialpedagogikk, May 2005.*

Austin, E. W. (1993), 'Exploring the effects of active parental mediation of television content', *Journal of Broadcasting and Electronic Media,* 37(2), p. 147–158.

Austin, E. W., Roberts, D. F. and Nass, C. I. (1990), 'Influences of family communication on children's television-interpretation processes', *Communication Research,* 17(4), p. 545–564.

Austin, M.J. and Reed, M.L.(1999), 'Targeting children online: Internet advertising ethics issues', *Journal of Consumer Marketing,* 16, p. 59.

Australian Broadcasting Authority, & NetAlert Ltd. (2005), *kidsonline@home:Internet use in Australian homes.* Sydney:ABA.

Australian Broadcasting Authority. (1993), *The People We See on TV: Cultural Diversity on Television.* Sydney.

Australian Broadcasting Authority. (1994), *'Cool' or 'Gross': Children's Attitudes to Violence, Kissing and Swearing on Television.* Sydney.

Australian Broadcasting Authority. (2003), *Understanding Community Attitudes to Radio Content.* Sydney.

Australian Government NetAlert. (n.d.). Retrieved March 1, 2008, from http://www.netalert.gov.au/home.html

Ayoob, K.T., Duyff, R.L. and Quagliani, D. (2002), 'Position of the American Dietetic Association: Food and Nutrition Misinformation', *Journal of the American Dietetic Association,* 102(2), p. 260–266.

Ayre, P. (2001), 'Child protection and the media: Lessons from the last three decades', *British Journal of Social Work,* 31(6), p. 887–901.

Baldaro, B., Tuozzi, G., Codispoti, M., Montebarocci, O., Barbagli, F., Trombini, E., et al. (2004), 'Aggressive and non-violent videogames: Short-term psychological and cardiovascular effects on habitual players', *Stress and Health,* 20(4), p. 203.

Ballard, M. E. and Lineberger, R. (1999), 'Video game violence and confederate gender: Effects on reward and punishment given by college males', *Sex Roles,* 41(7–8), p. 541–558.

Ballard, T. (2004), 'Television over the Internet: The boundaries of content regulation', *Computer and Telecommunications Law Review.*

Banks, M.A. (2003), 'Should Internet access be regulated? Yes', in A. Alexander and J.Hanson (eds.), *Taking Sides: Clashing Views on Controversial Issues in Mass Media and Society.* Guilford, Conn.: McGraw-Hill/Dushkin, p. 234–239.

Barak, A. (2005), 'Sexual harassment on the Internet', *Social Science Computer Review,* 23(1), p. 77–92.

Barak, A. and Fisher, W. A. (2003), 'Experience with an Internet-based, theoretically grounded educational resource for the promotion of sexual and reproductive health', *Sexual and Relationship Therapy,* 18(3).

Bardone-Cone, A. M. and Cass, K. M. (2007), 'What Does Viewing a Pro-Anorexia Website Do? An Experimental Examination of Website Exposure and Moderating Effects', *International Journal of Eating Disorders,* 40(6), p. 537–548.

Barker, M. (2004), 'Violence redux', in S. Schneider (ed.), *New Hollywood Violence.* Manchester: Manchester University Press.

Barker, M. (2005), 'Loving and hating Straw Dogs: The meanings of audience responses to a controversial film', Particip@tions, 2(2). Retrieved December 13, 2006, from http://www.participations.org/volume%202/issue%202/2_02_barker.htm

Barker, M. and Petley, J. (2001), *Ill Effects: The Media / Violence Debate,* 2nd ed., New York City, New York: Routledge.

Barker, M., Arthurs, J. and Harindranath, R. (2001), *The Crash Controversy: Censorship Campaigns and Film Reception.* London: Wallflower Press.

Barnes, S. B. (2006), 'A Privacy Paradox: Social Networking in the United States', *First Monday,* 11(9).

Barnett, S. and Seymour, E. (2000), *From Callaghan to Kosovo: Changing Trends in British Television News 1975–1999.* London: University of Westminster.

Barnett, S. and Thomson, K. (1996), 'Portraying sex: The limits of tolerance', in R. Jowell, et al. (ed.), *British social attitudes: the 13th report*: Dartmouth Publishing.

Bartholow, B. D., Bushman, B. J and Sestir, M. A. (2006), 'Chronic Violent Video Game Exposure and Desensitization to Violence: Behavioral and Event-Related Brain Potential Data', *Journal of Experimental Social Psychology*, 42(4), p. 532–539.

Bartholow, B. D. and Anderson, C. A.(2002), 'Effects of violent video games on aggressive behavior: Potential sex differences', *Journal of Experimental Social Psychology,* 38, p. 283–290.

BBC. (2005), *BBC Editorial Guidelines*: BBC. Retrieved 13 Dec, 2005 from http://www.bbc.co.uk/guidelines/editorialguidelines/

BBFC. (2005), *Guideline Research – Public opinion and the BBFC guidelines.* London: BBFC.

Beauregard, E., Lussier, P. and Prolux, J. (2004), 'An exploration of developmental factors related to deviant sexual preferences among adult rapists', *Sexual Abuse: A Journal of Research and Treatment,* 16(2), p. 151–163.

Beebe, T. J., Asche, S. E., Harrison, A. and Quinlan, K. B. (2004), 'Heightened vulnerability and increased risk-taking among adolescent chat room users: Results from a statewide school survey', *Journal of Adolescent Health,* 35(2), p. 116.

Bell, R. A., Berger, C. R., Cassady, D. and Townsend, M. S. (2005), 'Portrayals of Food Practices and Exercise Behavior in Popular American Films', *Journal of Nutrition Education and Behavior*, 37(1), p. 27–32.

Benesse Educational Research Institute (2002), 'In Chugakusei to media no sesshoku', *Monografu chugakusei no sekai*, (Vol.71). Tokyo: Benesse Corporation. Retrieved March 06, 2008, from http://www.childresearch.net/RESOURCE/DATA/MONO/EMS/index.html

Bennett, A. (2002), 'Music, media and urban mythscapes: A study of the 'Canterbury Sound', *Media, Culture and Society,* 24(1), p. 87–104.

Benson, R. (2004), 'Bringing the sociology of media back in', *Political Communication,* 21, p. 275–292.

Bensley. and Van Eenwyk, J.(2001), 'Video games and real-life aggression: Review of the literature', *Journal of Adolescent Health*, 29(4), p. 244.

Berelowitz, M. (2004), '*Children, young people and mobile phones*', Nestlé Social Research Programme.

Berg, F. M., & Rosencrans, K. (eds.). (2000), *Women Afraid to Eat: Breaking Free in Today's Weight-Obsessed World.* Hettinger, ND: Healthy Weight Network.

Berger, A. A. (2002), *Video Games: A popular culture phenomenon.* New Brunswick: Transaction.

Bessiere, K., Kiesler, S., Kraut, R. and Boneva, B. (2005), *Longitudinal Effects of Internet Uses on Depressive Affect: A Social Resources Approach.* Paper presented at the American Sociological Association, Philadelphia, PA.

Biely, E., Cope, K. M. and Kunkel, D. (1999), 'Sexual messages on television: Comparing findings from three studies', *The Journal of Sex Research,* 36(3), p. 230–236.

Bittle, S. (2002), 'Media treatment of hate as an aggravating circumstance for sentencing: The criminal code amendment and the Miloszewski case', *Canadian Ethnic Studies, XXXIV*(1), p. 30–50.

Blazak, R. (2001), 'White boys to terrorist men', *American Behavioral Scientist,* 44(6), p. 982–1000.

Blosser, B. J. and Roberts, D. F. (1985), 'Age-Differences in Children's Perceptions of Message Intent – Responses to TV News, Commercials, Educational Spots, and Public-Service Announcements', *Communication Research,* 12(4), p. 455–484.

Blumler, J. G. (1992), *The Future of Children's Television in Britain: An Enquiry for the Broadcasting Standards Council (No. 7).* London: Broadcasting Standards Council.

BMRB Qualitative and Social Research Unit. (2000), *Boundaries of Taste on Radio Report*. London: Broadcasting Standards Commission.

Bocij, P. (2003), 'Victims of cyberstalking: An exploratory study of harassment perpetrated via the Internet', *First Monday*, 8(10). Retrieved Dec 13, 2005, from http://www.firstmonday.org/issues/issue8_10/bocij/index.html

Bocij, P. and McFarlane, L. (2003a), 'Cyberstalking: A matter for community safety but the numbers do not add up', *Journal of Community Safety,* 2(2), p. 26–34.

Bocij, P. and McFarlane, L. (2003b), 'Online harassment: Towards a definition of cyberstalking', *Prison Service Journal,* 139, p. 31–38.

Bocij, P. and McFarlane, L. (2003c), 'Seven fallacies about cyberstalking', *Prison Service Journal,* 149, p. 37–42.

Bocij, P. and McFarlane, L. (2002),' Online harassment: Towards a definition of cyberstalking', *Prison Service Journal,* 139, p. 31–38.

Bodenhausen, G. V. and Garst, J. (1997), 'Advertising's Effects on Men's Gender Role Attitudes', *Sex Roles: A Journal of Research,* 36(9–10), p. 551–522.

Bogaert, A. F. (2001), 'Personality, individual differences, and preferences for the sexual media', *Archives of Sexual Behavior,* 30(1), p. 29–53.

Bolton, R. N. (1983), 'Modeling the impact of television food advertising on children's diets' in J. H. Leigh & J. C. R. Martin (eds.), *Current Issues and Research in Advertising.* Ann Arbor, MI: Division of research, Graduate School of Business administration, University of Michigan, p. 173–199.

Boone, G., Secci, J. and Gallant, L. (2007), 'Emerging Trends in Online Advertising', *Doxa Communication,* 5, p. 241–253.

Boots, K. and Midford, R. (2001), 'Mass media marketing and advocacy to reduce alcohol-related harm. In T. J. Peters & N. Heather (eds.), *International Handbook of Alcohol Dependence and Problems* (p. 805–822). New York: John Wiley & Sons Ltd.

Borden, R. J. (1975). Witnesses aggression: Influence of an observer's sex and values on aggressive responding', *Journal of Personality and Social Psychology,* 31, p. 567–573.

Borzekowski, D. L. G. and Robinson, T. N. (2007), 'Conversations, Control, and Couch-Time: The assessment and stability of parental mediation styles and children's TV and video viewing', *Journal of Children and Media,* 1(2), p. 162–176.

Borzekowski, D.L.G., Robinson, T.N. and Killen, J.D. (2000), 'Does the camera add 10 pounds? Media use, perceived importance of appearance, and weight concerns among teenage girls', *Journal of Adolescent Health,* 26(1), p. 36–41.

Boush, D. M. (2001), 'Mediating advertising effects' in J. Bryant & J. A. Bryant (eds.), *Television and the American Family.* 2nd ed., Mahway, New Jersey: Lawrence Erlbaum Associates, p. 397–412.

Boyd, D. (2006), 'Identity Production in a Networked Culture: Why Youth Heart MySpace', in American Association for the Advancement of Science, Retrieved March 05, 2008, from http://www.danah.org/papers/AAAS2006.html

Boyd, D. and Heer, J. (2006), 'Profiles as Conversation: Networked Identity and Performance on Friendster', in International Conference on System Sciences, Kauai, Hawaii, January 4–7, 2006, IEEE Computer Society

Boyd, D. (2004), 'Friendster and Publicly Articulated Social Networks', *Conference on Human Factors and Computing Systems (CHI 2004).* Vienna: ACM, April 24–29, 2004.

Boyle, K. (2000), 'The pornography debates – Beyond cause and effect', *Women's Studies International Forum,* 23(2), p. 187–195(189).

Boyle, R. and Hibberd, M. (2005), *Review of Research on the Impact of Violent Computer Games on Young People.* Department for Culture, Media and Sport. Retrieved March 05, 2008, from http://www.culture.gov.uk/NR/rdonlyres/3093C6FE-5932-41D5-B901-2BAF02810AC9/0/research_vcg.pdf

Boyson, A. and Smith, S. (2005), *The relationship between a predisposition to think about killing and media violence exposure: Exploring a new measurement model*. Paper presented at the 55th Annual Conference of the International Communication Association, New York.

Bragg, S. and Buckingham, D. (2002), *Young People and Sexual Content on Television*. London: Broadcasting Standards Commission.

Brin, D. (1998). *The Transparent Society: Will Technology Force Us to Choose Between Privacy and Freedom?* Reading, Mass: Addison-Wesley.

British Board of Film Classification, Independent Television Commission, & Broadcasting Standards Commission. (2001), *Wrestling: How do Audiences perceive TV and Video Wrestling?* London.

British Broadcasting Corporation, Broadcasting Standards Commission, & Independent Television Commission. (2002), *Briefing Update: Depiction of Violence on Terrestrial Television*. London.

Broadcasting Standards Authority (2008), *Children's Media Use, Exposure, And Response Research* Auckland: BSA Available at http://www.bsa.govt.nz/publications-pages/seenandheard.php

Broadcasting Standards Commission. (1998), *Codes of Guidance*.

Broadcasting Standards Commission. (2000), *Briefing Update No. 6: Matters of Offence*. London.

Broadcasting Standards Commission. (2001), *Briefing Update No. 8: Concerning Regulation*. London.

Broadcasting Standards Commission. (2003), *Briefing Update No.12: Ethnicity and Disability on Television 1997–2002*. London.

Broadcasting Standards Commission. (2003), *Briefing Update No.11: Depiction of Sexual Activity and Nudity on Television*. London.

Bronkhorst, S. and Eissens, R. (2004a), 'Anti-Semitism on the Internet: An overview: International Network Against Cyber Hate (INACH)', Retrieved December 13, 2005, from http://www.inach.net/

Bronkhorst, S. and Eissens, R. (2004b), *Hate on the Net: Virtual nursery for In Real Life crime*. International Network Against Cyber Hate (INACH). Retrieved December 13, 2005, from http://www.inach.net/

Brown, J. D. (2005), *Sexual media, sexual teens: Results of the teen media study*. Paper presented at the 55th Annual Conference of the International Communication Association, New York.

Brown, J. D., et al. (2006), 'Sexy Media Matter: Exposure to Sexual Content in Music, Movies, Television, and Magazines Predicts Black and White Adolescents' Sexual Behavior', *Pediatrics*, 117 (4), p. 1018–1027

Brown, J.D., Halpern, C. T. and L'Engle, K. L. (2005), 'Mass media as a sexual super peer for early maturing girl', *Journal of Adolescent Health*, 36(5), p. 420–427.

Brown, M. (1996), 'The portrayal of violence in the media: Impacts and implications for policy', *Australian Institute of Criminology*, 55(June).

Browne, B. A. (1998), 'Gender stereotypes in advertising on children's television in the 1990s: A cross-national analysis', *Journal of Advertising*, 27(1), p. 83–96.

Browne, K. D. and Hamilton-Giachritsis, C. (2005), 'The influence of violent media on children and adolescents: A public-health approach', *Lancet*, 365 (9460), p. 702–710.

Browne, K.D.and Pennell, A. (2000), 'The influence of Film and Video on Young People and Violence' in G. Boswell (ed.), *Violent children and adolescents: asking the question why*. London: Whurr, p. 151–168.

Brucks, M., Armstrong, G. M. and Goldberg, M. E. (1988), 'Children's use of cognitive defenses against television advertising – A cognitive response approach', *Journal of Consumer Research*, 14(4), p. 471–482.

Bryant, J. And Zillman, D. (2002), *Media Effects, Advances in Theory and Research*. Mahwah, New Jersey: Lawrence Erlbaum Associates.

Bryman, A. (1992), 'Quantitative and qualitative research: further reflection on their integration', in J. Brannen (ed.), *Mixing methods: qualitative and quantitative research*. Aldershot: Avebury, p. 57–80.

Buchanan, A. M., Gentile, D. A., Nelson, D. A., Walsh, D. A., & Hensel, H. (2002), *What goes in must come out: Children's media violence consumption at home and aggressive behaviors at school*: Paper presented at the International Society for the Study of Behavioural Development Conference, Ottawa, Ontario, Canada.

Buckingham, D. (1989), 'Television literacy: A critique', *Radical Philosophy,* 51, p. 12–25.

Buckingham, D. (1996), *Moving Images: Understanding Children's Emotional Responses to Television.* Manchester: Manchester University Press.

Buckingham, D. (2002), 'The Electronic Generation? Children and New Media' in L. Lievrouw and S. Livingstone (eds.), *The Handbook of New Media.* London: Sage.

Buckingham, D. (2005), *The media literacy of children and young people: A review of the research literature.* London: Ofcom.

Buckingham, D. and Bragg, S. (2003), *Young People, Media and Personal Relationships.* London: Advertising Standards Authority, British Board of Film Classification, British Broadcasting Corporation, Broadcasting Standards Commission, Independent Television Commission.

Buckingham, D. and Bragg, S. (2004), *Young People, Sex and the Media: The facts of life?* Basingstoke: Palgrave Macmillan.

Buckingham, D. et al. (2004), *Assessing the media literacy of children and young people: A literature review.* London: Ofcom.

Buijzen, M. and Valkenburg, P.M. (2003), The effects of television advertising on materialism, parent- child conflict, and unhappiness: A review of research. *Journal of Applied Developmental Psychology,* 24(4), p. 437–456.

Buijzen, M. and Valkenburg, M. (2003), 'The unintended effects of television advertising: A parent-child survey', *Communication Research,* 30(5), p. 483–503.

Buijzen, M., Molen, J. van den Wohl. and Sondij, P. (2007), 'Parental mediation of children's emotional responses to a violent news event', *Communication Research,* 34(2), p. 212–230.

Burn, A. and Willett, R. (2004), *'What exactly is a paedophile?' Children talking about Internet risk (Draft).* London: Institute of Education.

Burns, R.G. and Orrick, L. (2002), 'Assessing newspaper coverage of corporate violence: The dance hall fire in Qoteborg, Sweden', *Critical Criminology,* 11(2), p. 137–150.

Bushman, B. J. and Huesmann, L. R (2006), 'Short-Term and Long-Term Effects of Violent Media on Aggression in Children and Adults', *Archives of Pediatrics & Adolescent Medicine*, 160(4), p. 348–352.

Bushman, B. J. and Cantor, J. (2003), 'Media ratings for violence and sex: Implications for policymakers and parents', *American Psychologist,* 58(2), p. 130–141.

Bushman, B., J. and Anderson, C. A. (2002), 'Violent video games and hostile expectations: A test of the general aggression model', *Personality and Social Psychology Bulletin,* 28, p. 1679–1686.

Busselle, R.W. (2003), 'Television exposure, parents' precautionary warnings, and young adults' perceptions of crime', *Communication Research,* 30(5), p. 530–556.

Bybee, C., Robinson, D. and Turow, J. (1982), 'Determinants of parental guidance of children's television viewing for a special subgroup: Mass media scholars', *Journal of Broadcasting,* 26, p. 697–710.

Byron Review (2008), *Safer Children in a Digital World.* London: DCFS/DCMS. Retrieved April, 25, 2008, from http://www.dfes.gov.uk/byronreview/pdfs/Final%20Report%20Bookmarked.pdf

Calfee, J. E., and Scheraga, C. (1994), 'The influence of advertising on alcohol consumption: a literature review and an econometric analysis of four European nations', *International Journal of Advertising,* 13, p. 287–310.

Calhoun, C. (2002), *Dictionary of the Social Sciences.* Oxford Reference Online: Oxford University Press.

Calouste Gulbenkian Foundation. (1995), *Report of the Commission on Children and Violence convened by the Gulbenkian Foundation: Children and Violence.*

Calvert, S. (1999), *Children's Journeys Through the Information Age.* Boston: McGraw-Hill College.

Canadian Association of Broadcasters. (2005), *The Presence, Portrayal and Participation of Persons with Disabilities on Television Programming.*

Canadian Paediatric Society. (2003), 'Position statement: (PP 2003–01): Impact of media use on children and youth', *Journal of Paediatrics and Child Health,* 8(5).

Cantor, J. (2000), 'Media violence', *Journal of Adolescent Health, 27S*(2), p. 30–34.

Cantor, J. (2002), 'Fright reactions to mass media' in J. Bryant & D. Zillman (eds.), *Media Effects: Advances in Theory and Research.,* 2nd ed, Mahwah, NJ: Erlbaum, p. 287–306.

Carlsson, U. and Von Feilitzen, C. (1998), *Children and media violence.* Goteborg: Goteborg University.

Carnagey, N. L. and Anderson, C. A. (2004), 'Violent video game exposure and aggression: A literature review', *Minerva Psichiatrica,* 45(1), p. 1.

Carnagey, N. L. and Anderson, C.A. (2005), 'The effects of reward and punishment in violent video games on aggressive affect, cognition, and behavior', *Psychological Science*, 16(11), p. 882–889.

Carpenter, C. and Edison, A. (2005), *Taking it all off again: The portrayal of women in advertising over the past forty years.* Paper presented at the 55th Annual Conference of the International Communication Association, New York.

Carr, J. (2004), *Children's safety online: A digital manifesto*. London: Children's Charities' Coalition for Internet Safety.

Carrere. (2001), 'Tough guys: The portrayal of hypermasculinity and aggression in televised police dramas', *Journal of Broadcasting and Electronic Media*, 45(4), p. 615–634.

Carrigan, M. And Szmigin, I. (1999), 'In pursuit of youth: What's wrong with the older market?', *Marketing Intelligence and Planning,* 17(5), p. 230.

Carroll, T. E. and Donovan, R. A. (2002), 'Alcohol marketing on the Internet: New challenges for harm reduction', *Drug and Alcohol Review,* 21(1), p. 83 – 91.

Cassels, A., Hughes, M. A., Cole, C., Mintzes, B., Lexchin, J. and McCormack, J. P. (2003). 'Drugs in the news: An analysis of Canadian newspaper coverage of new prescription drugs', *Canadian Medical Association Journal,* 168(9), p. 1133–1137.

Celious, A.K. (2003), 'Blaxploitation blues: How Black women identify with and are empowered by female performers of hip hop music', *Dissertation Abstracts International. Section A,* 63(7–A), p. 2706.

CEOP. (2007), 'Strategic overview 2006–7: Making every child matter…everywhere', London: Child Exploitation and Online Protection Centre.

Chambers, S., Karet, N., Samson, N., and Sancho-Aldridge, J. (1998), *Cartoon Crazy? Children's Perceptions of 'Action' Cartoons.* London: Independent Television Commission.

Chang, N. (2000), 'Reasoning with children about violent television shows and related toys', *Early Childhood Education Journal,* 28(2), p. 85–89.

Charlton, T., Panting, C. and Hannan, A. (2002), 'Mobile telephone ownership and usage among 10- and 11-year-olds: Participation and exclusion', *Emotional Behavioural Difficulties,* 7(3), p. 152–163.

Chatterjee, B. B. (2005), 'Pixels, pimps and prostitutes: Human rights and the cyber-sex trade' in M. Klang & A. Murray (eds.), *Human Rights in the Digital Age*. London: Glasshouse Press, p. 11–26.

Children Now. (2005), *Interactive Advertising and Children: Issues and Implications*: Children Now.

Cho, C. H. and Cheon, H. J. (2005), 'Children's Exposure to Negative Internet Content: Effects of Family Context', *Journal of Broadcasting & Electronic Media,* 49(4), p. 488–509.

Coleman, A. M. (2001), *Dictionary of Psychology*. Oxford Reference Online: Oxford University Press.

Collins, R.L., Elliott, M.N., Berry, S.H., Kanouse, D.E., Kunkel, D., Hunter, S.B. and Miu, A. (2004), 'Watching Sex on Television Predicts Adolescent Initiation of Sexual Behavior', *Pediatrics* 114(3), p. e280–e289

Colmar Brunton. (2004), *Findings of a Complainants' Survey*. Wellington, New Zealand: Broadcasting Standards Authority.

Coltrane, S. and Messineo, M. (2000), 'The perpetuation of subtle prejudice: Race and gender imagery in 1990s television advertising', *Sex Roles,* 42(5/6), p. 363–389.

Colwell, J. and Payne, J. (2000), 'Negative correlates of computer game play in adolescents', *British Journal of Psychology,* 91(3), p. 295.

Comstock, G. A. and Scharrer, E. (2007), '*Media and the American Child*', Academic Press, Amsterdam; Boston.

Cooper, A., Delmonico, D., Griffin-Shelley, E. and Merthyr. (2004), 'Online sexual activity: An examination of potentially problematic behaviors', *Sexual Addiction and Compulsivity,* 11, p. 129.

Corrigan, W. (2004), 'Target-specific stigma change: A strategy for impacting mental illness stigma', *Psychiatric Rehabilitation Journal,* 28(2), p. 113–121.

Cottone, E. and Byrd-Bredbenner, C. (2007), 'Knowledge and Psychosocial Effects of the Film Super Size Me on Young Adults', *Journal of the American Dietetic Association,* 107(7), p. 1197–1203

Cottrell, L., Branstetter, S., Cottrell, S., Rishel, C. and Stanton, B. F. (2007), 'Comparing Adolescent and Parent Perceptions of Current and Future Disapproved Internet Use', *Journal of Children and Media,* 1(3), p. 210–226.

Cox Communications. (2007, March), *Teen Internet Safety Survey, Wave II.* Retrieved March 1, 2008, from http://www.cox.com/TakeCharge/includes/docs/survey_results_2007.ppt

Coyne, S. M. and Archer, J. (2005), 'The Relationship between Indirect and Physical Aggression on Television and in Real Life', *Social Development,* 14(2), p. 324–338.

Cragg, A. (2000), *R18 pornography. Are 'experts' in a position to say that children are harmed if they view R18 videos?* London: BBFC/Cragg Ross Dawson.

Cragg, A., Taylor, C. and Toombs, B. (2007), '*Video Games: Research to Improve the Understanding of What Players Enjoy About Video Games, and to Explain Their Preferences for Particular Games*', Retrieved March 1, 2008, from *BBFC* http://www.bbfc.co.uk/

Crano, W. D. (2000), 'The Multitrait-Multimethod Matrix as Synopsis and Recapitulation of Campbell's Views on the Proper Conduct of Social Inquiry' in L. Bickman (ed.), *Research design: Donald Campbell's legacy.* London: Sage, p. 37–62.

Crick, N.R. (1996), 'The role of overt aggression, relational aggression, and prosocial behavior in the prediction of children's future social adjustment', *Child Development,* 67, p. 2317–2327.

Crosier, K. and Erdogan, B. Z. (2001), 'Advertising complainants: Who and where are they?', *Journal of Marketing Communications,* 7(2), p. 109–120.

Cumberbatch, G. (2002), *Where do you draw the line? Attitudes and reactions of video renters to sexual violence in film.* Birmingham: The Communications Research Group.

Cumberbatch, G. (2004), *Video violence: Villain or victim?* London: Video Standards Council. Retrieved December 13, 2005, from http://www.videostandards.org.uk/video_violence.htm.

Cumberbatch, G. and Gauntlett, S. (2005), *Smoking, Alcohol and Drugs on Television.* London: Office of Communications.

Cumberbatch, G. and Howitt, D. (1989), *A Measure of Uncertainty: The Effects of the Mass Media.* London: John Libbey.

Cumberbatch, G. and Negrine, R. (1992), *The Images of Disability on Television*: Routledge.

Cumberbatch, G., Gauntlett, S. and Littlejohns, V. (2003), *A Content Analysis of Sexual Activity and Nudity on British Terrestrial Television 2002,* BBC, BSC, ITC.

Cupitt, M. (2000), *Community Views about Content on Free-to-Air Television.* Sydney: Australian Broadcasting Authority. Retrieved December 13, 2005, from http://www.aba.gov.au/newspubs/radio_TV/documents_research/community_views_free_to_air_99.pdf.

Dahlquist, J. P. and Vigilant, L. G. (2004), 'Way Better than Real: Manga Sex to Tentacle Hentai', in D. D. Waskul (ed.), *Net.seXXX: Readings on Sex, Pornography, and the Internet.* New York: P. Lang, p. 90–103.

Davie, R., Panting, C. and Charlton, T. (2004), 'Mobile phone ownership and usage among pre-adolescents', *Telematics and Informatics,* 21, p. 359–373.

Davies, H., Buckingham, D. and Kelley, P. (2000), 'In the Worst Possible Taste: Children, Television and Cultural Value', *European Journal of Cultural Studies,* 3(1), p. 5–25.

Davies, M. M. (1997), *Fake, Fact, and Fantasy: Children's Interpretations of Television Reality.* Mahwah, New Jersey: Lawrence Erlbaum Associates.

Davies, M. M. and Corbett, B. (1997), *The Provision of Children's Television in Britain: 1992–1996.* London: Broadcasting Standards Commission.

Davies, M. and Mosdell, N. (2001), *Consenting Children? The use of children in non-fiction television programmes*. London: BSC.

Davis, J. P. (2002), *The Experience of 'Bad' Behavior in Online Social Spaces: A Survey of Online Users*: Microsoft Research. Retrieved December 13, 2005, from http://research.microsoft.com/scg/papers/Bad%20 Behavior%20Survey.pdf

Davison, W. P. (1983), 'The third-person effect in communication', *Public Opinion Quarterly*, 47(1), p. 1–15.

De Lange, A. W. and Neeleman, J. (2004), 'The effect of the September 11 terrorist attacks on suicide and deliberate self-harm: A time trend study', *Suicide and Life Threatening Behavior*, 34(4), p. 439–447.

De Stempel, C. (2005), *Restricted Categories*: AOL.

De Wied, M. D., Hoffman, K. and Roskos-Ewoldsen, D. R. (1997), 'Forewarning of graphic portrayal of violence and the experience of suspenseful drama', *Cognition and Emotion*, 11(4), p. 481–494.

Deboelpaep, E. R. (2006), 'European Parliamentary Technology Assessment, Cyberbullying among Youngsters in Flanders', Retrieved March 4, 2008, from http://www.viwta.be/files/executive% 20overview%20cyberbullying.pdf

Dennis, T., Lowry, D. T., Nio, T. C. J. and Leitner, D. W. (2003), 'Setting the public fear agenda: A longitudinal analysis of network TV crime reporting, public perceptions of crime, and FBI crime statistics', *Journal of Communication*, 53, p. 61–73.

Department for Children, Schools and Families. (n.d.). 'Every Child Matters', Retrieved February 24, 2008, from Every Child Matters Web site http://www.everychildmatters.gov.uk/

Diamond, K. and Kensinger, K. (2002), 'Vignettes from Sesame Street: Preschooler's ideas about children with Down syndrome and physical disability', *Early Education and Development*, 13(4), p. 409–422.

Dibb, S. and Castell, A. (1985), *Easy to swallow, hard to stomach: The results of a survey of food advertising on television*. London: National Food Alliance.

Dickinson, G., Hill, M. and Zwaga, W. (2000), *Monitoring Community Attitudes in Changing Mediascapes*. Palmerston North, New Zealand: Broadcasting Standards Authority.

Diefenbach, D. L. and West, M. D. (2007), 'Television and Attitudes toward Mental Health Issues: Cultivation Analysis and the Third-Person Effect', *Journal of Community Psychology*, 35 (2), p. 181–195.

Dillon, P. (1998), 'Proactive or sensationalist? The media and harm reduction', *The International Journal of Drug Policy*, 9(3), p. 175–179.

Dixon, T. L. (2006), 'Psychological Reactions to Crime News Portrayals of Black Criminals: Understanding the Moderating Roles of Prior News Viewing and Stereotype Endorsement', *Communication Monographs*, 73(2), p. 162–187.

Dixon, T. L. and Maddox, K. B. (2005), 'Skin Tone, Crime News, and Social Reality Judgments: Priming the Stereotype of the Dark and Dangerous Black Criminal', *Journal of Applied Social Psychology*, 35(8), p. 1555–1570.

Dixon, T. L., Azocar, C. L. and Casas, M. (2003), 'The portrayal of race and crime on television network news', *Journal of Broadcasting and Electronic Media*, 47(4), p. 498–523.

Doering, N. (2001), 'Feminist views of cybersex: Victimization, liberation, and empowerment', *CyberPsychology & Behavior*, 3(5), p. 863.

Dohnt, H. and Tiggemann, M. (2006), 'The Contribution of Peer and Media Influences to the Development of Body Satisfaction and Self-Esteem in Young Girls: A Prospective Study', *Developmental Psychology*, 42(5), p. 929–936.

Dorr, A. (1986), *Television and Children: A Special Medium for a Special Audience*. Beverley Hills, CA: Sage.

Downs, E. and Smith, S. (2005), *Keeping Abreast of Hypersexuality: A Video Game Character Content Analysis*. Paper presented at the 55th International Communication Association, New York.

Drotner, K. (1992), 'Modernity and media panics' in M. Skovmand & K. C. Schroeder (eds.), *Media Cultures: Reappraising Transnational Media*. London: Routledge, p. 42–62.

Duimel, M and de Haan, J. (2006), *Nieuwe Links in het gezin: de digitale leefwereld van tieners en de rol van hun ouders (New links in the family: the digital world of teenagers and the role of their parents)*, Den Haag: SCP.

DuRant, R. H., Rome, E. S., Rich, M., Allred, E., Emans, S. J. and Woods, E. R. (1997), 'Tobacco and alcohol use behaviors portrayed in music videos: A content analysis', *American Journal of Public Health,* 87(7), p. 1131–1135.

Durham, M. G. (2005), *Myths of race and beauty in teen magazines: A semiological analysis.* Paper presented at the 55th Annual Conference of the International Communication Association, New York.

Durkin, K. (1995), *Computer Games: Their Effects on Young People*. Sydney: Office of Film and Literature Classification.

Durkin, K. (2006), 'Game Playing and Adolescents' Development' in P. Vorderer and J. Bryant, (eds.) *Playing Video Games: Motives, Responses, and Consequences*, Lawrence Erlbaum Associates

Durkin, K. and Barber, B. (2002), 'Not so doomed: Computer game play and positive adolescent development', *Journal of Applied Developmental Psychology,* 23(4), p. 373.

Dutton, W. H. and Helsper, E. J. (2007), 'The Internet in Britain', Oxford Internet Institute: University of Oxford, Oxford (UK).

Dworkin, A. (1997)', Sex, lies and videotape', *New Republic,* 217(13), p. 4–4.

Dwyer, C. (2007), 'Digital Relationships in the 'MySpace' Generation: Results from a Qualitative Study' in 40th Annual Hawaii International Conference on System Sciences (HICSS'07), Hawaii, http://doi.ieeecomputersociety.org/10.1109/HICSS.2007.176

Eastin, M. S., Greenberg, B. S. and Hofschire, L. (2006), 'Parenting the Internet', *Journal of Communication,* 56(3), p. 486–504.

Eastin, M. S., Yang, M.-S. and Nathansan, A. I. (2006), 'Children of the net: An empirical exploration into the evaluation of internet content', *Journal of Broadcasting & Electronic Media,* 50(2), p. 211–230.

Economist (2005, 8/4). Chasing the dream – Video gaming. *Economist, 376.*

Edwards, C., Oakes, W. and Bull, D. (2007), 'Out of the Smokescreen II: Will an Advertisement Targeting the Tobacco Industry Affect Young People's Perception of Smoking in Movies and Their Intention to Smoke?' *Tobacco Control,* 16(3), p. 177–181

Edwards, S. (2001), 'The Video Appeals Committee and the standard of legal pornography', *Criminal Law Review,* p. 305–311.

Egenfeldt-Nielson S. and Heide Smith, J. (2004), '*Playing with Fire: How do computer games influence the player?*', Nordicom: Gothenburg University.

Elchardus, M. and Siongers, J. (2003), 'Cultural practice and educational achievement: The role of the parents' media preferences and taste culture', *Netherlands Journal of Social Sciences,* 39(3), p. 151–171.

Ellis, J. (1992), *Visible Fictions* (Revised ed.), London: Routledge.

Ellison, N., Steinfield, C. and Lampe, C. (2007), 'The Benefits of Facebook: Friends, Social Capital and College Students' Use of Online Social Network Sites', *Journal of Computer-Mediated Communication,* 12(4). Retrieved March 1, 2008, from http://www.blackwell-synergy.com/loi/jcmc

Elvin, J. (2004), 'R V British Broadcasting Corporation ex parte ProLife Alliance: The Right to Free Speech, Standards of Taste and Decency, and the "truth" about Abortions', *Web Journal of Current Legal Issues.*

Emmers-Sommer, T. M., Pauley, P., Hanzal, A. and Triplett, L. (2006), 'Love, Suspense, Sex, and Violence: Men's and Women's Film Predilections, Exposure to Sexually Violent Media, and Their Relationship to Rape Myth Acceptance', *Sex Roles,* 55(5–6), p. 311–320.

Eneman, M. (2005), 'The new face of child pornography', in M. Klang. and A. Murray (eds.), *Human Rights in the Digital Age*. London: Glasshouse Press, p. 27–40.

Entertainment Software Association. (2005), *Essential Facts About the Computer and Video Game Industry*: Entertainment Software Association. Retrieved December 13, 2005, from http://www.theesa.com/files/2005EssentialFacts.pdf.

Esler, B. W. (2005), 'Filtering, blocking and rating: Chaperones or censorship?' in M. Klang & A. Murray (eds.), *Human Rights in the Digital Age* (). London: Glasshouse Press, p. 99–110.

Eurobarometer. (2004), *Illegal and Harmful Content on the Internet*. Brussels: European Commission. Retrieved December 13, 2005, from http://europa.eu.int/information_society/programmes/iap/docs/pdf/reports/eurobarometer_survey.pdf

European Commission (2007), *Safer Internet and Online Technologies for Children: Summary of the results of the online public consultation* p. 1–29. Retrieved March 2, 2008, from http://ec.europa.eu/information_society/activities/sip/docs/public_consultation_prog/summary_report.pdf

European Commission. (2007), *Summary of the results of the public consultation 'Child safety and mobile phone services'*, http://ec.europa.eu/information_society/activities/sip/public_consultation_

European Commission. (1997), *Green Paper on the Protection of Minors and Human Dignity in Audiovisual and Information Services*. Brussels: EU.

European Commission. (2007), *Public Consultation. Safer Internet and online technologies for children*. Retrieved March 1, 2008, from http://ec.europa.eu/information_society/activities/sip/docs/public_consultation_prog/pc_2007_info_en.pdf

European Commission. (2007, May), *Safer Internet for Children: Qualitative Study in 29 European Countries*. Retrieved March 1, 2008 from http://ec.europa.eu/information_society/activities/sip/docs/eurobarometer/qualitative_study_2007/summary_report_en.pdf

European Commission. 'Audiovisual and Media Policies', (n.d.). *Media Literacy*. Retrieved March 1, 2008, from http://ec.europa.eu/comm/avpolicy/media_literacy/index_en.htm

European Network and Information Security Agency. (2007, October), *Security Issues and Recommendations for Online Social Networks*. Retrieved March 1, 2008, from http://www.enisa.europa.eu/doc/pdf/deliverables/enisa_pp_social_networks.pdf

Eyal, K. and Kunkel, D. (2005, 30 May 2005), *The Effects of Sex on Television Drama Shows on Emerging Adults' Sexual Attitudes and Moral Judgments*. Paper presented at the International Communication Association 2005 Conference, New York City, New York.

Eyal, K. and Rubin, A. M. (2003), 'Viewer aggression and homophily, identification, and parasocial relationships with television characters', *Journal of Broadcasting and Electronic Media, 47*(1), p. 77–98.

Eyal, K., Kunkel, D., Biely, E. N. and Finnerty, K. L. (2007), 'Sexual Socialization Messages on Television Programs Most Popular among Teens', *Journal of Broadcasting & Electronic Media, 51*(2), p. 316–336

Farrar, K. M. (2006), 'Sexual Intercourse on Television: Do Safe Sex Messages Matter?', *Journal of Broadcasting & Electronic Media, 50*(4), p. 635–650.

Federal Communications Commission. (2007), *Violent television programming and its impact on children*. Retrieved February, 24, 2008 from http://hraunfoss.fcc.gov/edocs_public/attachmatch/FCC-07-50A1.pdf

Federal Communications Commission., Obscenity/Indecency/ Profanity Home Page. (n.d.). *Regulation of Obscenity, Indecency and Profanity*. Retrieved March 3, 2008, from www.fcc.gov/eb/oip

Federal Trade Commission. (2000), *Marketing Violent Entertainment to Children: A Review of Self-Regulation and Industry Practices in the Motion Picture, Music Recording & Electronic Game Industries*: Federal Trade Commission. Retrieved December 13, 2005, from http://www.ftc.gov/opa/2000/09/youthviol.htm

Federal Trade Commission. (2004), *Marketing Violent Entertainment to Children: A Fourth Follow-up Review of Industry Practices in the Motion Picture, Music Recording & Electronic Game Industries*: Federal Trade Commission. Retrieved December 13, 2005, from http://www.ftc.gov/os/2004/07/040708kidsviolencerpt.pdf

Federman, J. (1998), *National Television Violence Study Volume 3*. Santa Barbara, CA: Center for Communication and Social Policy.

Feilitzen, C. V. and Carlsson, U. (eds.). (2000), *Children in the New Media Landscape: Games, Pornography, Perceptions* (Vol. Yearbook 2000). Goteborg, Sweden: The UNESCO International Clearinghouse on Children and Violence on the Screen at Nordicom.

Ferguson, C. J. (2007), 'Evidence for Publication Bias in Video Game Violence Effects Literature: A Meta-Analytic Review', *Aggression and Violent Behavior, 12*(4), p. 470–482.

Ferguson, T., et al. (2005), 'Variation in the Application of the 'Promiscuous Female' Stereotype and the Nature of the Application Domain: Influences on Sexual Harassment Judgments after Exposure to the Jerry Springer Show', *Sex Roles*, 52(7–8), p. 477–487.

Fielder, A., Gardner, W., Nairn, A. and Pitt, J. (2007), *Fair Game?: Assessing commercial activity on children's favourite websites and online environments*. London: NCC

Finkelhor, D. and Hashima, Y. (2001), 'The Victimisation of Children and Youth' in J. White (ed.), *Handbook of Youth*: Kluwer Academic/Plenum Publishers.

Finkelhor, D., Mitchell, K. J. and Wolak, J. (2000), *Online Victimization: A report on the nation's youth*: Crimes against Children Research Centre.

Finkelstein, S. (2000), *Smartfilter – I've Got a Little List*. Retrieved November 18, 2005, from http://sethf.com/anticensorware/smartfilter/gotalist.php.

Firmstone, J. (2002), *Discerning Eyes: Viewers on Violence*. Bedfordshire, UK: University of Luton Press.

Fisch, S. M. and Truglio, R. T. (2001), *'G' is for Growing: Thirty Years of Research on Children and Sesame Street*. Mahwah, NJ: Erlbaum.

Fisher, W. A. and Barak, A. (2001), 'Internet pornography: A social psychological perspective on Internet sexuality', *The Journal of Sex Research*, 38(4), p. 312–323.

Fleming, M., Greentree, S., Cocotti-Muller, D., Elias, K. and Morrison, S. (2006), 'Safety in Cyberspace: Adolescents' Safety and Exposure Online', *Youth & Society*, 38(2), p. 135–154.

Flick, U. (1998). *An Introduction to Qualitative Research*. London: Sage.

Flood, M. (2007), 'Exposure to Pornography among Youth in Australia' *Journal of Sociology*, 43(1), p. 45–60.

Flood, M. and Hamilton, C. (2003a), *Regulating Youth Access to Pornography*: The Australia Institute.

Flood, M. and Hamilton, C. (2003b), *Youth and Pornography in Australia: Evidence on the extent of exposure and likely effects*: The Australia Institute.

Forsyth, R., Harland, R. and Edwards, T. (2001), 'Computer game delusions', *Journal of the Royal Society of Medicine*, 94(4), p. 184.

Fouts, G. and Vaughan, K. (2002), 'Locus of control, television viewing, and eating disorder symptomatology in young females', *Journal of Adolescence*, 25(3), p. 307–311.

Fowler, F. J. (2001), *Survey Research Methods*. Thousand Oaks, CA: SAGE.

Fowler, R. (1991), *Language in the News: Discourse and Ideology in the British Press*. New York: Routledge.

Fowles, J. (2003), 'Is television harmful for children? No' in A. Alexander & J. Hanson (eds.), *Taking Sides: Clashing Views on Controversial Issues in Mass Media and Society*. Guilford, Conn.: McGraw-Hill/Dushkin, p. 47–53.

Freedman, J. (2002), *Media Violence and Its Effect on Aggression: Assessing the Scientific Evidence*. Toronto: University of Toronto Press.

Freeman-Longo, R. E. (2000), 'Children, teens and sex on the Internet', *Sex Addiction and Compulsivity*, 7, p. 75–90.

Fried, C. B. (1999), 'Who's afraid of rap: Differential reactions to music lyrics', *Journal of Applied Social Psychology*, 29(4), p. 705–721.

Frith, K. (2005), *How advertisements in global women's magazines in China use stereotypes*. Paper presented at the 55th Annual Conference of the International Communication Association, New York.

Funk, J. B. (2005), 'Children's Exposure to Violent Video Games and Desensitization to Violence', *Child and Adolescent Psychiatric Clinics of North America*, 14(3), p. 387.

Funk, J. B., Baldacci, H. B., Pasold, T. and Baumgardner, J. (2004), 'Violence exposure in real-life, video games, television, movies, and the Internet: Is there desensitization?', *Journal of Adolescence*, 27(1), p. 23.

Funk, J. B., Jenks, J., Bechtoldt, H. and Buchman, D. D. (2002). An evidence-based approach to examining the impact of playing violent video and computer games. *SIMILE*, 2(4).

Furnham, A. and Mak, T. (1999), 'Sex-role stereotyping in television commercials: A review and comparison of fourteen studies done on five continents over 25 years', *Sex Roles: A Journal of Research,* 41(5–6), p. 413–437.

Fusanosuke, N. (2004), 'Japanese manga: Its expression and popularity', *ABD 2003,* 34(13).

Gale, J., et al. (2006), 'Smoking in Film in New Zealand: Measuring Risk Exposure', *Bmc Public Health,* p. 6.

Gardstrom, S. C. (1999), 'Music exposure and criminal behavior: Perceptions of juvenile offenders', *Journal of Music Therapy,* 36(3), p. 207–221.

Gaskell, G. and Bauer, M. W. (2003), *Qualitative Researching With Text, Image and Sound: A Practical Handbook for Social Research.* London: SAGE.

Gatfield, L. and Millwood Hargrave, A. (2003), *Dramatic Licence – Fact or Fiction?* London: Broadcasting Standards Commission.

Gauntlett, D. (1998), 'Ten things wrong with the 'effects model',in O. Linne, R. Dickinson & R. Harindranath (eds.), *Approaches to Audiences: A Reader.* London: Arnold.

Gee, J. P. (2003), *What Video Games Have to Teach Us About Learning and Literacy.* New York: Palgrave Macmillan.

Gentile, D. A. and Anderson, C. A. (2006), 'Violent video games: Effects on youth and public policy implications', in N. E. Dowd, D. G. Singer, and R. F. Wilson (eds.), *Handbook of children, culture, and violence.* Sage Publications, p. 225–246.

Gentile, D. A. (1998), *Parents Rate the TV Ratings.* Minneapolis, Minnesota: National Institute on Media and the Family.

Gentile, D. A. and Anderson, C. A. (2003), 'Violent video games: the newest media violence hazard' in Gentile, D.A. *Media violence and children.* Praeger, p. 131–151.

Gentile, D. A. and Stone, W. (2005), 'Violent video games effects on children and adolescents: A review of the literature', *Minerva Pediatrica, 2005,* p. 337–358.

Gentile, D. A., Lynch, P. J., Linder, J. R. and Walsh, D. A.(2004), 'The effects of violent video game habits on adolescent hostility, aggressive behaviors, and school performance', *Journal of Adolescence,* 27(1), p. 5.

Gerbner, G. (2001), 'Drugs in television, movies, and music videos' in Y. R. Kamalipour, and K. R. Rampal (eds.), *Media, Sex, Violence, and Drugs in the Global Village.* Lanham: Rowman and Littlefield Publishers, p. 69–75.

Gerbner, G., Gross, L., Morgan, M., and Signorielli, N. (1986), 'Living with television: The dynamics of the cultivation process' in J. Bryant and D. Zillman (eds.), *Perspectives on Media Effects.* Hillsdale, N.J.: Erlbaum.

Get Safe Online. (November 12, 2007), *Press release #8: Social networkers and wireless networks users provide 'rich pickings' for criminals.* Retrieved March 1, 2008, from http://www.getsafeonline.org/nqcontent.cfm?a_id=1469

Gibson, O. (2005, October 7), 'Young blog their way to a publishing revolution', *The Guardian.* Retrieved May 15, 2008, from http://www.guardian.co.uk/technology/2005/oct/07/media.pressandpublishing

Gilat, I. and Shahar, G. (2007), 'Emotional First Aid for a Suicide Crisis: Comparison between Telephonic Hotline and Internet', *Psychiatry-Interpersonal and Biological Processes,* 70(1), p. 12–18.

Gilbert, J. (1988), *A Cycle of Outrage: America's Reaction to the Juvenile Delinquent in the 1950's.* New York: Oxford University Press.

Gillespie, M. (1995), *Television, Ethnicity and Cultural Change.* London: Routledge.

Gillespie, M. (2002), *After September 11: TV News and Transnational Audiences*: London: BSC.

Gilliam, F. D., Valentino, N. A. and Beckmann, M. N. (2002), 'Where You Live and What You Watch: The Impact of Racial Proximity and Local Television News on Attitudes about Race and Crime', *Political Research Quarterly,* 55(4), p. 755–780.

Gilliam, F. D. and Iyengar, S. (2000), 'Prime Suspects: The influence of Local Television News on the Viewing Public', *American Journal of Political Science,* 44(3), p. 560–573.

Givens, G. H., Smith, D. D. and Tweedie, R. L. (1997), 'Bayesian data-augmented meta-analysis that accounts for publication bias issues exemplified in the passive smoking debate' *Statistical Science*, 12, p. 221–250.

Goddard, C. and Saunders, B. J. (2000), 'The gender neglect and textual abuse of children in the print media', *Child-Abuse-Review.Jan-Feb*, 9(1), pp 37–48.

Goldberg, D., Prosser, T. and Verhulst, S. G. (1998), *Regulating the Changing Media: A Comparative Study*. Oxford, UK, New York City, New York: Clarendon Press, Oxford University Press.

Goldberg, D. (2004), *An Exploratory Study About The Impacts That Cybersex (The Use Of The Internet For Sexual Purposes) Is Having On Families And The Practices Of Marriage And Family Therapists*. MSc. Virginia Polytechnic Institute and State University, Falls Church.

Gould, M., Jamieson, K.H., and Romer, D. (2003), 'Media contagion and suicide among the young', *American Behavioral Scientist*, 46(9), p. 1269–1284.

Government of South Australia. (n.d.) *Cyber bullying, e-crime and the protection of children*. Retrieved March 1, 2008, from http://www.decs.sa.gov.au/docs/documents/1/CyberBullyingECrimeProtec.pdf

Grabe, M. E., Zhou, S., Lang, A. and Bolls, D. (2000), 'Packaging Television News: The Effects of Tabloid on Information Processing and Evaluative Responses', *Journal of Broadcasting and Electronic Media*, 44(1), p. 1–18.

Graber, D. (1994), 'The infotainment quotient in routine television news: a director's perspective', *Discourse and Society*, 5(4), p. 483–508.

Graham, L. and Metaxas, T. (2003), 'Of course it's true: I saw it on the Internet': Critical thinking in the Internet era? *Communications of the ACM*, 46(5), p. 70–75.

Green, N. (2001), 'Who's Watching Whom? Surveillance, Regulation and Accountability in Mobile Relations' in R. Harper, B. Brown and N. Green (eds.), *Wireless world: social and interactional aspects of the mobile age*. London, New York: Springer.

Greenfield, M. (ed.), (2004), 'Developing and Children, Developing Media Research from Television to the Internet from the Children's Digital Media Center', *Journal of Applied Developmental Psychology*, 25(6), p. 627–769.

Greenwald, A. G. (1975),' Consequences of prejudice against the null hypothesis', *Psychological Bulletin*, 82(1), p. 1–20.

Griffiths, M. (2007), 'Videogame Addiction: Fact or Fiction?' in Willoughby, T. and Wood, E. (eds.), *Children's Learning in a Digital World*. Blackwell Publishing, Oxford, p. 85–103.

Griffiths, M. D. (2003), 'Internet Gambling: Issues, Concerns, and Recommendations', *CyberPsychology & Behavior*, 6(6), p. 577.

Griffiths, M. D. and Parke, J. (2002), 'The social impact of Internet gambling', *Social Science Computer Review*, 20(3), p. 312–320.

Griffiths, M. D., Davies, M. N. O. and Chappell, D. (2004), 'Online computer gaming: A comparison of adolescent and adult gamers', *Journal of Adolescence*, 27(1), p. 87.

Grimes, T. and Bergen, L. (2001), 'The notion of convergence as an epistemological base for evaluating the effect of violent TV programming on psychologically normal children', *Mass Communication and Society*, 4(2), p. 183–198.

Grimes, T., Bergen, L., Nichols, K., Vernberg, E. and Fonagy, P. (2004), 'Is psychopathology the key to understanding why some children become aggressive when they are exposed to violent television programming?' *Human Communication Research*, 30(2), p. 153–181.

Grimes, T., Vernberg, E. and Cathers, T. (1997), 'Emotionally disturbed children's reactions to violent media segments', *Journal of Health Communication*, 2(3), p. 157–168.

Gros, X. (1997), 'Understanding the Japanese society through mangas', *SDSK newsletter*, 30.

Grupo para el Estudio de Tendecnias Sociales. (2006), Coordinador: José Félix Tezanos. Dpto. Sociología III. Universidad Nacional de Educatcion a Distancia.

Grüsser, S.M., Thalemann, R., and Griffiths, M.D. (2007) Excessive computer game playing: Evidence for addiction and aggression? *Cyberpsychology & Behavior,* 10(2), p. 290–292.

Guldberg, H. (2003), *Challenging the precautionary principle*, Retrieved December 13, 2005, from http://www.countryguardian.net/The%20Precautionary%20Principle.htm

Gunter, B. (2002), *Media Sex:What Are The Issues?* Mahwah, NJ: Lawrence Erlbaum Associates.

Gunter, B. and McAleer, J. (1997), *Children and Television,* 2nd ed., London: Routledge.

Gunter, B., Charlton, T., Coles, D. and Panting, C. (2000), 'The impact of television on children's antisocial behavior in a novice television community', *Child Study Journal,* 30, p. 265–290.

Gunter, B., Oates, C. and Blades, M. (2005), *Advertising to Children on TV: Content, Impact, and Regulation.* Mahwah, New Jersey: Lawrence Erlbaum Associates.

Guy, K., Mohan, D. and Taylor, J. (2003), 'Do Schizophrenic Patients with a History of Violence express a preference for Screen Violence?', *International Journal of Forensic Mental Health,* 2(2), p. 165–171.

Haddon, L. (2007), '*Concerns about children and mobile phone communications: A review of academic research*', DWRC.

Hagell, A. and Newburn, T. (1994), *Young Offenders and the Media: Viewing Habits and Preferences.* London: Policy Studies Institute.

Häggström-Nordin, E., Hanson, U. and Tydén, T. (2005), 'Associations between pornography consumption and sexual practices among adolescents in Sweden', *International Journal of STD and AIDS,* 16(2), p. 102–107.

Haggstrom-Nordin, E., Sandberg, J., Hanson, U. and Tyden, T. (2006), ''It's Everywhere'! Young Swedish People's Thoughts and Reflections About Pornography', *Scandinavian Journal of Caring Sciences*, 20(4), p. 386–393.

Hald, G., and Malamuth, N. (2007), 'Self-Perceived Effects of Pornography Consumption', *Archives of Sexual Behavior*. DOI 10.1007/s 10508-007-9212-1

Halford, J. C. G., Gillespie, J., Brown, V., Pontin, E. E. and Dovey, T. M. (2004), 'Effect of television advertisements for foods on food consumption in children', *Appetite,* 42, p. 221–225.

Hamilton, J.T. (1998), *Television Violence and Public Policy*. Ann Arbor, Michigan: University of Michigan Press.

Hanley, P. (1998a), *Film Versus Drama: Relative Acceptability of the Two Genres on Television*. London: Independent Television Commission.

Hanley, P. (1998b), *Likely to Complain?* London: Independent Television Commission.

Hanley, P. (2002), *Striking a Balance: The Control of Children's Media Consumption*: ITC.

Hanley, P., Hayward, W., Sims, L. and Jones, J. (2000), *Copycat Kids? The influence of Television Advertising on Children and Teenagers*. London: Independent Television Commission, research conducted in conjunction with The Qualitative Consultancy.

Hargittai, E. (2007), 'Whose Space? Differences among Users and Non-Users of Social Network Sites', *Journal of Computer-Mediated Communication*, 13(1). Retrieved May 10, 2008, from http://www.blackwell-synergy.com/toc/jcmc/

Hargreaves, I. and Thomas, J. (2002), *New news, old news*, Retrieved December 13, 2005, from http://www.ofcom.org.uk/static/archive/bsc/pdfs/research/news.pdf

Hargreaves, I., Lewis, J. and Speers, T. (2003), *Towards a better map: Science, the public and the media*: ESRC.

Harrison, K. (2005, 29 May 2005), *Thinking Outside the Bun? Racial Differences in Food Advertisements Viewed by Children*. Paper presented at the International Communication Association 2005 Conference, New York City, New York.

Harrison, K. and Cantor, J. (1997), 'The relationship between media consumption and eating disorders', *Journal of Communication,* 47(1), p. 40–67.

Haste, H. (2005), *Joined up texting: The role of the mobile phone in young people's lives*: Nestle Social Research Programme.

Hastings, G., Stead, M., McDermott, L., Forsyth, A., MacKintosh, A., Raynor, M., Godfrey, C., Caraher, M. and Angus, K. (2003) *Review of the Research on the Effects of Food Promotion to Children*, Centre for Social Marketing, Glasgow, Scotland.

Healton, C. G., et al. (2006), 'Televised Movie Trailers – Undermining Restrictions on Advertising Tobacco to Youth', *Archives of Pediatrics & Adolescent Medicine*, 160(9), p. 885–888

Hearold, S. (1986), 'A synthesis of 1043 effects of television on social behavior' in G. Comstock (ed.), *Public Communications and Behavior,* Vol. 1, New York: Academic Press, p. 65–133.

Horst, H. A. and Miller, D. (2005), 'From Kinship to Link-up: Cell Phones and Social Networking in Jamaica', *Current Anthropology*, 46(5), p. 755–778.

Heim, J., et al. (2007), 'Children's Usage of Media Technologies and Psychosocial Factors', *New Media & Society*, 9(3), p. 425–454.

Heins, M. (2001), *Not In Front of the Children: 'Indecency,' Censorship and the Innocence of Youth*. New York: Hill and Wang.

Helsper, E. (2005), *R18 material: its potential impact on people under 18: An Overview of the Available Literature*. London: Ofcom.

Henderson, L. (2007), *Social Issues in Television Fiction*, Edinburgh University Press.

Hendy, D. J. (2000), *Radio in the Global Age*. Cambridge: Polity.

Henley, N. M., Miller, M. D., Beazley, J. A., Nguyen, D. N., Kaminsky, D. and Sanders, R. (2002), 'Frequency and specificity of referents to violence in news reports of anti-gay attacks', *Discourse and Society,* 13(1), p. 75–104.

Hill, A. (1997), *Shocking Entertainment: Viewer Response to Violent Movies*. Luton: University of Luton Press.

Hill, A. (2000), 'The language of complaint', *Media, Culture and Society,* 22(2), p. 233–236.

Himmelweit, H. T., Oppenheim, A. N. and Vince, P. (1958), *Television and the Child. An Empirical Study of the Effect of Television on the Young*. London: Oxford University Press.

Hinduja, S. and Patchin, W. (2007), 'Personal Information of Adolescents on the Internet: A Quantitative Content Analysis of MySpace', *Journal of Adolescence*, 31(1), p. 125–146.

Hitchings, E. and Moynihan, J. (1998), 'The relationship between television food advertisements recalled and actual foods consumed by children', *Journal of Human Nutrition and Dietetics,* 11(6), p. 511–517.

HMSO. (2003), *The Communications Act 2003*.

Hobbs, R. (1998), 'The seven great debates in the media literacy movement', *Journal of Communication,* 48(1), p. 6–32.

Hochstetler, A. (2001), 'Reporting of executions in U.S. newspapers', *Journal of Crime and Justice,* 24(1), p. 1–13.

Hoffner, C. and Buchanan, M. (2005), 'Young Adults' Wishful Identification with Television Characters: The Role of Perceived Similarity and Character Attributes', *Media Psychology*, 7(4), p. 325–351

Hoffner, C., Plotkin, R., Buchanan, M., Anderson, J. D., Kamigaki, S. K., Hubbs, L. A., et al. (2001), 'The Third-Person Effect in Perceptions of the influence of Television Violence', *Journal of Communication,* 51(2), p. 283–299.

Hogan, M. (2000), 'Media matters for youth health', *Journal of Adolescent Health,* 27(2), p. 73–76.

Holbert, R. L. and Stephenson, M. T. (2003), 'The Importance of Indirect Effects in Media Effects Research: Testing for Mediation in Structural Equation Modeling', *Journal of Broadcasting and Electronic Media,* 47, p. 556–572.

Holmstrom, A. J. (2004), 'The Effects of the Media on Body Image: A Meta-Analysis', *Journal of Broadcasting and Electronic Media,* 48(2), p. 196–218.

Hope, A. (2007), 'Risk taking, boundary performance and intentional school internet "misuse"', *Discourse: Studies in the Cultural Politics of Education,* 28(1), p. 87–99.

Huesmann, L. R., Moise, J., Podolski, C. P. and Eron, L. D. (2003), 'Longitudinal relations between children's exposure to TV violence and their aggressive and violent behavior in young adulthood: 1977–1992', *Developmental Psychology*, 39(2), p. 201–221.

Hughes, D. M. (2004), 'The use of new communications and information technologies for sexual exploitation of women and children' in D. D. Waskul (ed.), *Net.seXXX: Readings on Sex, Pornography, and the Internet*. New York: P. Lang, p. 109–130.

Hylmo, A. (2005), *Organizing girls on film? A critical examination of organizational socialization messages found in motion pictures targeting teenage girls.* Paper presented at the 55th Annual Conference of the International Communication Association, New York.

Independent Television Commission. (1998), *Television on Trial: Citizen's Juries on Taste and Decency*. London.

Information Commissioner's Office. (2007), Available via icopressoffice@trimediahc.com

Innes, M. (2004), 'Crime as a signal, crime as a memory', *Journal for Crime, Conflict and the Media*, 1(2), p. 15–22.

International Telecommunication Union. (2006), *Millennium Development Goals Storyline* International Telecommunication Union, p. 1. Available at http://www.itu.int/ITU-D/ict/mdg/material/MDGStory_ITU.pdf

Internet Crime Forum. (2000), *Chat Wise, Street Wise: Children and Internet Chat Services*. UK: The Internet Crime Forum IRC sub-group. Retrieved December 13, 2005, from http://www.Internetc.rime forum.org.uk/chatwise_streetwise.pdf

IPPR. (2004), *Media literacy and Internet safety: Report for the Association of Chief Police Officers arising from the seminar, 'Internet Safety', 30 January 2004*. London: IPPR.

IPSOS MORI on behalf of JISC (2007), The Student Expectations Study: Preliminary findings. Retrieved March 12, 2008, from http://www.jisc.ac.uk/publications/publications/studentexpectationsbp. aspx

ITC. (1995), *Television: The Public's View 1994*.

ITC. (1996), *Television: The Public's View 1995*.

Itzin, C. (1993), *Pornography: Women, Violence and Civil Liberties*. Oxford, UK: Oxford University Press.

Itzin, C. (2002), 'Pornography and the construction of misogyny', *Journal of Sexual Aggression*, 8(3), p. 4–42.

Itzin, C., Taket, A. and Kelly, L. (2007), *The evidence of harm to adults relating to exposure to extreme pornographic material: a rapid evidence assessment*. Ministry of Justice Research Series 11/07. London: Ministry of Justice.

James, A. (2003), *Cultural Diversity, Equality of Opportunity and Enterprise with Responsibility: Establishing a Regulatory Structure for Success in Electronic Media*: BSC/ITC.

James, S. (2008), 'Social Networking sites: Regulating the "Wild West" of Web 2.0', *Entertainment Law Review*, 19(2), p. 47–50.

Jancovich, M. (2002), 'Cult fictions: Cult movies, subcultural capital and the production of cultural distinctions', *Cultural Studies*, 16(2), p. 306–322.

Jenkins, H. (1992), *Textual Poachers: Television Fans and Participatory Culture*. Cambridge: Cambridge University Press.

Jenkins, P. (1999), *Synthetic Panics: The Symbolic Politics of Designer Drugs*. New York, NY: New York University Press.

Jensen, K. and Jankowski, N. (eds.), (1991), *A Handbook of Qualitative Methodologies for Mass Communications Research*. London: Routledge.

Jerslev, A. (2001), '"Video nights". Young people watching videos together – A youth cultural phenomenon', *Young*, 9, p. 2–17.

John, D. R. (1999), 'Consumer socialization of children: A retrospective look at twenty-five years of research', *Journal of Consumer Research*, 26(3), p. 183–213.

Johnson, J. D., Jackson, L. A. and Gatto, L. (1995), 'Violent attitudes and deferred academic aspirations: Deleterious effects of exposure to rap music', *Basic and Applied Social Psychology*, 16, p. 27–41.

Johnson, J.G., Cohen., Smailes, E.M., Kasen, S. and Brook, J.S. (2002), 'Television viewing and aggressive behavior during adolescence and adulthood', *Science*, 295(5564), p. 2468–2471.

Jordan, A. B., Hersey, J. C., McDivitt, J.A., and Heitzler, C.D. (2006), 'Reducing Children's Television-Viewing Time: A Qualitative Study of Parents and Their Children', Pediatrics, 118(5), November 2006, p. e1303-e1310 (doi:10.1542/peds.2006-0732)

Josephson, W.L. (1995), *Television Violence: A Review of the Effects on Children of Different Ages.* Ontario, Canada: Canadian Heritage; National Clearinghouse on Family Violence.

Kahlor, L. and Morrison, D. (2007), 'Television Viewing and Rape Myth Acceptance among College Women', *Sex Roles*, 56(11–12), p. 729–739.

Kaiser Family Foundation. (2001), *Parents and the V-Chip.* Kaiser Family Foundation.

Kaiser Family Foundation. (2003), *Growing up Wired: Survey on Youth and the Internet in the Silicone Valley*. Menlo Park: Kaiser Family Foundation.

Kaiser Family Foundation. (2005), *Generation M: Media in the Lives of 8–18 Year-olds.* Menlo Park: Kaiser Family Foundation.

Kaiser Foundation. (2000), 'U.S. Adults and Kids on New Media Technology' in C. Von Feilitzen and U. Carlsson (eds.), *Children in the New Media Landscape: Games, Pornography, Perceptions,* Vol. Yearbook 2000, Goteborg, Sweden: The UNESCO International Clearinghouse on Children and Violence on the Screen at Nordicom, p. 349–350.

Katz, E. and Szcesko, T. (eds.) (1982), *Mass Media and Social Change.* Beverly Hills: Sage.

Kaye, B. K. and Sapolsky, B. S. (2004), 'Offensive language in prime-time television: Four years after television age and content ratings', *Journal of Broadcasting & Electronic Media*, 48(4), p. 554–569.

Keen, A. (2007), *The Cult of the Amateur: How Today's Internet is Killing Our Culture.* Nicholas Brealey Publishing.

Kelley. P, Buckingham, D. and Davies, H.(1999), 'Talking dirty: Children, sexual knowledge and television', *Childhood,* 6(2), p. 221–242.

Kerr, M. and Stattin, H. (2000), 'What parents know, how they know it, and several forms of adolescent adjustment: Further support for a reinterpretation of monitoring', *Developmental Psychology*, 36, p. 366–380.

Khoo, N. and Senn, C. (2004), 'Not wanted in the inbox!: Evaluations of unsolicited and harassing e-mail', *Psychology of Women Quarterly,* 28(3), p. 204–214.

Kieran, M., Morrison, D. and Svennevig, M. (1997), *Regulating for Changing Values.* London: Broadcasting Standards Commission.

Kiewitz, C. and Weaver, J. B. (2001), 'Trait aggressiveness, media violence, and perceptions of interpersonal conflict', *Personality and Individual Differences,* 31(6), p. 821–835.

Kirsh, S. J. (2003), 'The effects of violent video games on adolescents – The overlooked influence of development', *Aggression and Violent Behavior,* 8(4), p. 377–389.

Kirsh, S. J. (2006), 'Cartoon Violence and Aggression in Youth', *Aggression and Violent Behavior*, 11(6), p. 547–557

Kirsh, S. J. and Olczak, P.V. (2000), 'Violent comic books and perceptions of ambiguous provocation situations', *Media Psychology,* 2(1), p. 47–62.

Kline, S. (2003a), 'Learners, spectators or gamers in the media saturated household? An investigation of the impact of the Internet on children's audiences' in J. Goldstein, Buckingham & G. Brougere (eds.), *Toys, Games and Media*: Lawrence Erlbaum.

Kline, S. (2003b), 'Media effects: Redux or reductive?', *Particip@tions,* 1(1). Retrieved December 13, 2005 from http://www.participations.org/volume%201/issue%201/1_01_kline_reply.htm

Knight, J. L. and Giuliano, T. A. (2001), 'He's a Laker; she's a "looker": The consequences of gender-stereotypical portrayals of male and female athletes by the print media', *Sex Roles,* 45(3–4), p. 217–229.

Koolstra, C. M. (2007), 'Source Confusion as an Explanation of Cultivation: A Test of the Mechanisms Underlying Confusion of Fiction with Reality on Television', *Perceptual and Motor Skills*, 104(1), p. 102–110.

Korner, H. and Treloar, C. (2004), 'Needle and syringe programmes in the local media: "Needle anger" versus "effective education in the community"', *International Journal of Drug Policy*, 15(1), p. 46–55.

Krahe, B. and Moller, I. (2004), 'Playing violent electronic games, hostile attributional style, and aggression-related norms in German adolescents', *Journal of Adolescence,* 27(1), p. 53.

Krcmar, M. and Hight, A. (2007), 'The Development of Aggressive Mental Models in Young Children', *Media Psychology*, 10(2), p. 250–269

Krcmar, M. and Vieira, E. T. (2005), 'Imitating life, imitating television: The effects of family and television models on children's moral reasoning', *Communication Research,* 32(3), p. 267–294.

Kunkel, D. (1990), *Children and TV Advertising: Research and Policy Linkages.* Paper presented at the International Communication Association, Dublin.

Kunkel, D. (1992), 'Children's television advertising in the multichannel environment', *Journal of Communication,* 42, p. 134–152.

Kunkel, D., Farinola, W. J. M., Donnerstein, E., Biely, E. and Zwarun, L. (2002), 'Deciphering the V-chip: An examination of the television industry's program rating judgments', *Journal of Communication,* 52(1), p. 112–138.

Kunkel, D., Wilcox, B., Cantor, J., Palmer, E., Linn, S. and Dowrick, P.(2004), *Report of the APA task force on advertising and children.* Reviewed January 20, 2006, from http://www.asu.edu/educ/epsl/ CERU/guildelines/ CERU-0402-201-RCC.pdf

Kuntsche, E. N. (2003), 'Hostility among adolescents in Switzerland? Multivariate relations between excessive media use and forms of violence', *Journal of Adolescent Health,* 34(3), p. 230–236.

L'Engle, K. L., Brown, J. D. and Kenneavy, K. (2006), 'The mass media are an important context for adolescents' sexual behavior', *Journal of Adolescent Health* 38(3), p. 186–192.

Lancaster, K. M. and Lancaster, A. R. (2003), 'The economics of tobacco advertising: Spending, demand, and the effects of bans', *International Journal of Advertising,* 22(1), p. 41–65.

Lange, G. (2007), 'The Vulnerable Video Blogger: Promoting Social Change through Intimacy', *The Scholar and Feminist Online*, 5(2). Retrieved March 1, 2008, from http://www.barnard.edu/sfonline/blogs/ lange_01.htm

Larson, M. S. (2003), 'Gender, race, and aggression in television commercials that feature children', *Sex Roles: A Journal of Research,* 48, p. 67–75.

Lavoie, F., Robitaille, L. and Herbert, M. (2000), 'Teen dating relationships and aggression: An exploratory study', *Violence Against Women,* 6(1), p. 6–36.

Lazarsfeld, F. (1941), 'Remarks on administrative and critical communications research', *Studies in Philosophy and Science,* 9, p. 3–16.

Lee, E. and Leets, L. (2002), 'Persuasive storytelling by hate groups online: Examining its effects on adolescents', *American Behavioral Scientist,* 45(6), p. 927–957.

Lee, K. M. and Peng, W. (2006), 'What Do We Know About Social and Psychological Effects of Computer Games?' in P. Vorderer. and J. Bryant, (2006), *Playing Video Games: Motives, Responses, and Consequences*, Lawrence Erlbaum Associates, p. 327–345.

Leets, L. (2001), 'Responses to Internet Hate Sites: Is Speech Too Free in Cyberspace?', *Communication Law & Policy,* 6(2), p. 287–317.

Leiss, W., Kline, S. and Jhally, S. (1990), *Social Communication in Advertising.* New York: Routledge.

Lenhart, A. (2005), *Protecting Teens Online*: PEW Internet & American Life. Retrieved December 13, 2005, from http://www.pewInternet.org/PPF/r/152/report_display.asp

Lenhart, A. and Madden, M. (2007), 'Social Networking Websites and Teens: An Overview', Pew Internet and American Life Project. Retrieved March 3, 2008, from http://www.pewinternet.org/PPF/r/ 198/report_display.asp

Leonard, D. (2003), '"Live in your world, play in ours": Race, video games, and consuming the other', *SIMILE,* 3(4).

Leung, L. (2007), 'Stressful Life Events, Motives for Internet Use, and Social Support among Digital Kids', *CyberPsychology & Behavior*, 10(2), p. 204–214. http://search.ebscohost.com/login.aspx? direct=true&db=buh&AN=25963259&site=ehost-live

Levin, D. E. and Carlsson-Paige, N. (2003), 'Marketing violence: The special toll on young children of color', *Journal of Negro Education,* 72(4), p. 427–437.

Levine, J. (2002), *Harmful to Minors: The Perils of Protecting Children From Sex.* Minneapolis: University of Minnesota Press.

Lewis, M. K. and Hill, A. J. (1998), 'Food advertising on British children's television: A content analysis and experimental study with nine-year olds', *International Journal of Obesity,* 22(3), p. 206–214.

Li, Q. (2005), 'New Bottle but Old Wine: A Research of Cyberbullying in Schools', *Computers in Human Behavior*, 23(4), p. 1777–1791. Retrieved March 1, 2008, from http://www.sciencedirect.com/science/article/B6VDC-4HR72DY-1/2/d7a395d06507a955c66376a918d0e228

Lightstone, S. N. (2004), 'The effect of bioterrorism media messages on anxiety levels', *Dissertation Abstracts International: Section B,* 65(1–B), p. 445.

Ling, R. (2004), *The Mobile Connection: The Cell Phone's Impact on Society.* San Francisco: Elsevier.

Ling, R. and Yttri, B. (2002), 'Hyper-coordination via mobile phones in Norway' in J. E. Katz & M. A. Aakhus (eds.), *Perpetual Contact.* Cambridge: Cambridge University Press, p. 139–169.

Linz, D., Donnerstein, E. and Penrod, S. (1988), 'Effects of long-term exposure to violent and sexually degrading depictions of women', *Journal of Personality and Social Psychology,* 55(5), p. 758–768.

Linz, D., Malamuth, N. M. and Beckett, K. (1992), 'Civil liberties and research on the effects of pornography' in P. Suedfeld & P. E. Tetlock (eds.), *Psychology and Social Policy.* New York: Hemisphere, p. 149–164.

Livingstone, S. (1996), 'On the continuing problems of media effects research' in J. Curran & M. Gurevitch (eds.), *Mass Media and Society,* 2nd ed., London: Edward Arnold, p. 305–324.

Livingstone, S. (1998), *Making Sense of Television: The Psychology of Audience Interpretation,* 2nd ed., London: Routledge.

Livingstone, S. (2002), *Young People and New Media: Childhood and the Changing Media Environment.* London: Sage.

Livingstone, S. (2005), 'Assessing the research base for the policy debate over the effects of food advertising to children', *International Journal of Advertising,* 24(3), p. 273–296.

Livingstone, S. (2007), 'Evaluating the online risks for children in Europe', *Telos,* 73, p. 52–69.

Livingstone, S. (2008), 'Taking risky opportunities in youthful content creation: teenagers' use of social networking sites for intimacy, privacy and self-expression', *New Media & Society,* 10(3), p. 459–477.

Livingstone, S. and Bober, M. (2004), *UK Children Go Online: Surveying the experiences of young people and their parents.* London: London School of Economics and Political Science. Available at http://eprints.lse.ac.uk/395/.

Livingstone, S. and Bober, M. (2005), *UK children go online: Final report of key project findings.* London: LSE Research Online. Available at http://eprints.lse.ac.uk/399/.

Livingstone, S. and Bober, M. (2006), 'Regulating the internet at home: Contrasting the perspectives of children and parents' in D. Buckingham and R. Willett (eds.), *Digital Generations* (93–113). Mahwah, NJ: Erlbaum. Available at http://eprints.lse.ac.uk/1016/

Livingstone, S., Bober, M. and Helsper, E (2005), *Internet literacy among children and young people.* Findings from the *UK Children Go Online* project. Available at http://eprints.lse.ac.uk/397/.

Livingstone, S. and Bovill, M. (1999), *Young People New Media.* London: London School of Economics and Political Science.

Livingstone, S. and Bovill, M. (2001), *Children and their Changing Media Environment: A European Comparative Study.* Lawrence Erlbaum Associates.

Livingstone, S., Bovill, M. and Gaskell, M. (1999), 'European TV kids in a transformed media world: Key findings of the UK study' in P. Lohr and M. Meyer (eds.), *Children, Television and the New Media.* Televizion: University of Luton Press.

Livingstone, S. and Helsper, E. (2004), *Advertising 'unhealthy' foods to children: Understanding Promotion in the Context of Children's Daily Lives. A review of the literature.* London: Ofcom.

Livingstone, S. and Helsper, E. J. (2006,) 'Does advertising literacy mediate the effects of advertising on children? A critical examination of two linked research literatures in relation to obesity and food choice', *Journal of Communication,* 56(3) p. 560–584. Available at http://eprints.lse.ac.uk/1018/

Livingstone, S., and Helsper, E. J. (2008), 'Parental mediation of children's internet use', *Journal of Broadcasting and Electronic Media,* 52(4) p. 581–599. Winter 2008.

Livingstone, S. and Lunt, P. (1994), *Talk on Television: Audience Participation and Public Debate.* London: Routledge.

Livingstone, S., van Couvering, E. J. and Thumim, E. (2005), *Adult media literacy: A review of the literature.* London: Ofcom.

Lobe, B., Livingstone, S. and Haddon, L., et al. (2007), 'Researching Children's Experiences Online across Countries: Issues and Problems in Methodology', *EU Kids Online Deliverable D4.1 Methodological Issues Review for the EC Safer Internet plus programme.* Available at www.eukidsonline.net.

Lord Chancellor's Dept. (2002), *Study Guide: Human Rights Act 1998*, Second Edition. London.

Lunt, P., Miller, L., Körting, J. and Ungemah, J. (2005), *The Psychology of Consumer Detriment: A Conceptual Review.* London: Office of Fair Trading.

MacBeth, T. M. (ed.),(1996), *Tuning in to Young Viewers: Social science perspectives on television.* Thousand Oaks, Cal: Sage.

Machill, M., Hart, T. and Kaltenhauser, B. (2002), 'Structural development of Internet self-regulation: Case study of the Internet Content Rating Association (ICRA)', *Info – The journal of policy, regulation and strategy for telecommunications,* 4(5), p. 39 – 55.

Machill, M., Neuberger, C. and Schindler, F. (2003), 'Transparency on the Net: functions and deficiencies of Internet search engines', *Info – The journal of policy, regulation and strategy for telecommunications,* 5(1), p. 52–74.

Malamuth, N. M. and Impett, E. A. (2000), 'Research on sex in the media: What do we know about effects on children and adolescents?' in D. G. Singer & J. L. Singer (eds.), *Handbook of Children and the Media.* Thousand Oaks, California: Sage Publications, p. 269–288.

Malamuth, N. M., Addison, T. and Koss, M. (2000), 'Pornography and sexual agression: Are there reliable effects and how might we understand them?' in J. Heiman (ed.), *Annual Review of Sex Research.*

Mancheva, G. (2006), *'Child in the Net' national campaign. The National Center for Studies of Public Opinion.* 12 September 2006. Full report unpublished but summary is available at: http://www.bnr.bg/RadioBulgaria/Emission_English/Theme_Lifestyle/Material/childinthenet.htm

Markert, J. (2001), 'Sing a song of drug use-abuse: Four decades of drug lyrics in popular music – from the sixties through the nineties', *Sociological Inquiry,* 71(2), p. 194–220.

Marshall, G. (1998), *'Causal modelling', Entry in a Dictionary of Sociology.* Oxford: Oxford University Press.

Martin, B. A. S. and Collins, B. A. (2002), 'Violence and consumption imagery in music videos', *European Journal of Marketing,* 36(7), p. 855–873.

Martin, M. C. (1997), 'Children's understanding of the intent of advertising: A meta- analysis', *Journal of Public Policy & Marketing,* 16(2), p. 205–216.

Martin, M. C. and Gentry, J. W. (2003), 'Is emphasis on body image in the media harmful to females only? Yes: Stuck in the model trap' in A. Alexander & J.Hanson (eds.), *Taking Sides: Clashing Views on Controversial Issues in Mass Media and Society.* Guilford, Conn.: McGraw-Hill/Dushkin, p. 58–67.

Marwick, A. (2007), 'The People's Republic of Youtube? Interrogating Rhetorics of Internet Democracy', AoIR 8, Vancouver, Canada.

Mastro, D. E. and Robinson, A. L. (2000), 'Cops and crooks: Images of minorities on primetime television', *Journal of Criminal Justice,* 28(5), p. 385–396.

Mathews, T. D. (1994), *Censored.* London: Chatto and Windus.

Mayo, E. (2005), *Shopping Generation.* London: National Consumer Council.

McCool, J. P., Cameron, L. D. and Petrie, K. J. (2005), 'The Influence of Smoking Imagery on the Smoking Intentions of Young People: Testing a Media Interpretation Model', *Journal of Adolescent Health*, 36(6), p. 475–485

McGuigan, J. (1996), *Culture and the Public Sphere*. London: Routledge.

McKenna, K. Y. A. and J. A. Bargh (1998), 'Coming out in the Age of the Internet: Identity 'De-Marginalization' from Virtual Group Participation', *Journal of Personality and Social Psychology*, 75, p. 681–694.

McQuail, D. (1987), *Mass Communication Theory: An Introduction*, 2nd ed., London: Sage.

McQuail, D. (2005), *Mass Communication Theory*. London: Sage.

McQuail, D. and Windahl, S. (1993), *Communication Models for the Study of Mass Communication*, 2nd ed., London: Longman.

Meadows, M., Forde, S., Ewart, J. and Foxwell, K (2007), *Community Medai Matters*. Brisbane: Griffiths University.

Meads, C. and Nouwen, A. (2005), 'Does Emotional Disclosure Have Any Effects? A Systematic Review of the Literature with Meta-Analyses', *International Journal of Technology Assessment in Health Care*, 21(2), p. 153–164.

Media Awareness Network. (2000), *Young Canadians In A Wired World*. Retrieved December 13, 2005, from http://www.media-awareness.ca/english/special_initiatives/surveys/index.cfm

Mediappro: The appropriation of new media by youth (2006), Retrieved March 13, 2008, from http://www.mediappro.org/publications/finalreport.pdf

Mediascope. (2001), *Teens, Sex and the Media: Issues Brief*. Mediacsope Press: Studio City: California.

Merriam-Webster Online, http://www.m-w.com/

Mesch, G. S. and Talmud, I. (2007), 'Similarity and the Quality of Online and Offline Social Relationships among Adolescents in Israel', *Journal of Research on Adolescence*, 17(2), p. 455–466.

Middleton, D., Elliot, I. A., Mandeville-Norden, R. and Beech, A. R. (2006), 'An investigation into the applicability of the Ward and Siegert Pathways Model of child sexual abuse with Internet offenders', *Psychology, Crime & Law,* 12(6), p. 589–603.

Millwood Hargrave, A. (1992), *Sex and Sexuality in Broadcasting*. London: Brad Ltd.

Millwood Hargrave, A. (1993), *Violence in Factual Television: Annual Review 1993*. London: Broadcasting Standards Council, John Libbey Publishing.

Millwood Hargrave, A. (1998), *Bad Language – What are the Limits?* London: Broadcasting Standards Commission.

Millwood Hargrave, A. (1999), *Sex and Sensibility*. London: Broadcasting Standards Commission.

Millwood Hargrave, A. (2000a), *Delete Expletives?* London: Advertising Standards Authority,

Millwood Hargrave, A. (2000b), *Listening 2000*. London: Radio Authority.

Millwood Hargrave, A. (2002), *Multicultural Broadcasting: Concept and Reality*. London: British Broadcasting Corporation, Broadcasting Standards Commission, Independent Television Commission, Radio Authority.

Millwood Hargrave, A. (2003), *How Children Interpret Screen Violence*. London: British Broadcasting Corporation. Available at http://www.ofcom.org.uk/static/archive/bsc/pdfs/research/how%20child.pdf

Millwood Hargrave, A. (2007), *Issues facing broadcast regulation*. London: Broadcasting Standards Authority. Available at http://www.bsa.govt.nz/publications/IssuesBroadcastContent-2.pdf

Millwood Hargrave, A. and Livingstone, S. (2006), *Harm and Offence in Media Content: A Review of the Empirical Literature*. Bristol: Intellect Press.

Millwood Hargrave, A. and Gatfield, L.(2002), *Soap Box or Soft Soap? Audience Attitudes to the British Soap Opera*. London: Broadcasting Standards Commission.

Mishara, B. L. and Weisstub, D. N. (2007), 'Ethical, Legal, and Practical Issues in the Control and Regulation of Suicide Promotion and Assistance over the Internet', *Suicide and Life-Threatening Behavior*, 37(1), p. 58–65.

Mitchell, K. J., Finkelhor, D. and Wolak, J. (2007), 'Online Requests for Sexual Pictures from Youth: Risk Factors and Incident Characteristics', *Journal of Adolescent Health*, 41(2), p. 196–203. Retrieved March 14, 2008 from http://www.sciencedirect.com/science/article/B6T80-4P72D8P-D/2/21eae2e2 f48711a0a798eb21fa94e01c

Mitchell, K. J., Finkelhor, D. and Wolak, J. (2003), 'The exposure of youth to unwanted sexual material on the Internet', *Youth & Society*, 34(3), p. 330–358.

Mobile Data Association. (n.d.), Retrieved March 1, 2008, from http://www.themda.org/ Page_Default.asp

Montgomery, K. (2001), *Children's Online Privacy Protection Act: The First Year*: Center for Media Education.

Moore, E. S. (2004), Children and the changing world of advertising. *Journal of Business Ethics,* 52(2), p. 161–167.

Moore, E. S. (2006), *It's Child's Play: Advergaming and the Online Marketing of Food to Children*. USA: The Kaiser Family Foundation. Retrieved March 07, 2008, from http://www.kff.org/entmedia/entmedia071906pkg.cfm

Moore, R. L. (1999), *Mass Communication Law and Ethics,* 2nd ed., Mahwah, NJ: Lawrence Erlbaum Associates.

Morrison, D. (1992), *Television and the Gulf war.* London: John Libbey.

Morrison, D. (1999), *Defining Violence: The Search for Understanding*. Bedfordshire, UK: University of Luton.

Morrison, D. and Svennevig, M. (2002), *The Public Interest, the Media and Privacy*. London: BBC/BSC/ICSTIS/ITC/IPPR/RA.

MSN (2006) *MSN Cyberbullying report*: MSN. Retrieved March 14, 2008, from http://www.msn.co.uk/ customercare/protect/cyberbullying/default.asp?MSPSA=1

Muggli, M. E., Hurt, R. D. and Becker, L. B. (2004), 'Turning free speech into corporate speech: Philip Morris' efforts to influence U.S. and European journalists regarding the U.S. EPA report on secondhand smoke', *Preventive Medicine,* 39(3), p. 568–580.

Muir, D. (2005, September), '*Violence against Children in Cyberspace: A contribution to the United Nations Study on Violence against Children*', Bangkok, Thailand: ECPAT International.

Murphy, P. (ed). (2003), *Blackstone's Criminal Practice*. Oxford University Press.

Murray, J. P. (1994), 'Impact of Televised Violence', *Hofstra Law Review*, 22(summer), p. 809–825.

Murray, J. P., Liotti, M., Ingmundson, T., Mayberg, H. S., Pu, Y., Zamarripa, F., et al. (2006), 'Children's brain activations while viewing televised violence revealed by fMRI', *Media Psychology,* 8(1), p. 25–37.

Nairn, A., Ormond, J. and Bottomley, P. (2007), *Watching, wanting and well-being: exploring the links*. London: National Consumer Council.

Nathanson, A. I. (1999), 'Identifying and explaining the relationship between parental mediation and children's aggression', *Communication Research,* 26(2), p. 124–143.

Nathanson, A. I. (2001), 'Parent and child perspectives on the presence and meaning of parental television mediation', *Journal of Broadcasting & Electronic Media,* 45(2), p. 201–220.

Nathanson, A. I. (2001), 'Parents versus peers: Exploring the significance of peer mediation of antisocial television', *Communication Research,* 28(3), p. 251–274.

Nathanson, A. I. (2004), 'Factual and evaluative approaches to modifying children's responses to violent television', *Journal of Communication,* 54(2), p. 321–335.

Nathanson, A. I. and Botta, R. A. (2003), 'Shaping the effects of television on adolescents' body image disturbance', *Communication Research,* 30(3), p. 304–331.

Nathanson, A. I. and Cantor, J. (2000), 'Reducing the aggression-promoting effect of violent cartoons by increasing children's fictional involvement with the victim: A study of active mediation', *Journal of Broadcasting and Electronic Media,* 44(4), p. 738–746.

Nathanson, A. I., Wilson, B. J., McGee, J. and Sebastian, M. (2002), 'Counteracting the effects of female stereotypes on television via active mediation', *Journal of Communication,* December.

National Center for Studying the Public Opinion, *First National Representative Study on the issues related with children's safety in internet.* SACP, Program 2003 'Internet and children's rights'. A summary is available at: http://cis-sacp. government.bg/sacp/CIS/content_en/index_en.htm

National Family Planning Institute. (2003), *Hard sell, soft targets?* UK: National Family and Parenting Institute.

NCH. (2005), *stoptextbully.com*. Retrieved June 7, 2005, from http://stoptextbully.com

NCH/Tesco Mobile. (2005), *Putting U in the picture: Mobile bullying survey*. Retrieved December 13, 2005, from http://www.nch.org.uk/information/index.php?i=237

Neilsen NetRatings. (2007), *Parents crack down on Internet safety, but there's still some way to go*. Retrieved March 08, 2008, from http://www.nielsen-netratings.com/pr/pr_071017_AU.pdf

NetSafe. (2005), *The Text Generation: Mobile phones and New Zealand Youth,* 2005. Retrieved June 7, 2005, from http://www.netsafe.org.nz/

Newman, J. (2004), *Videogames*. London: Routledge.

Nie, N., Simpser, A., Stepanikova, I. and Zheng, L. (2004), *Ten Years After The Birth Of The Internet, How Do Americans Use The Internet In Their Daily Lives?* Stanford: Stanford Center For The Quantitative Study Of Society.

Niemz, K., Griffiths, M. and Banyard, P. (2005), 'Prevalence of Pathological Internet Use among University Students and Correlations with Self-Esteem, the General Health Questionnaire (Ghq), and Disinhibition', *Cyberpsychology & Behavior*, 8(6), p. 562–570

Nightingale, V. (2000), *Children's Views about Media Harm: A collaborative project between the University of Western Sydney and the Australian Broadcasting Authority*. Sydney: Australian Broadcasting Authority.

Nightingale, V., Dickenson, D. and Griff, C. (2000), *Children's Views about Media Harm*. Sydney: University of Western Sydney, Australian Broadcasting Authority.

Nikken, P. and Jansz, J. (2006), 'Parental mediation of children's videogame playing: a comparison of the reports by parents and children', *Learning, Media and Technology,* 31(2), p. 181–202.

Nikken, P. and Jansz, J. (2007), 'Playing Restricted Videogames: Relations with game ratings and parental mediation', *Journal of Children and Media,* 1(3), p. 227–243.

Nikken, P., Jansz, J. and Schouwstra, S. (2007), 'Parents' interest in videogame ratings and content descriptors in relation to game mediation', *European Journal of Communication,* 22(3), p. 315–336.

Nobody's Children Foundation. (2006), *Child Abuse and Neglect in Eastern Europe. Research on risky behaviours of Polish children on the Internet*. Retrieved March 1, 2008, from http://www.fdn.pl/nowosci/?lang_id=2.

Noonan, R.J. (2007), 'The Psychology of Sex: A Mirror from the Internet' in Gackenbach, J. (ed.), *Psychology and the Internet : Intrapersonal, Interpersonal, and Transpersonal Implications*, 2nd ed., Elsevier/Academic Press, p. 93–141

Nordicom. (n.d.). *International Clearinghouse for Children, Youth and Media*. Retrieved February, 24, 2008, from http://www.nordicom.gu.se/clearinghouse.php

O'Connell, R. (2003a), *A Typology of Child Cybersexploitation and Online Grooming Practices*. Preston, Lancashire, UK: Cyberspace Research Unit. Retrieved December 13, 2005, from http://www.uclan.ac.uk/host/cru/publications.htm

O'Connell, R. (2003b), *Young People's Use of Chatrooms: Implications for policy strategies and programs of education*: Cyberspace Research Unit. Retrieved December 13, 2005, from http://www.uclan.ac.uk/host/cru/publications.htm

O'Connell, R., Price, R. and Barrow, C. (2004), *Emerging trends amongst Primary School Children's use of the Internet*: Cyberspace Research Unit. Retrieved December 13, 2005, from http://www.uclan.ac.uk/host/cru/publications.htm of *Applied Developmental Psychology,* 22(1), 73–86.

Ofcom. (2006), *Media Literacy Audit: Report on media literacy amongst children*. London: Ofcom. Available at http://www.ofcom.org.uk/advice/media_literacy/medlitpub/medlitpubrss/children/children.pdf

Ofcom. (2006,) *Online protection: A survey of consumer, industry and regulatory mechanisms and systems*. London: Ofcom. Available at http://www.ofcom.org.uk/research/telecoms/reports/onlineprotection/

Ofcom. (2006), *The Communications Market 2006*. London: Ofcom. Available at http://www.ofcom.org.uk/research/cm/cm06/cmr06_print/

Ofcom. (2007), *New News, Future News*. London: Ofcom. Available at http://www.ofcom.org.uk/research/tv/reports/newnews/newnews.pdf

Ofcom. (2007), *The Communications Market 2007*. London: Ofcom. Available at http://www.ofcom.org.uk/research/cm/cmr07/

Ofcom. (2004), *The Communications Market 2004*. London: Ofcom.

Ofcom. (2005), *A safe environment for children. Qualitative and quantitative findings*. London: Ofcom.

Ofcom. (2005), *A Safe Viewing Environment for Children*. London: Ofcom.

Ofcom. (2005), *Annual Report 2004/5*. London: Ofcom.

Ofcom. (2005), *Consultation with Young People on the Proposed Ofcom Broadcasting Code*. London: Ofcom.

Ofcom. (2005), Ofcom Annual Report 2004 – 05 Core Areas of Activity. Retrieved March 3, 2008, from http://www.ofcom.org.uk/about/accoun/reports_plans/annrep0405/core/?a=87101#tv

Ofcom. (2005), *Offensive Language and Sexual Imagery in Broadcasting*. The Fuse Group, London: Ofcom.

Ofcom. (2005), *Religious Programmes and the Ofcom Broadcasting Code*. London: Ofcom,

Ofcom. (2005), *Research into the Effectiveness of PIN Protection Systems in the UK: A Report of the Key Findings of Research Among School Children Aged 11–17, and a Separate Study of Parents*. Youth Research Group, London: Ofcom.

Ofcom. (2005), *The Broadcasting Code*. London: Ofcom.

Ofcom. (2005), *The Communications Market 2005*. London: Ofcom.

Ofcom. (2005), *The representation and portrayal of people with disabilities on analogue terrestrial television*. London: Ofcom

Ofcom. (2005, September 15), *Viewers and Voters: Attitudes to television coverage of the 2005 General Election* [Report]. London: Ofcom. Retrieved February 24, 2008, from http://www.ofcom.org.uk/research/tv/reports/election/election.pdf

Ofcom. (2007), *The future of children's television programming: Research Report*. London: Ofcom. Available at http://www.ofcom.org.uk/consult/condocs/kidstv/

Ofcom. (2008), *Social Networking: A quantitative and qualitative research report into attitudes, behaviours and use*. London: Ofcom. Available at http://www.ofcom.org.uk/advice/media_literacy/medlitpub/medlitpubrss/socialnetworking/

Office of Public Sector Information. (2003), *Communications Act 2003, 2003 CHAPTER 21*. Retrieved February 24, 2008, from Office of Public Sector Information Web site http://www.legislation.hmso.gov.uk/acts/acts2003/20030021.htm

Ogbar, J.O.G. (1999), 'Slouching toward Bork: The culture wars and self-criticism in hip-hop music', *Journal of Black Studies*, 30(2), p. 164–183.

Oliver, C. and Candappa, M. (2003), *Tackling bullying: Listening to the views of children and young people*. London: Department for Education and Skills.

Olson, C. K., et al. (2007), 'Factors Correlated with Violent Video Game Use by Adolescent Boys and Girls', *Journal of Adolescent Health*, 41(1), p. 77–83.

Oppenheim, A. N. (1992), *Questionnaire design, interviewing, and attitude measurement*. London: Printer Publishers.

Orgad, S. (2006), 'Media, Connectivity, Literacies and Ethics: Patients' Experience of Internet Environments: Storytelling, Empowerment and Its Limitations', EDS Innovations.

Orr, D. and Stack-Ferrigno. (2001), 'Childproofing on the World Wide Web: A Survey of Adult Webservers', *Jurimetrics*, 41(4), p. 465–475.

Ostrov, J. M., Gentile, D. A. and Crick, N. R. (2006), 'Media Exposure, Aggression and Prosocial Behavior During Early Childhood: A Longitudinal Study', *Social Development*, 15(4), p. 612–627.

Oswell, D. (1998), 'The place of childhood in Internet content regulation: A case study of policy in the UK', *International Journal of Cultural Studies,* 1(1), p. 131–151.

Palmer, T. and Stacey, L. (2004), *Just One Click: Sexual Abuse of Children and Young People Through the Internet and Mobile Telephone Technology.* Ilford: Barnardo's.

Panee, C. D. and Ballard, M. E. (2002), 'High versus low aggressive priming during video game training: Effects on violent action during game play, hostility, heart rate, and blood pressure', *Journal of Applied Social Psychology,* 32(12), p. 2458–2474.

Pardoen, J. and Pijpers, R. (2006), *Verliefd op Internet (In love on the Web).* Amsterdam: SWP.

Pardun, C. J., L'Engle, K. L. and Brown, J. D. (2005), 'Linking exposure to outcomes: Early adolescents' consumption of sexual content in six media', *Mass Communication and Society,* 8(2), p. 75–91.

Parents Television Council. (n.d.), TV Bloodbath: Violence on Prime Time Broadcast TV. A PTC State of the Television Industry Report. Retrieved March 1, 2008, from http://www.parentstv.org/ptc/publications/reports/stateindustryviolence/main.asp

Park, D. (2002), 'The Kefauver comic book hearings as show trial: Decency, authority and the dominated expert', *Cultural Studies,* 16(2), p. 259–288.

Park, S. H. (2002), 'Film censorship and political legitimation in South Korea, 1987–1992', *Cinema Journal,* 42(1), p. 120–138.

Pearson, G. (1983), *Hooligan: A history of Respectable Fears.* London: Macmillan.

Penfold, C. (2004), 'Converging content: Diverging law', *Information and Communications Technology Law,* 13(3), p. 273–290.

Pennell, A. E. and Browne, K. D. (1999), 'Film violence and young offenders', *Aggression and Violent Behavior,* 4(1), p. 13–28.

Perse, E. M. (2001), *Media Effects and Society.* Mahwah, NJ: Lawrence Erlbaum Associates.

Peter, J. (2004), 'Our long "return to the concept of powerful mass media" – A cross-national comparative investigation of the effects of consonant media coverage', *International Journal of Public Opinion Research,* 16(2), p. 144–168.

Peter, J. and Valkenburg, M. (2006), '"Adolescents" exposure to sexually explicit material on the internet', *Communication Research,* 33, p. 178–204.

Peter, J., Valkenburg, M. and Schouten, A. P. (2006), 'Characteristics and Motives of Adolescents Talking with Strangers on the Internet', *CyberPsychology & Behavior,* 9(5), p. 526–530. Retrieved March 1, 2008, from http://www.liebertonline.com/doi/abs/10.1089/cpb.2006.9.526

Peters, K. M. and Blumberg, F. C. (2002), 'Cartoon violence: Is it as detrimental to preschoolers as we think?', *Early Childhood Education Journal,* 29(3), p. 143–148.

Peterson, D. L. and Pfost, K. S. (1989), 'Influence of rock videos on attitudes of violence against women', *Psychological Reports,* 64, p. 319–322.

Peterson, E. E. (1988), 'The technology of media consumption', *American Behavioral Scientist,* 32(2), p. 156–168.

Peterson, P.E., Jeffrey, D. B., Bridgwater, C. A. and Dawson, B. (1984), 'How pro-nutrition television programming affects children's dietary habits', *Developmental Psychology,* 20(1), p. 5563.

Phau, I. and Prendergast, G. (2001), 'Offensive advertising: A view from Singapore', *Journal of Promotion Management,* 7(1/1), p. 71–90.

Philips. (2005), *World Encyclopedia.* Oxford Reference Online: Oxford University Press.

Phillips, D.A. (1986), 'Natural experiments on the effects of mass media' in Berkowitz, L. (ed.), *Advances in Experimental Social Psychology,* Vol. 19, New York: Academic Press.

Philo, G. (1993), 'Getting the message: Audience research in the Glasgow University Media Group' in Eldridge, J. (ed.), *Getting the Message: News, Truth and Power.* London: Routledge.

Pirkis, J., Francis, C., Blood, R.W., Burgess, P., Morley, B., Stewart, A., et al. (2002), 'Reporting of suicide in the Australian media', *Australian and New Zealand Journal of Psychiatry,* 36(2), p. 190–197.

Pointon, A. and Davies, C. (1997), *Framed: Interrogating Disability in the Media*. London: BFI Publishing.

Potter, J. and Mahood, C. (2005, 27 May 2005), *Justification in violent narratives: An exploration of individual interpretations*. Paper presented at the International Communication Association 2005 Conference, New York.

Potter, J. and Smith, S. (2000), 'The context of graphic portrayals of television violence', *Journal of Broadcasting and Electronic Media*, 44(2), p. 301–323.

Potter, W. J. (2004), *Theory of Media Literacy: A Cognitive Approach*. Thousand Oaks: Sage.

Potter, W.J. (2003), 'Is television harmful for children? Yes' in Alexander, A. and Hanson, J. (eds.), *Taking Sides: Clashing Views on Controversial Issues in Mass Media and Society*. Guilford, Conn.: McGraw-Hill/Dushkin. p. 34–46.

Prasad, V. and Owens, D. (2001), 'Using the Internet as a source of self-help for people who self-harm', *Psychiatric Bulletin*, 25(6), p. 222–225.

Prior, M. (2003), 'Any good news in soft news? The impact of soft news preference on political knowledge in', *Political Communication*, 20, p. 149–171.

QA Research. (2005), *Sounding Out, Find out what 14–17 year olds think about*.

Quayle, E. and Taylor, M. (2001), 'Child seduction and self-representation on the Internet', *CyberPsychology & Behavior*, 4(5).

Quayle, E. and Taylor, M. (2002), 'Child pornography and the Internet: Perpetuating a cycle of abuse', *Deviant Behavior*, 23, p. 331.

Quayle, E. and Taylor, M. (2003), 'Model of problematic Internet use in people with a sexual interest in children', *CyberPsychology & Behavior*, 6(1), p. 93.

Quinn, R. (2005), *Taste and Decency a review of national and international practice*. Dublin: Broadcasting Commission of Ireland.

Rada, J. A. (2000), 'A new piece to the puzzle: Examining effects of television portrayals of African Americans', *Journal of Broadcasting and Electronic Media*, 44(4), p. 704–715.

Ramsay, G. (2003), *The Watershed: Providing a Safe Viewing Zone*. London: British Broadcasting Corporation, Broadcasting Standards Commission, Independent Television Commission.

Reid, D. and Reid, F. (2004), *Insights into the Social and Psychological Effects of SMS Text Messaging*. Retrieved December 13, 2005, from http://www.160characters.org/documents/SocialEffectsOfTextMessaging.pdf

Retrieved March 1, 2008, from http://firstmonday.org/issues/issue11_9/barnes/index.htmls

Richards, F. (1997), *Lady Chatterley's Lover and Censorship in British Publishing*. http://apm.brookes.ac.uk/publishing/culture/1997/culture2.html#LINK9a

Richardson, C.R., Resnick, J., Hansen, D. L., Derry, H.A. and Rideout, V. J. (2002), 'Does pornography-blocking software block access to health information on the Internet?', *Journal of the American Medical Association*, 288, p. 2887–2894.

Richardson, J. W. and Scott, K. A. (2002), 'Rap music and its violent progeny: America's culture of violence in context', *Journal of Negro Education*, 71(3), p. 175–192.

RIS. (2006) *RIS 2006 – Gospodinjs tva (RIS-DCO-2006)*. Report available at: http://www.ris.org/uploadi/editor/1171361207InternetInSlovenskaDrzava2006.pdf

Roberts, D. F. (2000), 'Media and Youth: Access, Exposure, and Privatization', *Journal of Adolescent Health*, 27(2), p. 8–14.

Roberts, D. F. and Storke, T. M. (1997, 4–5 December 1997), *Media Content Labeling Systems: Information Advisories or Judgmental Restrictions?* Paper presented at the Violence, Crime and the Entertainment Media, Sydney, Australia.

Robinson, L. H. and Thoms, K. J. (2001), 'A longitudinal study of college student computer knowledge', *Journal of Computer Information Systems*, 42(1), p. 9–12.

Robinson, T., Popovich, M., Gustafson, R. and Fraser, C. (2003), 'Older adults' perceptions of offensive senior stereotypes in magazine advertisements: Results of a Q method analysis', *Educational Gerontology*, 29(6), p. 503–519.

Roedder, D. L. (1981), 'Age difference in children's responses to television advertising: An information processing approach', *Journal of Consumer Research,* 8, p. 144–153.

Rogala, C. and Tyden, T. (2003), 'Does pornography influence young women's sexual behavior?', *Women's Health Issues,* 13(1), pp, 39–43.

Rohlinger, D. A. (2002), 'Eroticizing men: Cultural influences on advertising and male objectification', *Sex Roles,* 46(3/4), p. 61–74.

Romer, D. and Jamieson. (2001), 'Advertising, smoker imagery, and the diffusion of smoking behavior' in P. Slovic (ed.), *Smoking: Risk, perception, and policy.* Thousand Oaks, Cal.: Sage, p. 127–155.

Romer, D., Jamieson, K. and Aday, S. (2003), 'Television news and the cultivation of fear of crime', *Journal of Communication,* 53, p. 88–104.

Romer, D., Jamieson, E. and Jamieson, K. (2006), 'Are News Reports of Suicide Contagious? A Stringent Test in Six US Cities', *Journal of Communication,* 56(2), p. 253–270.

Rosen, L, D. (2006), 'Adolescents in MySpace: Idenity Formation, Friendship and Sexual Predators.' Unpublished manuscript. California State University, Dominguez Hills.

Rosta, J. (2003), 'Alcohol in Danish and German educational print-media (1990–1998): A compariso', *Addiction Research and Theory,* 11(3), p. 169–176.

Rotfeld, H. J., Jevons, C. and Powell, I. (2004), 'Australian media vehicles' standards for acceptable advertising', *Journal of Advertising,* 33(4), p. 65–73.

Rowbottom, J. (2003), 'Article 10 and Election Broadcasts', *Law Quarterly Review,* 119(Oct).

Rowland, W. R. (1983), *The Politics of TV Violence: Policy Uses of Communication Research.* Beverley Hills: Sage.

Runciman, D. (2004), *The Precautionary Principle: David Runciman writes about Tony Blair and the language of risk.* Retrieved December 13, 2005, from http://www.lrb.co.uk/v26/n07/runc01_.html

SAFT. (2003), *Children's Study: Investigating online behaviour – Executive summary.* Retrieved 13 Dec, 2005 from http://www.saftonline.org

Salter, M. (2003), 'Psychiatry and the media: From pitfalls to possibilities', *Psychiatric Bulletin,* 27(4), p. 123–125.

Sancho, J. (2001), *Beyond Entertainment: Research into the Acceptability of Alternative Beliefs, Psychic and Occult Phenomena on Television.* London: Broadcasting Standards Commission, Independent Television Commission.

Sancho, J. (2003), *Disabling Prejudice: Attitudes Towards Disability and its Portrayal on Television.* London: British Broadcasting Corporation, Broadcasting Standards Commission, Independent Television Commission.

Sancho, J. and Glover, J. (2003), *Conflict Around the Clock: Audience Reactions to Media Coverage of the 2003 Iraq War.* London: Independent Television Commission.

Sancho, J. and Wilson, A. (2001), *Boxed In: Offence from Negative Stereotyping in TV Advertising.* London: Research conducted by The Qualitative Consultancy for the Independent Television Commission.

Sander, I. (1997), 'How violent is TV violence?', *European Journal of Communication,* 12(1), p. 43–98.

Sargent, J. D., et al. (2005), 'Exposure to Movie Smoking: Its Relation to Smoking Initiation among US Adolescents', *Pediatrics,* 116(5), p. 1183–1191

Sargent, J. D., et al. (2006), 'Alcohol Use in Motion Pictures and Its Relation with Early-Onset Teen Drinking', *Journal of Studies on Alcohol,* 67(1), p. 54–65

Sargent, J. D., et al. (2007), 'Exposure to Smoking Depictions in Movies – Its Association with Established Adolescent Smoking', *Archives of Pediatrics & Adolescent Medicine,* 161(9), p. 849–856.

Sargent, J. D., Tanski, S. E. and Gibson, J. (2007), 'Exposure to Movie Smoking among US Adolescents Aged 10 to 14 Years: A Population Estimate', *Pediatrics,* 119(5), E1167–E1176.

Savage, J. (2004), 'Does viewing violent media really cause criminal violence? A methodological review', *Aggression and Violent Behavior,* 10, p. 99–128.

Savin-Williams, R. C. and Ream, G. L. (2003), 'Suicide attempts among sexual-minority male youth', *Journal of Clinical Child and Adolescent Psychology,* 32(4), p. 509.

Saylor, C. F., Cowart, B. L., Lipovsky, J. A., Jackson, C., and Finch, A. J. Jr. (2003), 'Media exposure to September 11: Elementary school students' experiences and posttraumatic symptoms', *Am Behav Sci* 46:1622–1642.

Schlesinger, P., Dobash, R. E., Dobash, R. and Weaver, K. W. (1992), *Women Viewing Violence*. London: BFI Publishing.

Schlesinger, P. and Tumber, H. (1994), *Reporting Crime: The Media Politics of Criminal Justice*. Oxford: Clarendon Press.

Schramm, W., Lyle, J. and Parker, E. B. (1961), *Television in the Lives of Our Children*. Stanford: Stanford University Press.

Schroder, K., Drotner, K., Kline, S. and Murray, C. (2003), *Researching Audiences*. London: Arnold.

Schwandt, T. A. and Halpern, E. S. (1988), *Linking auditing and metaevaluation: enhancing quality.*

Seiter, E. (2005), *The Internet Playground: Children's access, entertainment, and mis-education*. New York: Peter Lang.

Sender, K. (2001), 'Gay readers, consumers, and a dominant gay habitus: 25 years of the Advocate magazine', *Journal of Communication*, 51(1), p. 73–99.

Seto, M. C., Maric, A. and Barbaree, H. E. (2001), 'The role of pornography in the etiology of sexual aggression', *Aggression and Violent Behavior*, 6(1), p. 35–53.

Shapira, N. A., Goldsmith, T. D., Keck Jr., P. E., Khosla, U. M. and McElroy, S. L. (2000), 'Psychiatric features of individuals with problematic Internet use', *Journal of Affective Disorders*, 57, p. 267–272.

Shaw, C. (1999), *Deciding What We Watch: Taste, Decency and Media Ethics in the UK and the USA*: Clarendon Press.

Shearer, J. (1998), *The Campaign for an Ethical Internet in Ethics and Social Impact*: ACM Policy '98.

Shearer, A. (1991), *Survivors and the Media*. London: BSC.

Sheese, B. E. and Graziano, W. G. (2005), 'Deciding to defect – The effects of video game violence on cooperative behavior', *Psychological Science*, 16(5), p. 354–357.

Sherry, J. L. (2001), 'The effects of violent video games on aggression. A meta-analysis', *Human Communication Research*, 27(3), p. 409.

Shim, J. W., Lee, S., and Bryant, P. (2007), 'Who responds to unsolicited sexually explicit materials on the Internet? The role of individual differences', *CyberPsychology and Behavior*, 10(1), p. 71–79.

Signorielli, N. (2003), 'Prime-time violence 1993–2001: Has the picture really changed?', *Journal of Broadcasting and Electronic Media*, 47(1), p. 36–57.

Signorielli, N. and Morgan, M. (eds.), (1990), *Cultivation analysis: New directions in media effects research*. Newbury Park, Calif. London: Sage Publications.

Silverstone, R. (1994), *Television and Everyday Life*. London: Routledge.

Simmons, B.J., Stalsworth, K. and Wentzel, H. (1999), 'Television violence and its effects on young children', *Early Childhood Education Journal*, 26(3), p. 149–153.

Singer, D. G. and Singer, J. L. (eds.), (2001), *Handbook of Children and the Media*. Thousand Oaks: Sage.

Skirrow, G. (1986), 'Hell vision: An analysis of video games', in McCabe, C. (ed.), *High Theory / Low Culture: Analysing Popular Television and Film*. Manchester: Manchester University Press, p. 115–142.

Slater, M. D., Henry, K. L., Anderson, L. L. and Swaim, R. C. (2003), 'Violent media content and aggressiveness in adolescents: A downward spiral model', *Communication Research*, 30(6), p. 713.

Slater, M. D. (2003), 'Alienation, aggression, and sensation seeking as predictors of adolescent use of violent film, computer, and website content', *Journal of Communication*, 53(1), p. 105–121.

Slater, M. D., Henry, K. L., Swaim, R. and Cardador, J. M. (2004), 'Vulnerable teens, vulnerable times: How sensation seeking, alienation, and victimization moderate the violent media content-aggressiveness relation', *Communication Research*, 31(6), p. 642–668.

Slaven, J. and Kisely, S. (2002), 'The Esperance primary prevention of suicide project', *Australian and New Zealand Journal of Psychiatry*, 36(5), p. 617–621.

Slone, M. (2000), 'Responses to media coverage of terrorism', *The Journal of Conflict Resolution*, 44(4), p. 508–522.

Slovic, P. (ed.), *Smoking: Risk, perception, and policy*. Thousand Oaks, Cal: Sage, p. 127–155.

Smith, A. (2007), '*"Teens & Online Stranger Contact?" Pew Internet & American Life Project*'. Available at http://www.pewinternet.org/

Smith, S. L. and Boyson, A. R. (2002), 'Violence in music videos: Examining the prevalence and context of physical aggression', *Journal of Communication*, 52(1), p. 61–83.

Smith, P., Mahdavi, J., Carvalho, M. and Tippett, N (2006), *An investigation into cyberbullying, its forms, awareness and impact, and the relationship between age and gender in cyberbullying: A Report to the Anti-Bullying Alliance*. Retrieved March 1, 2008, from http://www.anti-bullyingalliance.org.uk/downloads/pdf/cyberbullyingreportfinal230106_000.pdf

Sneegas, J. E. and Plank, T. A. (1998), 'Gender differences in pre-adolescent reactance to age-categorized television advisory labels', *Journal of Broadcasting and Electronic Media*, 42(4), p. 423–434.

Soanes, C. and Stevenson, A. (eds.), (2004), *The Concise Oxford English Dictionary*. Oxford University Press, Oxford Reference Online. Oxford University Press.

Southwell, B. G. and Doyle, K. O. (2004), 'The good, the bad, or the ugly? A multilevel perspective on electronic game effects', *American Behavioral Scientist*, 48(4), p. 391.

Sparks, R. (1992), *Television and the Drama of Crime: Moral Tales and the Place of Crime in Public Life*. Buckingham: OUP.

Spitzberg, B. H. and Hoobler, G. (2002), 'Cyberstalking and the technologies of interpersonal terrorism', *New Media Society*, 4(1), p. 71–92.

Sreberny, A. (1999), *Include Me In*. London: Broadcasting Standards Commission, Independent Television Commission.

Stacey, J. (1994), *Star Gazing: Hollywood Cinema and Female Spectatorship*. London: Routledge.

Stacey, J. (1994), 'Hollywood memories', *Screen*, 35(4), p. 317–335.

Staiger, J. (2005), *Media Reception Studies*. New York: New York University Press.

Stern, B. B., Russell C. A. and Russell D. W. (2007), 'Hidden Persuasions in Soap Operas: Damaged Heroines and Negative Consumer Effects', *International Journal of Advertising*, 26(1), p. 9–36.

Stern, S. R. (2005), 'Messages from Teens on the Big Screen: Smoking, Drinking, and Drug Use in Teen-Centered Films', *Journal of Health Communication*, 10(4), p. 331–346

Story, M., Neumark-Sztainer, D. and French, S. (2002), 'Individual and environmental influences on adolescent eating behaviors', *Journal of the American Dietetic Association*, 102(3), p. S40–S51.

Strom, P. and Strom, R. (2004), *Bullied by a Mouse*. Retrieved December 12, 2005, from http://www.childresearch.net/RESOURCE/RESEARCH/2004/MEMBER35.HTM

Stryker, J. E. (2003), 'Articles media and marijuana: A longitudinal analysis of news media effects on adolescents' marijuana use and related outcomes, 1977–1999', *Journal of Health Communication*, 8(4), p. 305–328.

Subrahmanyam, K., Kraut, R. E., Greenfield, M. and Gross, E. F. (2000), 'The impact of home computer use on children's activities and development', *Children and Computer Technology*, 10(2).

Sudak, H. S. and Sudak, D. M (2005), 'The Media and Suicide', *Acad Psychiatry*, 29, p. 495–499.

Sullivan, J. and Beech, A. (2004), 'A comparative study of demographic data relating to intra- and extra-familial child sexual abusers and professional perpetrators', *Journal of Sexual Aggression*, 10(1), p. 39–50.

Sutter, G. (2000), '"Nothing new under the sun": Old fears and new media', *International Journal of Law and Information*, 8(3), p. 338–378.

Svennevig, M. (1998), *Television Across the Years: The British Public's View*. Bedfordshire, UK: Independent Television Commission, University of Luton Press.

Tamborini, R., Chory-Assad, R. M. M., Lachlan, K. A., Westerman, D. and Skalski. (2005, 27 May 2005), *Talking Smack: Verbal Aggression in Professional Wrestling*. Paper presented at the International Communication Association 2005 Conference, New York.

Taveras, E. M., Rifas-Shiman, S. L., Field, A. E., Frazier, A. L., Colditz, G. A. and Gillman, M. W. (2004), 'The influence of wanting to look like media figures on adolescent physical activity', *Journal of Adolescent Health*, 35(1), p. 41–50.

Taylor, M. and Quale, E. (2003), *Child Pornography: An Internet Crime*. Hove: Brunner-Routledge.

Taylor, T. (2006), *Play Between Worlds: Exploring Online Game Culture*. MIT Press: Teenage Magazine Arbitration Panel. (2003), *Annual Report*.

Taylor, M. (ed.), (1988), *Britain and the Cinema During the Second World War*. Basingstoke: Macmillan.

The Commission for the Future of Multi-Ethnic Britain. (2000), *The Future of Multi-Ethnic Britain – the Parekh Report*: Profile Books.

Thiesmeyer, L. (1999), 'Racism on the Web: Its rhetoric and marketing', *Ethics and Information Technology*, 1, p. 117–125.

Thompson, R. and Scott, S. (1992), *Learning about sex: Young women and the construction of social identity*: WRAP.

Thompson, S. (2003), 'Adolescents as consumers of restricted media content: Empowering adults as mediators', *International Journal of Consumer Studies*, 27(3), p. 243–244.

Thompson, S. and Skrypnek, B. (2005), *Adolescents and Restricted Media Study: Selected Preliminary Findings and Their Implications for Film Classification*. Retrieved December 13, 2005, from http://www.oflc.gov.au/resource.html?resource=238&?lename=238.pdf.

Thornburgh, D. and Lin, H. S. (2002), Ch 6 – 'The Research Base on the Impact of Exposure to Sexually Explicit Material: What Theory and Empirical Studies Offer' in D. Thornburgh and H.S. Lin (eds.), *Youth, Pornography and the Internet: Can We Provide Sound Choices in a Safe Environment*: National Academy Press.

Tickner, J., Raffensperger, C. and Myers, N. (1999), *The Precautionary Principle in Action: A Handbook*. Retrieved December 13, 2005, from http://www.biotech-info.net/handbook.pdf

Tiggemann, M. (2005), 'Television and Adolescent Body Image: The Role of Program Content and Viewing Motivation', *Journal of Social and Clinical Psychology*, 24(3), p. 361–381.

Towler, R. (2001), *The Public's View 2001*. London: Independent Television Commission, Broadcasting Standards Commission.

Tsang, M. M., Hobs and Liang, T. P. (2004), 'Consumer attitudes toward mobile advertising: An empirical study', *International Journal of Electronic Commerce*, 8(3), p. 65–78.

Tuchman, G. (1981), 'Myth and the consciousness industry: A new look at the effects of the mass media' in Katz, E and Szcesko, T (eds.), *Mass Media and Social Change*. Beverly Hills: Sage.

Tumber, H. (1982), *Television and the riots*. British Film Institute.

Turow, J. (2001), 'Family boundaries, commercialism, and the Internet: A framework for research', *Journal of Applied Developmental Psychology*, 22(1), p. 73–86.

Tydén, T. and Rogala, C. (2004), 'Sexual behaviour among young men in Sweden and the impact of pornography', *International Journal of STD and AIDS*, 15(9), p. 590–593.

UCLA. (2000), *The UCLA Internet Report: Surveying the Digital Future – Year One*: UCLA Center for Communication Policy Retrieved December 13, 2005, from http://www.digitalcenter.org/.

UCLA. (2001), *The UCLA Internet Report: Surveying the Digital Future – Year Two*: UCLA Center for Communication Policy Retrieved December 13, 2005, from http://www.digitalcenter.org/.

UCLA. (2003), *The UCLA Internet Report: Surveying the Digital Future – Year Three*: UCLA Center for Communication Policy. Retrieved December 13, 2005, from http://www.digitalcenter.org/.

Uhlmann, E. and Swanson, J. (2004), 'Exposure to violent video games increases automatic aggressiveness', *Journal of Adolescence*, 27(1), p. 41.

UKHL 23. (2003), *R v British Broadcasting Corporation ex parte Pro Life Alliance*.

Unsworth, G. and Ward, T. (2001), 'Video games and aggressive behaviour', *Australian Psychologist*, 36(3).

United Kingdom Parliament. (2004), *Hansard Debates for 18 Mar 2004 (Column 169WH)*. Retrieved March 3, 2008, from http://www.parliament.the-stationery-office.co.uk/pa/cm200304/cmhansrd/vo040518/halltext/40518h01.htm

US TV watchdog banishes swearing. (2004, March 19). *BBC News.* Retrieved February 24, 2008, from http://news.bbc.co.uk/1/hi/entertainment/tv_and_radio/3549105.stm

Valkenburg, P. M. (2002), 'Kijkwijzer: The Dutch rating system for audiovisual productions', *Communications,* 27(1), p. 79–102.

Valkenburg, M. (2004), *Children's Responses to the Screen: A Media Psychological Approach.* Mahwah, New Jersey: Lawrence Erlbaum Associates.

Valkenburg, M. and Peter, J. (2007), 'Internet Communication and Its Relation to Well-Being: Identifying Some Underlying Mechanisms', *Media Psychology*, 9(1), p. 43–58. Retrieved March 09, 2008, from http://www.leaonline.com/doi/abs/10.1080/15213260701279556

Valkenburg, M. and Soeters, K. E. (2001), 'Children's positive and negative experiences with the Internet: An exploratory survey', *Communication Research,* 28(5), p. 652–675.

Valkenburg, M., Cantor, J. and Peeters, A. L. (2000), 'Fright Reactions to Television: A Child Survey', *Communication Research,* 27(1), p. 82–99.

Valkenburg, M., Peter, J., and Schouten, A. P. (2006), 'Friend Networking Sites and Their Relationship to Adolescents' Well-Being and Social Self-Esteem', *CyberPsychology & Behavior*, 9(5), p. 584–590.

Valkenburg, M., Krcmar, M., Peeters, A. L. and Marseille, N. M. (1999), 'Developing a scale to assess three different styles of television mediation: "instructive mediation", "restrictive mediation", and "social coviewing"', *Journal of Broadcasting and Electronic Media*, 43(1), p. 52–66.

Van Brunschot, E. G. and Sydie, R. A. (2000), 'Images of prostitution: The prostitute and print media', *Women and Criminal Justice,* 10(4), p. 47–72.

Van der Bulck, J., and van den Bergh, B. (2000), 'Parental guidance of children's media use and conflict in the family', in B. Bergh, Van Den & J.Bulck, Van Der (eds.), *Children And Media: Interdisciplinary Approaches.* Leuven-Apeldoorn: Garant, p. 131–150.

Van der haegen, T. (2003), *EU View of Precautionary Principle in Food Safety.* New York, NY: Agriculture, Fisheries, Food Safety and Consumer Affairs. European Commission Delegation.

van Dijk, T. A. (1991), *Racism and the Press.* London: Routledge.

van Evra, J. (1998), *Television and Child development.* London: Lawrence Earlbaum Associates.

Van Mierlo, J. and Van den Bulck, J. (2004), 'Benchmarking the cultivation approach to video game effects: A comparison of the correlates of TV viewing and game play', *Journal of Adolescence,* 27(1).

Vandewater , E. A., et al. (2007), 'Digital Childhood: Electronic Media and Technology Use among Infants, Toddlers, and Preschoolers', *Pediatrics*, 119(5), E1006–E1015.

Vandewater, E. A., Park, S. E., Huang, X. and Wartella, E. A. (2005), '"No – you can't watch that": Parental rules and young children's media use', *American Behavioral Scientist: Electronic Media Use in the Lives of Infants, Toddlers, and Preschoolers,* 48(5), p. 608–623.

Vega, V. and Malamuth, N. (2007), 'The role of pornography in the context of general and specific risk factors', *Aggressive Behavior*, 33, p. 104–117.

Veraldi, D. M. and Veraldi, L. (2000), 'Liability for PTSD-related violence', *American Journal of Forensic Psychology,* 18(1), p. 17–25.

Verhulst, S. (2002), 'About scarcities and intermediaries: The regulatory paradigm shift of digital content reviewed' in Lievrouw, L and Livingstone (eds.), *The Handbook of New Media: Social Shaping and Consequences of ICTs.* London: Sage, p. 432–447.

Verhulst, S. G. (April 2001), *Reflecting Community Values: Public Attitudes to Broadcasting Regulation.* London: Research conducted by the Programme in Comparative Media Law and Policy, Oxford University, for the Broadcasting Standards Commission.

Verwey, N. E. (1990), *Radio Call-Ins and Covert Politics: A Verbal Unit and Role Analysis Approach.* Aldershot: Avebury.

Vick, D.W. (2005), 'Regulating hatred' in Klang, M and Murray, A. (eds.), *Human Rights in the Digital Age.* London: Glasshouse Press, p. 41–54.

Viegas, F. B. (2005), 'Bloggers' expectations of privacy and accountability: An initial survey', *Journal of Computer-Mediated Communication*, 10(3), article 12. Retrieved March 07, 2008, from http://jcmc.indiana.edu/vol10/issue3/viegas.html

Villani, S. (2001), 'Impact of media on children and adolescents: A 10–year review of the research', *Journal of the American Academy of Child and Adolescent Psychiatry*, 40(4), p. 392–401.

Vincent, J. (2004, December), *11–16 Mobile: Examining mobile phone and ICT use amongst children aged 11 to 16*. Guildford: University of Surrey. Retrieved 13 Dec, 2005, from http:// www.surrey.ac.uk/dwrc/Publications/11–16Mobiles.PDF.

von Feilitzen, C. and Carlsson, U. (2004), *Promote or Protect? Perspectives on Media Literacy and Media Regulations.Yearbook 2003*. Göteborg, Sweden: Nordicom, Göteborg University.

Wahl, O., et al. (2007), 'The Depiction of Mental Illnesses in Children's Television Programs', *Journal of Community Psychology*, 35(1), p. 121–133.

Waller, D. S. (1999), 'Attitudes towards offensive advertising: An Australian study', *Journal of Consumer Marketing*, 16(3), p. 288–295.

Waller, D. S., Fam, K. S. and Erdogan, B. Z. (2005), 'Advertising of controversial products: A cross-cultural study', *Journal of Consumer Marketing*, 22(1), p. 6–13.

Walsh, D. A. and Gentile, D. A. (2001), 'A validity test of movie, television, and video game ratings', *Pediatrics*.

Warren, R., Gerke, P. and Kelly, M. A. (2002), 'Is there enough time on the clock? Parental involvement and mediation of children's television viewing', *Journal of Broadcasting and Electronic Media*, 46(1), p. 87–111.

Wartella, E. (1980), 'Children and television: The development of the child's understanding of the medium' in Wilhoit, C and DeBock, H. (eds.), *Mass Communication Review Yearbook*, Vol. 1, Beverly Hills: Sage.

Waskul, D. D. (2004), *Net.seXXX: Readings on Sex, Pornography, and the Internet*. New York: P. Lang.

Watson, N. A., Clarkson, J. P., Donovan, R. J. and Giles-Corti, B. (2003), 'Filthy or fashionable? Young people's perceptions of smoking in the media', *Health Education Research*, 18(5), p. 554–567.

Webb, T., Jenkins, L., Browne, N., Afifi, A.A., and Kraus, J. (2007), 'Violent Entertainment Pitched to Adolescents: An Analysis of Pg-13 Film', *Pediatrics*, 119(6), E1219–E1229.

Weber, R., Ritterfeld, U. and Kostygina, A. (2006), 'Aggression and Hostility as Effects of Playing Violent Video Games?' in Vorderer and Bryant, J. (eds.), *Playing Video Games: Motives, Responses, and Consequences*, Lawrence Erlbaum Associates, p. 346–361

Webwise 2006 (2006), *Webwise Survey of Children's Use of the Internet 2006: Investigating Online Risk Behaviour*. Ireland, July 2006. Available at: www.webwise.ie/GenPDF.aspx?id=1389

Wellings, K. (1996), *Briefing document: The role of teenage magazines in the sexual health of young people*: Teenage Magazine Arbitration Panel.

Wheeler, M. (2004), 'Supranational regulation: Television and the European Union', *European Journal of Communication*, 19(3), p. 349–369.

Widyanto, L. and Griffiths, M. (2007), 'Internet Addiction: Does It Really Exist? (Revisited)', in Gackenbach, J. (ed.), *Psychology and the Internet : Intrapersonal, Interpersonal, and Transpersonal Implications*, 2nd ed., Elsevier/Academic Press, p. 127–149.

Wied, M. D., Hoffman, K. and Roskos-Ewoldsen, D. R. (1997), 'Forewarning of graphic portrayal of violence and the experience of suspenseful drama', *Cognition and Emotion*, 11(4), p. 481–494.

Wigley, K. and Clarke, B. (2000), *Kids.net*. London: National Opinion Poll.

Will, E. K., Porter, B. E., Scott Geller, E. and DePasquale, J. P. (2005), 'Is television a health and safety hazard? A cross-sectional analysis of at-risk behavior on primetime television', *Journal of Applied Social Psychology*, 35(1), p. 198–222.

Willard, N. (2003), 'Off-campus, harmful online student speech', *Journal of School Violence*, 2(1), p. 65–93.

Williams, D. (2006), 'Virtual Cultivation: Online Worlds, Offline Perceptions', *Journal of Communication*. 56(1), p. 69–87.

Williams, D. and Skoric, M. M. (2005), 'Internet Fantasy Violence: A Test of Aggression in an Online Game', *Communication Monographs*, 72(2), p. 217–233.

Williams, K. D., Cheung, C. K. T. and Choi, W. (2000), 'Cyberostracism: Effects of being ignored over the Internet', *Journal of Personality and Social Psychology,* 79(5), p. 748.

Williams, N. (2001), *Are We Failing Our Children?* London: Childnet International Publications.

Williams, P. and Dickinson, J. (1993), 'Fear of crime: Read all about it: The relationship between newspaper crime reporting and fear of crime', *British Journal of Criminology,* 33(1), p. 33–56.

Wills, T. A., et al. (2007), 'Movie Exposure to Smoking Cues and Adolescent Smoking Onset: A Test for Mediation through Peer Affiliations', *Health Psychology*, 26 (6), p. 769–776.

Wilska, T.-A. (2003), 'Mobile phone use as part of young people's consumption styles', *Journal of Consumer Policy,* 26, p. 441–463.

Wilson, B. J., Smith, S. L., Potter, W. J., Kunkel, D., Linz, D., Colvin, C. M., et al. (2002), 'Violence in children's television programming: Assessing the risks', *Journal of Communication,* 52(1), p. 5–35.

Wilson, B. J. and Martin, N. (2006), 'The impact of violent music on youth' in Dowd, N. E., Singer, D. G. and Wilson, R. F. (eds.), *The handbook of children, culture and violence*. Thousand Oaks, CA: Sage, p. 179–202.

Winkel, S., Groen, G. and Petermann, F. (2005), 'Social Support in Suicide Forums', *Praxis Der Kinderpsychologie Und Kinderpsychiatrie*, 54(9), p. 714–727

Winston, B. (1996), *Media Technology and Society: A History – From the Telegraph to the Internet*. London: Routledge.

Wolak, J., Finkelhor, D. and Mitchell, K. J. (2005), *Child-Pornography Possessors Arrested in Internet-Related Crimes: Findings From the National Juvenile Online Victimization Study*: National Center for Missing & Exploited Children. Retrieved December 13, 2005, from http://www.missingkids.com/

Wolak, J., Finkelhor, D., Mitchell, K. and Ybarra, M.L. (2008), 'Online "Predators" and Their Victims: Myths, Realities, and Implications for Prevention and Treatment', *American Psychologist*, 63(2), p. 111–128.

Wolak, J., Mitchell, K. J and Finkelhor, D. (2006), *Online Victimization of Youth: Five Years On*. Crimes against Children Research Centre.

Wolak, J., Mitchell, K. J. and Finkelhor, D. (2003), *Internet Sex Crimes Against Minors: The Response of Law Enforcement*: National Center for Missing & Exploited Children. Retrieved Decembr 13, 2005, from http://www.missingkids.com/

Wolak, J., Mitchell, K. and Finkelhor, D. (2007), 'Unwanted and wanted exposure to online pornograpny in a national sample of youth internet users', *Pediatrics,* 119(2), p. 247–257.

Wood, R. T. A., Gupta, R., Deverensky, J. L. and Griffiths, M. (2004), 'Video game playing and gambling in adolescents: Common risk factors', *Journal of child and adolescent abuse,* 14(10), p. 77–100.

World Wireless Forum. (2004), *Mobile Youth 2004*.

Worrell, T. R., Rosaen, S., Greenberg, B. S., Salmon, C. T. and Volkman, J. (2005), *Will and Cake or the Young and the Hungry: An Examination of Eating and Drinking on Television*. Paper presented at the International Communication Association 2005 Conference, Sheraton New York, Empire Ballroom West.

Worth, K. A., Dal Cin, S. and Sargent, J. D. (2006), 'Prevalence of Smoking among Major Movie Characters: 1996–2004', *Tobacco Control*, 15(6), p. 442–446.

Wright, W. (1975), *Six Guns and Society: A Structural Study of the Western*. Berkeley: University of California Press.

Xiaoming, H. and Yunjuan, L. (2005), '*Media portrayal of woman and social change: A case study of "Women in China"'*. Paper presented at the International Communication Association 2005 Conference, New York.

Y. S. and Guba, E. G. (1985), *Naturalistic inquiry*. Beverly Hills, California; London: Sage.

Yanovitzky, I. and Stryker, J. (2001), 'Mass media, social norms, and health promotion effects: A longitudinal study of media effects on youth binge drinking' *Communication Research*, 28(2), p. 208–239.

Ybarra, M. L. (2004), 'Linkages between depressive symptomatology and Internet harassment among young regular Internet users', *Cyber Psychology & Behavior*, 7(2), p. 247.

Ybarra, M. L. and Mitchell, K. J. (2004a), 'Online aggressor/targets, aggressors, and targets: a comparison of associated youth characteristics', *Journal of Child Psychology and Psychiatry*, 45(7), p. 1308.

Ybarra, M. L., Mitchell, K. J., Finkelhor, D. and Wolak, J. (2007), 'Internet prevention messages: Targeting the right online behaviors', *Arch Pediatr Adolesc Med*, 161, p. 138–145.

Ybarra, M. L. and Mitchell, K. J. (2004b), 'Youth engaging in online harassment: Associations with caregiver-child relationships, Internet use, and personal characteristics', *Journal of Adolescence*, 27, p. 319–336.

Young, B. (1990), *Children and Television Advertising*. Oxford: Oxford University Press.

Young, B. (2003), 'Does food advertising influence children's food choices? A critical review of some of the recent literature', *International Journal of Advertising*, 22, p. 441–459.

Zahl, D. L. and Hawton, K. (2004), 'Media influences on suicidal behaviour: An interview study of young people', *Behavioural and Cognitive Psychotherapy*, 32(2), p. 189–198.

Zann, M. (2000), 'Children, television and violence', *Archives de Pediatrie*, 7(3), p. 307–311(305).

Zillman, D. (2000), 'Influence of unrestrained access to erotica on adolescents' and young adults' dispositions toward sexuality', *Journal of Adolescent Health*, 27S(2), p. 41–44.

Zillman, D. and Weaver, J. B. (1999), Effects of prolonged exposure to gratuitous media violence on provoked and unprovoked hostile behavior, *Journal of Applied Social Psychology*, 29(1), p. 145–165.

Zillmann, D. and Weaver, J. B. (2007), 'Aggressive Personality Traits in the Effects of Violent Imagery on Unprovoked Impulsive Aggression', *Journal of Research in Personality*, 41(4), p. 753–771.

Zillmann, D. and Bryant, J. (1982), 'Pornography, sexual callousness, and the trivialization of rape', *Journal of Communication*, 32(4), p. 10–21.

Zimmerman, F. J. and Christakis, D. A. (2005), 'Children's Television Viewing and Cognitive Outcomes – a Longitudinal Analysis of National Data', *Archives of Pediatrics & Adolescent Medicine*, 159(7), p. 619–625.

Zimmerman, F. J., Glew, G. M., Christakis D. A. and Katon, W. (2005), 'Early Cognitive Stimulation, Emotional Support, and Television Watching as Predictors of Subsequent Bullying among Grade-School Children', *Archives of Pediatrics & Adolescent Medicine*, 159(4), p. 384–388.

Zoller, H. M. and Worrell, T. (2006), 'Television Illness Depictions, Identity, and Social Experience: Responses to Multiple Sclerosis on the West Wing among People with Ms', *Health Communication*, 20(1), p. 69–79.

Zurbriggen, E. L., et al. Report of the APA Task Force on the Sexualisation of Girls. Washington: American Psychological Association. Retrieved March 11, 2008, from http://www.apa.org/pi/wpo/sexualizationrep.pdf

INDEX